Administering the School Personnel Program

WILLIAM B. CASTETTER

University of Pennsylvania

Administering the School Personnel Program

THE MACMILLAN COMPANY
NEW YORK

Fifth Printing, 1967

Library of Congress catalog card number: 62–7379

The Macmillan Company, New York
Collier-Macmillan Canada, Ltd., Toronto, Ontario

Printed in the United States of America

TO ROBERTA

Preface

The problem of improving the effectiveness of organizations has been the focus of lay and professional concern for almost a half-century. Many of the earlier studies of organization centered upon the nonpersonal dimension—facilities, budgets, programs, schedules, policies, and funds. The Hawthorne experiments led to an increasing emphasis on the personal dimension—to the conception that individuals are the most important part of an organization.

This book, which is primarily concerned with the personnel function in school administration, assumes that the individual and the organization are interrelated, and that total organizational effectiveness is improved by focusing attention on both the personal and nonpersonal dimensions of administration.

One of the major aims is to provide a conceptual framework for dealing with school personnel problems. Part I considers social change and its implications for personnel administration, examines the nature and scope of the personnel function, and points up problems created by individual needs and organizational demands. Parts II, III, and IV treat, in turn, the determination of personnel need, satisfaction of need, and maintenance and improvement of service. Emphasis is given throughout to the relationship of the personnel function to the total administrative process. Recognition is also made of the fact that school personnel consists of three groups—administrative, instructional, and noninstructional. Personnel problems associated with each group are treated in Parts II, III, and IV.

The author has drawn freely upon the writings, surveys, and researches of both practitioners and students of the subject under consideration, and their contribution is readily acknowledged. While there are many persons who have contributed in one way or another to the preparation of this book, and necessarily must go unnamed, the author wishes to acknowledge with special gratitude the assistance of Dr. Richard Heisler, whose suggestions and constructive criticisms have been extremely valuable, and the work of Sue Baetz and Paulette Mitchell, who assumed responsibility for preparation of the manuscript.

William B. Castetter

Ithan, Pennsylvania
May, 1961

Contents

PART THREE

Satisfaction of Personnel Need

PART FOUR

Maintaining and Improving Personnel Service

Figures

Tables

PART I

Fundamental Concepts

of School Personnel

Administration

School Personnel

AN OVERVIEW

CHAPTER ONE

Good Schools Require Adequate Staffing

It has been said many times before that continuance of the American way of life is closely dependent upon the effectiveness of its educational system. It is being said again, possibly with a great deal more conviction, and with a great deal more evidence to support this conviction as we reflect upon the world around us and the future ahead of us.

America has been witness in recent years to an interest in its educational system which is without parallel. While there has been marked disagreement about educational aims and methods for achieving these aims, there is general agreement on the need for maintaining a superior educational system and for removing the deterrents to the improvement of educational quality.

The problems involved in attaining education of fine quality in local school districts are formidable. Purposes must be defined, policies established, programs developed, personnel employed, facilities purchased, revenues obtained, and a host of separate operations coordinated. This work is done through people—professional educators, nonteaching personnel, librarians, doctors, psychiatrists, lawyers, business managers, and laymen. People, in the broadest sense, are the substance of the undertaking.

It is generally conceded that the success of any human endeavor is closely related to the quality of personnel who perform the tasks necessary to the achievement of purpose, as well as to the conditions which affect their physical and mental well-being. This assumption is as applicable to school systems as it is to any organization of human effort. The extent to which public education succeeds will depend, to a large extent, upon the quality of the personnel engaged in the educational process, and upon the effectiveness with which they discharge individual and group responsibilities. The school plant is important. Purposes count for more than a little. Money is significant. A well-designed program is essential. Leadership is vital. But the most crucial single element in the educative process is the competency of the personnel charged with the task of effecting desirable changes in children and youth. This, in essence, is the thesis which undergirds the textual material which follows.

Schools in a Changing Social Order

Developing and maintaining an effective school staff is one of the important functions of school administration. Any consideration of the manner in which this function can be improved must be tempered with the realization that the school is an instrument of society committed to the task of implementing its political ideals and of furthering individual self-realization.

Every major social change has educational implications. Indeed, one of the critical problems of educational administration is that of making the educational system more responsive to social change. A list of outstanding social trends in the nation, summarized by Pounds and Bryner, includes the following:

1. Increased leisure time made possible by technological efficiency.
2. Social lag of institutions behind material changes.
3. Increased necessity for cooperative action.
4. Increased necessity for long-range planning.
5. Increased dependence on social control.
6. Increasing remoteness of social control.

7. Increased need for specialization.
8. Increased differentiation in providing for individuals.
9. Weakening of traditional controls over human conduct.
10. Increased strains and tensions.
11. America in a position of world leadership.
12. Atomic energy and automation.[1]

It is no secret that these and other social forces have created educational problems of serious proportions. A brief review of the more obviously important social changes, their educational implications, and the impact they have had and will continue to have on school staffing is the subject of the discussion which follows.

Technological Revolution

One of the major contributors to social change is the development, application, and dissemination of scientific knowledge. Even a cursory examination of achievements in science within the present century reveals an advance of almost incredible magnitude. The vast range of scientific attainment—including aircraft, antibiotics, artificial satellites, atomic energy, automation, automobiles, mass-production techniques, nuclear power, radar, radio, rockets, sound storage, submarines, synthetics, and television—has given impetus to rapid and radical cultural change. Further, it would appear that mankind is on the threshold of new and exciting discoveries which will intensify world-wide change.

What science has done to the habits of people is considerable. We have changed from an agrarian to an industrial economy, to a standard of living higher than that ever before achieved by any civilization. Developments in transportation bring any terrestrial destination within reach from dawn to dusk. Mechanization has made the farm more productive, despite the decline in numbers of people selecting agriculture as a vocation. The surplus in food has reached scandalous heights. Medicine has reduced dramatically the infant mortality rate and has sharply increased life expectancy. Diseases which have plagued mankind for centuries have been brought under control. The automobile has changed the patterns of home and community living, symbolized in part by the two-income, two-car, middle-

[1] Ralph L. Pounds and James R. Bryner, *The School in American Society* (New York: The Macmillan Co., 1959), Chapter IV.

class suburban family. Government has become more complex, more
centralized, more concerned about the welfare of humanity. Large-
scale war has become irrational. So awesome is the power of man's
weapons of destruction that they have given greater impetus to ideas
of permanent peace among nations. The world which science has
created, it is said, is one which mankind is not yet socially prepared
to occupy.

Human Revolution

A second major factor behind the tidal wave of social change
which has engulfed the world is a revolt in the affairs of man. Great
segments of humanity are in open resistance to the way they are
governed, to continual domination, to discrimination, to inequality
of opportunity, to illiteracy, to an indecent standard of living, to a
denial of individual choice and judgment, to war, and to the status
quo and the value systems it represents. The impact of human aspira-
tion for change is without geographical limits. Anarchy, race riots,
strikes, crime, and juvenile delinquency are symptomatic of this
political and social unrest.

A clearly visible consequence of this movement is a changed
climate of opinion, a difference in men's relations, in their moral
and political outlook. The ascendancy of labor, collective bargaining,
civil rights and minimum-wage legislation, unemployment insurance,
economic assistance for the aged and disabled, the rising level of
education, and the willingness of the populace to be taxed to assist
the underdeveloped nations of the world—all are efforts indicative
of the growing consensus for man's humanity to man.

The Pressure of Numbers

Many of the problems of modern society, and especially those
involving the educational system, are associated with extraordinary
increases in population. A summary of population growth in the
United States between 1800 and 1960 is presented in Table 1.1, along
with projected figures for 1970 and 1980. Pertinent observations
which can be made of these data include the following:

1. The growth in population between 1940–1950 and 1950–1960
has been greater than any decade increase since 1800.

2. The rising birth rate since 1940 has created and will continue to create unprecedented educational demands in the form of new buildings, personnel, services, and programs.

3. One of the factors involved in the acute shortage of teachers during the 1950–1960 decade was the birth rate of the 1930's, during which time the population increase was lower than in any decade of the twentieth century.

4. Population growth between 1960 and 1980 will accentuate the demand for professional personnel in education.

Aside from the sheer changes in population growth, which, according to predictions will virtually double the nation's present population by the end of the century, there have been other notable changes which have social implications. These include increased population mobility, changes in age distributions, and in divorce, marriage, and death rates. Social consequences of population changes have been widespread, and their control will require intensive and extensive planning at all levels of government.

Table 1.1

Population Growth Trends in the United States, 1800–1980

Census Date	Population (in millions)	Index	Change in index by decades	Census Date	Population (in millions)	Index	Change in index by decades
1980 (Estimate)*	272,600,000	51.35	10.00	1890 (June 1)	62,979,766	11.86	2.41
1970 (Estimate)*	219,500,000	41.35	7.57	1880 (June 1)	50,189,209	9.45	2.19
1960 (April) †	179,323,175	33.78	5.27	1870 (June 1)	38,558,371	7.26	1.34
1950 (April 1)	151,325,798	28.51	3.61	1860 (June 1)	31,443,321	5.92	1.55
1940 (April 1)	132,164,569	24.90	1.69	1850 (June 1)	23,191,876	4.37	1.15
1930 (April 1)	123,202,624	23.21	3.24	1840 (June 1)	17,069,453	3.22	.80
1920 (January 1)	106,021,537	19.97	2.60	1830 (June 1)	12,866,020	2.42	.60
1910 (April 15)	92,228,496	17.37	3.01	1820 (August 7)	9,638,453	1.82	.46
1900 (June 1)	76,212,168	14.36	2.50	1810 (August 6)	7,239,881	1.36	.36
				1800 (August 4)	5,308,483	1.00	

Sources: 1800–1960: Bureau of the Census, *1960 Census of Population, Advance Reports, Final Population Counts,* PC (A1)–1 (Washington: Bureau of the Census, 1960), p. 3. 1970–1980: Bureau of the Census, *Illustrative Projections of the Population of the United States, by Age and Sex, 1960 to 1980,* Series P–25, No. 187 (Washington: Bureau of the Census, 1958), p. 2.
* Series I Projection.
† Includes 680,000 members of armed forces overseas.

Economic Revolution

The era through which we are passing has been referred to as "The Century of the Common Man." When viewed from an economic standpoint, there is no question that the citizenry of this nation has experienced greater advances in material progress and greater changes in ways of living than the inhabitants of any other period of history. Not only does the citizen have more to eat, drink, wear, spend, and save; he has choices in these matters. The income gap between the rich and the poor has been drastically reduced. The productivity of our economic system is such that it takes the American worker far less working time than those in other countries to purchase the necessities of life. The worker's ability to produce more goods and services in shorter periods of time gives promise of reaching new heights in the years ahead. In short, as a nation we have never been better off economically.[2]

The increasing real income of the nation has been accompanied by interrelated problems of education and economics. There are, for example, complicated economic questions of price stability, of removing inequities in the tax structure, of understanding the behavior of our economic system under various conditions and policies, of competing with other economic systems while maintaining and improving present living standards. Growing concern over the concentration of economic power in corporate enterprises and pressures for greater income security and for a more equitable distribution of the material and cultural goods of society give rise to questions of economic philosophy. Educational issues related to economic growth loom equally formidable. Schulz argues, for example, that the income and educational levels of a country are closely related, and that by removing sources of inefficiency in the educational enterprise the nation's economic growth can be increased.[3] As the national income and individual buying power increase, the nation's citizens will have more money to spend, more time to spend it, and presumably will be confronted with more choices on what it shall be spent. Education's role in helping youth to become more literate in the working of, and the problems in, the economic system, and more capable of making wise choices relative to the greater leisure and individual income which it produces, becomes increasingly important.

[2] Maloney identifies four economic revolutions which have occurred between 1940 and 1960. These include income, liquidity, price, and public-policy. Our fifth revolution in economic affairs, according to the author, will involve our relations with the outside world, and may turn out to be the greatest of all. See H. D. Maloney, "Four Economic Revolutions: 1940–1960," *Business Horizons*, 3, No. 1 (Spring, 1960), pp. 29–41.

[3] Theodore W. Schulz, "Education and Economic Growth" in National Society for the Study of Education, Sixtieth Yearbook, *Social Forces Influencing American Education* (Chicago: University of Chicago Press, 1961), Chapter III.

Changing Cultural Values

Within a half century America has changed in many ways, some of the gross features of which have been outlined previously. One of the less dramatic though highly significant changes is the shift in cultural values. Indeed, there are those who contend that the radical shift in values the nation has been experiencing represents the core of social change. Redefinition of the sexual roles, greater emphasis upon peer-group culture, changing relations within the family, the seeming disregard for authority and for traditional social taboos and sanctions are frequently singled out as examples of how values are undergoing modification. The direction of the shift, as viewed by Spindler, is summarized in Table 1.2. What relevance the shift in values has for education and for educators is a question which is being given increasing attention by philosophers, psychologists, educators, and anthropologists.[4] Among the emerging educational problems related to cultural values are the following:

1. To what extent should the school attempt to affect the values of children and youth? Should it attempt to offer appropriate value models for pupil identification and consideration?

2. Should the school attempt to open "closed areas of culture" (economics, race and minority-group relations, social class, sex, courtship, marriage, religion and morality, nationalism and patriotism)[5] for study?

3. How can the recruitment and selection processes be designed to identify value patterns of personnel which will have a negative impact on children and youth?

4. What are the implications of changing values for the school's program of in-service development for professional personnel?

5. What are the implications of changing values for curriculum change?

What the schools should or should not do about the implications of changing social values is beyond the scope and intent of this discussion. But the role of the school has been and will continue to be

[4] See "The Philosophical and Social Framework of Education," *Review of Educational Research*, XXXI, No. 1 (February, 1961).

[5] As defined by Maurice P. Hunt and Lawrence E. Metcalf, *Teaching High School Social Studies: Problems in Reflective Thinking and Social Understanding* (New York: Harper & Brothers, 1955), p. 230.

Table 1.2

Changing Values in American Culture

Traditional Values	Emergent Values
Puritan morality (Respectability, thrift, self-denial, sexual constraint; a puritan is someone who can have anything he wants, as long as he doesn't enjoy it!)	*Sociability* (One should like people and get along well with them. Suspicion of solitary activities is characteristic.)
Work-success ethic (Successful people worked hard to become so. Anyone can get to the top if he tries hard enough. So people who are not successful are lazy, or stupid, or both. People must work desperately and continuously to convince themselves of their worth.)	*Relativistic moral attitude* (Absolutes in right and wrong are questionable. Morality is what the group thinks is right. Shame, rather than guilt-oriented personality is appropriate.)
Individualism (The individual is sacred, and always more important than the group. In one extreme form, the value sanctions egocentricity, expediency, and disregard for other people's rights. In its healthier form the value sanctions independence and originality.)	*Consideration for others* (Everything one does should be done with regard for others and their feelings. The individual has a built-in radar that alerts him to other's feelings. Tolerance for the other person's point of view and behaviors is regarded as desirable, so long as the harmony of the group is not disrupted.)
Achievement orientation (Success is a constant goal. There is no resting on past glories. If one makes $9,000 this year he must make $10,000 next year. Coupled with the work-success ethic, this value keeps people moving, and tense.)	*Hedonistic, present-time orientation.* (No one can tell what the future will hold, therefore one should enjoy the present—but within the limits of the well-rounded, balanced personality and group.)
Future-time orientation (The future, not the past, or even the present, is most important. There is a "pot of gold at the end of the rainbow." Time is valuable, and cannot be wasted. Present needs must be denied for satisfactions to be gained in the future.)	*Conformity to the group* (Implied in the other emergent values. Everything is relative to the group. Group harmony is the ultimate goal. Leadership consists of group-machinery lubrication.)

Source: George D. Spindler, "Education in a Transforming Culture," *The Harvard Educational Review*, XXV, No. 3 (Summer, 1955), p. 149.

to help children to acquire appropriate social attitudes and values. The school's role in dealing with problems of social change raises questions not only about what values and what methods of teaching values, but also about what kinds of personnel are essential to this most significant task.

Control of Social Change

The extraordinary period of social change has created complex and varied problems calling for new and planned approaches to control the process of change. How, for example, can nuclear energy be controlled and utilized for the benefit of mankind? How are the steady depletions of natural resources to be halted? What measures are needed to bring the standards of living now enjoyed by many available to all? If the processes of change are to be controlled, can it be accomplished without regimentation—without infringing upon individual liberties and initiative? How can the political process be made to serve society more effectively? Unless there is the kind of daring and invention in the social sciences as that which has characterized the physical sciences, the gains of social change will be nullified. To put it in another way, good government is a necessary concomitant of technological and economic progress. An indispensable resource for developing the scientific and social skills basic to the process of orderly social change is an effective educational system.

Educational Implications of Social Change

The accelerated tempo of social change, as well as the basic principles of education to which this nation is committed, has presented the educational system with a staggering responsibility—and a magnificent opportunity. The concept of education for all stands as a monumental cultural contribution. Its implementation in the midst of sweeping social transformation, however, has presented problems which are as basic as those relating to national defense, inflation, unemployment, or taxation.

Shortages in Facilities

One of the more obvious consequences of the unprecedented growth in population is a critical shortage of school facilities. Throughout most of the decade of the fifties the number of pupils was far in excess of normal plant capacity. Not only has the demand outrun the supply of plant facilities; standards for construction and building costs have increased to the point where many local districts cannot afford to erect the necessary structures. This situation reflects in part an unwillingness of the nation to utilize an economy of abundance to solve a serious educational problem.

Shortages in Personnel

The present shortage of professional personnel in the field of education is closely related to the general manpower problem which has existed in certain forms throughout the nation since the beginning of World War II. The impact of the manpower shortage has been greatest in fields requiring specialized training. Demand for personnel in these areas has been well in excess of the supply.[6] Major areas in which specialized manpower shortages are anticipated in the years ahead are shown in Table 1.3.

Table 1.3

Estimates of Increase in Numbers of People Needed in the Occupations Where Shortages Will Be Most Severe—1965 over 1955

	1965 (Demand)	1955 (Supply)	Increase
Natural scientists (excluding college teachers)	280,000	200,000	80,000
Engineers (professional)	630,000	530,000	100,000
Physicians	255,000	210,000	45,000
College teachers	350,000	230,000	120,000
Nurses with college degrees	100,000	25,000	75,000
School teachers	1,685,000	1,200,000	485,000
Total	3,300,000	2,395,000	905,000

Source: Robert J. Havighurst, "Manpower and the Teacher Shortage," in *Teacher Education: The Decade Ahead*, National Commission on Teacher Education and Professional Standards (Washington: National Education Association, 1955), p. 34.

The acute shortage of teachers and other trained people is due to a combination of circumstances, the majority of which are traceable

[6] For every 100 skilled workers that the nation had in 1955, it will need 122 in 1965 and 145 in 1975. See "Shortage of Skills: It Grows Despite Unemployment," *Time Magazine* (March 10, 1961), p. 90.

to social change. The increasing demand for workers of the level under consideration is due largely to technological developments. Discoveries in science have created widespread innovations in many fields of endeavor, the result of which is an increasing demand for technical skills in fields such as medicine, engineering, industry, pure and applied sciences, and management. As the rate of industrial production increases, and the emphasis upon research in all fields continues, the manpower problem in these and other occupations will continue. The demand for teachers, on the other hand, is largely the result of increasing enrollments, as well as the expansion of educational programs.

The supply of teachers has been affected by a number of factors, including the increasing competition for trained manpower, the noncompetitive nature of compensation structures for school personnel, the unfavorable conditions of work which obtain in many school systems, and the fact that the population in the age group from which teachers are now recruited (20–29) was born in years when the birth rates were comparatively low.

Increasing Educational Demands

An expanding economy, along with a major transformation in the world of work, and the continued increase in the size of the population have placed new and unprecedented demands upon the educational system. Some indication of the numerical size of the educational task which faces the nation in the years ahead is reflected in Table 1.4. The future patterns of educational attainment, prepared by the Bureau of the Census, reveal:

A general improvement in the educational attainment of the population. By 1980, the median level of attainment for the adult population is expected to be the twelfth year of school. In 1950 the median years of schooling completed by the adult population was 9.3.

A sharp reduction in the number of persons with less than five years of schooling.

A sharp increase in the number of college graduates in the nation. The number of college graduates is expected to rise from 5,431,000 in 1950 to 10,078,000 in 1970. By 1980, the number is estimated to be 14,367,000, or approximately three times the number of college graduates in the population in 1950.

Table 1.4

Years of School Completed by Persons 25 Years Old and Over, for the United States: 1950, and Projections to 1960, 1970, and 1980 (in thousands)

Year, Age	Total Population	Years of School Completed								Median School Years Completed
		None	Elementary School			High School		College		
			1 to 4 Years	5 to 7 Years	8 Years	1 to 3 Years	4 Years	1 to 3 Years	4 Years or more	
1950 (Total, 25 years and over)	87,484	2,256	7,494	14,327	18,238	15,195	18,115	6,426	5,431	9.3
1960 (Total, 25 years and over)	99,042	1,771	6,255	13,169	17,310	18,701	26,147	8,167	7,522	10.8
*1970 (Total, 25 years and over)	110,033	1,359	5,003	11,404	14,564	21,913	35,427	10,288	10,078	12.0
*1980 (Total, 25 years and over)	130,783	1,101	4,062	9,471	11,987	26,194	49,804	13,800	14,367	12.3

Source: *Projections of Educational Attainment in the United States: 1960–1980*, Series P-20, No. 91. Current Population Reports, Population Characteristics, (Washington: U.S. Department of Commerce, Bureau of the Census), 1959, pp. 6–7.
* Series A Projection.

An increase in the number of high school graduates. By 1980, the number of high school graduates is expected to be 2½ times the number in 1950.

The task of providing funds, facilities, and faculties to meet the sheer numerical demands for education, formidable as it appears, is but a facet of the total problem. Continuous reorganization of the educational program in the schools of the nation has been necessary to cope with the accelerating rate of technological, economic, and cultural change. The rapid growth of knowledge, for example, has necessitated a reexamination of what is to be taught, how and why it is to be taught. The sequence of learning experiences which have been habitually employed at all levels of education are in continuous revision to meet the problems of an unfamiliar world which is rapidly emerging.

Educational demands of the modern labor force have changed drastically within a single generation. The development of a new product, for example, may call for research and experimentation carried on by highly specialized personnel. Its production may involve a change in the work content, as well as an increase in the skills involved in its performance. By the time the product is mass-produced and marketed, a variety of personnel with increasingly higher levels of educational attainments are required. Consequently, there are educational implications in rising employment standards, as there are in the problems posed by the steady decline of unskilled and low-skilled workers.

Education and the Interdependence of Nations

Another facet of the educational implications of social change is the necessity for establishing new understandings and new relationships in a world where a majority of the people are no longer isolated from each other by distance, by time, by lack of communication, or by foreign policy. Nations of the world have become interdependent for reasons such as defense, economics, and technical assistance. The global military and assistance commitments of the United States, for example, require greater understanding of languages, governments, and customs of many other nations. International trade and non-military missions among nations have made it necessary for people of different nations to live and to work together to achieve mutual objectives. Moreover, today's citizen has an extended obligation to understand not only his nation's problems; he has, in effect, a responsibility to people everywhere to contribute to the mutual solution of the vital problems upon which man's very existence and his cultural betterment depend. Education's role in helping people to understand that they can ill afford to ignore major problems of those who live beyond their shores is a major one.

Changing Demands for New and Extended Educational Services

The insistence of society upon placing a wide variety of obligations upon its educational institutions has been such that the schools have not been completely able to fulfill in every detail these rather lofty expectations. The school system has been extended in both directions to educate children from nursery school age to adulthood. Not only does the range of persons extend to virtually all age groups; the schools have attempted to provide educational opportunities for persons located at almost any point on the intellectual scale, including the mentally, physically, and emotionally handicapped. In addition, the modern school provides psychological, psychiatric, health, food, attendance, safety, transportation, recreation, summer school, camping, guidance, and a variety of other services.

The net result of extending the educational system and of broadening the services rendered by the schools has been a heavy increase in responsibilities without the concomitant financial resources to make so extensive a program fully effective, however noble its purpose.

If the educational system is to undertake the diverse and difficult tasks of providing equal educational opportunities for all, of creating a climate conducive to intellectual attainment, of coping with the many ramifications of social change, and of developing citizens capable of making wise decisions in an era of social tension and transition, there is much that remains to be accomplished. Thoughtful consideration of the emerging nature and scope of education's task suggests some challenging and perplexing problems ahead. The list of questions below, which is not intended to be exhaustive, points up policy and program issues in need of resolution:

1. To what extent should education attempt to cultivate moral and spiritual values? How should the curriculum be changed to help youth to choose and order value patterns?

2. If social change has rendered traditional programs of vocational education obsolescent, along what lines should they be reorganized?

3. What curriculum changes are implied by youth's changing economic, community, and family roles?

4. To what extent should the school assume responsibility for preparing youth to improve the effectiveness of social institutions?

5. What are the educational implications of automation? Should the school assume responsibility for helping adults to acquire new skills and competencies to replace those which have become obsolete as a result of automation?

6. What are the core values in our social heritage which should form the basis for education in civic competence?

7. What are the educational implications of the trend toward conformity in our society? Is the ideal of free minds for free men inconsistent with present realities?

8. Should schools intensify their efforts to improve international understanding?

9. In an era of increasing specialization, should the schools attempt to develop more specialists?

The extent to which these and other educational issues of equal significance can be solved satisfactorily depends upon availability of personnel capable of rendering a high level of educational service. The discussion which follows points up some of the difficulties involved in staffing schools in the wake of rapid social change, as well as some of the important personnel problems which need to be overcome in order to make the schools as effective as society wants them to be.

Impact of Change on School Staffing

That the forces of social change have affected the ability of educational institutions to provide satisfactory staffing is hardly a novel observation. The fact that the continuing personnel dilemma adds up to a major social crisis, however, is less well understood.

The gap between education's promise and its achievement is a concern of both citizens and educators. When the causes of the discrepancies between educational ideals and actualities are examined, the personnel factor appears to be highly contributory. It has been a fashionable and sometimes profitable pastime for persons in all walks of life to suggest what schools should do or should refrain from doing.

Much of this is pointless, however, if it fails to emphasize or to understand that the building of better educational programs depends heavily upon the quality and quantity of school personnel available for this purpose.

As noted in the following discussion, it will not be easy to maintain a sufficient supply of competent teachers and administrators to educate growing numbers of students capable of performing effectively and responsibly in an increasingly complex environment. It will require, among other things, a great deal more money, more staff, better conditions of employment, and more effective and imaginative administration.

Teachers for the Job

An indication of the trend in the demand for teachers in the United States is revealed by the numerical estimates contained in Table 1.5. Examination of these data affords some insight into the kinds and numbers of specific needs which make up the total teacher demand. What becomes strikingly clear from the trend data in Table 1.5 is the relative stability of the demand from year to year, even though there have been fluctuations in specific areas of need.

Table 1.5

Trends in Teacher Supply and Demand

	1958	1959	1960	1961
Replace those leaving	95,000	94,500	110,000	120,000
Relieve overcrowding	30,000	30,000	30,000	30,000
Serve increased enrollment	25,000	33,000	30,000	35,000
Add necessary services	10,000	20,000	20,000	25,000
Replace the unprepared	60,000	50,000	40,000	30,000
Total needed	220,000	227,500	230,000	240,000
New supply of college graduates	85,000	92,500	95,000	102,000
Net estimated shortage	135,000	135,000	135,000	138,000

Source: National Education Association, Research Division, *Teacher Supply and Demand in Public Schools,* 1958, p. 17; *1959,* p. 19; *1960,* p. 15; *1961,* p. 14 (Washington: The Association).

The composite picture of teacher demand in Table 1.5 indicates only the bare outline of a complicated problem, one which involves more than recruiting new teachers to replace those who leave the profession annually because of death, retirement, disability, and other miscellaneous reasons. To relieve overcrowding, to replace the unqualified, to provide for increasing enrollments, and to extend the instructional program and services would require more teachers than are needed for actual replacement purposes. The broad implication of these data is that despite efforts to reduce the recurring shortage of teachers, progress toward its solution has been painfully slow. More important, the situation not only affects the quality of existing programs; it actually prevents in many school systems initiation of new programs made necessary by the twentieth century revolution.

The supply of teachers upon which school systems depend to meet the demand described above must come largely, but not exclusively,[7] from newly qualified college graduates. According to the estimates in Table 1.5, the continuing spread between the supply of, and demand for, teachers is a wide one. The annual supply of new teachers, estimated at slightly below 100,000 in recent years, is in itself insufficient merely to meet replacement needs. The fact that less than three-fourths of the new college graduates qualified to teach actually become candidates for teaching positions lessens the prospects for reducing the gap between supply and demand. These and other estimates[8] imply nothing less than a massive effort to recruit and to retain well-qualified teachers if double sessions, overcrowding, recruiting of emergency teachers, and general erosion of educational programs are to be prevented.

Conditions of Employment

If this nation enjoyed an abundance of properly qualified school personnel, many systems would still be unable to attract the levels of teaching competencies for the educational task which lies ahead. Some of the factors conducive to this state of affairs are economic; some grow out of existing legal and administrative structures; some are related to conditions of employment which obtain in local school districts.

As noted earlier, competition for trained manpower has become

[7] Refers to former teachers, persons qualified to teach but without teaching experience, and persons unqualified to teach except for reasons of emergency. One out of every 14 teachers lacked full certification in 1960–1961.

[8] See The Fund for the Advancement of Education, *Teachers for Tomorrow,* Bulletin No. 2, 1955 (New York: The Fund).

and will remain increasingly keen. Local schools, in order to keep abreast of demands in the years ahead, will face stern competition from business, industry, defense agencies, government, and many other occupational endeavors for the limited supply of high-caliber personnel.

While substantial improvements in economic provisions for school personnel have been and are being made, it is widely recognized that existing compensation structures for many professional workers in education are less than satisfactory. Although other indices could be used to demonstrate the noncompetitive level of teachers' salaries, a comparison between the salaries in business and industry and those in education is one frequently employed. For example, the average *starting* salary for men in business and industry has been consistently higher than either the starting salary for new teachers or the average salary for new and experienced teachers combined.[9] Moreover, many believe that, through an unfortunate combination of forces, factors, and conditions, socialization of the economic status of the educator has become a reality.

Antiquated legal controls governing taxation, indebtedness, and expenditures have seriously hampered efforts of local school districts to make salaries more attractive. Students of school finance have long recognized the severe limitations of any approach which places the major burden for financing education exclusively on localities. Solution of the problems involved in financing education will require at least: (1) a minimum foundation program supported by federal, state, and local funds which will purchase for children an education which we as a people deem adequate for our times, and (2) legal arrangements which will permit greater flexibility in financing schools at the local level. These would include revision of property-taxing practices, freedom to experiment with nonproperty-tax sources, elimination of control of school budgets by noneducational agencies, revision of tax-and-debt limitation laws, and means for strengthening local participation in the budgetary process.

No stranger to the list of major educational deterrents is the small school district. Its inabilities are legion; its contribution to inequality

[9] For evidence on this point see: Frank S. Endicott, *Trends in the Employment of College and University Graduates in Business and Industry, 1961,* Fifteenth Annual Report. Evanston, Ill.: the Author (Director of Placement, Northwestern University), December, 1960. Also National Education, Research Division, *Estimates of School Statistics, 1960–61* (Washington: The Association), 1960.

of educational opportunity prodigious. The point of concern here
is that the small school district has been unable to attract and to
retain competent teachers, in part because the conditions of employment have been generally so unsatisfactory as to render the possibility
of career service virtually mythical. Another compelling reason for the
elimination of the small school district is that it is not conducive to
efficient utilization of school personnel. Data in Table 1.6 indicate

Table 1.6

**Size of School Districts in the United States
in Relation to Number of School Personnel**

Pupils	*Full-time Equivalent Employees per 1,000 Pupils Enrolled*	
	All Employees	Full-time Teachers
3,000 or more	55.0	39.4
1,200 – 2,999	56.8	41.5
600 – 1,199	61.3	43.7
300 – 599	67.4	46.8
150 – 299	72.1	50.6
50 – 149	74.3	53.0
Less than 50	99.3	76.9

Source: U.S. Department of Commerce, *1957 Census of Governments,* Vol. II,
No. 2 (Washington: U.S. Government Printing Office, 1957), p. 640.

the inverse relationship between school district enrollments and staff
size. The number of full-time teachers per 1000 pupils in very small
districts, for example, is almost double the staffing provisions per
1000 pupils in very large districts. If the broad purposes of education
are to be attained, the question of how much longer the nation can
afford to permit the very small school district to remain small deserves
continuing consideration. The wastefulness of school personnel in
small school districts during a period when trained personnel are in
short supply appears to be a defensible argument for increasing efforts
to secure more adequate administrative units. There are other reasons,
including greater capability of the larger district to plan, administer,
and finance more efficient and more effective educational programs.
    Conditions of employment other than those of an economic
nature often defeat efforts to recruit and to retain qualified school
personnel. Excessive teaching loads, assignments which are more cus-

todial than educational, absence of grievance machinery, failure of
school officials to give direction and meaning to school goals, inadequate housing, absence of provisions for individual and group improvement, preoccupation with administrative routine to the point
where difficult educational problems are chronically neglected, lack of
staff opportunities for participation in the development of educational
policy—these as well as other conditions not conducive to job satisfaction contribute to the erosion of the school staff and to attendant
effects upon instruction. There was a long time in the history of public
education during which little or no attention was given by administrative officers to the conditions under which school personnel rendered
service. Salary schedules, job security, tenure and retirement provisions, and concern for the personal and professional fulfillment of staff
members were not matters upon which systematic planning was
centered. But that time is past. The world of work, including the
professions, has come to realize that such provisions are not only
necessary to improve the conditions under which people render
service; it has learned that they are highly conducive to the attainment
of purpose. It has come to understand that while financial rewards
are essential to the improvement of performance, they do not alone
ensure this realization.

Implications for Personnel Administration

The growing belief that solution of the major problems of our
times will depend more upon brains, and less upon brawn and natural
resources, has enormous educational implications. The impact of
social changes outlined earlier in this discussion calls for efforts which
will require the cooperation and support of many persons within and
outside of the field of education.

For the nation it will mean, for one thing, a greater willingness
to utilize more of the fruits of our national productivity to pay for
the kind of education which the age we are living in demands. For
local communities it will mean wider participation in decisions which
affect the quality of the school program. For boards of education,
administrators, and staff members, it will mean, among other things,
a concerted effort to lift the salaries of the professional educator to a
substantially higher level. It will mean also immediate and long-span
planning which will encompass the entire range of activities involved

in administering the personnel program. How to attract, to retain, and to develop the human material responsible for directing the education of children and youth; how to bring about and maintain a climate where the staff member can and will release his creative energies; how to develop a staff which can make education a positive force for directing and controlling social change for human betterment—these are indicative of the areas within and the ends toward which personnel administration can wisely direct its efforts.

Suggested Reading

Allen, Frederick Lewis, *The Big Change; America Transforms Itself, 1900–1950* (New York: Harper & Brothers, 1952).

Carskadon, Thomas R., and George Soule, *U.S.A. in New Dimensions* (New York: The Macmillan Co., 1957).

Committee for Economic Development, *Paying for Better Public Schools* (New York: The Committee, 1960).

Counts, George S., *Education and American Civilization* (New York: Bureau of Publications, Teachers College, Columbia University, 1952).

Drucker, Peter F., *America's Next Twenty Years* (New York: Harper & Brothers, 1957).

Fortune editors, *The Fabulous Future: America in 1980* (New York: E. P. Dutton & Co., Inc., 1956).

National Conference of Professors of Educational Administration, *Automation: Its Meaning for Educational Administration* (New York: Bureau of Publications, Teachers College, Columbia University, 1957).

National Education Association, Department of Classroom Teachers, *Conditions of Work for Quality Teaching* (Washington: The Association, 1959).

National Education Association, Educational Policies Commission, *Manpower and Education* (Washington: The Association, 1956).

National Society for the Study of Education, Sixtieth Yearbook, *Social Forces Influencing American Education* (Chicago: University of Chicago Press, 1961).

Nordskog, John Eric, *Social Change* (New York: McGraw-Hill Book Co., 1960).

Norton, John K., "The Contemporary Scene," in *Administrative Behavior in Education,* edited by Roald F. Campbell and Russel T. Gregg (New York: Harper & Brothers, 1957), Chapter II.

Pounds, Ralph L., and James R. Bryner, *The School in American Society* (New York: The Macmillan Co., 1959).

Yoder, Dale, *Personnel Principles and Policies,* 2nd ed. (Englewood Cliffs, N. J.: Prentice-Hall, Inc., 1959).

The Personnel Function
in School Administration

CHAPTER TWO

If the reasons advanced in Chapter One in support of the urgent need for increasing the quantity and improving the quality of school personnel are valid, it follows that educational administration has a heavy responsibility in developing and applying intelligent action to the solution of personnel problems. The purpose of this chapter is to provide a perspective of the personnel function in school administration. By doing so it is also possible to (1) indicate its relationship to other major administrative tasks; (2) identify purposes of the personnel function; (3) outline essential elements in the personnel program; (4) provide suggestions for organizing the function; and (5) indicate the relationship of policies and plans to the realization of school expectations. It is written with the conviction that more reflection, discussion, and understanding are needed to guide fact finding, analysis, and decision making on personnel matters. The time is passing when regard for personnel will center around salary discussions at budget time. As the concern for improvement of the nation's schools becomes more intensive, educators inevitably will be drawn into a reexamination of educational policies, of courses of action being followed and of the results they yield. High on the priority list to undergo

25

scrutiny will be ways by which the personnel function can be improved, since the success of the entire enterprise rests squarely upon it.

As more citizens and educators sense the magnitude and implications of the personnel problem, as there is less temporizing and more planning, and as new approaches to personnel problems replace outmoded practices and constricted ways of dealing with them, the chances of achieving a higher quality of instruction for more children in more communities will increase.

The Personnel Function in Perspective

The major functions involved in administering an enterprise, whatever its reason for being, have been established in broad outline. Those common to administrative endeavors may be categorized in the following groupings:

Functions	Major Concerns
Planning	What are the present and future goals of the organization? What plans of action should be developed to attain the goals? What policies are necessary to implement and to guide the plans of action?
Allocating	What activities are required to attain the aims? How shall the activities be grouped? To whom shall the work be assigned? How shall it be performed? What funds and facilities are needed? How many persons are needed? What competencies? How shall they be recruited? What shall be the conditions of employment?
Coordinating	How can the diverse efforts of people be synchronized so that the work is performed according to plan?
Influencing	How can the behavior of persons be influenced so that it contributes maximally to the attainment of organization goals?
Appraising	Do the results measure up to established standards? What are the weaknesses of the operation? How can they be corrected?

When viewed in relationship to one another the specific tasks included in the foregoing list are referred to as the administrative process, or the series of decisions and actions taken to accomplish the goals of the organization. This grouping of administrative elements, which is intended to be illustrative rather than definitive, points up the interdependence of functions, the relationship of functions and objectives, the extent to which functions permeate the conduct of organizational affairs, and the necessity for their continuous application in the operation of an enterprise.[1]

The personnel function assumes an increasingly important place in the administration of a school system. Implicit in its performance are the number and kinds of people to employ, clarification of their duties and relationships, recruitment, selection, placement, compensation, coordination, security, as well as the maintenance of conditions and climate conducive to effective service. Thus, the people through whom the goals of education are achieved—their performance and its improvement, their creative talents, their welfare—constitute the very substance of the personnel function.

Purposes of the Personnel Function

Personnel administration has been defined in a variety of ways. In the narrowest sense it has meant the establishment of procedures for the employment and payment of personnel. A broader and more recent concept views it as one of the major functions in the general context of administrative responsibility. It means arranging conditions which will make possible greater self-direction by personnel in the performance of their work. It means an abiding administrative concern about people in the organization who are responsible for providing children and youth with educational opportunities of the highest possible quality.

Personnel administration cannot be divorced readily from the ultimate aims of education. It is a means to accomplish purpose. Responsibility for achievement of purpose rests primarily with employed personnel. A major premise of personnel administration is that the end results of the educative process will be determined by

[1] For an extended discussion of the administrative process, see Roald F. Campbell *et al.*, *Introduction to Educational Administration* (Boston: Allyn and Bacon, Inc., 1958), Chapter 7.

the effectiveness of school personnel. It also assumes that maximum effectiveness can be secured through deliberate and cooperative efforts, by the public, the board, and the staff to improve personnel provisions. This includes, among other things, continuous appraisal of the forces and factors conducive to a climate favorable to the achievement of the aims of the organization and to the satisfaction of the personal and professional interests of personnel.

Nature and Scope of the Personnel Function

One approach to understanding the nature and scope of the personnel function is through examination of the various activities generally recognized as being necessary to the achievement of its purposes. These activities, variously referred to as tasks, problems, or responsibilities, are grouped schematically in Figure 1 to portray the dimension and scope of the function, as well as to indicate its relationship to other major administrative functions.

The personnel function as conceptualized in Figure 1 includes three broad clusters of personnel activity: (1) determining personnel needs, (2) satisfying personnel needs, and (3) maintaining and improving service. Under each of these headings are listed a series of specific activities which, collectively, represent the major responsibilities common to the function. It should be mentioned also at this point that the three major areas listed in Figure 1 form the basis around which the separate chapters in Parts II, III, and IV have been organized.

There are useful generalizations to be derived from analysis of the activities which comprise the personnel function. Examination of Figure 1 suggests that (1) personnel activities are extensive and varied, (2) personnel are administration's preeminent concern, (3) many of the tasks are of a specialized nature, (4) there is wide involvement of persons in the conduct of the personnel program, (5) numerous decisions concerning personnel are required at different operational levels, (6) policies are necessary to guide the program, (7) continuous planning is basic to sustain the effectiveness of the program, and (8) the personnel function is closely related to all other administrative functions. These matters will be treated more fully in the sections which follow.

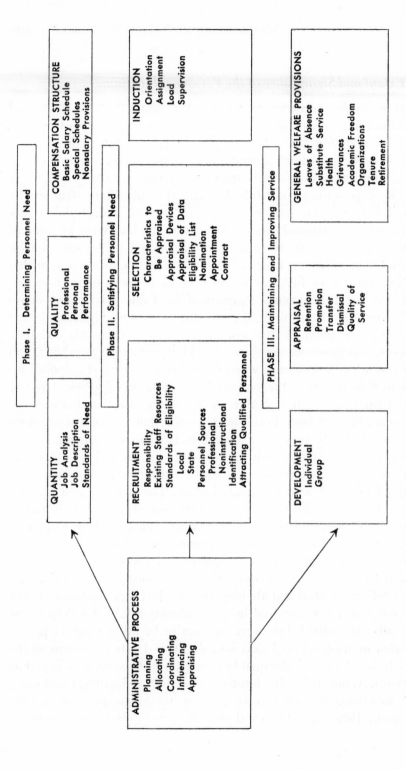

Phase I. Determining Personnel Need

QUANTITY
Job Analysis
Job Description
Standards of Need

QUALITY
Professional
Personal
Performance

COMPENSATION STRUCTURE
Basic Salary Schedule
Special Schedules
Nonsalary Provisions

Phase II. Satisfying Personnel Need

RECRUITMENT
Responsibility
Existing Staff Resources
Standards of Eligibility
    Local
    State
Personnel Sources
    Professional
    Noninstructional
Identification
Attracting Qualified Personnel

SELECTION
Characteristics to
    Be Appraised
Appraisal Devices
Appraisal of Data
Eligibility List
Nomination
Appointment
Contract

INDUCTION
Orientation
Assignment
Load
Supervision

PHASE III. Maintaining and Improving Service

DEVELOPMENT
Individual
Group

APPRAISAL
Retention
Promotion
Transfer
Dismissal
Quality of
    Service

GENERAL WELFARE PROVISIONS
Leaves of Absence
Substitute Service
Health
Grievances
Academic Freedom
Organizations
Tenure
Retirement

ADMINISTRATIVE PROCESS
Planning
Allocating
Coordinating
Influencing
Appraising

FIGURE 1 The personnel function and its relation to the administrative process.

29

Extent and Significance of the Personnel Function

It is hardly necessary to belabor the point that the personnel function is a vital part of school administration. Not only is it responsible for manning the enterprise and keeping it manned; decisions regarding the personnel program have major budgetary and educational implications. As any board member knows, salaries and wages of school personnel constitute the largest expenditure item in the school budget. Four out of every five current budget dollars are expended for personnel service. Moreover, the long-term investment required of a community to staff its schools is a sizable one. This is illustrated in Table 2.1, which contains data relating to the anticipated lifetime income of first-year teachers in 61 Pennsylvania school districts. While the incomes represented in Table 2.1 do not derive exclusively from local funds, the investment is substantial. Additional sums are expended by the local district for retirement, collateral benefits, and in-service development. Thus, personnel administration takes on added importance when viewed from a fiscal standpoint, for it is in this area that the potential for waste and inefficient use of school funds is greatest. Failure to employ competent personnel is an economic and educational waste, since staff competency and instructional quality are closely related. Retention of incompetent staff members represents not only an economic loss to society, it adds up also to a poor investment, for additional supervision is generally required for those who are unsatisfactory. The ultimate consequence of employing persons who are not professionally qualified is a compounding of losses in time, money, effort, and educational opportunities. The emphasis here is that personnel decisions so completely permeate every aspect of the school organiaztion and are so vitally related to educational outcomes that they must be regarded as administration's central and abiding concern. Just how extensive are the personnel decisions involved in administering a school system is not generally understood. For every position to be filled, whether professional or noninstructional, decisions are needed as to the nature of the work to be performed, the qualities needed for its performance, and its economic value. Plans for locating, selecting, inducting, developing, and appraising persons involve a variety of judgments and actions. Moreover, there are policies and procedures to be established regarding leaves of absence, organizations, academic freedom, substitute service, health, grievances, tenure, and retirements. In short, the continuous movement of personnel into and out of the school system requires constant and systematic attention if maximum educational returns are to be realized.

Table 2.1

Estimated Lifetime Income of First-year Teachers,* 1959–60

Estimated Income of Teachers with Bachelors' Degrees over a 40-Year Period	School Systems	
Above–$285,000	2	
$280,000– 284,999	0	
275,000– 279,999	1	
270,000– 274,999	1	
265,000– 269,999	1	
260,000– 264,999	1	
255,000– 259,999	1	High –$287,950
250,000– 254,999	2	Q_3 – 245,534
245,000– 249,999	7	Mdn.– 237,500
240,000– 244,999	10	Q_1 – 221,564
235,000– 239,999	9	Low – 207,000†
230,000– 234,999	3	
225,000– 229,999	5	
220,000– 224,999	4	
215,000– 219,999	2	
210,000– 214,999	4	
Below– 209,999	8	

Source: University of Pennsylvania, *School Personnel, 1959–60* (Philadelphia: Educational Service Bureau, 1960), p. 10.

* These data represent what first-year teachers in the study would receive over a 40-year period under existing salary schedules.

† Represents state minimum salary schedule.

Activities included in the personnel function are numerous and varied. Necessarily, they involve many people. The community, through its official representatives, must decide, for example, the metes and bounds of the personnel program, the policies which will guide its operation, and the financial support necessary for its implementation. At the administrative level, the administrator and his staff give expression to policies through plans, procedures, and programs. Principals and teachers are involved in performing certain personnel tasks, as well as in contributing ideas for program betterment. The related and routine tasks of record keeping, filing, and preparing payrolls involve the efforts of various types of noninstructional personnel. Some of the personnel tasks are specialized. Modern techniques for the selection of personnel, for example, require special preparation in testing, interviewing, and interpretation of data. Job analysis and descriptions also require special kinds of competence. As the occupational market continues to call for more highly trained personnel, the public schools will be in competition for various kinds of professional competencies which, in all probability, will remain for some time in somewhat restricted supply. As school enrollments rise and public demands for expended school services increase, school administration will be confronted constantly with personnel problems of one kind or another. Progress in meeting the challenge will be conditioned to a large extent by the interests and efforts of school administrators, by the command which they have of the subject matter of personnel administration, and by the increased skill which they develop in dealing with human beings and their problems.

Organization of the Personnel Function

The problem of allocating the work to be done and of defining what the working relationship among organizational personnel shall be is one with which administrators are constantly faced. There are different organizational patterns in public schools for administering personnel activities, ranging from the central personnel division in a large school district to the assumption of the major personnel responsibilities by a committee of the board of education in very small districts. The fact that many of the school districts in the nation are relatively small has created organizational and administrative difficulties which have prevented the introduction of desirable staffing practices. Even a casual inspection in both small and large school districts would reveal serious weaknesses in the manner in which personnel activities are organized and administered. Among the more important of these are (1) assumption of administrative responsibilities by the board of education, such as the recruitment and selection of teachers; (2) a dual system of control which places complete responsibility for all noninstructional personnel in the hands of an administrative agent not responsible to the superintendent of schools; (3) lack of personnel to undertake specialized personnel work; (4) unwillingness of the chief school administrator to delegate certain personnel responsibilities to subordinates; (5) numerical insufficiency of the administrative staff, which prevents effective performance of the total personnel function.

Indefensible personnel practices generally arise out of conditions such as the foregoing, characterized by:

1. Employment of personnel without due regard for the character of the work to be performed or for the qualifications needed to perform the work.

2. Performance of professional administrative tasks by nonprofessional agents.

3. Failure to define personnel policies.

4. Failure to plan and to coordinate personnel work.

5. Lack of definite policies or programs which encourage and stimulate professional performance.

6. Inattention to conditions of employment.

Certain fallacies regarding organization and administration of the personnel function have persisted over the years. One of the more serious is that personnel planning is unique to, and only necessary in, large school districts. Is it clearly evident, however, that regardless of the size of the operation the effectiveness of an organization and of the individuals in it demand systematic attention. It is true that the size of a school district will affect the nature and extent of the personnel program which can be put into effect. In very small school districts only limited provisions can be made toward the development of sound personnel programs. But even in small school systems, the basic concepts of personnel administration are applicable. This is not to argue in favor of retention of small school districts, since their capabilities for providing personnel programs which conform to acceptable standards are extremely limited.

A second fallacy of note is the assumption that the chief school administrator should and does possess all of the competencies necessary to perform all of the personnel-related responsibilities. It is not certain whether this line of reasoning has been responsible for the failure of many boards of education to provide sufficient staff assistance, both in number and in preparation, for effective performance of the personnel function. But it appears that inattention to central administrative staffing requirements has been a factor in the limited progress toward development of acceptable personnel programs.

In its best sense, the personnel function is a specialized staff activity under the direction of an assistant superintendent in charge of personnel. It exists to render advice and service to the administration and to personnel within the organization, and is comprised of subfunctions such as forecasting personnel needs; preparation of pertinent budget data; job analyses; salary and wage administration; record keeping; supervision of personnel benefits; advisement and assistance in the recruitment, selection, and placement of personnel; and continuous appraisal of employment conditions.

As a specialized staff function, personnel administration is the most recent to receive organizational emphasis. In a nation-wide study of central administrative personnel in 468 school districts, *The American School and University* reported that approximately 40 per cent had district-wide personnel positions.[2] No exact point on the size continuum at which schools differentiate the personnel function in the line of responsibility by assigning it to an assistant superintendent is as yet discernible. In general, the majority of schools which designate personnel as a separate staff function are those in which enrollments exceed 5000 pupils.

The foregoing discussion is not intended to convey the impression that organization is a panacea for the solution of personnel problems. Nor does it assume that organizational patterns for administering personnel activities will not differ from one school system to another. What is suggested, however, is that organization and personnel administration are interdependent, and the attainment of desired results will be affected by the extent to which these facets are skillfully synchronized.

Personnel Policy: Development and Application

The preceding discussion has treated the metes and bounds of school personnel problems and outlined the administrative process through which the personnel function is performed. In the remainder of this chapter attention is given to the development and application of personnel plans and policies. The major propositions advanced are as follows:

1. There are two ways to administer any organization of human

[2] Georgette N. Manla, "Administration in Transition," *American School and University,* 1960–61, 32nd ed. (New York: Buttenheim Publishing Corporation, 1960), pp. 148–149.

effort—by policy or by expediency. Experience has shown that there are distinct advantages in solving day-to-day and long-term problems by adherence to policy rather than to expedient action in response to complaints, pressures, or embarrassing comparisons.

2. School personnel are affected, directly or indirectly, by practically all administrative plans or decisions. Taking a course of action without reference to policy frequently entails hesitation and inconsistency, and ultimately affects personnel adversely.

3. Administration by expediency is an invitation to temporize or to ignore crucial problems.

4. There is an inherent relationship between purposes, policies, and programs. Specific plans of action are woven from the fabric of policy.

5. Absence of policy or the existence of inadequate policy quickly comes to the surface in the operation of a school system, calling for a sort of administrative fire brigade moving from crisis to crisis.

6. Commitment to administration by enlightened policy is a powerful motivational force for achieving the aims of the enterprise. It helps to guide, to control, to appraise, and to motivate organizational effort.

7. The school budget is a useful instrument for initiating, maintaining, appraising, and adjusting school policies.

8. Legally and theoretically, responsibility for formulation of community educational policy is the domain of the board of education; execution of policy is the responsibility of the chief executive officer. Operationally, policy formulation and implementation are not separable, and call for a high degree of reciprocity between the board and its executive officer.

9. Standing committees of the board of education and dual or multiple control systems are generally not conducive to effective policy formulation or execution.

Characteristics of Policy

Policy has become one of the more popular and fashionable terms in the administrator's vocabulary. To the undiscerning it is a formula for problem solving, with certain built-in features which eliminate much of the tribulation and disappointment in the life of a leader. Unfortunately, policy in itself will not produce organizational perpetuity. Problems are known to persist because of—even in spite of —policy.

The increasing interest in administration by policy is encouraging. Undoubtedly, boards of education will continue to hear more about, and to embrace, this idea which has an important bearing on the conduct of a school system. The discussion which follows centers around the meaning of policy, its chief characteristics, and the difference between it and practices and procedures.

Policy Reflects Intent

It has been observed in Chapter One that school systems are created to satisfy certain educational expectations. These expectations are made explicit in a variety of ways, including constitutional provisions, statutory enactments, charters, codes, and policy statements.

In general, policies are judgments which express organizational intentions for achieving expectations or purposes. They are authorative decisions which establish bases for administrative action. They represent the board of education's thinking as to lines along which the affairs of the school system should be conducted. They serve as practical guides to the administrator for thinking about and taking action on school matters with which he is constantly confronted. How does the administrator go about preparing the annual budget, for example, if there are no stated policies relative to teacher load, the professional qualities on which employment is to be based, the number of administrative assistants to be employed, or the collateral benefits to be paid to noninstructional personnel? True, these matters are often decided without policies, but the solutions are usually temporary, lead to confusion and indecision, and tend to impair the total organizational effort. If, on the other hand, the board's intentions are known, the administrator need not guess at what he thinks board policy is, nor make a decision on what he hopes it will turn out to be. As a matter of fact, absence of policy is most conducive to indecision, for the administrator is placed in the position of making decisions which he is never quite sure will result in approval or censure.

Policy Is Not Prescriptive

Since boards of education do not remain on the operational scene day in and day out to deal with administrative matters, firm bases need to be developed which will enable administrative agents to carry out board expectations. These bases, or policies, are formulated by the board to guide the school system along a preferred course of action. As such, they cannot be highly specific. They are not intended to provide answers to every problem which arises. They are meant to allow the administrator discretion in making decisions. They act to control decisions only to the extent that they indicate a preferred course of action. If, for example, it is the policy of the board to make adequate provisions for the in-service growth and development of all personnel, the manner in which the in-service program is to be established lies within the discretion of the chief administrator. The board does not specify the components of the program. The policy stated above broadly indicates its intentions with respect to in-service growth and development.

Policies are often confused with rules, regulations, procedures, and practices. The latter are the instruments which the administrator uses to translate broad policies into specific objectives and courses of action. They are administrative instruments through which individual rules are further defined. It may be the policy of the board to encourage leaves of absence for professional study. The eligibility requirements, financial arrangements, time limitations, and restrictions on the number of leaves allowed are procedures used to put the policy into effect. Practices and procedures, it should be noted, are in effect in every school system regardless of presence or absence of policies.

Policy Is Written

To be effectively and consistently applied, policy must be clearly understood. This is why boards of education are constantly urged to put their policies into written form so that they can be interpreted by school personnel, the public, and those groups which frequently participate in the task of improving the school.

A survey by the United States Office of Education indicated that, while the practice of developing written policies is far from universal, it has increased appreciably since 1946.[3] In effect, this means that efforts are increasing to make public those policies to which boards adhere in the conduct of school affairs. As a matter of fact, the con-

[3] Alpheus L. White, *Characteristics of Local School Board Policy Manuals*, Bulletin 1959, No. 14 (Washington: U.S. Department of Health, Education, and Welfare, 1959), p. 1.

viction is growing that publication and interpretation of school policies produce positive effects within and outside of the school system.

There are additional advantages to written policies. While the board has every right to deviate from a written declaration, the long-term effect of stated policies is to minimize sudden and unreasoning variations in board decisions. Another advantage is that serious departure from policy creates the necessity for explanation and justification. In a sense, the board is generally committed to follow the course of action which it has openly and officially adopted, for policy is a promise from which it is possible but not easy for school officials to disengage.[4]

Policy Is Constant

One of the hallmarks of sound policy is that it seldom fluctuates, since it constitutes the formal platform which reflects the board of education's position with respect to the conduct of the educational enterprise. If policy truly reflects the aspirations of the community for education, it need not be affected by changes in board membership. Policy is also constant in the sense that once established it is meant to be adhered to by all. It is not policy if exceptions to it are frequently granted, or if it can be suspended for reasons of external influence. It does not follow, of course, that policies are so permanent that they should not be revised in light of experience or changing conditions.

If policy is to have any semblance of firmness, and is meant to be more than a transitory expression of intent, long and studied considerations should attend its development. The tests with which the many policies in a school system are necessarily confronted are numerous, frequent, and often complex. Unless they are contrived by the best thinking available in the school organization and in the community, the chances are that they will fall short of intended purposes.

Policy-making Process

Much has been written about what educational policy should be, but the research devoted to how policy is actually developed and the

---

[4] For an excellent discussion of the value of published personnel policies see Charles R. Hook, "Improved Motivation through Published Personnel Policies," *Management Record*, XIX, No. 9 (September, 1957), pp. 314–315, 336–338.

problems attending its formulation is limited. Cunningham's [5] study of educational policy development resulted in the identification of five stages relating to the policy-making process. These are outlined below:

> *Stage One: Initiation.* The policy-making process begins when a problematic issue has been raised to a cognitive level.
> *Stage Two: Definition.* Problem is further identified and defined.
> *Stage Three: Deliberation.* Alternative solutions to the problem raised and considered.
> *Stage Four: Enactment.* Alternative is selected which stands as policy.
> *Stage Five: Consequences.* Consequences tested and evaluated in light of predicted results for the chosen policy alternative. Policy may be revised or discarded, depending on its contribution to goal attainment.

The significance to the administrator of an understanding of the policy-making process and its several stages is readily apparent. Not only does the administrator help the board to understand the importance of, and necessity for, policy formulation, he is also the key administrative agent in bringing to the board's attention the need for new, or the revision of existing, policies. He helps to define problems, suggests alternatives, furnishes appropriate information which will enable board members to understand the problem and implications of the several alternative courses of action, advises on the appropriateness of each alternative, and shares with the board the task of policy appraisal.

Frequently overlooked in discussions of policy development is the matter of community attitudes and values. To a very large degree, policies formulated by the board of education reflect values and attitudes of citizens about what their schools should or should not do. In attempting to formulate, let us say, a policy governing the teaching of controversial issues in a given school system, not all citizens or perhaps all board members will agree that it is educationally desirable to discuss controversial subjects. The outcome of policy deliberations (the third stage referred to in the policy-making process) will be affected by many factors, including individual values of board members,

[5] Luvern L. Cunningham, "The Process of Educational Policy Development," *Administrator's Notebook*, VII, No. 5 (January, 1959), University of Chicago: Midwest Administration Center, 1959.

of the chief executive, and of persons or groups within the community. This is to say that policy issues are ultimately decided by the complex interaction of people, the cultural values of those formally and informally involved in affecting decisions, their power in influencing community leaders and group opinion. McPhee's study,[6] which examined the relationship between the type of values which an individual holds to (1) the type of educational viewpoint to which he subscribes, and (2) the degree of school approval which he manifests, indicates:

1. The administrator can predict lower school approval from citizens whose educational viewpoints are most divergent from the superintendent's, are most traditional on educational matters, are members of labor unions, are in the lower occupational groupings and income levels, are over 50 years of age, and have had the least schooling.

2. The administrator can anticipate the greatest source of potential support for the schools from the following: citizens whose educational viewpoints are closest to the superintendent's, are most emergent in their educational beliefs, are P.T.A. members, are in the higher occupational categories and income groups, are between the ages of 30 and 50, and have received the most schooling.

While there is much to be learned about the relationship between cultural factors in the community and policy making, it is clear that the policy process does not operate independently of the citizens of the community and the values to which they give credence. It is well known that public opinion is an important determiner of school policy; that school officials are ultimately responsible to the citizens of the community for their actions; that a community consists of many subpublics among which there is not universal agreement as to the task of public education.[7] To be of maximum assistance to the board of education in policy matters the chief executive must be sensitive to cleavages in a community with respect to educational values, able to assess community value patterns, and to discern those aspects of policy in which agreement and disagreement are most likely to occur. Within

[6] Roderick F. McPhee, "Individual Values, Educational Viewpoint, and Local School Approval," *Administrator's Notebook*, VII, No. 8 (April, 1959), University of Chicago: Midwest Administration Center, 1959.

[7] See Roger C. Seager and Allen T. Slagle, "Sub-Publics View the Task of Public Education," *Administrator's Notebook*, VIII, No. 4 (December, 1959), University of Chicago: Midwest Administration Center, 1959.

the context of conflicting community values the school develops its position on policy matters. Never an easy task, it can be simplified by greater understanding of the social forces and factors involved in the resolution of policy issues.

By means of the flow chart illustrated in Figure 2, Campbell portrays educational policy as resulting from social, economic, political, and technological forces.

FIGURE 2   Flow chart on policy making in education.

I
Educational policy results from . . .

II
Basic social, economic, political, and technological forces, often national and world-wide in scope, which produce . . .

III
Political activity, extra-legal in nature. Many groups debate and seek information, and school leaders exert influence. These activities, usually interrelated at local, state, and national levels, culminate in . . .

IV
Formal, legal expression of policy which represents the value choices of influentials who participated in the process.

Source: Roald F. Campbell, "Processes of Policy Making within Structures of Educational Government," in *Government of Public Education for Adequate Policy Making* (Urbana, Ill.: Bureau of Educational Research, University of Illinois, 1960), p. 73.

The gist of the policy-making process, as conceived by Campbell, is that:

1. It has its origin in social change, e.g.: problems of national defense foster demands for improvement in science instruction.

2. It is nurtured by nation-wide antecedent movements, e.g.: movements to change educational policy, such as the Conant study and Rockerfeller report.

3. The antecedents and resulting proposals provoke debate and study in and out of government, e.g.: consideration of problem by means of mass communication, by professional associations, foundations, P.T.A., and governmental bodies.

4. It is formalized by local, state, or national government, e.g.: state education agency mandates teaching of a particular subject in the secondary schools, such as foreign languages.

Some of the difficulties encountered in the policy-making process include value confusion, lack of knowledge, and poor politics. Augmented research, better politics, and a local-state-national partnership in education are, according to the author, ways of improving policy making in education.[8]

Advantages of, and Obstacles to, Policy Development

Advantages of Policy Development

The concept of operating a school system on the basis of established policy is so appealing and so logical that the less than universal acceptance which it enjoys would appear to be somewhat of an oddity. The line of reasoning which argues for the establishment of policy is so obvious that it would seem to require only a few illustrations of its value and its promise. Summed up briefly, at least the following advantages result from established policies as they apply to personnel. They:

1. Provide a sense of security to personnel in that the intent of the board regarding personnel matters is on record.

2. Are conducive to operational stability. Policy does not change automatically when board membership changes.

3. Assure fair treatment to all personnel, which is in itself an appealing force.

[8] Campbell, *op. cit.*, pp. 59–76.

4. Save time, money, and effort in administration of the personnel function.

5. Facilitate decision making at the administrative level, since they are, in effect, criteria for weighing solutions to problems.

6. Minimize inconsistency in decisions by different administrative agents on similar problems.

7. Provide a basis for appraising existing or proposed plans for personnel.

8. Make known to all the intent of the board toward personnel in the organization.

9. Are positive in outlook—they foster action along lines considered appropriate for the attainment of personnel goals.

This is not to imply that policy, once developed, will yield through self-action returns such as those listed above. No mere body of value judgments can do that. The real test of policy is in its performance— the extent to which it serves as a basis for problem solving, how useful it is in helping the administrator to formulate specific plans of action, its value in probing issues, alternatives, and conflicting points of view, and the influence it has in guiding the organization along a preferred course. To put it another way, policies are not ornaments for display on special occasions. If they do not contribute to the improvement of organizational effort, of what value can they possibly be?

Obstacles to Policy Development

A prime obstacle to policy formulation and implementation in public education is lack of understanding by boards of education of policy function and potential. The human tendency to shy away from firm commitments is understandable. Expressing policies in written form, it is often argued, places the board of education in an exposed position from which it cannot readily make policy exceptions. Another objection is that making policies known leads to greater surveillance of board action, involving the need for continuous interpretation and defense of its official conduct. These and other attitudes toward policy are precisely why it is needed in school administration. Policies are written with the expectation that they will be adhered to; that there will be explanations when policy and practice are inconsistent.

Very few Americans would be willing to abandon the system of

local control under which schools operate. But the difficulties it poses
for policy development are formidable, though not insurmountable.
For illustrative purposes, consider the problem of policy making in a
local school system. Lay citizens comprising the board are not, by and
large, accustomed to defining policy and utilizing it in arriving at solutions to problems. Many members are not in a position to devote extended periods of time to the difficult task of policy consideration.
Add to this the shifting composition of board membership, the nar-
cotic of spur-of-the-moment decisions for which there is infrequent
accountability to a citizenry which may be indifferent to the administration of its schools, and the realities of making and adhering to policy
become imposing. All of this is not to suggest that boards of education are incapable of making and living with policy. Rather, the point
of emphasis is that continuous efforts need to be made to establish
policies which will endure beyond the traditional length of individual
board membership, and which will not atrophy because of inattention.
Means must also be employed to acquaint board members readily with
the need for, benefits of, and techniques in policy development, the
burden of which must, of necessity, rest with the chief executive.

Key Issues in Planning Personnel Policy

Planning is man's way of realizing his intentions. Because it deals
with concepts of the future, with problems requiring imagination and
choice, with deliberate forethought, with attainment by design, it
represents a most appealing and challenging endeavor. It is recognized
as organization's most reliable way of making happen what it wishes
to happen. It is the antithesis of expediency, laissez faire, and indirec-
tion. It is an effort to set a course of action and to guide its direction
in terms of a set of expectations.

It is easy to see that planning has a bearing on the personnel function. Why it is not applied more frequently and consistently in this
and other aspects of administration is not always clear. School officials
appear to be willing to invest almost any amount of money, time, and
effort to plan a new building. Similar enthusiasm for planning staff
needs, setting purposes, or making adjustments in the educational program is generally not apparent. Habitual concern with values, objectives, and policies is unusual, due perhaps to the range and complexity
of issues and problems, as well as to the fact that the process requires

consistent conceptual emphasis. Add to this the seeming unreality of aims to the practitioner steeped in manifold considerations, and the tendency to view planning negatively becomes understandable.

If planning is what is needed to give meaning and direction to the personnel function, what does it involve? Planning involves choosing from among alternatives the tasks which the school system should undertake, what policies are needed to guide day-to-day operations, what programs are most suitable for attaining objectives, how funds are to be secured, and the priorities for which they are to be expended. These are typical of choices which confront the planner.

Identifying the right questions to answer in personnel planning is equally as critical as formulating the right policies to aid administration in making the right decisions. Bringing the fundamental personnel problems into focus, encouraging the board, the staff, and the community to think them through, and developing a common understanding of what the nature and scope of the personnel plan should be is one of school administration's most challenging and, indeed, urgent considerations. To illustrate, let us consider some of the persistent and vexing personnel problems which require constant and simultaneous consideration:

1. What standards of personnel competency shall be established for the various classes of service to be rendered? The implications of this question are many, and, when answered, make possible the solution of a host of derivative problems and procedures. The recruitment and selection processes, the compensation structure, and the in-service program are but a few of the activities in the personnel function which are directly affected by policy established to govern the caliber of professional and noninstructional personnel employed by the district. The quality of instruction provided in the classroom, the efficiency with which supporting services are performed, the quality of leadership rendered—all are closely related to what undoubtedly is one of the most essential considerations in personnel planning.

2. What size staff is necessary to attain the objectives of the school system? The term "staff" as used herein includes more than teachers. It refers as well to administrators, supervisors, special service personnel, health, food, transportation, maintenance, operation, clerical, and secretarial workers—all of whom are important contributors to the work of the school.

The simplicity of the question raised fails to portray either its magnitude or its complexity. Before it can be resolved, decisions must be reached as to the breadth and depth of the educational program, the nature of the activities which will comprise the program, the manner in which instruction will be organized, and the work load which is most conducive to effective performance. As noted earlier, staff size is a major budgetary problem, and the question of how best to utilize the services of all personnel is one which ultimately enters into the determination of staff numbers.

3. What levels of compensation are needed to attract and to retain the kinds of personnel essential to the attainment of objectives? A compensation structure which will withstand the rigors of personnel grievances, public criticism, and at the same time have the competitive qualities to attract and retain competent personnel is difficult to come by. What the master salary schedule should be, the nature of special schedules for administrators and noninstructional personnel, payment for extra work and overtime, and the collateral benefit plan are fiscal facets which must receive appropriate attention and weight in the policies around which the total compensation structure is shaped. A concomitant consideration is the immediate and long-range financial implications of any compensation plan which is adopted, for there are certain built-in risks to policies not grounded in the realities of finance.

4. What provisions are needed to maintain and to improve the quality of the professional and noninstructional staff? The conviction is increasing that the educational institution does not exist today which prepares future teachers fully for the responsibilities which will confront them. More and more, local school systems are coming to the point of view that, to a large extent, improvement of personnel is their own responsibility. This indicates no lack of faith in teacher education institutions, but an emphasis upon staff development through participation in local program improvement.

The substantive elements of a development program for personnel are extensive and varied, involving board members, teaching and special service personnel, administrators, and noninstructional workers. Workshops, graduate study, consultant service, and curriculum revision are but a few of the in-service activities utilized for improving the effectiveness of staff members. Some of the important problems and issues in this area which must be resolved on the basis of policy include the following: To what extent should the local school system prescribe the development program? Should staff participation be optional or compulsory? Should there be a system of incentives and rewards for personnel development? What policies should govern the distribution of in-service improvement costs? How can the education of personnel be integrated with improvement of the curriculum-instructional program?

5. What provisions shall be made for the general welfare of school personnel? The conditions under which staff members render service are, in the final analysis, what school authorities want them to be. Those who intend to dedicate their careers to the cause of education have a right to expect that certain conventional arrangements which vitally affect their welfare will prevail, including plans for leaves of absence, substitute service, tenure, retirement, and academic freedom. That considerably more attention needs to be given to general welfare policies and the administration of them is well known. There is reason to believe that the high incidence of legal, community, and staff controversy in this area can be reduced by more effective planning.

Personnel policy decisions implicit in the foregoing questions are so important to the well-being of a school system that they cannot be made without careful consideration of each of the many items pertaining to each policy question, and without an examination of the collective soundness of all personnel policies. Balanced judgments are needed to determine whether the policies in effect are yielding the returns desired, whether the policy priorities are appropriate, and why the administration is doing what it is doing in every area of the personnel function.

Making Policy Work

The history of local school administration glitters with attempts to establish guides for the proper conduct of public education. It is also a matter of record that generally these efforts have come short of expectations. This is understandable. There is a strong inclination in organizations to seek easy and quick solutions to problems without giving serious thought to ultimate consequences. Willingness to adopt piecemeal answers to fit the time or the event instead of adhering to a body of value judgments calculated to yield more lasting results appears to be not only fashionable, but the only method of organizational conduct of which many in authority are cognizant.

There are abundant examples of adopted policies which, after exposure to the realities of difficult problems, have atrophied and become meaningless. Learning to live with policy is an exacting experience, especially because of the demand for group discipline. The major responsibility for making policy work rests with the board of education. This responsibility can neither be delegated nor ignored when difficult situations arise. To do so would be to shake the confidence of all interested parties in the integrity of the administration.

Policy planning is not only time consuming; it is a way of dealing with problems foreign to many laymen. Consequently, the task of putting policy into effect, especially in the initial stages, requires maintenance of initiative. Nursing the policy idea through to the point' where it becomes self-sustaining means that many policy statements will have to be added to, or changed, from time to time to convey board intent more clearly. Because of the constant necessity for adding to, and clarifying, policy statements, a policy manual which can be kept up-to-date is an indispensable tool. Another essential in policy application is continuous dissemination and interpretation of policy information through a wide variety of communications media, including the induction program for new personnel, policy handbooks, and discussions of policy during system-wide or individual school faculty meetings. Ample opportunities for staff participation in policy planning, as well as for discussions which encourage suggestions for implementing policy effectively and consistently, are also illustrative of activities conducive to policy maintenance and improvement.

Responsibility

An associated problem in policy implementation is that of clarifying the responsibilities of the board and its chief executive officer. As noted earlier, execution of policy is a responsibility which should be delegated the board's executive officer. It is mentioned here because one of the real difficulties in making policy work is that boards of education frequently assume responsibility for both policy making and execution. If, for example, the board appoints a personnel committee from among its members to interview and to nominate all candidates for teaching positions, it is engaging in administration of policy. If it assumes the responsibility for *selecting* school principals, it is performing a function which belongs to the superintendent. To be unequivocal, the board *elects* all personnel to school positions; the chief executive *selects* and *nominates* candidates for election by the board. Experience has shown that the more administrative responsibility a board assumes, the less likely it is to concentrate on the policy-making function.

Figure 3 illustrates a suggested working relationship between the board and its executive officer in matters pertaining to school personnel. This concept embodies these assumptions:

1. The board of education, as part of its legislative function, establishes and approves personnel policy.

2. The board operates as a committee of the whole, without standing committees to perform executive functions.

FIGURE 3

Illustration of board-superintendent relations in the personnel function.

THE PERSONNEL FUNCTION

To initiate, establish, administer, and appraise policies, programs, and procedures which will attract, retain, and develop the quality and quantity of personnel who can best promote the objectives of the school system.

FUNCTION OF THE BOARD OF EDUCATION

Establish and approve policies and programs which will promote the personnel function.

Delegate authority and responsibility to the superintendent of schools for the development of personnel programs and procedures which will implement the policy of the board of education.

FUNCTION OF THE SUPERINTENDENT OF SCHOOLS

Directs and administers established personnel policies and programs of the board of education.

Develops and recommends new personnel policies to the board of education.

Provides consultation and assistance to administrative personnel in the implementation of policy.

Develops programs and procedures (with board approval) relating to recruitment, selection, placement, compensation, orientation, retention, transfer, dismissal, development, and general welfare of personnel.

Assists board of education in appraising effects of personnel policies and programs in relation to personnel budgetary provisions, performance, and attainment of school objectives.

---

3. The board delegates the executive activity completely (unit control) to its executive officer and holds him responsible for the execution of board policy.

4. The chief executive delegates such authority and responsibility as he deems necessary to subordinate agents, and formulates plans, programs, procedures, rules, and regulations as are essential to attainment of desired results.

This arrangement neither advocates abdication nor abrogation of the legal function of the board of education. In essence, it simply means that the board establishes policy, verifies it in written form, and delegates its execution as a unit to the superintendent of schools.

In actual practice, the dividing line between who makes policy and who puts it into effect is a very tenuous one; the legal obligation for adoption of school policy rests squarely with the board on policy matters. As will be noted in the following section, the superintendent frequently proposes the adoption, extension, revision, or elimination of policies through the budget proposals which he submits for board consideration. Likewise, the board may wish to go beyond mere policy statement regarding certain personnel activities. Consider this illustration:

It is the policy of the Millville Board of Education to assist all personnel to become increasingly proficient in the performance of their work through continuous in-service education.

Can the administrator translate this policy statement into workable plans without some indication from the board as to the scope of the assistance it intends to provide, the nature of the in-service activities which should be wholly or partially supported at board expense? If policies and procedures are planned without staff participation, are they realistic and capable of engendering wholehearted support? The point is that formulation of policies and procedures is most effective when undertaken cooperatively, and with the desire to establish those conditions which will make possible the best educational opportunities which can be provided.

The Budget and Personnel Policy

Budgets—like purposes, policies, and programs—are plans employed by administration to guide and to control the many-faceted operations which characterize a school system. Before discussing the relationship between budgets and the personnel function, several terms should be defined. There are various kinds of budgets—annual, long term, capital, performance, building, department, special project. Irrespective of the name, the fundamental consideration behind any budget is that it is an instrument for putting purposes, policies, and programs into effect. Generally speaking, a budget defines a program for a given period to achieve established purposes. It includes an estimate of expenditures and the proposed sources of financial support. The *budget document* is the formal plan adopted by the governing body which binds the organization to its expenditure and revenue provisions. *The budgetary process*, on the other hand, is the method or methods by which the budget plan is initiated, prepared, adopted, and administered. It includes the persons and procedures involved in carrying the budget from the planning stages to the end of the fiscal period.

Advantages which can accrue to the administrator and staff members from skillful application of the budgetary process are extensive. Here are some examples:

1. The entire staff can participate in certain decisions, and contribute ideas to the personnel program to be incorporated in the budget.

2. Development of personnel provisions in the budget involves analysis of present plans to determine how suitable they are in terms of the work to be accomplished, how fully and effectively the present staff is utilized, and what budgetary revisions are needed to correct present shortcomings.

3. Long-range personnel needs can be analyzed and made the basis for a systematic recruitment program.

4. General objectives of the personnel program can be translated into specific short- and long-term budgetary plans, including the quality and quantity of personnel to be employed, their compensation, development, and conditions of employment.

While the foregoing opportunities for relating the budgetary process to the personnel function are not necessarily the most essential ones, they serve to emphasize an important point. School systems cannot improve personnel programs unless the central administrative staff has an understanding of, and makes appropriate use of, the budget for this purpose.

If policy is an expression of the board, and therefore community expectation concerning the conduct of school affairs, then it appears to be a fairly reasonable assumption that the budget is a most useful indicator of the extent to which policies have been translated into genuine plans of action. There are those who contend that budgetary provisions which prevail for school personnel are, to a large extent, what planners wish to prevail. They argue that even though legal and financial circumstances often prevent boards from establishing optimum personnel provisions, a budget generally manifests attitudes and efforts toward the formulation and implementation of sound policy. A budget cannot help but reflect policy, it is said, even if it has been prepared without reference to any policy and results in "policy by default."

Certainly any school budget provides at least outward manifestations of personnel policy, since a major portion of the current expenditure items is devoted to personnel in the form of salaries, wages, retirement, in-service development, and collateral benefits. The nature, scope, and, to some extent, the quality of personnel provisions are identifiable through budgetary analysis. Budgetary provisions for school personnel are known to vary widely among school districts, which may be attributed largely to variations in personnel policies.

Thoughtful consideration of the concept of the budget as a schematic plan for crystallizing organizational policies, plans, and resources will reveal its potential for appraising, initiating, adjusting, planning, integrating, and controlling policies and programs. The relationship between the school budget and personnel policies is a strong one, inasmuch as: (1) most policies lead to a price tag of some sort; (2) the budget forces translation of policies into specific plans involving precise dollar requirements; (3) the budgetary process makes possible an annual review of the effectiveness of existing policy; (4) the budget provides an important channel of communication for describing and clarifying policy; and (5) the unity, emphasis, and balance essential to policy planning are best realized through the medium of the budget.

Using the Budget in Personnel Planning

As experienced administrators know, putting policies into effect requires money. However impressive and potentially promising a plan may appear to be, and however painstakingly it may have been developed, it represents something of a mental exercise until a budget appropriation for its implementation has been formally approved.

A budget, in the final analysis, is a monetary expression of policy. Dollar signs before the various budget items are suggestive of board expectations. Even the absence of a particular item in the budget expresses board policy. The budget which appropriates more money for grass seed than it does for a program of in-service development of school personnel is an expression of policy. Such policy will be unwritten, but, to all intents and purposes, it indicates the course of action which has been adopted.

The budget is the most important instrument administration has to plan, to implement, to improve, and to control the many-faceted operations of a school system. It is a numerical storehouse of hundreds of large and small decisions which have been established to guide administrative action.

How can the administrator use the budget in personnel planning? While an extensive list could be developed, following are some guides which may be useful:

1. Developing a budgetary process which would enlist the judgment of the total staff in the formulation of the personnel program.

2. Encouraging the administration to review past budgetary practice in relation to the personnel program to determine whether the program and its support are adequate.

3. Planning the human and material resources to meet requirements of the total personnel plan.

4. Interpreting the personnel program through the proposed budget to the staff, board, and community.

5. Familiarizing board members with immediate and long-term personnel requirements.

6. Balancing personnel needs against those of the total program to determine budget priorities and emphases.

7. Making effective use of appropriations for personnel activities through a budgetary control system.

Hence, the budget and the process by which it is produced can be utilized extensively in personnel planning, not merely in quantifying organizational needs, but also in bringing about systematic examination of problems and issues. An example will illustrate this point. Consider the budgetary course of a single item pertaining to personnel, such as the need to adjust teachers' salaries to a wholesome level. Since this is in keeping with board compensation policy, the chief executive is asked to present his considered recommendations in the form of a budget proposal. Through an enlightened budgetary process the chief executive elicits staff, citizen, and board judgment as to salary and wage levels which should obtain, both in terms of recruiting potential and in terms of fairness to existing personnel. This approach would necessarily require a number of additional considerations, such as the long-term financial implications of the budget proposal, its effect upon other budgetary requirements, and willingness of the community to provide necessary fiscal support. Further discussion of the proposal, through budget hearings, and various types of group conferences afford opportunities for both proponents and opponents of the proposal to be heard. Board review of the entire budget before adoption permits appraisal of the soundness of the recommendation, whether or not it is fiscally feasible, and whether or not its approval would lead to neglect of other equally important priorities. In short, budgeting becomes an administrative and social refinery in which educational problems are resolved and find expression.

The budget, then, is more than a listing of expenditures and revenues to stay in business for another year. It should be viewed as a focal point around which there is a powerful interplay of forces, factors, and conditions which combine to determine the richness or meagerness of educational experiences available to children. It is worth emphasizing here that, while the budget is not all there is to planning education, it is a means through which virtually all planning decisions are put into operation.

To a greater or lesser extent every school district is compelled to prepare a school budget and to stay within its provisions. These tasks are not exacting if the budget is prepared merely to meet the letter and spirit of the law. But a budget which is carefully developed, and which relates each item to the attainment of administrative goals, is an entirely different consideration. Between the optimum and the minimum kinds of budgets there is an appreciable difference. Building the optimum budget calls for an understanding of its social, educational, economic, and administrative significance. It calls for a sound policy basis, balancing of many judgments, continuity of planning, and integration of hundreds of major and minor decisions calculated to provide an educational program which is in keeping with the demands of a society which becomes increasingly complex with the passing of time.

Suggested Reading

Coleman, James S., *Community Conflict* (Glencoe, Ill.: Free Press, 1957).

Hunter, Floyd, *Community Power Structure* (Chapel Hill: University of North Carolina Press, 1953).

Jonassen, Christen T., *The Measurement of Community Dimensions and Elements* (Columbus: Ohio State University, Center for Educational Administration, 1959).

National Industrial Conference Board, *Statements of Personnel Policy* (New York: The Board, 1959).

National Industrial Conference Board, *Personnel Procedure Manuals*, Studies in Personnel Policy, No. 180 (New York: The Board, 1961).

Ovsiew, Leon, and William B. Castetter, *Budgeting for Better Schools* (Englewood Cliffs, N. J.: Prentice-Hall, Inc., 1960).

Ridley, Clarence, *The Role of the City Manager in Policy Formulation* (Chicago: The International City Managers' Association, 1958).

Wayland, Sloan R., Edmund de S. Brunner, and Wilbur C. Hallenbeck, *Aids to Community Analysis for the School Administrator* (New York: Bureau of Publications, Teachers College, Columbia University, 1956).

White, Alpheus L., *Characteristics of Local School Board Policy Manuals*, Bulletin 1959, No. 14 (Washington: U.S. Government Printing Office, 1959).

The Human Element in
Personnel Administration

CHAPTER THREE

The administrative process can be perceived as having two dimensions. One is impersonal, relating to purposes, structures, policies, regulations, schedules, programs, funds, and facilities. The other dimension is personalistic, having to do with the satisfaction of human needs which are not necessarily related to organizational goals. While much of the content of this text is focused on the first dimension, it does not follow that the importance of the human factor in personnel administration is considered to be insignificant. As a matter of fact, administration is a complex mixture of personal and impersonal elements which are inseparable, even though much of the earlier emphasis in educational administration was devoted to its substantive aspects.

The first section of this chapter is devoted to human problems of school organizations, factors related to human satisfaction, organizational obstacles to need satisfaction, and the implications of these considerations for personnel administration. The second section treats important aspects of the administrative process involved in bringing individual needs and organizational demands into balance. These include communication, morale, supervision, group processes, organization, and administrative behavior.

Human Problems in Organizations

The Individual and the Organization

A school system may be described as an organization within which an essential social service is performed. Among the broad observations which can be made about the school organization, and around which this discussion is focused, are the following:

1. A school system is created to fulfill a set of expectations.

2. Expectations are made explicit through constitutions, statutes, and policy statements.

3. The legal and policy framework defines the nature of the activities and the roles of the system.

4. Roles are further defined by rules, regulations, procedures, practices, and programs.

5. Each individual in the organization has a task to perform which necessarily involves interaction with other individuals. These tasks are related in a manner conceived to achieve organizational expectations.

6. Each individual in the organization brings to his work certain needs which he seeks to satisfy.

7. When the needs of the individual and the demands of the organization are not congruent, problems arise which affect both the individual and the organization.

8. Seldom, if ever, are organizational demands and individual needs completely compatible. Causes of the disparity reside both in the individual and in the institution.

Characteristics of Individual Needs

Each individual brings to his role in the organization a pattern of needs which has been defined in various ways.[1] According to Davis, needs may be classified as primary or secondary. Primary needs are physiological, such as hunger, thirst, and sleep. Secondary needs de-

---

[1] Useful descriptions of human needs may be found in I. L. Heckmann, Jr., and S. G. Huneryager, *Human Relations in Management* (Cincinnati, Ohio: South-Western Publishing Co., 1960); also George Strauss and Leonard R. Sayles, *Personnel—The Human Problems of Management* (Englewood Cliffs, N.J.: Prentice-Hall, Inc., 1960).

rive from interaction with environment, are largely social, and have the following characteristics:

1. They are strongly conditioned by experience.
2. They vary in type and intensity among people.
3. They change within any individual.
4. They work in groups, rather than alone.
5. They are often hidden from conscious recognition.
6. They are nebulous feelings instead of tangible physical needs.
7. They influence behavior.

As illustrated in Figure 4, there are priority levels and a sequence of domination among human needs. The secondary needs, such as attention and self-realization do not assume importance until the primary or physical needs have been satisfied.[2]

This brings us to the question of the relevance of human needs to school administration. In a fundamental sense, the satisfaction of human needs is essential to the attainment of institutional objectives. The will of members of the school organization to cooperate in, or to resist, the attainment of objectives is strongly influenced by the extent to which each is able to experience work satisfaction.

It is axiomatic that work is necessary to satisfy physical needs, that is, to secure life's necessities. But in the process of earning a living, there are other needs which each individual seeks to satisfy. When opportunities do not exist to enable the individual to give expression to the secondary or social needs described earlier, feelings of discontent and dissatisfaction frequently develop which lead to behavior which is inimical to the work of the institution. The more fully work satisfies the individual, the greater will be his cooperation and productivity. To put the point more emphatically, an individual's work is an important means by which to satisfy fundamental human needs. These needs, it should be noted, are not necessarily related to the aims of the institution, but when opportunities in the work situation are not conducive to their satisfaction, the consequences to both the individual and the institution can be serious.

All who are involved in administration of an educational enterprise share the responsibility for understanding the relationship between human needs and work satisfaction, and for continuous efforts to improve working conditions and climate conducive to physical and

[2] Keith Davis, *Human Relations in Business* (New York: McGraw-Hill Book Co., 1957), pp. 38–39.

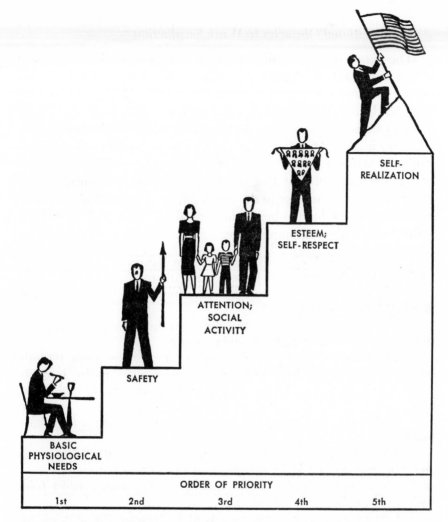

SELF-REALIZATION

ESTEEM;
SELF-RESPECT

ATTENTION;
SOCIAL
ACTIVITY

SAFETY

BASIC
PHYSIOLOGICAL
NEEDS

ORDER OF PRIORITY

| 1st | 2nd | 3rd | 4th | 5th |

FIGURE 4 **Priority of human needs.** From Keith Davis, *Human Relations in Business* (New York: McGraw-Hill Book Co., 1957), p. 41. By permission.

psychological satisfactions of school personnel. This understanding is especially important in school administration, since satisfaction of secondary needs of professional workers is assumed to be of a greater relative importance than it is for the nonprofessional.[3]

[3] Insights into ways in which satisfaction with the school system is related to personal characteristics of teachers and to administrative policies and practices are reported in a study by Francis S. Chase, "Factors for Satisfaction in Teaching," *Phi Delta Kappan*, 33, No. 3 (November, 1951), pp. 127–132.

Organizational Obstacles to Work Satisfaction

The nature of the organization to which an individual is attached has an important bearing on the extent to which he is able to satisfy his physical and psychological needs. Provisions which govern his job security, the extent and kind of supervision established, the amount of freedom he is able to exercise in the performance of his work, group relationships, opportunities for advancement, and incentives of various kinds frequently influence need satisfaction either positively or negatively. Argyris points out that organizational principles currently adhered to are not conducive to the development of characteristics which exemplify mature human beings in our culture. This position is illustrated in the following propositions:

1. There is a lack of congruency between the needs of healthy individuals and the demands of the formal organization.
2. The resultants of this disturbance are frustration, failure, short-time perspective, and conflict.
3. Under certain conditions the degree of frustration, failure, short-time perspective, and conflict will tend to increase.
4. The nature of the formal principles of organization cause the subordinates, at any given level, to experience competition, rivalry, intersubordinate hostility and to develop a focus toward the parts rather than the whole.
5. Employees react to formal organization by creating informal activities.
6. The employee adaptive behavior maintains individual self-integration and simultaneously facilitates integration with the formal organization.
7. The adaptive behavior of the employees has a cumulative effect, feeds back into the formal organization, and reinforces itself.
8. Certain management reactions tend to increase the antagonisms underlying the adaptive behavior.[4]

These propositions provide a general explanation of sources of conflict and behavioral consequences in an organizational setting. Solutions to the human problems of organization are more difficult and less certain. But it is clear that the administrator must be constantly alert to the impact of the organization on the individual em-

[4] Chris Argyris, *Understanding Organizational Behavior* (Homewood, Ill.: The Dorsey Press, Inc., 1960), pp. 14–18.

ployee. From the standpoint of staff relations he must understand the subtle relationships between the goals of the organization, the principles and practices employed in their attainment, and their impact on the individual. It can be assumed that provision for the primary needs of personnel in education are no longer a paramount concern, since arrangements have been made through minimum salary legislation, tenure provisions, social security, retirement, and leaves of absence to alleviate the problem. The greatest opportunities for educational administration to secure staff cooperation lie in organizational provisions to satisfy secondary needs. Few will deny that much can be done in every educational system to deal with organizational obstacles which interfere with the individual's desire for self-realization. In the discussion which follows we will examine certain aspects of the administrative process and how they are related to personnel cooperation. Before doing so, it should be noted that certain fallacies have developed about efforts to deal with human problems in organizations. Some have construed the concept of human relations as an effort to help people to be "happy." Others believe it is a means of improving race relations. Still others have taken it to mean "a democratic process" in which all members of an organization should participate in decision making. While there is a kernel of truth in these conceptions, the problems of human beings in an organization, and the ways in which these problems are solved, are more extensive considerations. Getzels and Guba summarize the administrative implications of human relations concisely by noting that:

> The unique task of administration, at least with respect to staff relations, is just this: to integrate the demands of the institution and the demands of the staff members in a way that is organizationally productive and individually fulfilling.[5]

Achieving Cooperation: Communication

Communication and Cooperation

Having said that attainment and institutional expectations is dependent upon personnel cooperation, it will be helpful to examine an essential element in sustaining and improving the will of a school staff

---

[5] J. W. Getzels and E. G. Guba, "Social Behavior and the Administrative Process," *The School Review*, LXV, No. 4 (Winter, 1957), p. 430.

to work together. This element is referred to as communication, or the process through which explanations, ideas, information, directions, attitudes, and feelings are transmitted from person to person and group to group.

It can be seen readily that personnel performance and organizational communication are closely related. The individual's understanding of what the organization expects to accomplish; how it plans to achieve its aims; what it expects him to do; how, when, where, why, and with what and whom it expects him to do it; and whether it considers his work satisfactory depends upon the efficiency of the communication system.

The number of instances of failure in communication within an organization are literally legion, resulting in grievances, unsatisfactory individual performance, misunderstandings, resignations, lack of concern for system-wide goals, and a general decline in unified behavior. In effect, communication is organization's connective tissue. The clearer the understanding that effective communication in an organization is essential to the satisfaction of physical and psychological needs, as well as to the attainment of purpose, the more apparent is the need for efforts to improve it.

Characteristics of Communication in Organizations

The work of organizations is carried on largely through oral and written forms of communication. The primary function of communication from an organizational standpoint is to influence behavior in ways conducive to attainment of purpose. The form of behavior which the organization expects as a consequence of communication, however, does not always materialize, especially if the receiver's response is unfavorable.

The direction of organizational communication may be downward, upward, or horizontal. Downward communication usually parallels the line of responsibility, and is essential to the continuity of organizational life. Official educational policies, programs, standards, definition of assignments, and schedules of various kinds are examples of information which is transmitted along the superior-subordinate axis. Upward communication indicates the transmission of information from the subordinate through the administrative hierarchy. There are several important reasons why administration should encourage the upward flow of information. The first is to determine the extent to which the goals of the school system are being attained, the problems which arise in the conduct of the work of the school, and the corrective action which is needed. A second, and one which is being examined with increasing frequency, is to determine whether organizational arrangements are conducive to personnel cooperation. By such means as grievance machinery, workshops, small group conferences, surveys, faculty meetings, and committee work greater emphasis is being placed on the flow of information from the bottom to the top of the organization structure. For purposes of coordination, horizontal communication to personnel at the same operating level, such as those who perform staff functions, is necessary.

Informal communication is also a characteristic of the process by which information is transmitted and received within an organization. The work which is carried on in a single school building through interpersonal relationships requires communication. Informal face-to-face contacts among teachers, principals, supervisors, and custodians are important means by which formal communications are analyzed, interpreted, disseminated, and through which personnel are motivated. The "grapevine" is an important element in informal communication, and one which tends to operate to the disadvantage of organization in the absence of proper formal communication. A central task of administration is to integrate the formal and informal systems of communication in order to promote the mutual cooperation between the individual and the organization which is essential to achieving organizational aims and to satisfying individual needs.

Personnel cooperation can be furthered when the factors which inhibit effective communication are understood, and when efforts are made to minimize persistent barriers. These include: (1) preventing downward channels of communication from being overloaded; (2) encouraging the free flow of ideas and information in all directions, (3) developing a sensitivity among members of the administrative staff to the need for understanding the psychological barriers to effective communication; and (4) planning programs to help members of the administrative staff with some of the fundamental problems of communication with which they are confronted.

There is no easy answer to the communication problems involved in administering a school system. Through careful attention to communication roadblocks, analyzing the reasons why they develop, and searching for possible solutions, gains can be achieved which ultimately lead to greater organizational efficiency.[6]

Achieving Cooperation: Supervision

Supervision and Personnel Adjustment

If every member of the school organization is to fulfill his role satisfactorily, there are at least three kinds of personal adjustments which need to be made. First is the adjustment of the individual to the work which he is expected to perform. Second is the adjustment to the persons with whom the work is performed. The third adjustment is to the administrator who is primarily reponsible for directing or coordinating his work. The emphasis in the discussion which follows is focused on the importance of effective supervision in helping organization personnel to make the foregoing adjustments.

The term "supervision" has acquired various meanings in the language of educational administration. As used herein, it refers to those activities which are designed to facilitate the adjustment of professional and noninstructional personnel. As such, supervision is not limited to personnel who hold the title of "supervisor." It includes all staff personnel who are engaged in assisting people to fulfill their work assignments. Hence, the building principal, the director of transportation, the business manager, and the director of personnel are conceived as supervisors in the sense that they have an important responsibility for helping other staff members to make those adjustments essential to competent performance. Cues to the relationship between supervision and individual adjustment are provided in the following quotation:

When an individual performs up to role expectations, we may say that he is *adjusted* to the role. Conversely, when an individual fulfills all his needs, we may speak of him as integrated. Ideally, the individual should be both adjusted and integrated, so that he may by one act fulfill both the nomothetic, or institutional, requirements and the ideographic, or personal

---

[6] For detailed treatments of communication in organization, see the following: Jack A. Culbertson, Paul B. Jacobson, and Theodore L. Reller, *Administrative Relationships: A Casebook* (Englewood Cliffs, N.J.: Prentice-Hall, Inc., 1960), Chapter 5; I. L. Heckman, Jr., and S. G. Huneryager, *Human Relations in Management* (Cincinnati, Ohio: South-Western Publishing Co., 1960), Part 5; Willard V. Merrihue, *Managing by Communication* (New York: McGraw-Hill Book Co., 1960).

requirements. This would obviously be the case if institutional expectations and personal needs were absolutely congruent, for the individual would always will what was mandatory, and both his adjustment and his integration would be maximized. But absolute congruence of expectations and needs is seldom, if ever, found in practice, and as a consequence there is inevitably a greater or lesser amount of strain for the individual and the institution.[7]

Implicit in the concept of personnel adjustment is the fact that the satisfaction of individual needs is a continuous process throughout the employment cycle. Supervision contributes materially to the total administrative effort to satisfy both organizational expectations and personnel physical and psychological needs. The section which follows considers how supervision can be used in achieving these ends.

Implications for Supervision

The occupational phases of a professional career in public education can be viewed as consisting of three stages, including the probationary, tenure, and terminal periods.[8] Throughout each of these phases, various kinds of personnel adjustments are necessary. A major task of supervision is to provide assistance to members of the school organization in solving the problems with which they are constantly confronted during the employment period. Supervision is highly essential during the probationary period, from the time of recruitment until the organization decides whether the individual is capable of fulfilling role expectations. More specifically, supervision can help the organization clarify the position requirements and the qualifications necessary for successful performance. It can assist in the selection process through assessment of personnel potential to meet position requirements. Once the individual has been selected, it is a prime responsibility of supervision to orient him to the work he is to perform, to acquaint him with his associates, and to help him to understand the goals of the school system and how his particular assignment is related to them. The process of helping the new teacher to make initial adjustments also includes interpretation of organizational policies and

[7] J. W. Getzels and E. G. Guba, *op. cit.*, p. 431.

[8] Sociologists identify five phases in the occupational career pattern of the typical industrial worker—preparatory, initial, trial, stable, and retirement. See Delbert C. Miller and William H. Form, *Industrial Sociology* (New York: Harper & Brothers, 1951), pp. 517 ff.

procedures, school and community relationships, and other facets of organizational life.[9] Throughout the probationary period, the supervisor is responsible for appraising the new teacher's performance, for helping him to master the technology of the work assignment, for helping him to establish the necessary working relationships with his colleagues, and for facilitating his personal and professional development. In general, effective supervision helps to minimize the factors which are conducive to personnel anxiety and insecurity during a period when the adjustment demands are formidable.

During the tenure period an important supervisory task relates to motivation of the individual teacher. By encouraging members of the organization to accept responsibility for self-development and creativity, supervision helps them to fulfill the role of the professional, during the course of which organizational demands are fulfilled and human needs, such as self-realization, recognition, and status can be satisfied.

Dealing with personnel maladjustment, which is expressed in various forms of personal behavior such as aggression or regression, and which is not conducive to satisfactory work performance, is an important supervisory task. Changes in work assignments, unsatisfactory superior-subordinate relationships, lack of promotion, nonacceptance by associates, and repetitive work are illustrative of situations which frequently create individual maladjustment. Effective supervision can neither solve all personnel problems nor bring about the adjustment of all problem personnel. But it can contribute materially to the minimization of tension and strain within the school system by improving efforts for identifying and dealing with the sources of personnel maladjustment, including the nature of the individual. Dubin questions the assumption that all people like to work, and points out that the supervisory approach to the work-oriented person should be different than that used with the nonwork-oriented person.[10] In short, supervision must deal increasingly with the complexities of human nature and its implications for organizational behavior.

The terminal period of occupational employment refers to the time when personnel approach retirement age. Since this represents a period of transition for personnel, new forms of adjustment prob-

---

[9] See Chapter 9 for an extended discussion of orientation problems and procedures.
[10] Robert Dubin, *The World of Work: Industrial Sociology and Human Relations* (Englewood Cliffs, N. J.: Prentice-Hall, Inc., 1958), pp. 254–258.

lems emerge. In some cases it involves a change in the standard of living, disruption of the social aspects of work, and diminishment of work-connected satisfactions. With increasing frequency, supervision is assuming greater responsibilities for providing assistance to potential retirants so that they can understand and deal effectively with adjustment problems.[11]

Achieving Cooperation: Group Work

The quest for ways by which groups can be organized to benefit both the institution and those who perform its work has been an interesting administrative development. So extensive is the effort to apply the findings of group processes to educational administration that school personnel rarely experience a working day without some form of group involvement.

The term group processes, often referred to as group dynamics, is construed throughout this discussion to mean the face-to-face participation of school personnel in small groups who come together to perform a service or task related to the operation of the school system. Although there are numerous kinds of groups formed in a school system, including conferences, assemblies, seminars, workshops, faculty and administrative meetings, the emphasis in the following discussion is focused on small work groups and committees. Functions of such groups, their significance for the organization and for the individual, their limitations, and administrative implications will be examined in turn.

Functions of Groups

The universal administrative practice of forming groups to facilitate the work of school systems stems from a variety of reasons. These include growth in size and complexity of school organizations, the urgency to adjust educational programs to the realities of social change, the necessity for developing improved means for securing personnel cooperation, and demands for democratization of the administrative process. In addition, it should be noted that the work of

[11] Supervisory principles and practices are dealt with extensively in Herbert J. Chruden and Arthur W. Sherman, Jr., *Personnel Management* (Cincinnati, Ohio: South-Western Publishing Company, 1959), and Kimbal Wiles, *Supervision for Better Schools*, 2nd ed. (Englewood Cliffs, N.J.: Prentice-Hall, Inc., 1955).

a school system is centered largely around professional personnel upon whom the institution depends heavily for the creativity essential to educational change.

Involvement of the staff in organizational problems has led to substantial increases in the number of groups and the frequency with which they meet. General functions which groups are asked to perform are indicated in the following list:

Function	Activities
1. Planning	Designing educational specifications for a new school building; formulating a system-wide development program for personnel.
2. Appraising	Appraising the effectiveness of a course of study, a curriculum, or the existing compensation structure.
3. Communicating	Explaining the provisions of social security and retirement to members of the school staff.
4. Advising	Recommending features essential to policies governing academic freedom.
5. Educating	Acquiring and interpreting to staff information about trends in secondary school mathematics.

The manner in which and the results achieved through the use of small groups to perform the functions illustrated above vary widely among and even within school systems. Group productivity depends upon many things, including the competency of its members, the nature of the task with which it is confronted, the processes employed in the conduct of the work, the extent to which groups are permitted to use initiative in solving problems, and administrative integrity in dealing with group suggestions, decisions, or recommendations.

Significance of the Group to the Institution

There are many recorded beliefs as to why the school organization should foster participation of groups in the conduct of its affairs. It is widely held, for example, that the most practical approach to securing personnel cooperation is through their involvement in the conduct of school affairs. Other benefits which are said to accrue to the organization when groups are properly organized include the development of better understanding of organizational goals, more effective solutions to problems, encouragement of creativity, improved motivation and morale, opportunity for the identification and development of leadership, and better communication.

Significance of Group Work to the Individuals

Group activity within the institution offers considerable opportunity for satisfying the secondary or social wants of the individual. Under appropriate conditions the group environment is conducive to individual expression, innovation, and development of creative capacities. The group can serve as a useful device for the individual to contribute ideas and suggestions for improving the way things are done in the organization, for correcting what he believes to be its shortcomings. It is the avenue by which he helps and is helped by his colleagues; it is a means for gaining recognition and status; it can be the escalator to his aspirations. The group is potentially useful to the individual as a learning laboratory where he gains skill in communication and cooperation, comes to see the problems of the institution in a different perspective, extends his interpersonal relations, and obtains a broader understanding of the institution and his role in it.

Limitations of Group and Committee Work

It is generally conceded that the group is important to the work of the organization, and provides a means for satisfying individual wants. But there are some misconceptions of, and limitations to, group work which deserve consideration. At its magnificent best, group deliberation is never a simple process. The mere act of forming a committee to solve a problem does not ensure solution. What is more, the group, in its efforts to reach agreement, often blunts the individual creativity which it is supposed to encourage. Whyte sums up the problem in this way:

Think for a moment of the way you behave in a committee meeting. In your capacity as a group member you feel a strong impulse to seek common ground with the others. Not just out of timidity but out of respect for the sense of the meeting you tend to soft-pedal that which would go against the grain. And that, unfortunately, can include unorthodox ideas.

A really new idea affronts current agreement—it wouldn't be a new idea if it didn't—and the group, impelled as it is to agreement, is instinctively hostile to that which is divisive. With wise leadership it can offset this bias, but the essential urge will still be to unity, to concensus.[12]

If we look at the use of committees in school systems, it will be noted that there is considerable room for improvement. The tendency to deify the committee, to place in its collective lap problems which do not rightfully belong there, or problems which remain there much longer than they ought to, is all too common. The committee decision has also been used as a subtle device which makes identification of its responsibility virtually impossible.

Group meetings can be wasteful of time, money, and effort when not properly organized for, and oriented to, a given task. In brief, it should be recognized that the success of the organization depends heavily upon effective group work. But group work has its limitations, a major one being that it is not a device which relieves the administrator of the necessity for making decisions which are unpopular. Nor is it conceived to be the only environment conducive to sound judgment.

Conditions of Group Effectiveness

Until the laws and principles of group behavior are perfected, group activity need not be suspended. The school system will go on, but will go on more effectively if educational administration reconsiders how, when, and for what purposes groups should be formed to assist in the conduct of school affairs.

From what has been learned about committee work in educational institutions, it seems clear that neither the needs of group participants nor the expectations of administration will be fulfilled when:

1. The purposes for which the group is formed are not clarified or are purposely concealed.

2. The nature of the tasks assigned to the group is not conducive to the satisfaction of participant needs.

3. The function of the group is executive rather than advisory. For example, difficulties often arise when a committee is given responsibility to administer a program.

[12] William F. Whyte, Jr., *The Organization Man* (New York: Simon and Schuster, Inc., 1956), p. 58.

4. There is misunderstanding about the extent of group authority.

5. The number of committees in the school system poses serious problems of coordination.

6. The work of a committee is not given due recognition, or its recommendations discounted by administration without explanation.

It is very probable that administrative concern with group work will increase rather than lessen. Emergence of team-teaching and lay-advisory groups in public education adds to the necessity for greater understanding of the complex problem of helping groups to function in a manner that will promote personnel cooperation, contribute to organizational goals, and at the same time provide satisfaction for the participants.

Achieving Cooperation: Organization

Elements of Organization

Examination of any organized activity will reveal the existence of at least three elements which are closely related to each other. These include:

1. The purpose or goal of the activity: to create a specific product, to care for the sick, to provide educational opportunities.

2. The work or activities necessary to the attainment of the purpose. This includes not only what work is to be done, but, in general, how it is to be done, where it is to be done, funds and facilities necessary to do the work, how the work tasks are related, and the methods for ensuring that they are carried out effectively. These arrangements comprise the organizational structure.

3. The people who do the work.

These elements of organization are symbolized in Figure 5 by an equilateral triangle, in which the base represents *purpose*, and the two sides *structure* and *personnel*. If the organization is to be effective, the three elements must be closely integrated. Purpose must appeal to those employed to attain it; the structure must be conducive to effective work, and the people in the organization must find satisfaction in the work they perform. How to arrange the components of organization into an effective plan for achieving a collective purpose, then, is both a persistent and challenging administrative problem.

At first glance, there would seem to be little or no relationship of

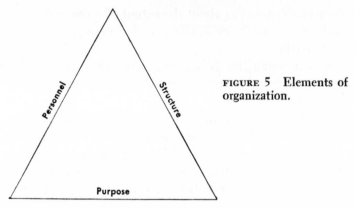

FIGURE 5   Elements of organization.

an organization to the behavior of its personnel. The more closely we examine the matter, however, the more apparent it is that organizational arrangements have both positive and negative effects on the individual. The discussion which follows aims to describe major characteristics of school organizations, the impact of structure upon personnel, and the implications of organization for personnel administration.

Formal Organization

Formal organization refers to arrangements made for getting work done. It may be conceived as the division of labor or allocation of tasks, in the process of which decisions are made as to who shall do the work and who shall direct those who do it. The broad features of formal organization can be identified by examination of Figure 6, which illustrates the line-staff type of organization structure. The line of authority and responsibility, as depicted by the heavy black line constitutes the framework for the organization structure. It indicates those directly responsible for achieving the objectives of the school system. The staff officers, identified by the light black lines, serve the organization in advisory, control, and service capacities.

The type of organization shown in Figure 6 is frequently referred to as the tall or pyramidal type of organization, in which there are several levels of authority between the classroom teacher and the chief executive officer.

A second type of organization structure is illustrated in Figure 7. This is known as the flat type of organization, since the number of

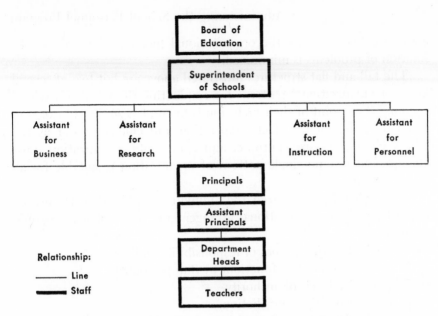

FIGURE 6　Illustration of line-staff type organization.

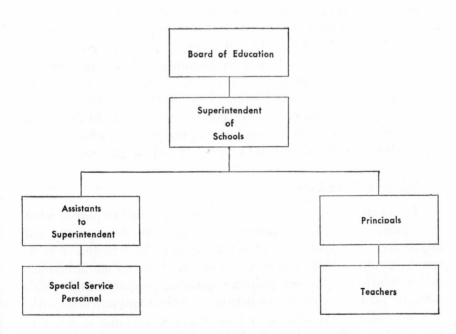

FIGURE 7　Illustration of flat type of organization.

73

administrative levels in the organizational hierarchy involved in the solution of problems is minimized.

The tall and flat structures illustrated above are but two of several kinds of organizational patterns for conducting the work of a school system.[13] The point of their inclusion is to emphasize that (1) organizational arrangements affect cooperation and efficiency; (2) as the school changes in size, purpose, and complexity, organization must change; and (3) no single pattern of organization is suitable for all school systems.

It is generally recognized that human complications are precipitated by certain organizational arrangements, a list of which would include:

1. Lack of clarity in lines of responsibility and authority.
2. Assumption of line functions by staff personnel.
3. Excessive levels of authority.
4. Dual or multiple jurisdiction.
5. Lack of understanding of organizational relationships.
6. Lack of coordination.
7. Failure to grant authority to make decisions at the point of action. If we add to this list the organizational arrangements not conducive to opportunities for the individual to experience variety in his work, independence of thought and action, reasonable freedom from authority, and sufficient leeway in planning and carrying out his assignment, the significance of organizational structure as a conditioner of personnel behavior becomes increasingly apparent.

Thus, one of administration's continuous tasks is to develop a framework designed to minimize human problems, and which secures cooperation by will rather than by authority and exhortation.

Informal Organization

The organization charts illustrated above are used to portray what is frequently referred to as formal organization. By definition, formal organization is a systematic plan for unifying the activities of individuals to accomplish a collective purpose. It is an administrative design which presupposes purposes, policies, programs, and which indicates planned relationships between positions and functions with-

[13] See Cooperative Development of Public School Administration in New York State, *Modern Practices and Concepts of Staffing Schools* (Albany: New York State Teachers Association, 1956).

out reference to specific individuals. It establishes lines of authority and communication, as well as reporting relationships.

While the formal structure of a school system helps us to understand how the mutually dependent organizational components are supposed to be grouped and arranged, it does not reveal anything about the individual and how he fulfills his role. It is possible, for example, to develop an organization chart before personnel are selected to occupy the positions. This leads to the observation that an organization cannot be fully understood until we learn something about the behavior of the people who fill the positions on the organization chart.

We know from experience that individuals and groups in an organization become associated with each other. These interpersonal relationships give rise to a second dimension of organization known as informal organization. It comes into being and maintains itself through the interaction of members of a group or clique whose associations are determined by factors such as work location, insecurity, common interests or values, and similarity in points of view or beliefs. The latter element, it should be noted, is central to the existence of informal groups.

Informal groups arise and exist to satisfy the mutual needs of members created in part by, but not wholly satisfied through, formal organization. Consider this illustration. Foxcroft school district has developed an indefinite leave-of-absence plan for all school personnel. After the leave plan was in operation for one year, several teachers abused the leave privilege by being absent for what appeared to other professional personnel to be an excessive number of days. Informal groups in each of the schools in the system became aware of this situation through the "grapevine." Consequently, several groups decided to take informal action against those few persons abusing the privilege. The groups called upon the violators and succeeded in convincing them that continuance of such behavior would jeopardize one of the most unique leave-of-absence plans available to school personnel.

This illustration affords further generalization about the informal organization. We note that the informal groups are not established by formal organization. They arise from the interaction of people in the performance of work, and depend on the "grapevine" as the communication system. Informal organization is spontaneous, indefinite, variable, and in a constant state of transition. The life cycle of an informal group may be short or long, depending upon how successful it is in attaining its goals.

In effect, the informal organization is a behavior system which operates in a variety of ways to satisfy personal needs. Deficiencies in the formal structure, such as autocratic administration, conditions of work, lack of grievance machinery, injustice to staff members, and a faulty compensation plan may precipitate formation of informal groups whose goals are usually to seek remedies to work-related problems.

The informal organization is capable of helping or hindering attainment of a collective purpose. It can work for or against the administration, for example, when efforts are made to introduce changes in policies, procedures, and programs.

It is certain that informal organization is a permanent and integral feature of the total organizational structure. Since it influences the behavior of personnel, as well as the attainment of organizational ends, it is of primary significance to personnel administration.

To ignore the existence or potential of informal organization is to invite conflict. To deal with it intelligently, the reasons for its existence must be understood. Quite often the circumstances which give rise to informal organization are the product of ineffective arrangements in the formal organization.

Ideally, formal and informal organization should complement each other. The informal organization should be construed as a positive rather than negative force, one which can be relied upon to exert constructive actions for the welfare of the organization. If this is to be done, however, administration must accept the existence of informal groups, understand the nature of their expectations, help them to pursue constructive ends and to redefine those which appear to be destructive. In sum, administration should encourage informal organization, recognizing it is a means through which fulfillment of individual needs and organizational functions can be sought.[14]

Achieving Cooperation: Administrative Behavior

It has been observed earlier that every school system establishes an administrative structure consisting of prescribed positions, functions,

[14] For a more complete presentation of informal organization in school systems see Daniel E. Griffiths, *Human Relations in School Administration* (New York: Appleton-Century-Crofts, Inc., 1956), Chapter 16.

and levels of authority. We are concerned in the following discussion with the individuals in the administrative hierarchy—such as superintendents, principals, supervisors, directors, and department heads— vested with authority to make decisions relating to the work of the school.

The positions in the administrative hierarchy form the nerve center of the school system. Each position carries with it some degree of authority to direct the activities of other persons. Each position has certain role expectations attached to it: the organization expects the position incumbent to meet certain standards of administrative behavior; each administrator in turn knows what he expects in the way of professional and personal behavior of the staff members responsible to him; and staff members have various expectations for the administrators under whom they serve, including competence, humanness, and the ability to help them fulfill their wants and needs.

The Administrator's Concept of Administration

The concept which administrators in a school system have of their roles, and the manner in which they perform administrative functions, has considerable impact on the behavior of individual staff members. The theories and viewpoints of principals, for example, define to a significant degree the roles of teachers and special service personnel. Campbell's study of teacher-principal agreement on the teacher role indicates that the nature of the teacher-principal relationship is instrumental in determining teacher satisfaction, effectiveness, and confidence in leadership. Highly satisfied teachers, according to the study, consistently referred to certain attributes of their principals, such as general competency, making teachers feel worthy, guidance without interference, making it easy for teachers to teach, and maintaining good discipline. Highly dissatisfied teachers *failed to mention the principal,* but referred to a variety of contributory annoyances, such as an unwanted class, shortage of equipment and supplementary materials, nonparticipation in defining school goals, and too much clerical work.[15]

It may be useful at this point to generalize about types of ad-

[15] Merton V. Campbell, "Teacher-Principal Agreement on the Teacher Role," *Administrator's Notebook,* VII, No. 6 (February, 1959), University of Chicago: Midwest Administration Center, 1959.

ministrative behavior. Getzels and Guba point out that leadership-followership styles can be grouped into three categories:

Nomothetic Style: places emphasis on the requirements of the institution, the role, and the expectation rather than on the requirements of the individual, the personality, and the need-disposition.

Ideographic Style: emphasizes requirements of the individual, the personality, and the need-disposition rather than the requirements of the institution, the role, and the expectation.

Transactional Style: Expectations are defined as sharply as they can be but not so sharply as to prohibit appropriate behavior in terms of need-dispositions. Role conflicts, personality conflicts and role-personality conflicts are recognized and handled. The standard of administrative excellence is individual integration and efficiency, satisfaction, and institutional adjustment and effectiveness.[16]

It can be seen that the orientation of administrative behavior will differ, depending in part upon the administrator's perception of his role, as well as the manner in which the organization as a whole expects him to perform the functions of the position. When either the demands of the organization or the needs of staff members are given exclusive consideration, the result is organizational imbalance. The administrator who frowns upon textbook writing by members of his staff or attendance at professional meetings because such activities interfere with the work of the school gives little consideration to the satisfaction of individual needs; the administrator who attempts to satisfy staff desires to the exclusion of goal achievement jeopardizes his status. In brief, the administrator is "the man in the middle." An emerging viewpoint among educators is that greater effort and understanding are needed in educational administration to develop administrative behavior (transactional style) which seeks to bring organizational demands and individual needs into a condition of balance. The capacity of an organization to maintain cooperation depends upon the extent to which member wants and needs are satisfied. The ability of the administrator to enlist the cooperation of personnel depends not so much upon manipulating the individual for organizational ends, but on achieving goals through maintenance of an organizational climate conducive to individual self-realization.

[16] J. W. Getzels and E. G. Guba, *op. cit.*, pp. 435–436.

Administrative Behavior and Personnel Cooperation

In the pursuit of understanding how administrative behavior can help school personnel to derive maximum satisfaction from work-related activities and to give consistently their best efforts to the organization, no universally applicable solutions have been developed. But there are some guidelines which, if applied by administration in the conduct of school affairs, will improve its ability to deal with the complex human, economic, and educational problems with which it is daily confronted.

If educational administration expects to achieve the aims of the school through the cooperation of personnel, a point of beginning is at the administrative level. Not only must the administrator be knowledgeable about the impersonal dimension of the administrative process, he must also acquire greater understanding of the personal or human dimension. This suggests that systematic attention needs to be given by the entire administrative staff to the human problems in the school organization and the means for their solution. It suggests that criteria for the selection of administrators include an understanding of human behavior in the school setting. It suggests that opportunities for improving the skill of administrators in diagnosing and dealing with human problems in organization be given a high priority in the in-service program. It suggests, in short, that the strength of an organization and its ability to progress toward its goals depend largely upon the understanding administrators have of human behavior and its motivation.

There is a little evidence to indicate that there is more need for better understanding by the administrator of his own administrative behavior. Hencley's study of conflicts which arise between school administrators and their reference groups (teachers and principals, boards of education, P.T.A., etc.) indicated tendencies of school superintendents (1) to believe that there were no differences between their own views and the views of others when, in reality, such differences existed; (2) to define reference group expectations accurately even though they did not concur with these expectations; and (3) to see conflicts where none existed.[17]

---

[17] Stephen P. Hencley, "The Conflict Patterns of School Superintendents," *Administrator's Notebook,* VIII, No. 9 (May, 1960), University of Chicago: Midwest Administration Center, 1960.

It goes without saying that there is much to be learned about human behavior as it relates to organization, and how this knowledge can be applied by administrators under actual conditions. How to exercise wisely the authority vested in an administrative position, how to improve communication among members of the organization, how to minimize personnel resistance to the constant changes which confront educational institutions, how to provide maximum opportunity for personnel self-fulfillment consistent with organizational requirements—all are problems which require a better understanding of what administrative behavior is and how it can be made more effective.

Achieving Cooperation: Morale

The word "morale" is one to which various meanings have been applied. To some it means the zeal or enthusiasm with which an individual performs his work. Others insist that morale is the willingness of a group to work toward a collective purpose. Most observers of organizational behavior consider morale to be something more than an individual's state of mind. They conceive it to be a group phenomenon, or the relations among individuals in a group which result in a willingness to work together for a common end.

It is generally agreed that maintenance of personnel cooperation is not achieved by improving this or that organizational function. Improving the compensation structure is important, but not all-important. Many administrators labor under the misapprehension that, by applying a particular remedy, it will in some mysterious way bring about better morale. Dubin points out that there is no clear-cut evidence to indicate a high relationship between high morale and organization effectiveness. He also suggests that "under certain circumstances . . . it may be that high morale is not an important organization goal, and authority holders need to give little conscious attention to its development and maintenance." [18]

From an administrative point of view, it appears that instead of directing efforts toward the development and maintenance of morale, the task might be looked upon as developing and maintaining organizational health. This is to say that the organization does not set out

[18] Robert Dubin, "Human Relations in Formal Organizations," *Review of Educational Research*, 29, No. 4 (October, 1959), pp. 362–363.

consciously to build morale; rather, it seeks to bring the organizational requirements and the needs of the individual into a state of balance. Roethlisberger, in discussing morale in a business organization, views it in two parts:

1. The daily problem of maintaining internal equilibrium within the organization, that is, maintaining that kind of social organization in which individuals and groups through working together can obtain human satisfactions that will make them willing to contribute their services to the economic objective of cooperation; and

2. The daily problems of diagnosing possible sources of interference, of locating sore spots, of liquidating human tensions and strains among individuals and groups, of helping people to orient themselves to their work groups, of spotting blockages in the channels of communication. These are the two "human controls" exercised by the administrator.[19]

As most school administrators have learned, the personnel or human problems which daily confront them are numerous and complex. They realize full well that the solutions which they devise are never perfect, never final. They know that there is no "do-it-yourself-kit" for building morale. In the final analysis, that happy state of affairs when personnel unite to gain a collective purpose is achieved through planning. It is realized by the combined effect of all of the provisions which are developed to improve the personnel function. To sum up: every aspect of the personnel program should contribute to morale betterment. This implies that both the personal and impersonal dimensions of the administrative process present opportunities for encouraging personnel cooperation. The personal dimension, which has been emphasized in this chapter, can be conceived as an administrative sector wherein the focus of attention is on human problems in the organization and what can be done to solve them. The impersonal dimension, which is treated in the text following, deals with problems of compensation, quality and quantity of personnel, recruitment, selection, development, and general welfare. Although these two dimensions are treated separately, they are in fact inseparable. When we look at the personnel function in the larger content of educational administration, we see it as a function designed to assist the organization to achieve its purpose and to make possible

---

[19] F. J. Roethlisberger, *Management and Morale* (Cambridge, Mass.: Harvard University Press, 1955), p. 192.

maximum personnel satisfaction. Involved in this function is the necessity for continuous appraisal of the effects of all organizational conditions in terms of the impact they have on the will of personnel to give their best to organization purpose.

Suggested Reading

Argyris, Chris, *Personality and Organization* (New York: Harper & Brothers, 1957).

Chruden, Herbert J., and Arthur W. Sherman, Jr., *Personnel Management* (Cincinnati, Ohio: South-Western Publishing Co., 1959).

Greenewalt, Crawford H., *The Uncommon Man: the Individual in the Organization* (New York: Harper & Brothers, 1959).

Niles, Mary Cushing, *The Essence of Management* (New York: Harper & Brothers, 1958).

Northcott, C. H., *Personnel Management*, 4th ed. (New York: Pitman Publishing Corp., 1960).

Pigors, Paul, Charles A. Myers, and F. T. Malm, *Readings in Personnel Administration* (New York: McGraw-Hill Book Co., 1959).

Strauss, George, and Leonard R. Sayles, *Personnel: The Human Problems of Management* (Englewood Cliffs, N. J.: Prentice-Hall, Inc., 1960).

The International City Manager's Association, *Municipal Personnel Administration*, 6th ed. (Chicago: The Association, 1960).

PART II

Determining Need

Staff Personnel:

QUANTITY

CHAPTER FOUR

Providing the amount and kind of school personnel needed to operate a school system is both difficult and significant. It is difficult because of the variety of factors that enter into staffing decisions, some of which are illustrated in the following questions: Who shall be educated and for what? What should be the nature and extent of the educational program and services? How shall instruction be organized? What methods of teaching shall be employed? To what extent are supervisory services needed? What standards of professional competency shall be established? What standards of plant maintenance and operation are desirable? What are the personnel implications of enrollment trends? Is the community willing and able to support a staff, in accordance with criteria such as those established by the Educational Policies Commission. (See p. 92.) Is the administrative unit sizable enough to provide a comprehensive educational program? To what extent can certain educational services be provided by cooperative arrangements among several school systems? The task is also significant because effectiveness of personnel service is critically dependent upon, and influenced by, the quality of decisions made in relation to the size and competency of the school staff.

As conceptualized in Figure 1, establishment of need is the foundation of the personnel function, as well as the basis for program planning and budgeting. This chapter and the two which follow deal sequentially with determination of personnel need and concomitant fiscal requirements. Each chapter identifies problems involved in establishment of need and suggests ways of dealing with them in better and more lasting form through application of principle.

The discussion is focused upon three groups of school personnel—teaching, administrative, and noninstructional—in keeping with the idea that personnel planning should encompass all persons employed by the school system, regardless of the nature of service rendered.

Size of the Instructional Staff

The number of human components needed for instructional purposes in local school systems has never been solved satisfactorily, on either a theoretical or operational basis. Inconclusiveness of the evidence regarding the influence of class size on pupil achievement, the variety of staffing policies and practices now in existence, and the extensive experimentation currently in progress regarding organization of instruction at all educational levels reflect the complexity of the problem. This does not mean that many of the present staffing patterns for instruction are ineffective. It does suggest, however, that traditional staffing assumptions are open to question. We cannot be sure, for example, that present plans for the organization of instruction will continue indefinitely. As will be shown later, there are signs which point to the contrary. Prominent considerations in determining instructional staff size have been implied in the foregoing questions. These will be examined in the sections which follow.

School Purposes

The central consideration in determining staff need is the educational aims of the school system. That the abilities, skills, knowledges, and attitudes which children and youth are expected to acquire under the guidance of the school affects the size of the instructional staff is evident to even the most obtuse observer. Yet the extent to which this factor is ignored in determining staff need is so widespread that its implications for staffing, as well as for all educational planning, must be reexamined continuously. Goals of an enterprise are the substance from which educational programs are derived. They determine the educational opportunities which the school provides, and, in turn, affect the size of the school staff necessary for their implementation. It is worth restating here what has been said many times before—that goals have little value unless they can be translated into realistic, attainable objectives. As the understanding of school aims increases, it will be possible to make better decisions as to what is to be taught, how it is to be taught, who is to be taught, as well as to the amount and kind of staff required to provide instruction.

Nature and Scope of the Educational Program

A basic issue which has both policy and procedural implications for instructional staff size and composition is the nature and scope of the educational program. Examination of Figure 8 points up the relationship between fundamental policy decisions concerning the educational program and requisite staffing provisions. Determination of the educational program, it should be noted, involves selection from a number of alternatives, because local school districts provide both mandated and permissive educational opportunities ranging from late infancy through adulthood. The nature and extent of the educational program which the administration decides to put into effect should be made against a background of existing plans, facilities, community character and composition, social and educational change, and fiscal potential of the administrative unit. These and other factors are conducive to wide variations in breadth and depth of educational opportunities, staffing practices, and expenditure levels which exist among school districts across the nation.[1] Existing knowledge indicates that as the level of educational service increases, there is a corresponding increase in expenditure level and staffing demand. The educational plan, then, greatly influences the size and composition of the school staff, which, in turn, conditions the kind and amount of educational services available to pupils.

[1] The Metropolitan School Study Council reports that in 1960–61 the net current expenditure levels among 62 school districts ranged from a high of $989 per pupil to a low of $358. Similarly, the number of professional staff members per 1000 pupils ranged from a high of 81.4 to a low of 43.8. See Metropolitan School Study Council, *Financing Council Schools, 1960–61* (New York: The Council, 1961), pp. 47–51.

FIGURE 8   Illustration of decisions involved in determining staff size.

1 What persons in what age groups shall be educated at public expense? Within what age limits shall pupils be compelled to attend school? What pre- and postcompulsory age groups shall be included in the educational program?

2 How shall the educational program be organized? Should it be similar to, or different from, the following pattern?

Nursery school	4– 5 years of age
Kindergarten	5– 6 years of age
Elementary school	6–12 years of age
Junior high school	12–15 years of age
Senior high school	15–18 years of age
Junior college	18–20 years of age
Adult education school	16 years upward

3 What should be the educational goals of each of these instructional divisions?

4 How shall the program of instruction in each division be organized? Should the grade be continued as the basic unit for the division of school work in the elementary school? Should the team-teaching concept be applied at the secondary level? Elementary level? Should the self-contained classroom be adopted as the pattern for organizing instruction in the elementary school?

5 What should be the composition of the instructional staff in each of the divisions? Should there be teachers for special subjects?

6 Which of the following services should be provided in each of the divisions? Guidance, psychological, health, co-curricular, library, food, transportation, safety, camping education, and services for children with special needs. To what extent should they be provided?

7 What system-wide services to teachers should be provided, such as in-service education, supervision, professional library, curricular and instructional aids. To what extent?

8 What central administrative services are necessary, such as: pupil personnel, staff personnel, business, plant, research, planning, and coordination? To what extent?

Organization of Instruction

The manner in which pupils are grouped for educational purposes affects the size and composition of the school staff. Throughout the history of American education many plans have been employed for the formation of instructional groups. These include, particularly at the elementary school level, the Departmental, Platoon, Winnetka, Dalton, and Cooperative Group plans. Other schemes for organizing instruction include ability grouping, the self-contained classroom, team teaching, special classes, and the all-year school, each reflecting viewpoints on instructional means for attaining educational objectives.[2]

It should be evident that any grouping plan should be developed in terms of educational objectives. If an educational plan places sole emphasis upon acquisition of subject matter, the grouping scheme will be different from that which obtains in a school which stresses, along with the fundamental skills, human relationships, individual differences, critical thinking, citizenship, and personality development.

Grouping and staffing are closely interrelated. Decisions affecting the size, number, kinds, duration, and purposes of instructional groups have significant staffing implications, particularly in relation to staff size, composition, and function. If the grouping plan is to have a real impact upon the educational progress of children, the staffing considerations which are related to it cannot be taken for granted. People, in the last analysis, are more important than structure.

Class Size

Class size refers to pupil membership in a group organized for instructional purposes.[3] The question of how many pupils should be assigned to an instructional group has been and still remains the subject of serious concern by all who are interested in the nation's

[2] Shane identifies 32 types of, or approaches to, grouping in the elementary school which have developed during the past century. See Harold G. Shane, "Grouping in the Elementary School," *Phi Delta Kappan*, XLI, No. 7 (April, 1960), pp. 313–319.

[3] Class size refers to the number of pupils enrolled in a class or instructional group. Average class size is the average number of pupils enrolled in all classes in a school attendance or administrative unit. Teacher-pupil ratio is the number of pupils enrolled per full-time teacher.

schools. There are several reasons why so much significance is attached to the class-size question. The first is the educator's quest to provide grouping arrangements most conducive to learning and study. While it is clear that a given class size is no absolute guarantee of the educational progress of all children, many educators are convinced that the grouping plan is an important contributor to educational attainment.

A second reason for attaching so much importance to class-size policies is the matter of cost. There is a vast difference between the budgetary requirements of a school system which decides that it needs a classroom for every 20 pupils as compared with one which sets the class size at 40 pupils. As noted earlier, the major share of the current budget is allocated to staffing requirements. A recent study by the National Education Association Research Division of class size in urban elementary schools indicates, for example, that to reduce classes in excess of 25 children each to that size would require 92,000 additional classrooms and teachers; to reduce classes larger than 30 to that size would require more than 28,000 classrooms and teachers.[4] To get the maximum educational return for every dollar invested, questions about class-size policy are always in order. If a class of 25 is as effective for educational purposes as a class of 20, is adherence to the former figure educationally and fiscally defensible? Wide diversity in practice regarding size of school classes is partially indicative of the uncertainty of the answer to the question.

Lack of qualified teachers today is a third reason for continuing concern over class size. If by some magic schools could secure enough funds to establish the number and kinds of groups deemed optimum for instructional purposes, it is certain that the staff needed would be unavailable. But the gap between the supply of, and demand for, qualified teachers has helped to focus attention on ways by which staffs can be utilized more effectively, a subject which will be dealt with in a subsequent section of this chapter.

Until there is better evidence about the most effective size and composition of groups for attaining specific educational objectives, decisions on class size will have to be made in terms of existing knowledge, and in terms of the many unique factors which prevail

[4] National Education Association, Research Division, Research Report 1960–R10, *Class Size in Urban Elementary Schools, 1959–60* (Washington: The Association, 1960), p. 5.

in the local school system. There are some important generalizations which have been derived from studies of, and experiments with, class-size problems over the last century. Among the more useful are these:

1. Research studies favor smaller classes over larger classes at the ratio of two to one.

2. Class size may properly vary with the subject taught, the characteristics of the student body, and the number of professional personnel available to supplement the teacher's efforts in guiding pupils.

3. Numerical staff adequacy (number of professional staff members per 1000 pupils) is a better predictor of school quality than average class size.

4. Research does not point to any specific number of pupils in a class as being optimum for all educational purposes.

5. Class size should be planned in terms of educational objectives. Certain kinds of objectives may best be realized in small classes, others in larger classes.

6. No grouping scheme will eliminate the need for teaching excellence, for adjusting the methods and materials of instruction to the needs of the individual pupil, for making provisions for those exceptional children whose adjustment will be difficult under any classification plan.

7. Regardless of the grouping plan, every school system needs a staff which is large enough to provide every pupil with reasonable instructional services.[5]

Staff Size

Staff size, as defined here, refers to the number of professional staff members per 1000 students. This index is preferable to class size or to pupil-teacher ratio statistics, since its meaning is straightforward. Average class size fails to reveal the diversity of class sizes, while one is never quite sure whether the pupil-teacher ratio includes only classroom teachers or all professional, licensed staff members.

[5] Summarized from Donald H. Ross and Bernard McKenna, *Class Size: The Multi-Million Dollar Question* (New York: Metropolitan School Study Council, 1955), pp. 21–22; National Education Association, Educational Policies Commisson, *An Essay on Quality in Public Education* (Washington: The Association, 1959), pp. 14–16.

An illustration of the manner in which staff size is computed is provided in Table 4.1. For the particular school system under consideration, the size of the professional staff amounts to 47 members for every 1000 pupils. Whether or not this school system is satis-

Table 4.1

Computation of Staff Size *

A. Goodville School District has the following pupil membership:

Grade	Resident Membership	Non-resident Membership	Total Membership	Resident Pupils for Whom Tuition Is Paid in Another District	Staffing Units
K	939	1	940	0	470.0
1–6	4,065	39	4,104	0	4,104.0
7–12	3,397	25	3,422	1	3,764.2
Total	8,401	65	8,466	1	8,338.2

B. The district has 392 professional employees, including superintendent, principals, classroom teachers, administrative assistants, special teachers, psychologists, nurses, teachers of special subjects, and librarians.

C. To compute the number of staffing units in the system: Use the average daily membership, which includes pupils sent *by* other districts; exclude resident pupils sent *to* other districts.
1. Divide total kindergarten membership (940) by 2 (half day)
2. Multiply total secondary membership by 1.1 to account for the difference in secondary over elementary school staffing (3,422 × 1.1)
3. Compute total staff units (470.0 + 4,104.0 + 3,764.2 = 8,338.2)

D. Professional Staff Size:

$$\frac{\text{Professional employees} \times 1{,}000}{\text{Staffing pupil units}} = \frac{392}{8{,}338.2} = 47 \text{ professional staff members for every 1,000 pupils}$$

* Staff size is defined as the number of staff members per 1000 students.

factorily staffed cannot, of course, be answered categorically. According to the Educational Policies Commission, the minimum number of professional staff members in good school systems is about 50 per 1000 pupils.[6] Data from two different studies have been combined in Table 4.2 to illustrate variations in staffing practices in 125 school

[6] National Education Association, Educational Policies Commission, *An Essay on Quality in Public Education* (Washington: The Association, 1959), p. 17.

systems in and around New York City and Philadelphia. Examination of these data indicate wide diversity in staffing provisions, some systems having more than twice the number of professional staff member per 1000 pupils than others. Many schools fall below the criterion of 50 professionals per 1000 pupils suggested by the Educational Policies Commission.

Table 4.2

Distribution of Sizes of Professional Staff

Professional Staff per 1000 Weighted Pupils	Metropolitan School Study Council	Philadelphia Suburban School Study Council
81–83	1	
78–80	0	
75–77	0	
72–74	3	
69–71	3	
66–68	4	1
63–65	7	0
60–62	13	1
57–59	6	3
54–56	8	3
51–53	7	13
48–50	3	11
45–47	4	21
42–44	1	8
39–41		6
36–38		1
33–35		0
30–32		0
27–29		1
Median	60.2	47.5

Source: Metropolitan School Study Council, *Financing Council Schools, 1960–61* (New York: The Council, 1961), pp. 41–45; Philadelphia Suburban School Study Council, *School Personnel, 1960–61* (Philadelphia: The Council, 1961), p. 25.

It is hardly necessary to argue the point that expectations which society has for its public schools demand a wide variety of specialists in addition to classroom teachers. Nor would it seem imperative to debate the proposition that more can be accomplished educationally for children with a staff of 70 professionals per 1000 pupils as compared with one half that size. Experience has shown that when the

Table 4.3

Illustration of Staffing Guidelines Based on a Ratio Study of Noninstructional Professional Personnel

Personnel Classification	Ratios in the Literature [a]	Ratios in Practice [b]	Requested Adjusted Ratios [c]	Suggested Guideline Ratios [d]
1. Asst. Superintendent	1 per 100 teachers	1 per 157 teachers	†	1 per 100 teachers (more or less)
2. Principals	1 per 6–30 teachers	1 per 21 teachers	‡	1 for each school of 6 or more teachers
3. Art Specialists	1 per 20–50 teachers	1 per 59.5 teachers	1 per 28.5 teachers	1 per 30 or less teachers
4. Music Specialists	1 per 20–50 teachers	1 per 58 teachers	1 per 40 teachers	1 per 40 or less teachers
5. Physical Education	1 per 50 teachers	1 per 81 teachers	1 per 49 teachers	1 per 50 or less teachers
6. Reading	1 per 40 teachers	1 per 66 teachers	1 per 39 teachers	1 per 40 or less teachers
7. Librarian	1 per 200–1000 students	1 per 1100 students	1 per 1000 students	1 per 500 students
8. Nurses	1 per 500–2000 students	1 per 1600 students	1 per 1100 students	1 per 1000 or less students
9. Physicians (part-time)	1 per 2400–5000 students	*	1 per 2160 students	1 per 2200 students or less
10. Dental Hygienists	1 per 1600–5000 students	1 per 2500 students	1 per 1700 students	1 per 1700 students
11. Psychologists	1 per 1200–5000 students	1 per 4000 students	1 per 2500 students	1 per 2500 students
12. Speech Correctionists	1 per 750–850 students	1 per 2000 students	1 per 1500 students	1 per 750–850 students
13. Home and School Visitor	1 per 1200–5000 students	1 per 3400 students	†	1 per 3400 or less students

Source: Stanley R. Duda, A Ratio Study of Non-Instructional Professional Personnel in Selected Public Schools of Pennsylvania (Pittsburgh: University of Pittsburgh, Doctor of Education Dissertation, 1959), p. 98.

[a] These figures are extreme ranges of ratios representing recommendations of authorities.

[b] These figures represent current status median ratios.

[c] These figures are adjusted ratios based on reduced service loads requested by respondents.

[d] These figures are based on substantial agreement between [a] and [c] above except for items 1, 7, and 12 which are reflected in the literature and appear to be more reasonable.

* Indeterminate.

† Requests insignificant.

‡ Of the teaching principals 87.5 per cent request relief from teaching regardless of size of school.

Note: Items 9, 10, and 10 per cent of 11 and 12 each represent individual case loads.

level of educational service increases, more and better educational opportunities can be provided.

The futility of attaining the broad goals of American education without specialists in guidance, counseling, health, and other services is recognized by the overwhelming majority of school administrators. Not all are agreed as to what services should have top priority. As indicated by the data shown in Table 4.3, not all are agreed as to the exact number of specialists needed in a school system of a given size. But most will agree that if theory and practice are to be consistent, the number of professional staff members in most school systems needs to be increased. When this happens, the chances are good that the gifted as well as the retarded will be better served, career counseling will be more extensive, special aptitudes of children will be given increased attention, and provisions for meeting the needs of individuals at all points along the intellectual scale will be improved.

Balance in Instructional Service

In addition to the problem of staff size, let us now consider two other appropriate planning questions relating to the instructional staff: What should be the distribution of the staff members in terms of instruction and special services? What priorities should be established in planning special instructional services? One question has to do with the preservation of a reasonable balance between classroom instruction and the special services needed to make instruction more effective; the other with choosing from among the many kinds of services those which should have top priority and those which are desirable but cannot, for financial reasons, be budgeted simultaneously.

Because of a combination of circumstances, including the high incidence of small school districts, financial limitations, unavailability of special service personnel, and the classroom teacher shortage, these questions have been, for the most part, academic. Few school districts have been in a position to examine critically what an equitable staff distribution between classroom teachers and staff specialists should be for a school district of a given size and for a given educational program. Few would debate the contention that more school systems need to test continuously for both balance and adequacy the system-wide and individual building staffing arrangements. No less difficult are those decisions involved in planning special instructional services

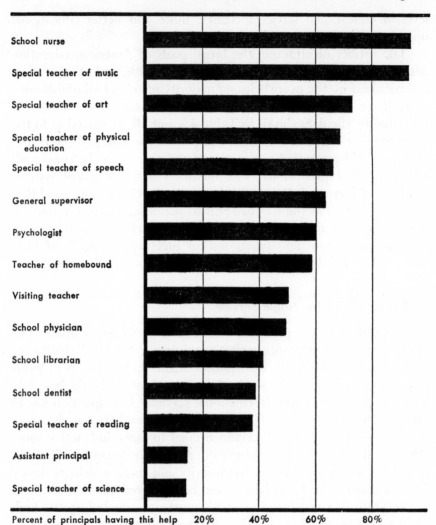

Percent of principals having this help   20%   40%   60%   80%

FIGURE 9 Resource Personnel Available to Some Supervising Principals. National Education Association, Research Division, *Research Bulletin* 36 (December, 1958), p. 109.

to supplement the work of the teacher. Figure 9, which contains data from a National Education Association study of special resource personnel available to elementary schools, brings the problem of personnel priority into focus. According to these data there is a wide diversity in the decisions reached by school officials as to the amount and kinds of essential instructional services. The task of establishing a ra-

tional basis for determining the extent and variety of special instructional services is occasionally complicated by the existence of state aid
laws which encourage local school systems through financial incentives
to establish certain types of special education. Local pressure groups,
too, have often interfered with planning efforts by insisting on a particular kind of service regardless of its relationship to the over-all educational program. The fact that educational services to the mental and
physically handicapped are socially necessary, for example, does not
mean that the educational program and related staffing plans should be
dominated by this consideration.

McKenna, in reviewing studies concerned with patterns of staff
deployment related to school quality, cites five conclusions which
have a bearing on staff selection and allocation:

1. Adaptable school systems do not choose between (a) small classes
and few professional specialists, and (b) large classes and many specialists.
They tend to keep classes small on both elementary and secondary levels
in addition to backing up the teachers with a goodly number of non-
classroom professionals. The most adaptable systems employ, on the
average, 18 such professionals for each 1000 pupil units.

2. The average practice for a group of highly adaptable school systems
is elementary class size of 26 and secondary class size of 22.

3. Professional, non-classroom specialists contribute more when they
are assigned to either the elementary or secondary level, and less when they
operate on a system-wide basis.

4. Those professionals who seem to contribute most to school system
adaptability when present in greater numbers are: librarians, psychologists
and psychiatrists, health personnel, and guidance counselors.

5. Approximately 9 clerical personnel per 1000 pupil units are associated
with the most adaptable school systems.[7]

Every plan for staffing schools must take cognizance of the objectives of education, immediate and long-term enrollments, various
aspects of the educational program which are to be emphasized, the
manner in which instruction is to be organized, and methods of
instruction to be employed. The important task is to plan a staffing
program with definite priorities and to have it adopted by school
officials as a part of the long-term educational plan. Having done

[7] Bernard H. McKenna, "Patterns of Staff Deployment Related to School Quality,"
Institute of Administrative Research, Teachers College, Columbia University, *Research
Bulletin,* Vol. 1, No. 3 (April, 1961), p. 8.

this, an enlightened budgetary procedure would then better the chances that certain steps will be taken in each fiscal year to attain the staffing pattern desired. This approach holds far more promise than the typical practice of adding personnel in piecemeal fashion in response to pressures, sentiment, fads, state financial incentives, and, it should be added, without regard to purpose.

Staff Utilization

Staff utilization is many things. It is devising ways whereby the ablest teachers can be made available to more students. It is assessing staff competencies and maximizing them for instructional purposes. It is conserving the energies and talents of the staff for genuine educational tasks. It is recognizing staff differences and making teaching assignments accordingly. It is relieving the instructional staff of routine work which can be performed effectively by personnel employed for this purpose, such as clerical and instructional assistants. It is supporting the professional functioning of teachers through greater and more imaginative use of modern technological aids to instruction.

Staff utilization involves all of these things and, at its best, represents a systematic effort to utilize fully and economically the competencies, time, and energies of personnel to the utmost instructional advantage.

It is clear that size and composition of the school staff will be affected by staff utilization. But the whole problem of staff utilization is so interrelated with the organization of instruction that it is difficult to determine categorically just what optimal staff utilization should be for a given school system. That concepts of staff composition and utilization are changing is illustrated in the proposal by Trump shown in Table 4.4. Over and above the intrinsic merit of this proposal as a conceptual scheme for the organization of instruction are the implications it poses for staffing schools. The type of staff envisioned here, it should be noted, will be utilized differently than the staff of the traditional secondary school. Operationally, classes are not conceived to be of uniform size, teaching assignments are varied, and much of the routine work is assigned to personnel below the professional level. The key idea is to enable the professionally trained teacher to render more professional service more effectively to more students.

Table 4.4

Instructional Staff in a Secondary School with 400 Students—or for Each 400 Students in a Larger School

TYPE OF STAFF	FUNCTIONS AND EMPLOYMENT	TRAINING	NUMBERS
Professional Teachers: including Teacher Specialists and General Teachers	Direct learning activities; plan methods and materials of instruction; teach concepts and appreciations; counsel and consult; supervise evaluation; assist with student activities; provide specialized services for which competent and interested (employed on full-time basis—also year-around if able and interested)	Masters degree and beyond with specialization as needed	10
Instruction Assistants	Perform specific aspects of teaching below professional level of teachers and above clerks; read and evaluate some English themes, science reports, etc.; confer with students about their progress and provide teachers with reports; serve as laboratory assistants; supervise specific out-of-school projects; assist with student activities (typically employed 10–20 hours per week)	Usually college graduates but always trained for specific duties assigned	200 hours services per week
Clerks	Type; duplicate materials; check materials and prepare reports; grade objective tests; keep records; check and distribute supplies; attendance and perform other routine services; other clerical duties (employed on 40-hour per week basis)	High school graduate: business education	100 hours services per week
General Aides	Control and supervise students on school grounds, in cafeteria, corridors, auditorium, etc., and at extraclass activity functions; work with students in developing maximum self-controls; assist in student activities when competent (typically employed 10 to 20 hours per week)	High school graduate: some general courses; some college desirable	50 hours services per week
Community Consultants	Lecture; consult; make tapes, records, kinescopes, slides, films, etc.; typically volunteers, although might be paid (used whenever needed or desirable to provide special information and services)	Unusual competence; selected from file of available persons	Indefinite depending on local circumstances
Staff Specialists	Special services in such areas as guidance, research, health, reading, aid to exceptional children, audio-visual materials, and curriculum development; supplement work of professional teachers (full-time persons who might serve several schools as needed)	Highly trained in area of specialty	Indefinite depending on local circumstances

Source: J. Lloyd Trump, *Images of the Future: A New Approach to the Secondary School* (Urbana, Ill.: Commission on the Experimental Study of the Utilization of the Staff in the Secondary School, 1959), pp. 20–21.

The foregoing observations serve to reenforce the point that determination of instructional staff size involves many considerations, not the least of which are the educational program and instructional organization. Research has provided certain useful insights and practices for the practitioner regarding staff size. But this does not preclude the necessity for each school district to examine the forces, factors, and conditions germane to the problem and to deduce therefrom the staffing policies which are reasonable in the local situation.

Schedules and Work Load

The school schedule is an administrative device for realizing the aims of the educational program. Its construction involves decisions governing the kinds of instructional activities which will be provided, number of personnel needed, sizes of instructional groups, length of instructional periods, staff work load, and assignment of duties appropriate to staff interests, training, and competencies. Unfortunately, its significance is not always fully appreciated. Unless there is effective scheduling of pupils, plant, staff, and programs, much of the effort which goes into budgeting, recruiting, selecting, and developing school staffs will be wasted.

The fact must be recognized that scheduling, especially at the secondary level, is an important determiner of staff size. If the work load of each individual staff member is not carefully planned, both in terms of equity and utility, there is waste. If instructional activities are scheduled which are of dubious value, there is a question as to whether this is the wisest use of staff time and tax funds. A high incidence of small classes or an exceedingly small pupil-teacher ratio increases unnecessarily school staff and expenditures. An excessive number of staff specialists may lead to imbalance in the instructional staff. In short, the schedule involves a weighing of so many factors affecting educational progress—grouping, staff utilization, program breadth and depth, cost, staff size—that careful appraisal of its effects is decidedly one of administration's primary and continuous concerns.

The work load of each staff member has been the subject of discussion and research for many years. Its measurement is extremely difficult because of the intangibles which must be taken into account, including out-of-school activities, community demands, curriculum variations, pupil differences, variations in the number of class prepara-

tions, and school-related duties above and beyond the normal assignment. The list of solutions for making the load of the teacher
reasonably equitable is a long one, ranging from the centralization
of clerical work such as the recording of attendance data to the use
of teacher aides for grading themes and reports, and supervising study
halls and cafeterias.[8] So variable are the factors which affect the
teacher's work within a single school or from one school to another
that the possibility of their incorporation into a load formula which
is universally applicable appears to be out of the question. The core
problem which must be dealt with in making work load reasonably
equitable is staff size. If the staff is not sizable enough to carry out
the educational program, overburden cannot be resolved by manipulating a formula. A formula developed by the local administration
and professional staff, however, can be a useful device in studying
ways to maintain balance and equity in staff load. Such analyses will
help to identify load imbalance and its causes, and to provide a basis
for planning solutions to the load problem.

Size of the Administrative Staff

The problem of administrative staff size is one which has continuously engaged the attention of students of school administration.
It has long been argued, and with complete justification, that most
schools are suffering from administrative deprivation. Sargent and
Belisle, for example, state that:

. . . with some possible exceptions, school systems in general and irrespective of size are basically suffering from a deprivation of administrative resources. . . .

Coupled with this basic premise, however, the authors raise the question as to:

. . . whether present educational administrative knowledge and thought
are capable of developing the requisite imaginative pictures of the human
components and relational design of administrations, let us say, of *twice*

---

[8] An extensive discussion of the factors affecting the teacher's work load may be
found in Department of Classroom Teachers of the National Education Association,
Department of Classroom Teachers, *Conditions of Work for Quality Teaching* (Washington: The Association, 1959), pp. 42–73.

the present size in relation to enrollments in a given school system—which we are holding as a tentative yardstick. This problem is underscored by the amorphousness of thought with respect to definitions of the functions-and-structure of knowledge and activities involved in public school administration, together with the evidence in numerous school systems of inability to use effectively the specialized knowledge and personal resources which they possess. Somehow, it would appear, there may have to be something resembling a *leap* in knowledge-and-practice in educational administration, in such a way that the goals of development defined for this field may more nearly correspond to the implications of the idea of public education itself. Without increased understanding, is there any assurance that increased finances for schools will bring about educational achievement which is either corresponding or adequate to the survival problems of the society? [9]

The task of defining how large an administrative staff should be for a local school system is complicated by many factors. There is great diversity among school systems—in size, educational programs, financial ability, location, community expectancy for education—all of which make for differences in administrative personnel provisions. Hence, there is no precise yardstick, such as the pupil-administrator ratio, to indicate what the optimum size of the administrative staff should be.

Public support for increasing administrative assistance has generally lagged, both in local budgets and in state aid formulas. The burden of responsibility for gaining public acceptance for increasing the size of administrative staffs lies, in the final analysis, with the professional administrator. Until he is able to demonstrate convincingly to the public why administrative assistance is necessary, how it will be employed, and how it will make a significant difference in the progress of children, there is little likelihood that greater support for this purpose will be forthcoming.

In developing policy governing administrative staffing, it is not too much to expect school officials to be clear about what it really expects of an administrative staff. The complexity of the administrative task in public education is such that school boards must begin to secure the professional staff behavior necessary to direct a modern school system; to provide a compensation structure which will attract and retain

[9] Cyril G. Sargent and Eugene L. Belisle, *Educational Administration: Cases and Concepts* (Boston: Houghton Mifflin Co., 1955), pp. 444–446.

administrative competency; to marshal the necessary funds, facilities, and operating structure which will enable the chief executive and his staff to engage in professional planning directed toward the attainment of community educational purposes. For too long the chief administrator has been deluged with details which he has not been able to delegate because sufficient administrative resources have not been available. This has led frequently to an administrative emphasis on a multitude of immediate problems to the neglect of those which are more fundamental.

Despite the lag in administrative staffing, considerable effort is being exerted to extend and to improve school administrative structures. A study of central office administrative personnel in 468 school systems indicates that:

1. One public school administrator in four holds a position that has been created within the past five years. Of the 694 district-wide administrative positions reported, thirty-five percent were added in the last half decade.
2. Three school districts out of four will make a change in their administrative organization in the next five years.
3. There is a rising degree of specialization among members of the administrative staff.
4. Sizes of administrative staffs vary widely irrespective of the size of districts by enrollment.
5. As the number of districts decrease because of reorganization, the demand for personnel continues to increase.[10]

Appraising Administrative Resources

The role of administration has been recognized as a matter of genuine importance in every kind of social institution. Indeed, effectiveness of any organization depends heavily upon its administrative structure, including the amount and kinds of administrative staff members and the manner in which they are organized to perform administrative tasks.

Periodic review of the administrative structure of a school system is a continuous responsibility of leadership to make certain that ad-

[10] Georgette N. Manla, "Administration in Transition," *American School and University 1960–61*, 32nd ed. (New York: Buttenheim Publishing Corporation, 1960), pp. 145–155.

ministrative arrangements are appropriate for attaining the aims of the enterprise. No one disputes the usefulness of appraisal in school administration, but its absence in the area of administrative staffing is noteworthy, as indicated by the following dispositions of local school officials:

To keep the size of the administrative staff intact, despite sharp increases in school enrollments.

To be skeptical of all budgetary requests for increasing the size of the administrative staff.

To minimize the effects of social change on administrative responsibility.

To suspect that adding staff specialists has no relationship to improvement in the quality of education.

To resist the idea that a considerable amount of administrative time should be devoted to planning—both immediate and long term.

To view proposals for additions to the administrative staff as not being conductive to economy.

To accept as valid the belief that results increase if the size of the administrative staff is held to a minimum.

To regard the administrative structure as the one area in the school system least in need of improvement.

Confronted with these and other dispositions regarding the administrative staff, many chief executives have had to tolerate administrative inertia and to accept as inevitable the neglect and inefficiency which attends understaffing. But regardless of the roadblocks to improvements in administrative staffing, and no matter how dim the prospects for organizational change appear to be, there are many good reasons why every school system should develop plans as to what its administrative structure should be at the present time as well as in the future. Most administrators find that if they want to develop the administrative structure, it is necessary to prepare plans for this purpose. This includes identifying administrative personnel needed, when they will be needed, and making necessary budgetary proposals as need occurs. It is also recognized that a clearly defined plan for administrative staffing is conducive to improved personnel administration. When administrative personnel needs are established, greater consideration can be given to selecting and developing personnel to fill administrative positions provided for in the organization. Another advantage in planning for the administrative staff needs is that operational efficiency can be improved by clarifying relationships among administrative personnel. Hence, it is reasonable to assume that every school system can profit from continuous appraisal of its administrative staffing plan, just as it could conceivably profit from an appraisal of educational achievement, the school plant, or the educational program.

Organization Analysis

The problem of determining for a school system of a given size the optimum number, types, and competencies of administrative personnel capable of exerting maximum influence upon the educational development of children involves a variety of considerations. In undertaking this task perhaps the most important single question to consider at the outset is this: What is the organization expected to accomplish? When organization can clearly identify its objectives, which are reflected in policies and programs, it can then concentrate on the administrative functions to be performed, specific tasks related to each function, and number and types of personnel needed to perform the functions.

Careful analysis of current organization structure will help to determine its suitability for accomplishing established goals. Among the questions to be raised in appraising the current administrative structure are the following:

1. What is the present administartive staffing pattern?
2. What types of administrative positions now exist?
3. What are the functions of the various administrative positions?
4. How are activities of the various positions coordinated?
5. Are relationships among administrative positions clarified so that duplication of effort and neglect of essential responsibilities are minimized?
6. Are administrative resources sufficient to carry out immediate and projected responsibilities?
7. Does the administrative staff have enough time to develop and to initiate new plans?
8. What organization of administrative personnel will most help them to do their work?

The assumption on which the foregoing appraisal is recommended is that doing what is best for the administrative staff is doing what is best for the entire organization, the children, the community, and society. This is not only sound administrative policy, it is sound economic policy. The expenditures called for in school budgets today are such that it is foolhardy not to provide qualitative and quantitative administrative resources to assure maximum returns from the investment.

Function Analysis

Plans for establishing the size of the administrative staff can be improved by analyses of administrative functions which must be performed to enable the organization to meet its objectives. This involves a study of the current administrative structure, how and by whom major and subsidiary administrative functions are performed, as well as the flow of authority and accountability. Data for making an analysis of organization practice are derived from several sources, including organization charts, manuals, position guides, interviews with position incumbents, and specially designed questionnaires and check lists.[11]

Table 4.5, which illustrates an abridged job responsibility chart of administrative functions, has been included to lend greater specificity to the foregoing discussion. This scheme may be employed to:

1. Identify and relate major administrative functions and positions.
2. Indicate authority and accountability.
3. Provide data for studying current and foreseeable administrative structures.
4. Develop intermediate and long-range organizational plans.
5. Project administrative staff needs.
6. Aid in the preparation of organization charts and position guides.
7. Focus attention on those administrative functions not fully staffed.
8. Detect administrative overburden.
9. Arrange functions so that administrative personnel can perform their tasks more effectively.[12]

[11] Detailed procedures for organization analysis are contained in: Council for Administrative Leadership in New York State, *Handbook for the Study of Administrative Staff Organization* (Albany: New York State Teachers Association, 1957), and National Industrial Conference Board, *Preparing the Company Organization Manual* (New York: The Board, 1957), pp. 62–83. Principles of school organization are fully developed in Daniel E. Griffith, David L. Clark, D. Richard Wynn, and Lawrence Iannaconne, *Organizing Schools for Effective Education* (Danville, Ill.: The Interstate Printers and Publishers, Inc., 1961).

[12] The original study identified 54 administrative functions which were categorized under the four headings shown in Table 4.5.

Job Responsibility Chart of Administrative Functions (Abridged)

Planned for 2600 Enrollment

1 Jr.-Sr. H.S. Building (1,200)	10 Administrative Staff Members
3 Elementary Buildings (1,400)	1–260 Administrator-Pupil Ratio
111 Teachers	1–11 Admininstrator-Teacher Ratio
1–24 Teacher-Pupil Ratio	

Key to Symbols

x Work is done
1 General supervision
2 Direct supervision over work done
3 Supervision with coordination
4 Decision on points specifically submitted
5 Person must be consulted
6 Person must be notified
7 Person may be called in for exchange of views

Symbol followed by "D" indicates activity limited to personnel of particular department

	Staff							
	Chief School Administrator	School Business Officials	Jr.-Sr. H.S. Principal	Asst. Prin.—Sr. H.S.	Asst. Prin.—Jr. H.S.	Elementary Principals	Coordinator of Cur. and Guidance	Director-Special Services
A. TO IMPROVE EDUCATIONAL OPPORTUNITY								
1. Revision of curriculum and selection of curriculum materials	1	–	5	7	7	5	x	7
2. Assisting teachers in diagnosing the learning difficulties of pupils	7	–	x	7	7	x	7	–
3. Helping teachers in planning effective remedial instruction	7	x	7	x	x	7	7	–
B. TO OBTAIN AND DEVELOP PERSONNEL								
1. Selection and recommendation to the Board of Education for employment of professional staff personnel	x	1	5	7	7	5	5D	5D
2. Induction and orientation of professional staff personnel	1	–	x	7	7	x	xD	xD
3. Supervision of professional staff personnel	1	x	7	x	x	7	xD	xD
C. TO MAINTAIN EFFECTIVE INTERRELATIONSHIPS WITH THE COMMUNITY								
1. Helping the Board of Education to determine the educational needs of the community	x	5	5	7	7	5	5	5
2. Direction of program for use of school facilities by non-school groups	x	6	5	6	5	5	6	6
3. Preparation of special reports and bulletins for general distribution	1	x	7	x	x	7	x	x
D. TO PROVIDE AND MAINTAIN FUNDS AND FACILITIES								
1. Debt service management	2	x	–	–	–	–	–	–
2. Control of budget	2	x	6	6	6	6	6	6
3. Plant planning and construction	x	5	7	5	5	7	7	7

Source: *A Study of the Organization and Administration of the Kennett Consolidated School District* (Kennett Square, Pennsylvania: The Board of Education, 1957), pp. 47–50.

The purpose of the foregoing illustration of administrative analysis, is not, of course, to furnish categorical or unequivocal solutions to staffing problems, even if this were possible. Rather, it is illustrative of one approach to a problem of genuine importance in many school systems.

Continuous review of organization practice will enable school officials to determine the extent to which the current structure varies from what they consider to be an optimum organizational design, and, at the same time, lessen the possibility of unsatisfactory coverage of administrative positions.

Size of the Noninstructional Staff

Noninstructional personnel include those persons who render services, which, for the most part, are indirectly related to the instructional process. School clerks and secretaries, cafeteria and lunchroom workers, building service personnel, and safety and transportation employees are usually grouped in this category. The number of noninstructional employees in relation to the total school staff varies considerably, ranging from no noninstructional to more noninstructional than instructional staff. Due to a wide variety of factors, determination of size and distribution of the noninstructional staff is equally as formidable a problem as are those involved in determining administrative and instructional personnel needs.

An illustration of the nature of some of the problems involved in determining the size of the noninstructional staff is provided by the data shown in Table 4.6. These data show the relationship between custodial standards adopted by Center City School District and the actual number of custodians assigned to each school building. The number of custodians exceeds the standard in some instances, and is below it in others. Questions posed by the data in Table 4.6 include the following:

1. Is the standard of 20,000 square feet of floor space a valid index of work load?

2. Should a different index of work load be established, since the present standard is based upon floor areas of the building, and does not take into consideration work to be performed outdoors, such as on lawns, play yards, and sidewalks?

3. If the standards are revised, to what extent will the size of the present staff increase or decrease?

Table 4.6

Relationship Between Custodial Standards and Number of Custodians
Center City School District, 1960–61

School	Square Feet of Floor Space	Standard *	Number of Custodians Employed †
1	141,927	7.1	8.5
2	61,849	3.1	2.0
3	31,001	1.6	1.0
4	57,374	2.9	3.5
5	199,608	10.0	11.5 [a]
6	233,000	11.7	10.5 [a]
7	29,297	1.5	2.0
8	71,112	3.6	5.0
9	87,753	4.4	5.0
10	130,643	6.5	5.0 [a]
11	117,106	5.9	7.0
12	129,276	6.5	6.0 [a]
13	129,366	6.5	6.0
14	130,643	6.5	6.0
15	92,965	4.6	4.5
16	32,247	1.6	1.0
17	7,912	.4	1.0
18	16,871	.8	1.0
19	32,247	1.6	1.0
20	12,234	.6	1.0
21	18,901	1.0	1.0
22	19,216	1.0	1.0
23	21,313	1.1	1.0
24	57,698	2.9	3.0
25	37,988	1.9	1.5
26	62,960	3.1	3.5
27	13,760	.7	1.0
28	8,004	.4	1.0
29	8,285	.4	1.0
30	18,656	.9	1.0
31	37,542	1.9	1.5
32	10,622	.5	1.0
33	93,006	4.7	6.5 [b]
34	45,986	2.3	1.5
35	31,615	1.6	1.0
36	18,592	.9	1.0
37	6,987	.3	1.0
38	13,676	.7	1.0
39	25,299	1.3	1.5
40	17,464	.9	1.0

[a] Laundry men, firemen, bath matrons not included.

[b] Playground problem.

* One custodian for each 20,000 square feet of floor space; one woman cleaner for each 10,000 square feet of floor space.

† Two women cleaners regarded as equivalent of one custodian.

Note: Standards established by school system.

4. Would elimination of some of the very small schools be conducive to better utilization of custodial personnel?

5. To what extent would custodial service be impaired by shifting custodians in those schools where the standard is exceeded to schools below the standard?

6. If additional personnel are required to achieve satisfactory custodial service, will the educational program be affected adversely?

Considerable effort has been devoted during the past three decades to improving approaches such as the one illustrated in Table 4.6 for determining manpower requirements for school plant operational service. Finchum has classified various formulas for measuring custodial workload in terms of the following concepts: time units, room equivalents, over-all duties, job frequency and worker skill, and measured work technique.[13]

An illustration of one of the types of formulas listed above (over-all duties) as reported by the California Association of School Business Officials is given below:

1. *Given:* 1 custodian for each 8 teachers, find the teacher factor.

$$\frac{\text{Number of teachers}}{8} = \text{Teacher factor (correct to two decimal places)}$$

2. *Given:* 1 custodian for each 225 pupils, find the pupil factor.

$$\frac{\text{Number of pupils}}{225} = \text{Pupil factor (correct to two decimal places)}$$

3. *Given:* 1 custodian for every 11 rooms * to be cleaned, find the room factor.

$$\frac{\text{Number of rooms}}{11} = \text{Room factor (correct to two decimal places)}$$

4. *Given:* 1 custodian for every 15,000 square feet of building area, find the square foot factor.

$$\frac{\text{Total square feet of building}}{15,000} = \text{Square foot factor (correct to two decimal places)}$$

5. *Given:* 1 custodian for each two acres of upkept ground, find the grounds factor.

$$\frac{\text{Total acres of upkept grounds}}{2} = \text{Grounds factor (correct to two decimal places)}$$

[13] R. N. Finchum, "Determining Custodial Personnel Requirements," in *Administering the Custodial Program* (Washington: U.S. Government Printing Office, 1961), p. 11.

6. Add the five factors and divide the total by 5 to find the actual number of cleaning custodians needed.

$$\frac{\text{Total of 5 Factors}}{5} = \text{Cleaning custodians needed (correct to two decimal places)}$$

* All rooms to be cleaned by custodians are included: offices, storage rooms, toilets, classrooms, gymnasiums, etc. An average classroom was defined as one containing 1000 square feet. This standard is used to break large area rooms, such as gymnasiums and multi-use rooms into equivalent classrooms.[14]

Despite emergence of refined approaches to determining custodial personnel requirements, certain factors have precluded universal acceptance by school districts, including inattention to standards of custodial performance, lack of funds, and unsuitability of any formula to all school districts under all circumstances.

Factors Influencing Staff Size

The extent of noninstructional service, in the final analysis, is a matter of judgment. Some of the major factors which affect determination of staff need, and which must be weighed in making decisions on this matter, include the following:

1. Standards of service established for building, secretarial, clerical, food service, transportation, and safety personnel.
2. Plans for personnel utilization.
3. Personnel competency.
4. Extent to which certain services are performed on contractual basis by nonschool agencies, such as catering of food service, cleaning, and snow removal.
5. Availability of labor saving devices.
6. Union relationships.
7. Number and capacity of units in the school plant.
8. Use of nonschool agents for school functions (safety personnel to control traffic).
9. Use of part-time and temporary personnel.
10. Variable building factors.

Certain of these factors will vary among school districts, which decreases the likelihood that sound decisions concerning the size of the

[14] California Association of Public School Business Officials, "Custodial Load Formula," *Journal of School Business Management* 21, No. 1 (July, 1955), pp. 16–17.

noninstructional staff can be arrived at through the use of arbitrary ratios or formulas. Some school districts have need for extensive transportation services, others not at all. Some districts have a good service program for every attendance unit; in others, the service may extend to some units and not to others. This list could be extended to indicate variations among school districts in all areas of noninstructional service, but the point of emphasis is that only through careful analysis of noninstructional service, and only after taking into account the key factors which affect the number of personnel needed, can reasonable judgments be reached.

There are at least two premises which enter into decisions on noninstructional service. The first is that expenditures for noninstructional personnel should not be increased at the expense of the educational program. Every dollar expended for this service beyond minimum need is one which is diverted from instruction—the sole purpose for the school's existence. The second premise is that noninstructional service should be sufficient to meet the requirements of the educational program and to provide for the health, comfort, and safety of pupil and staff personnel. Essentially the problem is one of maintaining a defensible balance between necessary service, on the one hand, and of attaining economical use of the operating force, on the other.

The problem of noninstructional service involves critical examination by administration of the essential amount and kinds of service necessary to support the educational program. This means that there must be a definition of what maintenance, operation, transportation, secretarial, clerical, food, and safety services are to be provided, and of standards of service to be maintained.

Planning Procedures

The basis upon which noninstructional services are predicated is the educational program, the soundest which can be conceived within the conditions and limitations imposed upon the organization by society. More specifically, noninstructional services should be planned in terms of fundamental educational policies established by the board of education. The number of personnel needed for maintenance and operation, for example, must be judged in terms of policies governing the size of elementary and secondary attendance units. This latter factor also affects, to some extent, the number of clerical and secretarial employees required. In other words, decisions affecting noninstructional service cannot be divorced from educational policies.

A useful approach to determination of amount and kinds of noninstructional service to be provided throughout the school district is to review the present program. Among the initial problems to be considered are the following:

1. What noninstructional services are now provided?
2. Do present services make an effective contribution to achievement of objectives of the educational program?
3. To what extent and for what reasons do present service provisions deviate from desired practice?
4. To what extent are any of the services overemphasized or underemphasized?
5. Are existing personnel fully utilized?
6. Can the imbalance in some services be corrected by making defensible economies in others?
7. Can the size of the working force be reduced through more effective planning?

Review of the status of noninstructional services will provide administration with data which form the basis for decisions concerning changes in the plan of action. Fundamental to the analysis, however, are the development and application of criteria, standards, and measures which will yield meaningful information concerning the sufficiency and efficiency of noninstructional service. Analysis of the work to be performed in each area of service, how and by whom it is now performed, the current cost of providing service, suitability of existing standards of performance, the manner in which personnel are now utilized—all are illustrative of areas in which probing is necessary to develop a picture of the current plan of noninstructional service in terms of its strengths and limitations.

Having established the standards or levels of service deemed appropriate for the school system, and having appraised existing provisions in terms of these standards, administration is then in possession of information on which to make decisions as to what the future plan for noninstructional service should be, which services have the greatest priority, and how these priorities should be phased over a period of years to achieve an orderly improvement in the service program.

Advantages of Personnel Planning

The benefits to be derived from the personnel planning process outlined above, both direct and indirect, are numerous. They include the following: (1) it helps administration to think through and to specify its objectives for noninstructional service on a current and long-term basis, (2) it makes realistic the task of establishing necessary operating policies to attain objectives, (3) it facilitates planning of current and long-term budgets, (4) it involves review of the relationship of noninstructional service needs to those of the total operation, (5) it helps to focus attention on resources required to carry out policies, (6) it provides organization with information on additional personnel requirements in advance of employment, (7) it furnishes opportunities to appraise how fully the noninstructional staff is utilized, and (8) it focuses attention upon the nature of the work to be performed and development of standards of performance.

The broad implication of these considerations is that personnel planning is indispensable to effective and economic operation of a school system. It is the best means of ensuring that there will be constant surveillance of personnel plans and policies against an acceptable level of service designed to realize objectives of the educational program.

Suggested Reading

Burke, Arvid J., *Financing Public Schools in the United States*, rev. ed. (New York: Harper & Brothers, 1957), pp. 156–162.

Finchum, R. N., *Administering the Custodial Program* (Washington: U.S. Government Printing Office, 1961).

National Education Association, Department of Classroom Teachers, *Conditions of Work for Quality Teaching* (Washington: The Association, 1959).

National Industrial Conference Board, *Preparing the Company Organization Manual* (New York: The Board, 1957).

Otto, Henry J., *Elementary-School Organization and Administration*, 3rd ed. (New York: Appleton-Century-Crofts, Inc., 1954), Chapters 4 and 5.

Yeager, William A., *Administration of the Noninstructional Personnel and Services* (New York: Harper & Brothers, 1959).

Staff Personnel:

QUALITY

CHAPTER FIVE

Schools are interested in—indeed dependent upon—competent personnel. Ever since the ideal of universal schooling was conceived, the task of developing professional and supporting personnel has been ubiquitous. In many different ways, and for many years, scores of people inside and out of the profession have worked diligently to attract and to improve the quality of personnel to whom the education of children and youth are entrusted. Despite efforts of educators, governments, statesmen, laymen, professional associations, independent commissions, and assemblies over an extended period of time, the problem of how to attract and to retain enough capable personnel for our schools amounts to something of a national dilemma.

The Problem Has Many Dimensions

The complexities involved in providing personnel for the nation's schools are formidable. Even a cursory examination of the problem indicates that:

1. The supply of qualified personnel has not kept pace with the increase in school enrollment.

115

2. Greater competition for the supply of trained manpower has affected education's ability to recruit enough qualified teachers.

3. Thousands of unqualified teachers are now employed in the public schools.

4. The conditions of work in many school systems throughout the nation are not conducive to attracting and retaining competent personnel.

5. Many school districts cannot initiate new programs or services because of a lack of qualified personnel.

6. Standards of teacher employment in many states encourage professional mediocrity.

In view of conditions such as the foregoing, and in light of the pressing demands of social change upon the educational system, efforts need to be intensified along many lines to improve the quality of teaching staffs. This includes making education more attractive as a career to greater numbers of competent persons, increasing efforts to recruit college graduates of outstanding ability, improving the compensation structure, reorganizing the preservice preparation of teachers, strengthening standards for admission to the profession, bettering working conditions for staff personnel in local school districts, and developing improved procedures for selecting, placing, and utilizing personnel in tasks appropriate to their training and capabilities.

Educators alone cannot solve the problem of better school staffing. While the root of the matter is financial, improvement of teacher competency requires both governmental and lay action on a wide variety of related issues. Closer cooperation among federal, state, and local units of government is essential to solution of the financial problem. No less significant are improvement of policies relating to manpower, teacher preparation, certification, and general conditions affecting the holding power of the teaching profession. In short, the task is national in scope. Governments, laymen, educational institutions, and professional associations share responsibility for removing social, economic, political, and legal barriers to the improvement of staff quality.

Control of Personnel Quality at the Local Level

It has been observed previously that many of the major forces, factors, and conditions related to the problem of personnel competency cannot be controlled by the local school district. Preservice preparation, manpower demands and distribution, financial ability to support education, and licensing are but a few of the elements which can be cited to illustrate this point. But local school districts, willing to engage in the planning necessary to improve staff quality, can do much to facilitate its attainment.

As yet there is no single approach which will guarantee staff quality, but there are at least some fairly certain and time-tested procedures which are helpful in the process. As a matter of fact, every aspect of the personnel function is designed to employ staff members fully capable of rendering effective performance throughout their terms of service. The major premise of this chapter, however, is that control of the quality of school personnel logically proceeds from an understanding of (1) the nature and scope of activities to be performed in the operation of a school system; (2) duties and responsibilities attached to each position, job, or service; and (3) the competency dimensions of each position, job, or service. As we shall see later, analysis of the work to be done and the competencies necessary to perform the work constitute no more than a first step toward staff improvement. Other provisions such as compensation, recruitment, selection, placement, and in-service programs contribute materially to this purpose. But this first step is central to much of the decision making which goes into the staff-improvement process.

Public Education Requires a Variety of Personnel and Services

According to the data contained in Table 5.1, the total instructional staff in the public schools has increased 53.3 per cent over the past decade, or at an average gain of about 4 per cent a year. If administrative and noninstructional personnel were included in these figures it is reasonable to assume that the total school staff would be in excess of two million.

Not only are the number of workers in education increasing; there is an astonishing variety of work to be performed, calling for different skills, knowledges, and levels of preparation. Moreover, there is ample evidence to warrant the assumption that the number and types of public school personnel will increase, along with an emphasis upon staff improvement.

The attainment of staff quality is definitely the most fundamental and vexing task confronting local school officials. Faced with a definite

shortage in professional personnel in the years to come, school districts will have to give more attention to ways of increasing the supply
of competent employees and to work toward this goal by continuous
planning. For many decades persons have been employed in the
public schools without due regard for the work to be done or for the
qualifications possessed by the employee to do the work. This approach
has produced in many instances something less than staff quality and
has tended to compound rather than to minimize personnel problems.

Table 5.1

Instructional Staff Trends in the Public Schools 1950–51 to 1960–61

School Year	Instructional Staff *	Per cent gain	
		Over 1950–51	Over Previous Year
1950–51	995,241	—	—
1951–52	1,012,384	1.7%	1.7%
1952–53	1,050,613 †	5.6	3.8
1953–54	1,098,320	10.4	4.5
1954–55	1,150,755 †	15.6	4.8
1955–56	1,213,459	21.9	5.4
1956–57	1,271,191	27.7	4.8
1957–58	1,333,332	34.0	4.9
1958–59	1,394,913 †	40.2	4.6
1959–60	1,464,930 †	47.2	5.0
1960–61	1,526,079 †	53.3	4.2

Source: National Education Association, Research Division, Research Report 1960–
R15, *Estimates of School Statistics, 1960–61* (Washington: The Association, 1960),
p. 11.
   * Classroom teachers, principals, supervisors, other instructional staff.
   † Estimated.

The discussion which follows provides suggestions for improving
staff quality through a series of analyses designed to (1) describe the
function of each position in the organization, (2) identify the major
responsibilities of each position, (3) indicate organizational relationships of the position, (4) establish qualifications needed to render
effective service in the position, and (5) provide standards to be employed in appraising the performance rendered by the holder of the
position. In short, suggestions are provided for controlling staff quality

through analyses of the services to be rendered by school personnel and by the establishment of qualifications deemed necessary for effective performance.

Preparation of Position Specifications

The foundation of any plan to improve staff quality is a system for gathering and analyzing information relating to the various kinds of work activities—the mental and physical effort—needed to carry out organization purposes. Techniques employed for this purpose are referred to as position classification; job analysis, description, or specification; and position guide preparation.

Organization analysis of positions, extensively used in government and industry as the basis for wage and salary administration, has had limited application in public education. This may be explained in part by the relatively small size of public school staffs, the homogeneous nature of much of the teaching activity, differences in nature of work performed, and the narrow range of most school compensation structures.

As the following discussion attempts to make clear, public education can make effective use of the position analysis concept. Development of position descriptions will help to: (1) facilitate recruitment, selection, and placement; (2) point up overlapping and duplication of functions; (3) provide a basis for compensation planning; (4) enable personnel to understand their duties and responsibilities; (5) clarify organizational relationships; (6) determine staffing adequacy; (7) minimize neglect of established responsibilities; (8) make planning for in-service programs more effective; (9) provide a basis for budgeting personnel needs; (10) make the task of supervision more realistic; (11) make available information for decisions relating to transfer and promotion; and (12) furnish a guide for appraisal of personnel performance. Apparent as these advantages may seem, it is not to be implied that they can be gained quickly through emulation of position classification plans used in noneducational enterprises. But there is every reason to believe that there are certain benefits to be derived by school administration from a careful and continuous analysis of the positions to be filled and the qualifications needed to fill them. Although position analysis can be applied more readily to administrative and noninstructional positions, it is clear that analysis of the similarities and differences in instructional positions will be helpful in administering the personnel program. The wide variety of instructional personnel required in the modern school program, calling for professionally trained instructors with many different kinds of knowledges, skills, and abilities, lends support to the argument that an understanding of the duties and requirements of each position will better enable school administration to recruit personnel with requisite qualifications.

Position Analysis

Analysis of the positions in a school system generally begins with a study of the existing plan of organization, that is, with what work is now being performed, and under what division of labor. The initial problem is to identify each of the various positions, as well as the duties and responsibilities attached thereto. The three main categories of positions in a school system—administrative, instructional, and noninstructional—provide a practical basis for the grouping of positions, particularly in light of the fact that different compensation plans are usually developed for each of these three personnel categories. As noted earlier, information relating to these positions can be gathered by means of questionnaires, check lists, interviews, observation, and through studies of organization charts and manuals.

Position Function

Those who have thought carefully about the kinds of information which position analysis should yield are in agreement that a knowledge of the major function of each position is indispensable. When the ends for which the position has been created can be stated in concise and meaningful terms, the foundation upon which to base related decisions has been laid. It enables administration to (1) visualize how the function of the position is related to the common purpose of the organization; (2) consider the duties and responsibilities necessary to performance of the function; and (3) clarify for the position incumbent how the position fits into the over-all plan of organization. A subsidiary value in stating position functions is the broader understanding which personnel derive from participation in the process.

Position Responsibilities

Once the primary functions have been developed, a guidepost is established for translating the position function into specific duties or responsibilities. Several observations need to be made here. Analysis of responsibilities is not concerned with who is doing the work now, with methods by which the work is performed, nor with the minute details inherent in the task. Rather, the purpose is to outline the work which ought to be accomplished, and the major tasks involved in getting it done successfully.

The simplest way to characterize responsibilities of a position is to identify key factors involved in its performance, then to organize descriptions around these elements. Some school districts, for example, have analyzed responsibilities of all administrative positions in terms of the following categories: (1) improvement of educational opportunity, (2) personnel administration, (3) community relations, and (4) provision of funds and facilities. A check list of administrative duties, similar to the one shown in Table 4.5, is then constructed to establish the necessary administrative task in each category and to designate which should be assigned to each member of the administrative staff. It is assumed, of course, that each administrator will have certain responsibilities assigned to him in each of the four categories listed above, the nature of which will depend upon requirements of the position.

Position Relationships

The third element in the problem of position analysis is determination of the relationship of one position in the organization to another. Several of its aspects deserve mention here. All positions in an organization are assumed to have a reporting relationship, that is, the position incumbent is responsible to at least one other person for the performance of assigned responsibilities. Clarification of this relationship is essential not only from the standpoint of preventing conflicts in assignments, but also to eliminate duplication of effort and to enable administration to hold personnel responsible for the performance of designated duties.

Another matter to be clarified is the line or staff function of the position. Line positions are those directly charged with the responsibility and accorded the necessary authority for initiating and implementing organizational aims, policies, and procedures. The principal of an attendance unit, being a line officer, is generally conceded to have the authority and responsibility to put into effect the educational program established for the unit, and to organize personnel and facilities in a manner conceived to attain the broad goals of the school program. Staff positions, on the other hand, are those established to render advice and service to the line positions. Conflicts frequently arise when staff personnel assume line functions and vice versa, or when a particular responsibility is not discharged because of failure to delegate it specifically to either line or staff personnel. Experience has shown that personnel performance can be improved when the scope of each position is made clear, when the limits of authority and responsibility for each position are defined, and when supervisory relationships are clearly delineated.

Position Qualifications

Controls over qualifications of school personnel may be categorized as either internal or external. Qualifications established by the local administrative unit are referred to as internal controls. Employment conditions established by extraschool board agencies, such as civil service units, unions, and state departments of education, are in the nature of external controls. The discussion which follows emphasizes the nature and importance of internal controls to staff improvement, recognizing, of course, that boards of education must comply with employment requirements of legal agencies and with those of trade organizations with whom they have contractual agreements.

The basis for establishing employment requirements rests firmly upon a clear understanding of the kind and quality of service which the administration expects to be rendered in each position. Such information can be derived through position descriptions. These descriptions provide a starting point for consideration of qualifications needed by the individual to succeed in the position. From the position descriptions must be deduced the qualities necessary to perform the service in each of the positions of the three work categories under consideration—instructional, administrative, and noninstructional.

Employment Standards for the Instructional Staff

So much has been written about the qualities which contribute to instructional success that it seems superfluous to catalogue here what has come to be a rather extensive and not necessarily valid list of traits. The question of which traits, and in which degree each one is essential for effective teaching and guidance of children, is one which has both baffled and intrigued educators for many years. Efforts continue to develop a master list of traits to characterize good teachers. But the administrative staff needs more information than a set of traits to guide it in the selection of instructional staff members. Certainly the position descriptions will reveal that there are differences in subjects, pupils, programs, purposes, and teaching conditions. Those who select the instructional staff have the difficult task of judging what qualities are necessary to meet the demands of the position variations mentioned above. In other words, it seems unlikely that teaching positions are so standardized that they can be performed by anyone possessing a generalized set of traits, especially in view of the wide variety of teaching and service positions associated with a modern educational program.

It is generally recognized that the characteristics of the modern instructional staff are different than they were a quarter of a century ago, because the range of staff responsibilities has been extended. Schools have always sought and will continue to seek personnel with more than average intelligence, who are personally mature, professionally competent, who possess mental and physical vitality, who have acquired a liberal education, and who show promise of professional growth. But the modern teacher is expected to be more than technically competent in the classroom. More and more, professional staff members are expected to participate in the solution of school- and district-wide problems relating to purposes, programs, facilities, policies, and procedures. The broad front of education beyond the administrative unit also has genuine implications for all professional personnel for engaging in extraclass activities which contribute both to individual improvement and to the solution of larger educational issues.

A point that should be made clear about establishing qualifications is the need for excluding those factors which have no particular rela-

Non valid characteristic note

tion to staff quality. <u>Political affiliation, sex, marital status, color, religion, residence, and age are characteristics yet to be proven as being detrimental to teaching competence. Those who are responsible for developing eligibility requirements need</u> to take into consideration specifically those characteristics which the position description indicates are necessary for competent performance. To do otherwise would be to negate the entire concept of position description.

Specific characteristics suggested for inclusion in a guide for instructional staff positions are outlined in Figure 10. The reasons for selecting these particular elements were developed in previous sections of this chapter. The purpose of the guide is to enable both the candidate and school officials to understand what competencies are needed to perform specific duties and responsibilities effectively.

FIGURE 10   Outline of position guide for instructional staff.

POSITION TITLE:

English Instructor, Senior High School: Position No. IN-82.

PRIMARY FUNCTION:

To participate as a member of an instructional team to direct learning activities of three sections of high-ability senior high school students in the attainment of subject, school, and system objectives.

MAJOR RESPONSIBILITIES:

(1) instruction, (2) classroom management, (3) guidance and counseling, (4) school organization and administration, (5) professional development, and (6) school-community relations.

ILLUSTRATION OF KEY DUTIES:

(1) INSTRUCTION: (a) provide adequate educational experiences to enable pupils to develop, interpret, and transmit ideas effectively; (b) provide opportunities for pupils to develop ability to solve problems, to think critically, to study effectively; (2) CLASSROOM MANAGEMENT: (a) establish a classroom climate conducive to effective learning and study; (b) routinize clerical duties so that instructional process is uninterrupted; (3) GUIDANCE AND COUNSELING: (a) assist pupils in dealing with academic, personal, social, and vocational problems; (b) work closely with guidance counselor and with instructional team on specific problems of individual pupils; (4) SCHOOL ORGANIZATION AND ADMINISTRATION: (a) contribute to continuous improvement of educational program by initiating suggestions for staff consideration; (b) serve on committees appointed to appraise and to improve curriculum; (5) PROFESSIONAL DEVELOPMENT:

FIGURE 10   Outline of position guide for instructional staff (*Cont.*).

(a) engage in appropriate studies and activities to improve professional competence; (b) contribute to solution of educational problems at state and national levels; (6) SCHOOL-COMMUNITY RELATIONS: (a) work closely with parents in guiding growth and development of pupils; (b) work with community agencies to better the welfare of the children and youth.

QUALIFICATIONS:

(1) EDUCATION: (a) graduate of four-year accredited college, master's degree in English; (b) major course work in creative writing and speech; (2) SKILLS, KNOWLEDGES, ABILITIES: (a) function effectively as a member of instructional team (four members); (b) direct all instructional activities in English and speech for which instructional team is responsible; (b) work effectively with small seminar groups; (c) serve as team consultant in English instruction; (d) utilize wide variety of instructional aids, devices, and methods; (3) EXPERIENCE: three-years' teaching experience in English and speech.

ORGANIZATIONAL RELATIONSHIPS:

(a) accountable to the instructional team leader for performance of assigned responsibilities; (b) coordinates work with members of instructional team.

Use of position guides in personnel administration is not without limitations. This is especially true when applied to the instructional staff. Some educators argue that the competency dimensions for most instructional positions are so similar that position analysis and description are not only unnecessary, but absurd. Others believe that it is futile to attempt to describe in detail the many tasks involved in the teaching-learning process. The inability or unwillingness of boards of education to allocate funds necessary to attract personnel with the qualifications called for in the position guide is also a powerful deterrent to the plan. Quite clearly, there are few advantages to be gained by use of position guides unless funds are provided to realize their intent. Availability of guides for all instructional positions makes possible comparison of similarities and variations in performance demands, enables school officials to establish qualifications in terms of position difficulty, and provides a basis for determining which measures are most likely to yield appropriate data for determining the acceptability of applicants.

There is little question of the value of the position guide in helping school officials to identify factors to be considered in matching persons to positions. Its superiority over traditional employment procedures in public education must be conceded. But the position guide is merely a device to enable the administrator to relate the man and the job. The skill of the members of the selection team in developing information about the potential of a candidate to perform successfully in a position is equally as important as careful preparation of the position guide.

Employment Standards for the Administrative Staff

Nothing is more essential to the progress of a school system than a competent administrative staff. It is generally agreed that the greatest contribution a board of education can make to the welfare of children is to establish provisions and procedures for attracting capable leader-

FIGURE 11   Outline of position guide for administrative staff.

POSITION TITLE:

Assistant to Superintendent: Business Affairs. Position No. A-3.

PRIMARY FUNCTION:

To provide advice and service to all elements of the school district on business and financial affairs.

MAJOR RESPONSIBILITIES:

(1) financial planning; (2) purchasing and supply control; (3) school facilities; (4) school-community relations; (5) personnel administration; (6) in-service development; (7) maintenance and operation; (8) food services; (9) records and reports; (10) office management.

ILLUSTRATION OF KEY DUTIES:

(1) FINANCIAL PLANNING: (a) collect and interpret appropriate data for use by all elements of the school system for preparing annual and long-term budgets; (2) PURCHASING AND SUPPLY CONTROL: (a) prepare specifications and standards for purchasing school supplies and equipment; (3) SCHOOL FACILITIES: (a) initiate studies to determine present and future school plant needs; (4) SCHOOL-COMMUNITY RELATIONS: (a) prepare financial reports to develop community understanding of district fiscal operations; (5) PERSONNEL ADMINISTRATION: (a) recruit, select, induct, and supervise all noninstructional personnel, guided and limited by

FIGURE 11   Outline of position guide for administrative staff (*Cont.*).

over-all employment standards established by district; (6) IN-SERVICE DEVELOPMENT: (a) develop and maintain plan for in-service development of noninstructional personnel; (7) MAINTENANCE AND OPERATION: (a) develop work program for maintenance and operation employees; (8) FOOD SERVICES: prepare plans for operating school lunch program; (9) RECORDS AND REPORTS: (a) direct the recording and reporting of all school fiscal operations; (10) OFFICE MANAGEMENT: (a) plan the internal organization of the business office.

QUALIFICATIONS:

(1) EDUCATION: (a) doctor's degree; (b) specific preparation in finance and business administration; (2) SKILLS, KNOWLEDGES, ABILITIES: (a) competency in supervising data processing equipment; (b) ability to direct maintenance, operative, and food service programs; (c) understanding of state and local tax structures; (d) knowledge of the legal implications of local school finance; (e) evidence of unusual personal integrity; (f) ability to coordinate school financial planning with city financial planning; (3) EXPERIENCE PRIORITIES: (a) at least seven years of successful experience in business, industry, and/or education; (b) at least five years of appropriate and satisfactory school experience; (c) at least two years of administrative or supervisory responsibilities in school systems.

ORGANIZATIONAL RELATIONSHIPS:

(a) staff position; (b) reports to and is accountable to superintendent of schools; (c) provides advice and service to all elements of the school organization; (d) establishes and maintains such contacts as are necessary to the fulfillment of the function.

---

ship. Three essential steps in the process of securing administrative personnel include: (1) position description, (2) procedures designed to secure a continuing supply of administrative talent from which selection can be made, and (3) a selection process which provides the kinds of information needed to match the qualifications of the individual with the position description. It is trite, but necessary, to point out that position description is an indispensable tool in the process of assessing administrative potential. There is little reason for school districts, whether small or large, to select persons for administrative posts without either party knowing something of the performance expectations. Of the total number of personnel in a school system, only a small percentage are administrators. Hence, the task of describing administrative positions is both possible and feasible in almost any system. With so much at stake in the employment of administrators, and with the knowledge that administrative positions are capable of definition, the belief that the "right" administrator will emerge by letting nature take its course cannot be seriously regarded.

The position guide for administrative positions, an outline of which is shown in Figure 11, indicates major elements for which definitions and specifications are needed. While most job description forms or guides are fairly similar, it is quite unlikely that the actual nature of administrative duties and responsibilities in two school systems will be identical. In one a principal may be responsible for student fund accounting. Other schools may assign this function to teachers or to the business manager. Briefly stated, each system must describe administrative positions in terms of needs and conditions peculiar to them.

Although considerable research has been devoted to development and validation of criteria for predicting success in administrative positions, results are inconclusive.[1] Representative of the factors which investigators have taken into consideration in attempting to identify essential administrative competencies are the following: (1) intellectual ability; (2) physical and emotional stamina; (3) leadership qualities, such as the ability to influence an organization to define and to achieve its goals; (4) professional competence; (5) skill in human relations; (6) ability to conceptualize; (7) skill in communication; and (8) evidence of success in past administrative performances. In establishing standards for selection of administrators, these as well as other attributes cannot be written off as being unimportant, despite the fact that research does not point to a single trait, nor even to a combination of traits as being the most effective determinant of administrative success.

While the search for better measures to judge administrative effectiveness goes on, so must the very practical business of selecting administrative personnel in public school systems across the nation. Those who are charged with the responsibility can proceed by making certain that standards used for selection are flexible, since the process

---

[1] See Roald F. Campbell and Russell T. Gregg, editors, *Administrative Behavior in Education* (New York: Harper & Brothers, 1957), Chapters IX, XI.

of judging administrative competency is largely subjective. The position guide, then, should be regarded as a starting point to consider (1) the nature and scope of the position; (2) what the individual who fills it must know, do, and be; and (3) the social setting with its extensive network of cooperative relationships within which the individual is expected to perform effectively.

Employment Standards for the Noninstructional Staff

Results which have been accomplished in business, industry, and public education by the use of job descriptions and employment standards for nonprofessional positions have been effective enough to create extensive adoption of these practices wherever sizable groups of people are employed. Indeed, the position classification system, which goes well beyond the position guide concept previously discussed in connection with professional personnel, is the central feature of many personnel programs. To be more specific, under the position classification system jobs are grouped into classes, depending upon the kind and level of work. Employment standards are established for each class of positions, and the compensation structure designed accordingly. Recruitment, selection, promotion, transfer, and development plans are carried out in terms of the position classification system.

As is evident from analysis of Figure 12, employment standards for noninstructional personnel are, for the most part, less difficult to establish than are those for professional personnel. Not only does the work to be done lend itself more readily to description, but measures for screening the presence or absence of essential competencies to perform the work are generally available. This is especially true of routine operations, such as typing, clerical assignments, machine operation, and other activities which do not involve decision making or influencing group behavior toward the attainment of certain goals. This generalization does not mean that all is known that needs to be known about criteria for selection of noninstructional personnel. Rather, it points out that position description is less complicated as the level of work difficulty decreases.

Major elements to be considered in establishing qualification standards for noninstructional personnel—education, skills, knowledges, abilities, experience, personal qualifications—are quite similar to those discussed for other personnel categories. The crucial problem is to determine which of the foregoing factors is essential to job performance, in what degree each is essential, and whether certain combinations of factors are more desirable than others. If this information were available for each position, the task of setting specific standards could be more readily accomplished.

The assumption underlying qualification standards is so straightforward, so defensible that its acceptance as a useful device in personnel administration can hardly be questioned. It holds that the quality of personnel performance can be improved by careful analysis of the work to be done, and of the human competencies needed to do the work. While neither of the two kinds of requirements are generally isolated to the extent that is desirable, adherence to the principle is vital to staff improvement.

FIGURE 12   Outline of position guide for noninstructional staff.

POSITION TITLE:

Administrative or Junior High School Secretary to Principal Position: Secretary II, Grade IV.

PRIMARY FUNCTION:

To render administrative and secretarial service to a junior high school principal, an assistant principal in the high school, or a staff administrator in the central administration.

MAJOR RESPONSIBILITIES:

(1) secretarial; (2) administrative; (3) supervisory.

ILLUSTRATION OF KEY DUTIES:

(1) SECRETARIAL: (a) act as secretary to the principal or assistant to the superintendent; (b) take and transcribe dictation and minutes of administrative meetings; (2) ADMINISTRATIVE: (a) interpret policies and procedures for the professional staff, public, and pupils; (b) compose, edit, and prepare bulletins, schedules, and correspondence; (c) prepare secretarial, payroll, enrollment, and statistical reports regarding personnel, requisitions, and pupils; (3) SUPERVISORY: (a) supervise clerical and/or student assistants.

QUALIFICATIONS:

(1) EDUCATION: (a) graduation from high school, including or supplemented by secretarial and business training; (2) SKILLS, KNOWLEDGES, ABILITIES: (a) ability to take dictation at 90 words per minute; (b) ability to type at net correct speed of 50 words per minute; (c) sufficient computational ability to compile statistical records; (d) under-

FIGURE 12   Outline of position guide for noninstructional staff (*Cont.*).

standing of modern office techniques; (e) knowledge of elementary bookkeeping; (4) EXPERIENCE: at least three years of recent, full-time, paid, directly related office experience.

LINES OF PROMOTION:

From: Secretary II to: Secretary I (Grade 5) Senior High School Principal;

To: Executive Secretary (Grade 6) Superintendent-Business Manager.

SALARY SCHEDULE:

(Grade 4) $3450–$4344; (Grade 5) $3,924–$4,824; (Grade 6) $4,356 to $5,406. Salary increases are on merit, based on annual evaluation of employee by immediate supervisor. Evaluation subject to review by superintendent and/or business manager, and by board of school directors.

WORK SCHEDULE:

Position calls for 37.5 hour week, 8:00 A.M. to 4:30 P.M.

ORGANIZATIONAL RELATIONSHIPS:

(a) reports to and is accountable to administrative officer to whom assigned; (b) supervises clerical and/or student assistants assigned to this position; (c) maintains contact with business manager, who is responsible for establishing conditions of employment for all noninstructional personnel.

Position Planning: Some Generalizations

A school system rests on the shoulders of its planners. Since every position in the system has been established for a particular purpose, systematic planning is necessary to make certain that purpose is realized.

There is nothing mysterious about position planning. Every school has the obligation to fill each position with a competent functionary. Many pages have been devoted to discussion of reasons why staff quality in education is less than satisfactory. But despite numerous obstacles, it is fair to assume that the problem of improving staff quality will be one of perennial interest.

The treatment in this chapter relating to the improvement of school personnel by the use of position analysis and description has been necessarily brief. Only the main elements of various techniques available for position planning have been outlined, since standard reference works are available on the subject.[2] The extent to which a local school district can and should undertake to employ techniques for position planning described herein is a difficult one to answer. More and more, outside consultant service has proved to be advantageous in establishing position classification systems, especially for noninstructional personnel. Regardless of the size of the system, the need for preparing qualification standards for personnel exists. How the need can best be satisfied is a matter which local districts must decide.

Although the task of preparing position descriptions is a major one, the plan is doomed to fail if constant efforts are not made to improve its administration. Creation of new positions frequently means reallocation of duties in existing positions. The point of emphasis is that duties and responsibilities in an organization are constantly changing, and the position descriptions and qualification standards must be adjusted accordingly. Constant appraisal of the effectiveness of existing standards in recruiting, selecting, and retaining personnel will provide the administrator with information for considering the validity of present practices.

Suggested Reading

American Association of School Administrators, *Professional Administrators for America's Schools* (Washington: The Association, 1960), Chapter VI.

Byers, Kenneth M., Robert Mantilla, and Elmer V. Williams, *Elements of Position Classification in Local Government* (Chicago: Civil Service Assembly, 1955).

Campbell, Roald F., John E. Corbally, Jr., and John A. Ramseyer, *Introduction to Educational Administration* (Boston: Allyn and Bacon, Inc., 1958), Chapters 10, 11, and 12.

The International City Manager's Association, *Municipal Personnel Administration*, 6th ed. (Chicago: The Association, 1960), Chapters III and IV.

Morphet, Edgar L., R. L. Johns, and Theodore L. Reller, *Educational Administration: Concepts, Practices, and Issues* (Englewood Cliffs, N.J.: Prentice-Hall, Inc., 1959), Chapter IV.

[2] Readings are suggested on pages 132, 133, 382.

National Education Association, *New Horizons in Teacher Education and Professional Standards* (Washington: The Association, 1960).

National Industrial Conference Board, *Organization of Staff Functions,* Studies in Personnel Policy, No. 165 (New York: The Board, 1958).

National Industrial Conference Board, *Selecting Company Executives,* Studies in Personnel Policy, No. 161 (New York: The Board, 1957).

United States Civil Service Commission, *Less Paperwork in Position Classification,* Personnel Management Series No. 15 (Washington: U.S. Government Printing Office, 1959).

United States Department of Agriculture, Office of Personnel, *Classification in a Nut Shell* (Washington: U.S. Government Printing Office, 1959).

The Compensation Structure

CHAPTER SIX

The compensation structure is introduced here to emphasize its sequential importance in the personnel function. Simply stated, this means that when the board of education establishes policies on the quality and quantity of the school staff it must, at the same time, establish correlative fiscal policies. The chief executive cannot develop an effective recruitment program, for example, unless the total compensation structure for all personnel has been clearly defined. Moreover, its structural characteristics must be designed to attract and retain the kinds of competencies envisioned by the board as being essential to the conduct of the school program. The chief executive should be able to enter the personnel market armed with whatever budgetary provisions may be necessary to implement board personnel policy. To expect him to act as a bargainer to secure talent in exchange for charm and vague promises is to expect the impossible.

The compensation structure of a school system refers to provisions governing salaries, wages, and collateral benefits of school personnel. Economic provisions within the structure generally apply to three per-

134

sonnel categories. These categories, as well as the schedules or provisions usually applicable to each category, are listed in Table 6.1.

Table 6.1

Outline of the Local School Compensation Structure

Provisions	Group I Teaching Personnel	Group II Administrative Personnel	Group III Noninstructional Personnel
Master Salary Schedule	x		
Special Salary Schedules		x	x
Nonsalary Provisions	x	x	x

Factors Affecting Salaries of School Personnel

Professional salaries to attract well-qualified teaching and administrative personnel seem to be an old problem, ever new. There is an increasing array of evidence to support the contention that professional earnings in education are not high enough to attract and retain competent personnel. Some pertinent facts are as follows:

1. The income of teachers does not compare favorably with that of other professions.

2. The rate of increase in the income of school personnel has exceeded the rate of increase in the cost of living in the last decade, but the relative economic status of teachers in comparison with other professional and nonprofessional occupational groups has not changed significantly.

3. The earnings of teachers are neither commensurate with the service they render nor sufficiently rewarding in relation to certification standards.

4. The present lifetime income expectancy from teaching will not attract enough persons who possess desirable personal and professional qualifications.

5. School personnel have not benefited materially from gains made in the national economy, despite the strong relationship between education and economic productivity.

The unfavorable economic status of professional school personnel, however, is only one of a number of facets involved in a rather complex problem. The question of how to improve the economic lot of public education has brought forth a wave of exhortations, admonitions, essays, debates, suggestions, and declarations. Some of these have amounted to irrationalism.

The hard fact of life is that we cannot continue to treat low salaries as though they were unrelated to larger complexes of conditions. Indeed, the problem has many dimensions. It is not as simple as just getting more money this year and next year. It involves more than adding another hundred dollars or two to either the low or high end of the salary schedule. It is a problem more complex than money itself. It is related, for example, to: (1) earnings in other occupations; (2) national productivity; (3) supply of and demand for professional personnel; (4) standards governing entrance into the profession; (5) federal, state, and local provisions for public education; and (6) units of school government.

The point of view held here is simple to state as a generalization—though its parts are not so simple: the generalization is that the profession must become much more intimately concerned with solving a complex of interrelated socioeconomic-educational problems and must expect that the economic status of school personnel will improve only as the profession and the educational enterprise both gain in strength and vigor. Some of the factors related to the improvement of personnel salaries are discussed in the following section.

Pertinent Salary Determinants

It has been noted previously that salaries and wages of school personnel are determined by an interaction of social and economic forces and factors. With this in mind let us examine some of the more pertinent determinants as they relate to the problem out of which this discussion originated—the school compensation structure. Unfortunately, it is not possible to cover all of the ramifications of salaries and wages for school personnel in a single chapter. The discussion, however, will concentrate on several factors which bear heavily on the compensation structure.

Supply and Demand

Pervading the professional salary problem in education is a determinant which, in the opinion of many students of the matter, has not been given proper emphasis. In the long run, salaries and wages are determined by the supply of and demand for a given quality of personal service. According to Thomas,[1] this means that the price of labor tends to be set by the interaction of (1) the number of potential employees who have the desired productive competence and who can be induced to sell their competence at certain rates of pay, and (2) the effective demand, as interpreted by employers and expressed by them through wage offers and related perquisites, for such qualified employees.

When existing salary provisions for teachers are examined in light of the law of supply and demand, an interesting question emerges: If the shortage of qualified teachers is as acute as it appears to be, why are teachers' salaries as low as they are? Presumably they should be much higher. Although it must be admitted readily that there is a shortage of qualified teachers, there is apparently no shortage of unqualified teachers, many of whom are now manning the classrooms of the nation. Several decades ago Morrison noted:

> The compensation of personal services in the form of wages, or in the form of salaries, which constitute only a special case of wages, obeys the general law of supply and demand. . . . Teaching feels the operation of the law, in the excess supply of workers available in the large labor reserve which is permitted to exist.
>
> The age-old attitude of the public toward teaching is one of underevaluation, if not contempt. . . . The effect is that the public as a whole, in a democratic country, come to demand standards but slowly. The result is that practically anybody can teach somewhere, or try to teach, or pretend to teach, who desires to do so, with either no preparation at all or next to none. The outcome is a labor reserve which, save at short intervals of abnormal industrial activity, has been a characteristic feature of the calling throughout our whole school history. When any young girl can teach somewhere, if she can get a job, until she is married, and any young man who is too inept for industry, the potential labor surplus in teaching is the whole body of such young people in the nation.
>
> This labor reserve constitutes the basal factor in the determination of salary levels, even in our best and most efficient districts.[2]

[1] Lawrence G. Thomas, *The Occupational Structure and Education* (Englewood Cliffs, N.J.: Prentice-Hall, Inc., 1956), p. 83.
[2] Henry C. Morrison, *The Management of School Money* (Chicago: University of Chicago Press, 1932), pp. 224, 227–228.

A more recent statement by Lieberman emphasizes the same dilemma:

The difficulty of trying to raise the economic status of teachers while teachers' organizations are engaged in an intensive campaign to recruit teachers should be obvious. No major professional group has been able to drastically improve its status, economic or otherwise, while simultaneously engaging in an intensive drive for more practitioners. There is no reason to think that teachers will succeed in the process. Furthermore, the experience of the professions and of most occupational groups suggests very strongly that concentrating upon legislative action to set minimum salaries (the course of action followed by most educational organizations today) is unlikely to succeed in raising teachers' salaries to professional levels. Restricting entry on the basis of professional qualifications has proved a far more effective method of recruitment, of improving the quality of professional services, and of raising the economic status of the practitioners.[3]

All of this analysis says much the same thing: that desired economic levels in education will not be achieved until professional standards are made what they ought to be. This has been the history of every profession. Until education begins to make entry into the ranks more restrictive, to extend the length and intensity of training, it must endure the pangs of a hungering profession.

Before a clear-cut solution to the problem of respectable compensation for educators is achieved, the profession must find remedies to a complex of social and economic problems. The matter which we have been considering—professional control over the supply of professional workers—ranks high among the factors in need of regulation if the economic status of school personnel is to be improved.

Economic Productivity

The local school district payroll is met largely by revenues from taxation. Tax yields are closely linked to the economic productivity of the nation. Historically the Gross National Product (GNP), an index of the nation's economic activity, has increased at an average rate of about 3 per cent a year. Estimates of the nation's future economic activity, reported by the National Industrial Conference Board,

[3] Myron Lieberman, *Education As a Profession* (Englewood Cliffs, N.J.: Prentice-Hall, Inc., 1956), p. 415.

indicate that, if the present rate of growth persists, we can expect a trillion dollar economy in the 1980's. Estimates of the GNP from 1959 to 2000, as reported by the Conference Board, are shown in Table 6.2.

Table 6.2

Gross National Product, 1959–2000, Projected at 3% Growth Rate

	Gross National Product	Gross Private Domestic Investment	Personal Consumption Expenditures	Government Purchase of Goods and Services
	Billions of 1959 Dollars			
1959	479.5	71.1	311.6	97.6
1965	545.4	80.7	346.3	115.1
1970	632.4	93.6	401.6	133.4
1975	733.3	108.5	465.6	154.7
1980	850.2	125.8	539.9	179.4
1985	985.8	145.9	626.0	208.0
1990	1,143.0	169.2	725.8	241.2
1995	1,325.2	196.1	841.5	279.6
2000	1,536.5	227.4	975.7	324.2

Source: Gertrude Deutsch, "Looking Ahead at the Nation's GNP," *The Conference Board Business Record*, XVII, No. 6 (June, 1960), p. 16.

The economic potential of the nation, then, is assumed to be an expanding one. Moreover, most fiscal experts agree that the nation has the financial ability to increase substantially its allocation of economic resources for public education.

Productivity can be viewed also from the standpoint of the teacher. It can be argued that teachers of our children have every justification to share in the economic output, for productivity depends upon education.

The paradox of salary anemia in a land and a time when the standard of living is higher than any civilization has ever experienced is a matter of record. It poses several fundamental problems. If national productivity develops according to the expectations as shown in Table 6.2, and school personnel do not share in the increase, shortages are inevitable.[4] Solution of the problem in more lasting fashion may well call for an approach vastly different to those which have been pursued for so long without success. It may involve more regulation of such factors as the supply of school personnel, a minimum income level appropriate for professional educators, and closer linkage between teachers' salaries and national income. Whatever the approach may be, and there is need for developing various lines of inquiry, it is certain that the profession must improve its economic status, not only to prevent greater erosion of school staffs, but to attract and to retain enough competent people to provide more and better education for the increasing number of children anticipated in the years immediately ahead.

The District System

The system by which the nation's school districts are organized should be included in the list of school personnel income determinants. During the 1960–61 school year the number of basic administrative units totaled 37,153; 13,392 superintendents of schools were employed in these units. The number of units ranged from 3,250 in Nebraska to 1 in Hawaii.[5] Many administrative units do not contain a sufficient number of children or have the financial ability to maintain anything resembling a comprehensive educational program. Since community size and level of training of school personnel are positively related, it is not surprising that the majority of the temporary (emergency) teachers are located in small rural schools where salaries are generally low.

These conditions create competition for school personnel among districts which does little to improve, and often retards, economic betterment in education. The small district, in many cases, cannot afford to provide salaries good enough to attract competent personnel. Consequently, this situation leads to competition among unqualified persons for low salaries, not for salaries commensurate with quality performance.

The small district described here is one which, under the existing

[4] For an interesting summary of the interaction between education and productivity, see Committee on Tax Education and School Finance, *Citizens Speak Out on School Costs* (Washington: National Education Association, 1959), pp. 19–22.

[5] See National Education Association, Research Division, *Estimates of School Statistics, 1960–61*, Research Report 1960–R15 (Washington: The Association, 1960), p. 19.

system of school organization, cannot now or in the future afford to pay the cost of essential staffing. It will perpetuate low salaries and low qualifications, and prevent economical use of funds.

Taxation

Throughout these pages, repeated inferences have stressed the point that improvement of the economic status of school personnel is more than a problem of money. Other determinants, of which the district system is one, must be dealt with realistically and simultaneously if the American public school system is to maintain and enhance its proven values. As school systems are reorganized into larger units capable of providing comprehensive programs of education, tax systems at all levels of government need to be overhauled to provide economic assistance to schools. The billions of dollars lost in the federal tax system by congressional willingness to maintain tax loopholes, for example, would contribute materially toward initiation of a national minimum foundation program for public education, which in turn would contribute to the improvement of the economic status of school personnel.[6]

Similar revamping of the state and local tax systems are long overdue. Improvement of the local property tax would yield many millions of dollars sorely needed by local school systems. Antiquated tax and debt limitations need to be modernized to permit local schools more fiscal flexibility. Unnecessary budgetary controls and other financial obstacles at the state level could be added to the foregoing list of conditions, which, if remedied, would help provide economic resources so vital to the cause of public education.

The State and School Personnel

While a sound state fiscal plan for public education is essential to development of improved compensation structures at the local level, there are several factors of a nonfiscal nature which should be mentioned that relate to the economic well-being of school personnel.

[6] Major loopholes in the federal tax system include those which: (1) allow a person living on investments to pay less taxes than a wage or salary earner; (2) permit deductions for luxury expense account expenditures and certain travel expenses; (3) permit depletion allowance for oil and gas; (4) do not require taxes on dividends and interest to be withheld at the source. From the Senator's Chair, *Report from The Capitol by Senator Joseph S. Clark* (July 17, 1959), mimeographed.

Many states exercise certain broad controls over school personnel in the form of regulations governing certification, tenure, retirement, and teacher education. The matter of the supply of qualified school personnel, for example, depends largely upon state certification policy. Continuous investigation and regulation by the state of the balance between supply and demand are essential to maintenance of a defensible economic status for teachers within the state. When unrestricted competition creates a serious imbalance between supply and demand, the inevitable result is a lowering of salaries.

Tenure bears an indirect relationship to economic status. While the need for tenure is generally recognized, the state has a responsibility for protecting all parties from the incompetent employee. Absence of sound tenure policies is an open invitation to the unqualified and incompetent. The result here, as in the case of ineffective certification policies, is maintenance of salary levels for public school personnel which are unrealistic.

Finally, brief mention must be made of state control of teacher education institutions. It is a matter of record that when the state does not develop an effective design for developing and controlling teacher education institutions, serious problems develop. These include: (1) existence of institutions not equipped to offer appropriate education for school personnel; (2) absence of central direction and control in relating supply to demand; (3) failure to coordinate aims, standards, and efforts of teacher education institutions; and (4) competition among institutions resulting from decentralized control.

Solution of these problems is fundamental to attainment of the purpose of the state personnel function, which is to meet the qualitative and quantitative staffing needs within the state. It is also fundamental to attainment of an improved economic status for school personnel, inasmuch as there is a tendency for salary schedules to improve as standards for entrance into the profession are strengthened.

Considerations in Developing the Compensation Structure

The previous section dealt briefly with several major determinants of salaries and wages of school personnel. Many of these factors are beyond immediate control of the local school district. Every district, however, develops some sort of pay plan, regardless of the wealth or poverty of its economic resources. The importance of a well-designed compensation structure should not be overlooked, because the pay check which it makes possible is related to satisfaction of individual needs, status, and motivation.

The compensation structure, as the term is used herein, includes salaries, wages, and nonsalary benefits of school personnel, both professional and noninstructional. The discussion which follows has been arranged so as to present a series of considerations for the development of the local school compensation structure. These are grouped arbitrarily under four headings: (1) general considerations; (2) master salary schedule; (3) special salary schedules; and (4) nonsalary provisions.

Each of these divisions embraces an important phase of the total problem. The treatment of each is of a general nature designed to: (1) ensure a general knowledge and understanding of the various problems involved in developing the compensation structure; and (2) point up the interrelationships of the various elements, and the relationship of these elements to the total problem.

This approach may disappoint the practitioner interested in specific answers to salary and wage problems, not principles or generalizations. If the treatment brings about awareness or sensitivity to various facets of personnel compensation, and generates insights into ways by which existing designs can be improved, its aim will be served.

General Considerations

1. *The compensation structure should be designed to include personnel working in every capacity, regardless of income level or job responsibility.* Preoccupation with the master salary schedule is so pervasive that systematic schemes for compensating administrators and noninstructional personnel often come as an afterthought. This condition is reflected in educational literature, in which there is a paucity of reported research, innovation, and experimentation relating to compensation plans for these personnel groups. Competition in the labor market for all types of personnel would seem to be reason enough to justify the principle under consideration, although there are many other purposes to be served by a comprehensive compensation plan for all personnel.

2. *Position guides should be prepared for all positions in the school system.* This principle is based on the assumption that a fairly determined salary or wage must be based on certain facts, such as responsibilities of the position, experience, training, skill, and other qualifications clearly essential to proper determination of salary. This is not to argue for abolition of the single salary schedule, so prominent in public education. As noted in previous chapters, position descriptions are vital to the total personnel function. While it is granted that position guides have not been employed widely in developing the master salary schedule for teachers, they are decidedly applicable in the case of administrative and noninstructional positions. Position guides are especially useful in relating qualifications of a given position to board policies on the quality of personnel to be employed. Personnel standards will, of course, influence salary considerations.

3. *Income levels for all positions should be competitive, in keeping with the responsibilities and duties of the position, and sufficiently high enough to attract and to retain the caliber of personnel capable of attaining the objectives of the service for which they are employed.* It is recognized that implementation of this principle is not without practical problems. Competitive salaries and wages for school personnel are not an issue which can be put up for bargain. To a large extent, the answer lies in an enlightened citizenry which understands the social implications of low school salaries. To make this principle fully operative, coordinated governmental action—federal–state–local—is necessary, along with vigorous professional efforts to define and to support appropriate means for achieving higher income levels.

4. *Satisfactory service should be the criterion for advancement in income.* Salary and wage increases should be granted on the basis of satisfactory service, whatever the level of income or job responsibility. Individuals should advance in income only as they actually prove their value. It is hardly the intent of a salary schedule to make financial rewards automatic, regardless of the nature of the contribution of the individual to the attainment of purpose.

5. *Quality of service should be rewarded.* This principle supports the belief that those school agents who make outstanding con-

tributions to attainment of purpose should be rewarded financially. While there is considerable agreement that the principle is sound, there is controversy over the fairness, validity, and reliability of implementation procedures currently employed. Some think that we do not know what constitutes quality in instruction; others think that we know what quality of teaching performance is, but we have no way of measuring it. And still others contend that any plan for rewarding quality of service will have a harmful effect upon teacher morale and level of performance.

There is no question that much remains to be done to improve methods for appraising teaching effectiveness. It is also granted that an attractive salary schedule is essential to the success of any plan for rewarding competence. It would appear to be a mistake, however, to assume that existing obstacles to rewarding competency are so great that they can never be overcome, that experimentation in any form is futile. High and equal pay for unequal performance is a belief so contrary to logic that its defenders are placed in a footless position.

6. *Collateral benefits should be an inherent feature of the compensation structure.* The employee benefit program is becoming a recognized aspect of occupational life in the United States. If public education must compete in the employee market for qualified personnel, it must recognize this growing social trend to provide collateral benefits as an essential part of the compensation structure.

7. *Continuous planning is basic to development and maintenance of a sound compensation structure.* Reference has been made previously to the fact that salaries, wages, and benefits are a complex of various administrative and social problems. Constant social change affects salary and wage levels. Problems created by the forces, factors, and conditions affecting salaries and wages can be solved best through systematic planning. The compensation structure is a sort of delicate mechanism which needs constant attention to keep it in working order, for problems recur in the best of compensation plans. Without continuous review and adjustment, taking into account, for example, such factors as trends in earnings in other professions and in the cost of living, the structure loses its competitive qualities.

Once in existence, the structure is best maintained and improved through an effective system of budgeting. The annual and long-term budgets are useful instruments for planned change. The budgetary process provides the means for anticipating compensation problems, and for developing policies and programs aimed at their solution. Stated another way, compensation problems are not solved by hope, by luck, or by expediency. They are solved through foresight—through anticipation of what lies ahead and planning for it.

Master Salary Schedule

The master salary schedule refers to the salary payment plan for classroom teachers. It involves the majority of school personnel and claims the greatest share of the current budget.

There are two basic types of salary plans for classroom teachers, the most prominent of which is the single salary schedule. Adoption of the single salary schedule, which means equivalent salaries for equivalent preparation and experience, has been practically universal in urban school systems. The position type schedule, which bases salaries on classification of positions within the school system, has lost favor over the years, mainly because the assumptions upon which it was based were unacceptable to most school personnel.

A number of school systems have built upon the single salary schedule to produce what might be termed a preparation-experience-merit schedule. Many varieties of merit have been combined with the single salary plan.

1. *The design of the master salary schedule should be built around its purposes or objectives.* The conventional approach to salary scheduling is to determine what kind of schedule can be developed for X dollars. A more meaningful approach is to determine what the salary schedule should accomplish. Having determined this, the schedule should then be developed to achieve its stated aims. Questions such as these are involved: What should be bought with the schedule? What will it cost to buy it? Is the community able and willing to buy the personal services reflected in the stated purposes?

As stated frequently throughout these pages, school funds should be designed to attract, retain, and improve competent personnel. This is the basic purpose of any salary schedule. It would appear to be the test of schedule validity.

2. *Minimums, maximums, and lifetime earnings should be competitive with other occupational groups which require equivalent preparation and experience.* One of the recurrent problems throughout the history of American public education has been that of establishing a competitive beginning salary level for teachers. According to the Educational Policies Commission:

An adequate starting salary is one which is reasonably competitive with those of other professional occupations and other teaching positions open to candidates. It approximates the average of beginning salaries in occupations for which a college degree is required.[7]

Certainly one of the purposes of any master salary schedule should be to attract competent new college graduates into public education. The local school district must be prepared to base its schedule upon this or reasonably similar standards if it expects to develop and maintain a capable school staff. Recommendations by the Educational Policies Commission are shown in Table 6.3.

Table 6.3

Hypothetical Salary Distributions

In a School System with High Salary Levels	In a Less Favored Setting	In a Still Less Favored Setting
5% of staff at starting level	10% of staff at starting level	15% of staff at starting level
10% at 1.25 times the starting level	20% at 1.25 times the starting level	15% at 1.25 times the starting level
15% at 1.50 times the starting level	20% at 1.50 times the starting level	20% at 1.50 times the starting level
20% at 2.00 times the starting level	20% at 2.00 times the starting level	20% at 1.75 times the starting level
20% at 2.25 times the starting level	20% at 2.25 times the starting level	25% at 2.00 times the starting level
20% at 2.50 times the starting level	10% at 2.50 times the starting level	5% at 2.50 times the starting level
10% at 3.00 times the starting level		

Source: Educational Policies Commission, *An Essay on Quality in Public Education* (Washington: National Education Association, 1959), p. 28.

[7] Educational Policies Commission, *An Essay on Quality in Public Education* (Washington: National Education Association, 1959), p. 18.

The foregoing data illustrate one of many approaches to the implementation of the competitive salary principle. For the most part, they are based on judgment rather than on factual evidence. This is to be expected, since salaries and wages within the entire occupational structure are to a large extent the product of both fact and judgment.

3. *Incentive differentials among salary classes should be wholesome enough to make possible retention and improvement of competent school personnel.* The master salary schedule groups teachers of equivalent preparation into what are known as salary classes. A salary class is usually defined in terms of academic degrees or years of professional preparation. To illustrate:

Class	Level of Training
1	no degree
2	bachelor's degree
3	master's degree
4	master's degree plus
5	doctorate

Each salary class specifies minimum salaries, the number and amount of annual increments, salary steps in recognition of experience, and maximum salaries. Incentive differentials among the salary classes should be attractive enough to encourage educational advancement. This is a common failing in many schedules, in some cases the differentials being too small for the teacher to recover in a short period of time the added expenses incurred for additional academic preparation. One report [8] suggests a difference of from 10 to 15 per cent between minimums, mid-points, and at the maximums of two adjacent salary classes.

A minimum number of salary classes emphasizing completion of degrees rather than accumulation of credits, as well as establishment of a bachelor's degree as the minimum level of preparation for professional employment, are important considerations in designing the schedule.

[8] National Association of Manufacturers, *Satisfying the Salaried Employee* (New York: The Association, 1957), p. 21.

4. *Opportunities are available to advance toward the maximum within a reasonable period of satisfactory service, and at an accelerated rate for those who complete required levels of training.* Controls exercised over the advancement of school personnel within the range of a salary class, or from one salary class to another, should be positive in character. The typical salary schedule contains 12 to 13 increments, which, it should be noted, is a modal figure rather than a standard. Arrangement of increments should be such as to facilitate recruitment and retention of personnel. Transition from one class to another should be conducive to continuous professional growth.

5. *Opportunities are provided for personnel to earn continuous financial rewards for satisfactory performance throughout the entire service period.* This principle is based upon the belief that teaching should be viewed as a career profession; its recruitment, selection, and rewards based on a career of service. The problem is not that there are—as some have said—too many women in teaching. Rather, it is that too many of the women—and men—who start do not intend to stay—and, even more important, that many who might, never do start, because they do not perceive teaching as a continuously rewarding career.[9]

Salary schedules are frequently designed to enable personnel to reach the maximum in a relatively short period of time, say within the first third of a teacher's academic life. It is worth considering whether it would be wiser to spread increments over 40 years to maximums much higher than any which are conceived as appropriate in 12 or 14 years. Education, as other professions—and this is characteristic of professional status— ought never to put an earnings ceiling appropriate to youth and immaturity on the prime years of power and service. It ought to be possible for a classroom teacher to see himself growing in power, in stature, and in earnings throughout his professional life. Earnings should be consistent with the concept of a pro-

[9] Thorndike and Hagen's extensive study of men who remained in and left teaching indicates that those who were academically capable and more talented tended to drop out of teaching and that those who remained as classroom teachers in elementary and secondary schools were the less intellectually able. See Robert L. Thorndike and Elizabeth Hagen, *Characteristics of Men Who Remained in and Left Teaching* (New York: Teachers College, Columbia University, 1961), p. 10.

fession which rewards career service. As noted earlier, the total lifetime income of a salary schedule is a more meaningful measure of its provisions than the maximum at 12, 14, or some other arbitrarily designated number of years.

There are a variety of plans for continuous rewards for service during the academic lifetime of school personnel. Whether the principle of continuous rewards for satisfactory service is implemented through merit, career increments, super maximums, and so on, it is the principle, and not the mechanics, that matters most.

In developing compensation plans for professional personnel, increasing use is being made by school systems of an *index* or *ratio salary schedule*. As illustrated in Table 6.4, this is a technique by which a

Table 6.4

Illustration of Index Salary Schedule for Classroom Teachers *

Year	B. A.	M. A.	M. A. + 30	Doctorate
1	1.00	1.10	1.25	1.45
2	1.05	1.15	1.30	1.50
3	1.10	1.20	1.35	1.55
4	1.15	1.25	1.40	1.60
5	1.20	1.30	1.45	1.65
6	1.25	1.35	1.50	1.70
7	1.30	1.40	1.55	1.75
8	1.35	1.45	1.60	1.80
9	1.40	1.50	1.65	1.85
10	1.45	1.55	1.70	1.90
11		1.60	1.75	1.95
12			1.80	2.00
13				2.05

* Annual increments of 5 per cent and preparation differentials of 10, 15, and 20 per cent of base salary (B. A. minimum).

system of multipliers is used to establish increments and preparation differentials in relation to a base salary. Index salary schedules may be used for administrative and supervisory positions as well as for instructional personnel. Among the advantages of this approach are the following:

1. It enables schedule planners to concentrate on the development of principles to be incorporated in the compensation structure before adoption of dollar amounts.

2. It makes for ease of understanding structural interrelationships.

3. It is a means for making a compensation plan for administrative and supervisory positions definitive and interrelated with schedules for instructional personnel.

4. Dollar amounts can be altered without changing established relationships.

Variations in existing index schedules are both considerable and commendable. While the index plan must be viewed as a means to an end, and will not in itself improve the compensation structure, it offers a systematic approach to the solution of salary schedule problems.[10]

Special Salary Schedules

Administrative Personnel

There is general recognition today that compensation for public school administrators is both inadequate and inequitable. Concern over failure of local communities to assure economic satisfaction of its educational leaders was heightened by the published findings of Ruml and Tickton [11] on the long-term trend in the financial status of school administrative positions. Deterioration of the economic status of administrative personnel has been so great over a 50-year period, according to the report, that attractiveness of these positions as careers for able young men and women has diminished.[12]

Reasons why administrative salaries are one of the least well-defined aspects of the public school compensation structure are fairly easy to perceive. The increase in population has created the greatest personnel increases at the classroom level. Administrative positions have not increased correspondingly. Hence, the master salary schedule has been accorded a high priority on available financial resources.

[10] Current use of index schedules for teachers is described in National Education Association, Research Division, Research Memo 1961-12, *Index or Ratio Salary Schedules for Teachers* (Washington: The Association, 1961).

[11] Beardsley Ruml and Sidney G. Tickton, *Teaching Salaries Then and Now* (New York: The Fund for the Advancement of Education, 1955), pp. 18–19.

[12] A second report by Tickton in 1961 indicates that the salary picture for educators has changed somewhat between 1953 and 1959, and the deterioration in the relative purchasing power of education as compared to industry has stopped for the time being. See Sidney G. Tickton, *Teaching Salaries Then and Now—A Second Look* (New York: The Fund for the Advancement of Education, 1961).

Noninstructional functions have also expanded considerably over the years. The net result has been to satisfy the nonadministrative compensation needs and to neglect or to minimize problems relating to administrative compensation. Few boards of education have been willing to risk reactions which might emerge from a policy of purchasing top administrative talent, especially if it means less funds for teachers' salaries. A policy of this kind, however, would seem to possess investment character, because funds needed in most local school systems to improve administrative salaries would be relatively insubstantial. It would also take cognizance of the idea that a substantial part of the superintendent's larger salary is in consideration of his non-tenure status. This approach would tend, in the long run, to yield returns of a nature inconceivable under current administrative salary patterns.

It has been argued by some that past practice in administrative compensation was the best that could be done under prevailing circumstances. It can also be argued that past or even current practice is not a solution.

To this primary premise that school administration is undervalued, socially and economically, should be added strong emphasis upon the educational losses to society which are inevitable so long as this situation prevails.

This discussion does not lead to specific price tags for school administrative salaries. It is aimed at clarification and understanding, not persuasion. The knowledge intended is more in the way of appreciation than application. It is saying, quite simply, that responsibilities of educational leadership are constantly increasing. Society expected more of its school administrators in the fifties than it did in the forties. It will expect more in the sixties. The administrator must know more today than he did a generation ago, for the rate of social change has accelerated, leaving in its wake problems in education which call for constant adjustment.

It would appear reasonable to contend, in light of ever increasing responsibilities and challenges involved in educational administration, that the quality of school administrators must be improved, not lowered. People who are willing to assume administrative responsibilities at low salaries probably will never be in short supply. But in view of the level of leadership which can be purchased for low salaries, and in view of the educational and social losses which are likely to occur under poor leadership, the price of employing inferior administrators frequently proves to be inordinately high.

Having said this, it is now necessary to attempt to point the way to something better than the time-honored, random approach to compensation programs for administrators. Some of the criteria to be kept in mind in formulating plans to assure economic satisfaction to administrative personnel are stated below in question form:

1. Are the salaries commensurate with the kinds of staff members desired?

2. Are the salaries commensurate with duties and responsibilities administrators are asked to assume?

3. Have position guides been prepared to indicate the level of difficulty and responsibility of each administrative position?

4. Does the salary schedule for any administrative position exceed the maximum salary for any teacher?

5. Is the salary of the superintendent of schools substantial enough to offset the insecurity inherent in the position?

6. Does the salary plan reflect the board's intention to employ administrative leadership rather than managerial service?

7. Is the compensation plan for administrators objective enough to eliminate bargaining?

8. Does the plan provide for salary increases over a period of years upon evidence of satisfactory service?

9. Is the plan internally consistent and externally competitive?

10. Does the plan have safeguards to prevent favoring persons with long tenure rather than those who meet performance standards?

As shown in Table 6.5, several types of compensation plans for school administrators were in effect in 1960–61. A proposal by Wynn [13] for determining administrative salaries involves development of a "job ratio" and a "man ratio." These are derived by numerical ratings of major elements in administrative positions (responsibility, complexity, conditions of employment) and ratings of qualifications of individuals occupying these positions (preparation, experience, personal qualifications). The average of the job and man ratio scores, when multiplied by the maximum salary for teachers, indicates the actual salary to be paid administrators.

[13] Richard Wynn, *Guides to the Solution of Administrative Staffing Problems* (Danville, Ill.: The Interstate Printers and Publishers, 1958), pp. 14–25.

Table 6.5

Per Cent of Districts by Type of Salary Schedule for Administrators, 1959–60 and 1960–61

Type of Schedule	GROUP I		GROUP II	
	1959–60	1960–61	1959–60	1960–61
Independent administrative schedule	88.5%	80.8%	53.2%	42.3%
Dollar—differential schedule	7.7	3.8	20.7	20.5
Ratio—differential schedule	3.8	11.6	26.1	34.6
Dollar—and ratio-differential schedule	—	3.8	—	2.6
Number of schedules	26	26	92	78

National Education Association, Research Division, "Maximum Salaries for School Administrators," *Research Bulletin*, 38 (December, 1960), p. 122. Group I: Population 500,000 and over; Group II: No. 4, Population 100,000 to 499,999.

Note: Descriptions of salary schedules for administrators are contained in *National Education Association, Research Division, Research Report 1961–R5, Salary Schedule Maximums For School Administrators, 1960–61, Urban School Districts 30,000–99,999 in Population* (Washington: The Association, 1961). See also National Education Association, Salary Consultant Service, *The Use of Index Ratios to Determine Salaries and Salary Schedules of Supervisory and Administrative School Personnel* (Washington: The Association, Undated).

Another approach, proposed by Howsam, Morphet, and Ross for the Anchorage Independent School District, is expressed in the following formula: [14]

$$S = T [M + E (M \times R)],$$

where S = the *administrator's salary*

T = the *time ratio* between the regular school year for teachers and the length of the year for which administrators are employed

M = the *maximum teachers' salary* in the column where the administrator would be placed on the basis of his professional preparation

E = the *experience ratio* for administrators and supervisors

R = the *responsibility ratio* for administrators and supervisors

[14] Robert B. Howsam, Edgar L. Morphet, and John G. Ross, *Proposed Salary Schedule for the Professional Staff of the Anchorage Independent School District* (Anchorage, Alaska: Board of Education, 1959, mimeographed), p. 40.

Steps in building a compensation plan for administrators should include the following:

1. Determine the objectives which the plan is intended to meet.

2. Make provisions for evaluating and describing elements of each position, such as responsibility, level of difficulty, extent of decision making, need for creative thinking.

3. Decide the relative importance of each administrative position in terms of position descriptions.

4. Establish salary ranges and increments for the several classes of positions.

5. Decide how the transition should be made from the old to the new schedule.

6. Make plans to evaluate the new plan periodically, to take into account changes in or creation of new positions, and adjustments which need to be made in administrative salaries as the master salary schedule for teachers' increases.

One final point on the matter of administrative salaries. Point systems, conversion factors, formulas, and rating schemes will not improve low salary levels. Quantification of job factors and qualifications, useful as it is, cannot be employed exclusively to decide the monetary worth of administrative posts. Numbers are aids to decision making. In the matter under consideration they should be recognized as such. The concern at the moment is to raise salary levels to the point where they will secure executive talent needed in public education. Numbers not related to this concept generally lead to delusion rather than to problem solving.

Noninstructional Personnel

Until recent years the problem of compensation for noninstructional personnel has been characterized by public and administrative inattention. Various explanations of this condition are offered: (1) lack of funds to assure all personnel economic satisfaction; (2) selection of personnel on political considerations; (3) dual control, which often prevents unified planning; (4) the small school district with few noninstructional employees; (5) an abundant labor supply; and (6) a general undervaluation of the role of these employees.

The reasoning behind the economic and social worth of noninstructional employees is curious and vulnerable. The value of school property with which they are entrusted generally amounts to millions of dollars. Their efforts are vital to the health and safety of school children. Their character, conduct, and effectiveness influence the entire school operation.

Table 6.6 contains actual data from a school system relating to turnover in noninstructional personnel during a 12-month period. No claim is made that these data are representative of school systems across the nation. They do indicate, however, difficulties which personnel changes of this type create in maintaining satisfactory service. Since most of these changes have been traced to low compensation levels, and since these data reflect what has come to be a serious personnel problem in many school systems, the matter deserves more than cursory consideration.

Table 6.6

Turnover in Noninstructional Personnel, Moraine School District
1960–61

Description	Positions	Personnel Changes During the Year
Clerical	16	15
Maintenance-operation	29	8
Cafeteria	8	1
Business office	3	4

There are several additional reasons why a positive personnel program should be established for noninstructional personnel. The competencies public education seeks in these employees are the same competencies other occupations seek. If education hopes to attract personnel of high caliber, it must be prepared to compete in an open labor market for their services.

The ever-increasing school population will require more, not fewer, noninstructional personnel. This fact, coupled with the steady reduction in the number of school administrative units in the nation, plus the growing demand for additional services, foreshadows personnel needs which can be attained best by carefully planned change.

Principles for developing a sound compensation structure are considered to be as applicable to noninstructional as they are to professional personnel. Techniques for implementing these principles in a sound pay plan for noninstructional personnel, however, differ considerably from those employed in preparing the single salary schedule for professional employees. This is due in large measure to the variety of occupations, levels of training, and diversity of functions performed by noninstructional as compared to professional personnel.

Position Classification—A Basis for Compensating Noninstructional Personnel

The foundation of an effective compensation plan for noninstructional employees is the position classification concept. Essentially this scheme is based on the assumption that there should be equal pay for equal work. Steps in the position classification plan include: (1) making a detailed analysis of each position, especially duties and responsibilities involved; (2) assigning each position to an appropriate class; (3) stating the duties and requirements of each position; (4) establishing qualification standards to fill the positions; and (5) setting salary ranges for positions in a given category or classification.[15]

The steps outlined above provide the framework within which the position classification plan is formulated. Techniques and procedures of position classification have been subject to extensive experimentation during the past three decades, both in government and industry.[16]

It should be said, by way of summary, that the way out of chaos and expediency in compensating noninstructional personnel is the shaping of an instrument which will assist administration in formulating salary and wage policies. The classification idea provides a useful tool for this purpose. It has these advantages:

1. Provides a systematic basis for establishing salary and wage differentials for the various classifications.
2. Serves as the basis for expression of fiscal policy for noninstructional employees.

[15] Descriptions of pay plans related to position classification are contained in (1) Alvin N. Zachrich, "How to Develop a Sound Salary Schedule for Non-Professional Personnel," *School Management* (September, 1959), pp. 49–54, and (2) "How to Develop A Single Salary Schedule for all Non-Teaching Personnel," *School Management*, 4, No. 10 (October, 1960), pp. 65–70.

[16] Roelfs's study identifies the following legal bases for classifying noninstructional personnel in cities over 200,000 population: board of education policy, state constitution or general statutes, city charter or municipal ordinance, state law and city charter, special state legislation, and federal civil service. R. M. Roelfs, *Job Classification Procedures for Non-Certificated Positions in Large City School Systems* (unpublished doctoral dissertation, University of Colorado, 1951), p. 284.

3. Is a valuable planning aid, especially in the preparation of current and long-term budgets.

4. Is a useful control device in that salaries and wages are not subject to bargaining and manipulation.

5. Provides a means for appraisal of compensation equity among positions within a given class, and among the several classes. It also makes possible appraisal of the plan in relation to prevailing rates in other areas and occupations.

6. Forms the basis for recruitment, selection, and promotion for noninstructional personnel.

7. Removes administration of noninstructional personnel from the expediency level and raises it to one of direction and control.

8. Promotes economy and efficiency in that it is designed to employ only the number of employees needed to perform the services, and to attract and retain personnel who are competent to perform them.

9. Clarifies relationships within the school organization, since duties and responsibilities are clearly defined.

10. Enables administration to establish qualification standards for noninstructional personnel, which, incidentally, makes for a more realistic compensation policy.

One of the difficulties in developing a compensation plan for noninstructional employees is that of controlling expenditures so that they do not affect the salary levels of professional employees. This possibility can be minimized by careful planning, which involves taking measures such as the following:

1. *Employment of noninstructional personnel solely on the basis of established need.* This approach is not so obvious as it sounds. It involves, primarily, job analyses to determine the work to be done and the number of personnel required to perform the work. It also envisions studies to determine whether certain types of work can be performed more economically by special contract than by regularly employed personnel.

2. *Sound recruitment and selection procedures.* While this problem will be treated in detail in Chapter 7, it should be noted here that recruitment and selection procedures which attract competent individuals, especially those with multiple skills, will help to minimize outlays for noninstructional personnel, and at the same time provide essential services.

3. *Maximum utilization of personnel.* Carefully planned work schedules, laborsaving equipment, effective employee supervision, and

training opportunities are a few of the many practices employed to secure maximum returns for noninstructional expenditures.

A comprehensive, competitive compensation structure includes provisions relating to extra pay for extra work as well as to collateral benefits. These matters are treated separately in the text following.

Nonsalary Provisions: Extra Pay for Extra Work

Professional Personnel

Educative experiences provided under school auspices in American public education appear to become more extensive with each passing year. Some of these are prescribed by state law, whereas others are optional. While major components of the educational program included in the normal schedule are conducted within the classroom, many nonclassroom activities are sponsored by schools beyond what is generally defined as the school day.

For the most part, school staffs have not increased in proportion to increases in enrollments and educational activities. In such cases, heavier teaching loads have been inevitable. In order to minimize load inequities, a variety of measures have been applied, ranging from load adjustment to extra compensation for service in excess of load policy.

Studies of extra pay for extra work indicate that the practice appears to be gaining acceptance among school districts.[17] While most educators would probably not accept the extrapay practice as a permanent solution to the problem, they are likely to contend that policies regarding extra pay are necessary until the ideal staffing situation is attained. Even if staffing conditions are optimum, it is conceivable that problems of staff load will arise which necessitate a clearly defined extrapay policy.

Actually, the extrapay problem does not appear to be a major issue in developing the compensation structure. McClain in an extensive study of extrapay practices, notes that:

The practice of extra pay for extra-curricular activities has increased and will probably continue to do so since a substantial percentage of

[17] National Education Association, Special Memo Research Division, *Teacher Personnel Practices, Urban School Districts,* 1955–56 (Washington: The Association, 1956). Also National Education Association, Educational Research Service, *Extra-Pay Provisions in 1959–60 Salary Schedules,* Educational Research Service Circular No. 4 (Washington: The Association, 1960).

schools having extra pay report the practice as working satisfactorily. Administrators favor the practice because it assures better response and cooperation on the part of teachers and facilitates administrative assignment of duties.

As a whole, the amounts being paid for extra-curricular activities do not appear to be high, nor do they seem out of proportion to salaries received by teachers for classroom instruction.

Extra pay for extra-curricular activities is consistent with practices in other professions and does not violate the concept of the single salary schedule. Teaching does not become non-professional when practices of extra pay are introduced.[18]

Extracompensation assignments are generally those conceded to have positive educational values—values to the extent that they should be recognized as an integral part of the educational program. In developing extrapay provisions the following principles are applicable:

1. Teaching, like most other professions, involves assignments which often exceed an established load. Every teacher should be expected to render a reasonable amount of additional service as part of his contractual obligation, without benefit of extra compensation.
2. Contractual obligations of every teacher should be clearly defined by the board of education. While these obligations may vary somewhat, depending upon the teaching assignment, it is to the interest of all concerned that this matter be clarified before policies governing extra compensation can be established.
3. The board of education should compensate personnel who render service clearly in excess of contractually established duties.
4. Activities in which any teacher may engage for extra compensation should be limited.
5. Compensation for service rendered should be based upon the current salary of the professional employee concerned.
6. Compensation provided for extracontractual services should be specified in a supplementary contract.

[18] Warren J. McClain, "A Study of Current Practices in Extra Pay for Extra-Curricular Activities in Secondary Schools of the Northeastern States," New Jersey School Development Council, *Research Bulletin*, 3, No. 2 (December, 1958), pp. 15–17, New Brunswick: Rutgers: The State University.

7. Compensation derived from extra services should not be considered a part of the regular salary.
8. Activities should be subjected to job evaluation, including such factors as responsibility, time, and pupil load in order to develop quantitative indices to determine amounts to be paid for each activity.
9. Supplementary activities should be evaluated each year prior to formal adoption of the budget for the ensuing year.
10. Compensation for supplementary activities should be limited to rostered, long-term activities, administered by the responsible head of each school.
11. Only those activities should be sponsored which contribute to the purposes for which the school exists.
12. Teaching and administrative personnel, to whom the rules and regulations governing extra compensation will apply, should participate in their formulation.
13. Administrators and assistants who receive salaries for performing administrative functions should not be included in the extracompensation plan.

Noninstructional Personnel

Whether or not noninstructional employees should be compensated for work required beyond the established workday or work week is no longer an issue in the majority of school systems. The principle is so firmly established and so universally recognized as standard practice that the main concern of educational administration is to establish sound policies and practices for control purposes.

It must be recognized that there will be occasions in most school systems which require certain noninstructional employees to work beyond the regular schedule. It should be recognized also that unless proper controls are established, the practice of paying for overtime is often abused.

In keeping with a principle established earlier to the effect that the fundamental purpose of every school system is the improvement of the quality of instruction, every effort should be made to allot as much of the budget as is possible for this purpose. Funds spent for noninstructional purposes, necessary as they are, are funds which cannot be used for instructional purposes. This in no way implies that school districts should be penurious in expending money for non-instructional services; it implies that the funds should be spent wisely.

Experience indicates that when the practice of paying overtime is initiated, such expenditures increase annually, suggesting that overtime may be artificially created in many instances.

Practices for paying for overtime vary from compensatory time off to double time. Whichever it may choose, the administration should seek, first of all, to minimize the practice. Procedures should be established defining overtime, eligibility, assignment responsibility, restrictions on the amount of overtime any employee is permitted to work, and requiring board ratification of all overtime employment.

Non-Salary Provisions: Collateral Benefits

A collateral or "fringe" benefit, as the term is used herein, refers to certain direct or indirect forms of compensation initiated by the board of education, generally on behalf of all personnel, which do not

Table 6.7

Types of Collateral Benefits for School Personnel

	Types of Benefits	
Time Off with Pay	*Protection*	*Incentive and Improvement*
Vacations	Life insurance	Tuition refunds
Holidays	Health and accident	Tuition payments
Military training	insurance	Scholarships
Personal absences	Hospital and medical	Incentive increment
Professional ab-	insurance	Professional improvement
sences	Liability insurance	credit
Expense allowances	Retirement	Noninstructional training
	Social Security	programs
	Severance allowances	Expense allowances
		Professional affiliations

require additional services to be performed by personnel beyond those required under the basic compensation structure. Various kinds of collateral benefits are listed in Table 6.7. As a broad generalization, practice would seem to indicate:

1. Collateral benefits policies in public schools are generally kept separate from compensation policies.

2. Certain benefits apply only to professional personnel; some apply only to noninstructional personnel; others apply to all school personnel.

3. Certain benefits are governed by statute; others by board policy.

4. Benefits are paid partially or fully by public funds, depending on board policy and/or state regulations.

Collateral benefits, as the term implies, are related to, but less important than, the basic compensation paid to school personnel. Moreover, benefits which public school systems are able to provide do not now equal package-benefit plans utilized so extensively in industry. It is quite likely that they never will, since the benefits must be paid, not from profits, but from taxes of one sort or another. This is not to contend, however, that the benefit concept cannot be utilized as a quasi-compensation device in public education.

Benefit Theory

Comprising, as they do, a minor or indirect aspect of compensation, questions of the purposes which benefits serve often arise. Why are they needed if salary structures are internally consistent and externally competitive? If the compensation levels are too low, shouldn't these expenditures be employed to improve salaries and wages? Are benefits devices for maintaining low salary and wage levels?

The assumptions behind collateral benefits may be viewed properly from the standpoint of both the board of education and school personnel. Benefits should be conceived as serving both interests. From a realistic standpoint the board must understand that benefits are necessary from a competitive standpoint. The current shortage of professional personnel is such that the board must not only compete for skilled manpower in a restricted market, but it must deal with college graduates who are, on the whole, mature in economic matters. Since the society in which we live has come to recognize the benefit concept as an essential part of the occupational structure, boards are forced to compete for personnel under existing occupational mores. Admittedly, this is realism, not theory, but there are occasions when realism must be served.

There is an all-important reason for benefits from the board standpoint which goes beyond the realm of realism. It can be stated somewhat as follows: *benefits are established by the board of education*

for no other reason than to assist it in attaining institutional purposes.
It is the board's way of saying that all school personnel have a particular function to perform, a role to play which contributes to the objectives of the educational enterprise. This contribution, it says, can be enhanced if personnel are provided with certain professional growth incentives and secured against certain economic risks. The board, in the final analysis, hopes that collateral benefits will make a difference in the quality of education which children receive. It conceives the benefit program, not only as a contribution to current compensation, but as a means of helping to recruit, hold, and appropriately motivate personnel to achieve the fundamental objectives of public education. From this vantage point, then, the benefit program is not a substitute for anything. It is not a tool for making a weak salary schedule strong; it is not a gift for past performance; it is not a stratagem which involves something for nothing. Rather, it is a tool for securing competent performance in the interests of children and youth.

What do benefits mean to school personnel? Economic and psychological objectives are as important to school personnel as institutional objectives are to the board of education. Both interests must be served. Collaterial benefits, if properly administered, can be useful tools for achieving both institutional and personal aims.

From the employee's vantage they reduce economic problems incident to illness, disability, retirement, death, absences, and professional improvement. With the minimization of personal problems through collateral benefits, the chances are favorable for the development of a staff which will be more efficient, stable, and cooperative. So, at least, are the assumptions upon which collateral benefits rest.

Among the advantages attributed to collateral benefits are these: (1) they are not subject to taxation; (2) they are economical, since they can be mass-purchased; (3) efforts to incorporate collateral benefits into the compensation structure encounter less resistance than proposals for salary increases; (4) they contribute to staff security; and (5) they place school districts in a better competitive position to attract new college graduates.

Each collateral benefit serves a somewhat different purpose; each varies in effectiveness in achieving purpose; each, it is assumed, produces certain side effects, such as improved motivation and morale. One of the tasks of school administration is to design each benefit to the end that it will have investment character—that it will realize certain objectives for the individual as well as for the institution.

Suggested Reading

Benson, Charles S., *The Economics of Public Education* (Boston: Houghton Mifflin Co., 1961).

Burke, Arvid, *Financing Public Schools in the United States* (New York: Harper & Brothers, rev. ed. 1957), pp. 152–162.

Johns, Roe L., and Edgar L. Morphet, *Financing the Public Schools* (Englewood Cliffs, N.J.: Prentice-Hall, Inc., 1960), Chapter 15.

Michael, Lional B., *Wage and Salary Fundamentals and Procedures* (New York: McGraw-Hill Book Co., 1950).

Mort, Paul R., Walter C. Reusser, and John W. Polley, *Public School Finance* (McGraw-Hill Book Co., 3rd ed. 1960), Chapter 21.

National Industrial Conference Board, "Assuring Economic Satisfaction," *Management Record*, XX, No. 5 (May, 1958), pp. 162–165.

O'Meara, J. Roger, "The Neglected Side of Fringes," *Management Record*, XXI, No. 4 (April, 1959), pp. 120–123.

Weissinger, T. E. "Equitable Salary Structures for Professionals," *Management Record*, XX, No. 5 (May, 1958), pp. 158–170.

PART III

Satisfaction of

Personnel Need

Recruitment of Personnel

CHAPTER SEVEN

Introduction

The term recruitment, as used herein, refers to those activities in school administration designed to attract the quantity and quality of personnel necessary to satisfy established need. As such, the recruitment phase of personnel administration has both short- and long-term implications. The short-range problem involves those activities carried on to meet current personnel demand, such as that which continually exists in every school system when positions are vacated due to death, promotion, resignation, retirement, leaves of absence, dismissals, and the creation of new positions.[1] The long-range problem involves those

---

[1] The rate of staff turnover varies considerably among school systems. A study involving 8664 teachers in 43 New England school systems indicated a range in turnover rates from 1.2 per cent to 21.4 per cent. The over-all rate of turnover was 9.8 per cent. See New England School Development Council, *Teachers' Salaries: The Process of Change in Forty-Three Metropolitan School Systems* (Cambridge, Mass.: The Council, 1959), p. 47. A similar study involving 9839 professional personnel in 69 Pennsylvania school districts revealed a turnover rate of 12.1 per cent. See University of Pennsylvania, *School Personnel, 1960–61* (Philadelphia: Educational Service Bureau, 1961), p. 26.

activities engaged in by the local school system to assure a continuous supply of qualified professional and noninstructional personnel.

Relationship of Recruitment to Personnel Function

The total personnel function, as conceived in Figure 1, consists of three phases: *determination of need, satisfaction of need,* and *maintenance and improvement of service.* These phases necessarily overlap in the sense that they do not always occur serially. An important advantage of viewing the personnel function in this way is that it helps administration to conceive the totality of the personnel function, as well as its salient elements.

From this vantage, recruitment becomes the first step in satisfaction of personnel need. It is important to mention, at the risk of being redundant, that recruitment should not be considered as the first step in personnel administration. Rather, it is one of several activities undertaken to implement personnel policies previously established. How, for example, can the chief executive and his staff develop a systematic plan for recruiting personnel if the board has not clarified its intentions with respect to quantity and quality of personnel? How can those responsible for recruitment answer questions of a prospective applicant if decisions concerning the compensation structure are left in abeyance? As a matter of fact, the recruitment program stands or falls on policies previously established for the total range of personnel considerations.

Among the premises upon which an effective recruitment program rests, and around which this chapter is organized, are the following:

1. The board of education is the prime mover in the local recruitment program. This implies a complex of positive attitudes and actions on the part of this body leading to development of employment conditions calculated to attract qualified personnel.

2. The board of education delegates responsibility for implementation of its recruitment policy to its executive officer.

3. Nomination of all persons to positions of employment in the system is a responsibility of the chief executive officer; the board makes appointments.

4. Specific duties of the chief executive officer in the recruitment program include: (a) determination of immediate and long-term quantitative and qualitative personnel needs; (b) establishment of

employment qualification standards for all personnel; (c) preparation of budgetary plans, both current and long term, which embrace provisions calculated to satisfy personnel needs; and (d) development of a systematic plan to locate and to attract qualified persons for service in the system.

5. The recruitment program is conceived as a carefully planned, continuous, long-term activity.

6. The search for qualified personnel is not restricted to specific institutions or geographic areas.

7. Staff participation in formulating and implementing the recruitment program is encouraged.

8. The local school system shares responsibility for increasing the supply of new teachers throughout the nation. This implies increased counseling services for prospective teachers, and cooperation with governmental, institutional, and professional organizations in a variety of efforts to increase the number and to improve the quality of school personnel.

9. The recruitment program is conceived as an essential, but not an isolated, aspect of the total personnel function.

Responsibility

The Board of Education

In matters pertaining to recruitment, as well as in other educational considerations, functions of the board of education are those involving policy development and appraisal. The hypothesis advanced here is that while recruitment will go on in some fashion in every school system, it will go on better and attain more lasting results if the board of education's viewpoint is positive and forward looking. All this is not said to point out to the reader the well-known principle that policy making is the board's function. The broader implication is that unless the board takes initiative to establish conditions and climate for administrative action on a sound recruitment program, the chances are good that the best of intentions and plans will be abandoned subsequently.

The board and its chief executive are confronted with questions such as these: What types of personnel do we need to accomplish the goals of the system? What qualifications should they possess? What conditions of employment are necessary to attract the kinds of

personnel we have under consideration? Where can these competencies be located? These considerations, it will be noted, must be
translated by the board into policies governing the recruitment program. Also worth mentioning is that these issues need to be resolved
well in advance of the time that the chief executive begins to formulate specific plans putting policies into operation.

The magnitude and complexity of these problems are such that
they deserve extended analysis before recruitment policies can be
stipulated. Size and quality of the present staff, staff load and deployment, situations in which additional personnel are warranted, and
cost implications for staff improvement are suggestive of appraisals
involved in formulating goals and determining means by which they
can be realized.

By clarifying its intent toward the recruitment program, by dele-
gating its administration in full to the chief executive and holding
him accountable for results, and by providing means to attain ends,
major steps will have been taken to define and to give direction to
recruitment plans and procedures.

The Chief Executive

When we turn our attention to problems involved in recruiting
school personnel, we are quickly led to an appreciation of their importance. It is not difficult to realize that the investment made in
every school employee is considerable; that the success of the local
school system depends upon a continuous flow of qualified personnel;
that future educational leadership is related to present recruitment
policies; that the potential for waste of every kind is enormous if
recruitment programs are ineffective; and that solutions to today's
recruitment problems do not possess unchanging validity.

It is for these and other reasons that the leadership role of the
chief executive in the recruitment program is an extremely crucial one.
Of his many obligations in recruitment planning, the following are
representative:

1. Provides the board with relevant data, counsel, and recommendations in shaping recruitment policies.

2. Initiates studies of immediate and long-term personnel needs.
(See Table 7.1.)

3. Formulates, with the help of the staff and with board approval,

qualification standards for professional and noninstructional personnel.

4. Provides organization and funds to locate candidates capable of meeting qualification standards.

5. Continually explores various avenues for bringing the system's personnel needs to the attention of potential candidates.

6. Recognizes the importance of sound budgetary procedures through which the objectives of the personnel function are realized.

7. Is sensitive to the shortage of properly qualified professional personnel, and encourages the school staff to counsel with precollege students concerning teaching as a career.

8. Cooperates with teacher education institutions in helping them to prepare the kinds of personnel with the competencies the system seeks.

9. Studies developments in the manpower field and their impact upon recruitment.

10. Is alert to the need for establishing employment conditions conducive to effective recruitment.

11. Employs a variety of communications media to develop understanding of recruitment program objectives.

How the superintendent of schools carries out responsibility for dealing with matters pertaining to the satisfaction of personnel need depends to a large extent upon the administrative organization. If the system is small, this responsibility is generally administered personally by the chief executive; if it is large the likelihood is that responsibility will be delegated to an agent or division in the central administrative office.[2] There is a changing concept at work in public school administration in regard to the assistance which the chief executive needs in fulfilling personnel requirements of the school system. Briefly stated, this concept views personnel administration as a strategic task. It embraces the idea that if schools of modest size and means can afford an assistant to the superintendent for business and an assistant for instruction, it should also provide assistance to carry out the personnel function. The argument has force when one considers the importance of personnel to the operation of the enterprise.

[2] According to a National Education Association Research Division survey of nearly 2000 school systems in 1955–56, only a small percentage employed a director of teacher personnel or other official whose duties relate chiefly to personnel administration. National Education Association, Research Division, *Teacher Personnel Practices, Urban School Districts, 1955–56*, Special Memo (Washington: The Association, 1956), p. 4.

Personnel Planning and Recruitment

Recruitment is an essential part of a comprehensive plan to develop and to maintain a staff capable of attaining institutional purpose. The more today's superintendent of schools considers the educational problems which he is expected to solve, the more clearly he sees that his organization cannot function successfully unless it is fully and competently staffed. He also recognizes that a competent personnel corps is not a matter of luck or happenstance. Indeed, he realizes the close association between planning and educational returns, and views his primary task as one involving setting of objectives and planning ways by which they can best be realized.

Experience has shown that the most effective kind of personnel planning is that which goes beyond one school year. It has also demonstrated that personnel planning goes on better when it is meshed with other system-wide planning efforts. This point can be readily understood by analyzing the data contained in Table 7.1, which illustrates one approach to forecasting professional school personnel requirements. In order to establish minimum personnel requirements shown in Table 7.1, it was necessary to make certain assumptions or estimates concerning enrollment trends, acceptable staffing standards, replacement rates, staffing costs, and future staff utilization. Completion of these tasks provided information which could be translated into estimates of the amount and kinds of personnel to be recruited during the planning period.

Although the method outlined above represents one of many viewpoints regarding long-term planning of personnel needs, the major aim of this or other approaches is to induce those who are responsible for personnel decisions to undertake a critical analysis of staffing objectives and policies needed for their attainment. When administration has defined staffing standards to which it intends to adhere for the present as well as for the future, it can then be determined what types of personnel will be needed, the number of each type to be recruited, what the annual staffing requirements will be, what the personnel plan will cost, and, hence, what the long-term personnel plan for the district should be.

It may be well to point out also that a long-term personnel plan need not and should not be confined to professional personnel. A

Table 7.1

Illustrative Summary—Minimum Professional Personnel Requirements Forecast, Foxcroft School District, 1960–1967

	(Actual) 1960–61	1961–62	1962–63	1963–64	1964–65	1965–66	1966–67
1. Enrollments (Most Probable)							
K – 6	1,136	1,221	1,329	1,433	1,511	1,602	1,700
7 – 9	405	450	462	469	501	533	560
10 – 12	314	342	363	386	431	443	450
Total	1,855	2,019	2,154	2,288	2,433	2,578	2,710
2. Staffing Requirements							
A. Instructional Personnel	64	72	80	88	98	103	108
B. Administrative Personnel	7	8	9	10	12	13	15
C. Special Service Personnel	4	5	6	7	8	9	10
D. Total Professional Personnel	75	85	95	105	118	125	133
3. Personnel Ratios *							
A. Pupil-Instructional Personnel	28:1	28:1	26:1	26:1	24:1	25:1	25:1
B. Pupil-Administrative Personnel	265:1	252:1	239:1	228:1	203:1	198:1	180:1
C. Pupil-Special-Service Personnel	463:1	403:1	359:1	326:1	305:1	286:1	271:1
D. Pupil-Professional Personnel	24:1	23:1	22:1	21:1	20:1	20:1	20:1
E. Numerical Staff Adequacy per 1000 Weighted Pupils †	41	42	44	46	48	49	49
4. Recruitment Requirements							
A. Replacements (Death, Retirement, Resignation, Leaves, Dismissal)							
(1) Instructional Personnel		7	8	8	10	10	11
(2) Administrative Personnel		0	2	1	0	0	1
(3) Special Service Personnel		0	1	0	1	0	1
(4) Total Professional Personnel		7	11	9	11	10	13
B. New Positions							
(1) Instructional Staff		8	8	8	11	5	5
(2) Administrative Staff		1	1	1	2	1	2
(3) Special Service Staff		1	1	1	1	1	1
(4) Total Professional Staff		10	10	10	14	7	8
C. Total Personnel to be Recruited		17	21	19	25	17	21

Assumptions: Pupil-instructional personnel ratio should be reduced from 28:1 in 1960-61 to 25:1 in 1966-67. Turnover rate for instructional personnel will approximate 10 per cent. Four administrative staff members will retire during period forecast.

* Fractions omitted.

† See Table 4.1 for explanation of numerical staff adequacy.

175

genuine planning effort should encompass all personnel, just as it should envelop the whole range of activities which are essential to the operation of the system.

Recruitment and the Career Service Concept

The striking personnel dilemma which has confronted public education during the past three decades must be recorded as one of its most expensive and poignant experiences. Despite extensive efforts to recruit and retain competent personnel, a lasting solution to the problem is not yet at hand. At the root of the problem are many causes—undervaluation of public education, lack of money, variations in employment standards, and lack of concerted effort to make public education a truly career service. It is to this latter element that the following discussion will be devoted, since it weighs so heavily in the recruitment process.

A career service program may be defined as one which is planned to attract competent youth to pursue with satisfaction careers in public education from induction to retirement. The broader meaning of a career service program may be explained by the results expected from it, such as:

1. An expectation for young men and women that they may find opportunities for economic, professional, and personal satisfaction.

2. An assurance that there is opportunity to advance within the system to positions of greater rewards and responsibilities.

3. A knowledge that the system will provide opportunities for improving and rewarding professional competence.

4. An assurance of protection of academic freedom, and from dismissal on personal, racial, religious, and political grounds.

5. An understanding that employment is based on a fair system of selection, which emphasizes high qualifications.

6. A mature staff which is able to plan intelligently and cooperatively toward attainment of school objectives.

7. A community which can rest assured that its school system has in its employ the professional competencies needed to direct the education of its youth.

A more extensive catalogue of results which could be expected from a career service program, while possible, would probably belabor the idea. It is sufficient to state here that the recruitment program, indeed the total personnel program, should be conceived with these ends in mind. In this time of critical shortages in school personnel this statement is pious, but it is important. It is important because it is a demonstrably workable concept, the evidence for which may be seen in certain communities throughout the nation.

Preservice Recruitment

Although the major portion of this chapter is devoted to a discussion of recruiting personnel who have completed training programs, mention should be made of the responsibility of the local school system for furthering the career service concept at the preservice level. It is the conviction of many students of teacher education that teacher recruitment is a major responsibility of the state and of the members of the teaching profession. The local school system, through appropriate efforts, can make an important contribution to increasing the supply of qualified personnel.

A program for seeking out able youth who will enter training for a career of service in teaching will have many facets. Some of the specific approaches which have been reported by local school districts include:

1. Programs designed to give students an understanding of the rewards and requirements of teaching.

2. Chapter of the Future Teachers of America in the local school district.

3. Cadet teacher experiences.

4. Guidance booklets.

5. Assembly programs to dramatize teaching.

6. Programs for parents in which teaching as a profession is discussed.

7. Local scholarships for youth with career intentions in education.

8. Units on teaching in courses in occupations.

9. Faculty-student committees to explore means for identifying able students, and for encouraging these students to undertake teaching careers.

10. Career days during which university representatives explain admission and graduation requirements for teaching.

11. Audiovisual materials to portray the importance of teaching as a career.

These and other efforts which may be undertaken in a local school district are needed to aid in the solution of one of the nation's more pressing problems. They are part of the unified effort which must be made, both in and out of the profession to maintain and to improve the professional status of teaching.

Standards of Eligibility

Recruitment of school personnel is undertaken within a control system established by state and local agencies of government. To be eligible for employment in the public schools, professional personnel, in general, must meet certification requirements established by the state. These requirements may vary according to the type of certificate which the applicant is seeking. In addition, the applicant must meet requirements established by the local board of education, which may be stated in the form of general rules for employment and/or in the form of position specifications. Noninstructional personnel, of which there are both certificated and noncertificated, must meet whatever state and local requirements that have been established. School physicians, dentists, nurses, psychologists, psychiatrists, dental hygienists, business managers, architects, and engineers, are illustrations of noninstructional personnel who perform professional services in the public schools, and for whom certificates or licenses may be established, depending upon the state under consideration. Furthermore, it should be noted that for certain classes of noninstructional workers, especially in large cities, employment may depend upon requirements established by state or local civil service commissions, constitutions, statutes, and city charters or ordinances. The point to be made here is that the recruiting process must be fashioned in terms of the state and local legal framework, as well as local board personnel policy. Whatever controls exist governing employment in the local school system should be part of the information which the recruiting agent or agency communicates to, and clarifies for, prospective applicants.

State Requirements

In carrying out the education function, every state exercises certain controls affecting all school personnel. These generally relate to teacher preparation, certification, and welfare. In controlling entrance of persons into the profession, the state is actually acting in behalf of all school districts to improve the quality of education. It acts to protect society from incompetent personnel in the same manner that it protects it from unqualified physicians, dentists, lawyers, and other unqualified professional personnel.

The following statements have been included to serve as a summary of salient facts relating to state certification—facts which are important in dealing with the broad problem of personnel recruitment:

1. Certification, broadly defined, is the act of granting official authorization to teach. Such authorization is usually delegated to the state department of education by the legislature, generally carrying with it the power to issue, to renew, or to revoke teachers' certificates. Certificates may be permanent or temporary, limited to special fields, subjects, or levels of instruction, and generally apply to those rendering professional services.

2. Certification of professional personnel is not controlled by professional educators. Other professional groups exercise far greater control over the licensing of its members than do educators.

3. Bases of certification, although varying considerably among the states, include requirements relating to an earned college degree or a specified number of semester hours, U.S. citizenship, minimum age, oath of allegiance or loyalty, special courses, health and age requirements, and, in some cases, recommendations from the college or employing officer.

4. Recent trends in teacher certification include a marked movement toward centralization of teacher certification authority in state education agencies; improvement in certification reciprocity; a decline in the examination system; national progress toward higher certification standards; an increase in extralegal bodies, broadly representative of the teaching profession, created to recommend requirements which should be enforced for the issuance of certificates; simplification of the certification process; closer working relations between state education agencies and teacher education institutions; a decrease in the number of types of certificates issued by state education agencies; and extended requirements for certification in special subject areas, such as administration, supervision, and special education.

Despite the relatively large number of teachers now holding emergency certificates, the long-term trend in the certification of teachers indicates that substantial progress has been made in the last century to strengthen requirements for service in the field of education. According to Toy:

Ninety years ago elementary school teachers (fewer than 200,000 in all) rarely had any education beyond that acquired in the schools in which they taught.

Fifty years ago not more than 20 per cent of all teachers (there were about a half million) had any special training for teaching.

Forty years ago one-third of all teachers (under 700,000 total) had no more than two years of education beyond the eighth grade and half of them had no more than four years.

Twenty-five years ago when there were about 850,000 teachers, most teaching certificates were still issued at the local and county level, which meant few standards were maintained or enforced.

Twenty years ago there were about 875,000 teachers, but a quarter of the states required only high school graduation or less for elementary teacher certificates.

Today state certification laws require college training ranging from one year to four years, with a bachelor's degree as a minimum for the well over one million classroom teachers.[3]

The foregoing summary, while indicative of steady progress in the improvement of certification requirements, gives no cause for complacency. Improvement in the area of personnel certification is a responsibility of the profession, one which requires a unified and coordinated effort on local, state, and national levels. It is the key to the solution of the many subsidiary problems which are related to the larger problem of selective recruitment.

Local Requirements

It is universally recognized that state certification requirements represent minimum levels of preparation for school personnel. Local districts are permitted to prescribe eligibility standards within state certification patterns. These often include provisions relating to examinations, age limits, teaching experience, professional preparation, nepotism, physical handicaps, marital status, outside interests, and residency. For noninstructional personnel, local requirements for employment depend upon board policy, as well as state or local pro-

[3] Henry Toy, Jr., "Now Is the Time," *Teachers College Record*, 59, No. 1 (October, 1957), p. 4.

visions which may be in effect. These items provide a description of local requirements for employment of school personnel. But the illustration further serves to emphasize what has been said in Chapter Five—that general requirements simply will not enable a school system to match the man and the job. To be sure, general requirements are helpful, but by themselves they do not provide satisfactory devices for screening applicants.

Position Guides: Their Function in Recruitment

The need for position guides in recruitment is reemphasized here because its absence has been a notable failing in the recruitment process. Stripped of the usual verbiage, a position guide is a tool to assist administration in defining, prior to seeking available applicants, the kinds of competencies which personnel should possess to perform the services under consideration. Obvious as it may sound, recruitment procedures usually in effect in local school systems have not been based upon job descriptions, partly because of the critical shortage of qualified teachers. Rare is the administrator who has not been compelled to recruit and to accept personnel without too much regard for the competencies which are required by the job.

Despite the shortage of qualified school personnel, there is increasing evidence to indicate that school staffs can be improved through the use of position analysis, description, and classification. Even in small school systems, where an elaborate plan of position classification would be superfluous, there is reason to believe the careful description of all positions would prove helpful in the recruitment process.

Position guides subject administration to an examination of school purpose. What the school intends to achieve will affect the kinds of personnel selected to provide services essential to purpose. Variations in purpose call for different kinds of competencies. The point of emphasis here is that the administrator must have a clear conception of the particular teaching and service functions for which he is recruiting personnel, and this conception must be translated into job specifications so that, on the one hand, he knows what to look for, and, on the other hand, the applicant knows what the school system is seeking.

An intelligent recruitment program, designed to locate personnel who can meet state and local requirements, borders on expediency unless it is based upon careful planning. Recruitment planning re-

quires preparation of information about duties of the position, quali-
fying requirements, and measures used to determine which applicants
can best meet requirements.

This planning emphasis suggests that the gathering of information
and its evaluation will facilitate the recruitment process if data-gathering devices are developed so as to enable school officials to determine
more readily the suitability of the applicant for the position under
consideration. It also argues against use of the typical application form
which provides general information about the candidate and little
else. What is needed is information which will help relate qualifications of the applicant to the position.

A practical approach to informing candidates of the requirements
of a position and the qualifications needed to fill it is the preparation
of a position guide which is attached to the application form and
forwarded to prospective candidates. Major items included in the
position guide and the application form are listed in Table 7.2. While
there are many additional items which may be included in the
categories shown in Table 7.2, the plea is that the position description
and application form should be dovetailed as closely as possible so
that they will yield a maximum amount of pertinent information
during the selection process.

Table 7.2

**Outline of Major Items to Be Considered in Preparing Position
Guides and Application Forms**

Position Guides	*Application Form*
Nature and scope of position	Academic qualifications
Basic function	Professional qualifications
Duties, responsibilities, objectives	Educational experience
Required knowledges, skills, abilities	Nonteaching experience
Organizational relationships	General experience
Special requirements	Personal qualifications
Working conditions	Social qualifications
Desirable preparation and experience	Scholastic record
Compensation	Special qualifications for position

Staff Participation

The point is worth making, too, that preparation of position
guides is a cooperative effort, one which involves the collective

wisdom of the entire school staff. This is in keeping with the principle stated earlier—that school personnel should participate in formulation of personnel policies and procedures. Moreover, administration must rely heavily upon the school staff for preparation of position descriptions. The building principal, department head, and supervisors are obviously involved in the recruitment task, since they are vitally interested in specifications to be employed in determining the composition of the school staff.

An approach to recruitment in these terms is a departure from conventional practice, but it has much to offer. Use of position guides will help to strengthen administrative efforts to eliminate the practice of employing personnel for reasons of favoritism or political pressure. It also makes it possible to deal with the recruitment problem systematically and openly. Moreover, position guides provide applicants and teacher education institutions with a clearer understanding of school personnel requirements and qualifications. In the final analysis, any device which helps administration to define its aims, and to interrelate these aims to required personnel competencies, is worth more than the casual cognizance it has been given in school staff development.

Appraising Existing Staff Resources

Need for Staff Balance

The goal of school personnel recruitment is primarily that of total staff improvement. Its attainment will involve, prior to recruitment, several kinds of analyses of existing staff resources. The purpose of these analyses is to disclose imbalances in the makeup of the total staff. There may exist, for example, staff shortages in certain kinds of competencies, in the number of out-of-district or out-of-state employees, as well as a lack of ethnic, religious, geographic, cultural, and philosophical diversity. There is need for a wholesome variation in traits, skills, qualities, points of view, and backgrounds which staff members possess, since these contribute considerably to total staff strength and balance.

The measures listed in Table 7.3 are those employed by the Central School Boards Committee for Educational Research in a study comparing staff characteristics of different school systems.

Table 7.3

Illustration of Measures of Staff Characteristics

Elementary Staff Characteristics	*Secondary Staff Characteristics*
a. Per cent 36–60 years of age	a. Per cent males
b. Per cent with more than 2 years training	b. Per cent 36–60 years of age
c. Per cent with 5 or more years training	c. Per cent with 5 or more years training
d. Per cent with undergraduate courses in 3 or more areas	d. Per cent with some college training within past 3 years
e. Per cent from outside the district but in the state	e. Per cent without any college training within past 9 years
f. Per cent from outside the state	f. Per cent with courses in 3 or more areas
g. Per cent traveling over 500 miles in any one trip in the past 8 years	g. Per cent from outside the state
h. Per cent traveling over 1200 miles in any one trip	h. Per cent traveling over 500 miles in last 8 years
i. Average number of foreign countries visited	i. Average number of foreign countries visited
j. Per cent owning more than 150 non-professional books	j. Per cent buying 12 or more non-professional books in the last 3 years
k. Per cent buying 7 or more professional books in the last 3 years	
l. Per cent subscribing to 1 or more professional magazines	

Source: Central School Boards Committee for Educational Research, *Quality Control Guide* (New York: Teachers College, Columbia University, 1958) p. 17.

While these measures are not to be considered as being perfect indicators of good and poor staffs, they are indicative of the nature of staff data which can be compiled and analyzed in connection with the recruitment process. They will yield helpful insights into past and present staffing practices, weaknesses in staff composition, and hints for recruiting new staff members. These and other measures should also be helpful devices for minimizing staff inbreeding and provincialism.

The recruitment process should be aimed also at providing balance in the number and kinds of staff generalists, specialists, and administrators. This will involve a continuous survey of personnel requirements to assure adequacy and diversity of human resources in the staff as a whole as well as in each of its separate components.

Personnel Sources

After personnel specifications have been developed by the superintendent of schools and his staff, and have been approved by the board of education, the recruitment process advances sequentially to the work of locating candidates who can best meet the established requirements. Personnel sources may be categorized as either experienced or nonexperienced. Experienced personnel are those who are employed within the system, in other systems, or who are experienced but not currently employed in the profession. The general sources of teaching personnel may be classified as follows:

1. College and university placement bureaus.
2. Commercial teacher placement agencies.
3. Individual applications.
4. Other school systems.
5. State education agency placement bureaus.
6. State teachers' association placement bureaus.
7. Inquiries, formal or informal.

There are reasons for believing that regardless of the number of new teachers who enter the ranks of public education each year, the supply will fall short of demand. It is generally recognized that every local school system, regardless of its size, must give continuous consideration to the problem of making greater use of the potential teaching resources in our society which are not now being utilized. As the search for better methods of organizing instruction and utilizing staffs goes on, it is quite likely that a wider variety of personnel will be needed, including instructional assistants, clerks, aides, consultants, and specialists. Not all staff members will need exactly the same kinds of training and competencies. Not all of the tasks will be concerned directly with instruction. Not all tasks will require the services of full-time personnel. The point toward which this discussion is leading, then, is that there are qualified, capable persons in our society whose talents can be utilized in certain capacities in the service of education. Former teachers, women college graduates, and persons whose unique competencies can be secured for certain kinds of service are illustrative. To avoid misinterpretation, it should be made clear that the foregoing statements do not suggest recruitment of persons who will reduce the quality of the professional staff. Rather, they suggest that every school system should attempt to attract qualified, competent personnel for certain types of educational service.[4]

Budgeting Funds for Recruitment

If the recruitment process is seriously pursued, it usually calls for expenditures of one kind or another. It may involve, for example, expenditures for publications which describe existing vacancies and position specifications; for visits to observe candidates in other school systems; for visits by candidates to school districts; for published announcements of vacancies; for consultant service in establishing position guides, as well as other activities or projects which involve expenditures of public funds. It may well involve relatively large sums if the board follows the practice of some school systems, which selectively recruit each year a "cadet corps" of new teachers, and provides this group with ample supervision and consultant service during the initial year of employment.

Staff building is so important to the welfare of any organization that it calls for systematic planning. Since the budget is the most effective planning device available to the administrator, it should be utilized to define recruitment plans and to translate these needs into funds necessary for their support.

Attracting Competent Personnel

In order to bring the recruitment cycle to full circle, a thorough search is undertaken to locate potential candidates and to provide them with appropriate information concerning existing vacancies and employment requirements. A study by the National Education Association Research Division [5] of first year teachers indicates that the methods of getting their first teaching job include:

[4] The Educational Policies Commission, in its review of manpower and its relation to education, suggests qualified married women, older members of the community, and members of minority groups as sources from which to recruit persons capable of rendering satisfactory educational service. See National Education Association, Educatonal Policies Commission, *Manpower and Education* (Washington: The Association, 1956), pp. 116–118.

[5] National Education Association, Research Division, "First Year Teachers In 1954–55," *Research Bulletin*, 34, No. 1 (February, 1956), p. 30.

	Per cent
Personal application	54.9%
Placement agency of college or university	35.4%
Placement agency of teachers' association	1.8%
Commercial employment agency	1.8%
Some other way	6.1%

While the figures on personal applications are not reported in detail, it is possible that many resulted from employer solicitation. The study further indicates that large school districts have been more successful than small districts in getting their choice of the teaching supply, due in part to more extensive recruitment and higher beginning salaries.[6]

Communication

Communication, in its broadest sense, is the key to successful recruitment. The local district must devise ways and means by which to inform prospective candidates of existing vacancies, and to arouse their interest in making applications. This involves use of a variety of communication media to reach personnel sources listed earlier in the chapter.

Every candidate applying for a position is entitled to certain information, including a description or characterization of the position, duties, compensation, and qualification requirements. Suggestions for extending the scope of the information furnished to prospective candidates include the following:

1. An explanation of the compensation structure.
2. Descriptions and pictures of school facilities.
3. Special services for pupils and teachers.
4. Explanation of the organization of instruction.
5. Administrative services.
6. Community structure—government, cultural opportunities, church facilities, transportation, recreation, industry.
7. The in-service program.
8. The educational program.

[6] A study by Williams indicates the importance of wholesome conditions of employment in the recruitment and retention of teachers. See Meta F. Williams, "To Attract and Hold Good Teachers," *The School Executive*, 79, No. 1 (September, 1959), pp. 66–68.

9. Living accommodations.

10. General welfare provisions, including: retirement, tenure, leaves of absences, grievance machinery, and academic freedom.

The manner in which such information is prepared and directed to reach personnel sources depends upon the nature of recruitment needs and funds available for publicizing the needs. Regardless of the size of the school district, preparation and distribution of printed materials to inform personnel sources of existing vacancies is an administrative necessity. It goes without saying that published materials for recruiting personnel can be vastly improved. Not only should they be attractive and informative; they should be such as to arouse the interest of the prospective candidate to make inquiries concerning vacancies.

These materials, even when skillfully designed, represent only one of the multidirectional approaches employed to attract qualified personnel. Letters of invitation, visits with potential candidates by staff members, personal contacts with placement officials in colleges and universities, visits to college campuses or to other districts, and directing announcements of vacancies to professional organizations or acquaintances are among the approaches which have been used effectively.

Extending the Search

Modern transportation and communication facilities enable employing officials to extend the market area in which to search for suitable applicants. It is neither necessary nor advisable to select candidates from a limited geographic area, nor from a single college or university placement service. As the search is extended, the likelihood is that the personnel potential will be greater. The nature and extent of college recruitment programs developed by business and industry have implications for public education.

A strong case can be made for increasing the scope of recruitment, especially if one is to give credence to the assumption that the educational program can be no better than the composition of its staff.

No administrator needs to be reminded of the fact that the burden of filling an opening with competent talent rests with the school district, not the applicant. The school must do the seeking, and if it is not willing to make a determined effort to secure personnel with the type of training and background desired, it cannot expect to develop a high-caliber staff.

Suggested Reading

Ayars, Albert L., *Administering the People's Schools* (New York: McGraw-Hill Book Co., 1957).

Eastmond, Jefferson N., *The Teacher and School Administration* (Boston: Houghton Mifflin Co., 1959).

Elsbree, Willard S., and E. Edmund Reutter, *Staff Personnel in the Public Schools* (Englewood Cliffs, N.J.: Prentice-Hall, Inc., 1954).

Huggett, Albert J., and T. M. Stinnett, *Professional Problems of Teachers*, 2nd ed. (New York: The Macmillan Company, 1956).

The International City Managers' Association, *Municipal Personnel Administration* (Chicago: The Association, 1960).

National Industrial Conference Board, *Selecting Company Executives* (New York: The Board, 1957).

Weber, Clarence A., *Personnel Problems of School Administrators* (New York: McGraw-Hill Book Co., 1954).

Selection of Personnel

CHAPTER EIGHT

As the process of securing competent personnel for the local school system moves from the recruitment to the selection phase, a number of formidable problems will confront the personnel administrator. These include determining the kinds of data needed to select competent applicants, deciding what devices and procedures are to be employed in gathering the data, securing staff participation in appraising the data and the applicants, relating the qualifications of the applicants to the position specifications, screening the qualified from the unqualified, preparing an eligibility list, and selecting and nominating suitable candidates for appointment by the board of education. In brief, he is responsible for developing, initiating, and maintaining an effective process for selecting school personnel.

It is axiomatic that the selection process does not operate independently of the recruitment process. Unless the number of applicants exceeds the number of placements to be made, a selection process becomes an exercise in futility. Recruitment and other phases of the personnel program are conditioned by general personnel pol-

FIGURE 13   The selection process.

DEFINE BEHAVIORAL CHARACTERISTICS TO BE APPRAISED

Describe in detail the mental, physical, professional, personal, and social characteristics to be appraised. Indicate responsibility for and procedures to be followed in appraisal, including the kinds of information to be compiled, appropriate questions to be asked, and appraisal devices to be employed.

COMPILE APPROPRIATE DATA

Collect and record data relevant to behavioral characteristics under consideration from application blanks, transcripts, recommendations, examinations, interviews, observations, and personality assessment techniques. Verify data to extent possible.

APPRAISE DATA AND APPLICANTS

Prepare profile chart and appraisal report for screening purposes. Selection team estimates recommended. Relate qualifications of applicants to position guides. Eliminate unqualified.

PREPARE ELIGIBILITY LIST

Place candidates fulfilling qualifications on eligibility list. Develop priority ratings. Check certification status.

NOMINATE

Superintendent nominates personnel for employment from eligibility list.

APPOINTMENT

Board confirms or disapproves nomination. In event of board disapproval, superintendent nominates another selectee. Formal election of appointees recorded in minutes, candidates notified, contracts tendered.

---

icies. The number and quality of personnel which the recruitment program attracts, for example, will depend upon the quality of policies covering the entire personnel program.

Figure 13 has been included to enable the reader to visualize the personnel selection process as a whole. It illustrates the sequential development of the process, and serves as an outline for discussing each of the steps involved.

Objectives of Selection

The primary aim of personnel selection is to fill existing vacancies with personnel who meet established qualifications, and who appear likely to succeed on the job. When properly planned, many side effects flow from this central task. It enables the school district to exercise an important responsibility to the community and to the profession—the elimination of candidates who, in the considered judgment of the staff, are not likely to succeed. It helps to minimize the waste of time, money, and effort which must be invested in developing a school staff. It provides a rational and uniform basis for personnel selection, which, when consistently applied, provides the applicant as well as the community with the assurance that merit, not favoritism, not influence, not political considerations, is the determining factor. It provides the board of education with an instrument of control to maintain and to improve the quality of the staff. And it provides the chief executive, who is ultimately responsible for the selection of all personnel, with a basis by which he can justify his selections should they be questioned or contested.

Appraisal of Teacher Characteristics

A systematic plan for selecting personnel, one which is planned before the recruitment process is initiated, is essential to the success of the selection process. Minimum essentials of any plan require definition of the factors on which candidates are to be appraised, the instruments or procedures to be employed in securing data relating to each characteristic, and the assignment of appraisal responsibilities.

The object of any appraisal must be identified in clear and understandable fashion. If one needed to evaluate a course in science, for example, he would first identify the objectives of the course, such as ability to draw inferences, to apply principles, or to develop functional information. The same principle should be invoked in appraising candidates for teaching positions. The staff must define, first of all, the characteristics or qualities to be appraised, then settle upon the instruments and procedures which are to be employed in the appraisal. If, for example, the academic background of the candidate is to be examined, the data-gathering devices must be designed to secure this information. In short, the design for collecting the necessary data must be clarified prior to the selection process, and the application blanks, recommendation forms, examinations, interviews, and other procedures fashioned to yield data and observations on the characteristics under consideration. This point seems too obvious to merit the attention it has been accorded here, but the fact that some school systems overlook it would seem to be reason enough to justify its inclusion.

Who Appraises?

Responsibility for appraisal is determined by board policy, which in turn is conditioned by the nature of the school organization. If the school district is small, the likelihood is that the chief executive will make the appraisal. In larger systems where, for example, administration is confronted annually with the task of appraising several hundred applicants, the personnel function is likely to be specialized in a personnel department.

Table 8.1

Interviewing Applicants for Teaching Positions

Practice	Number of Districts	Per cent
Who interviews the applicants?		
Superintendent of schools	1754	89
Principal or other supervisory officer to whom the teacher may be responsible	1231	63
Members of the board of education	198	10
An assistant superintendent or personnel officer	405	21
A committee of school officers designated for the purpose	97	5
A committee of the school staff, including classroom teachers	94	5

Source: National Education Association, Research Division, *Teacher Personnel Practices, Urban School Districts, 1955–56,* Special Memo (Washington: The Association, 1956), p. 12.

Selection practices reported by the National Education Association are summarized in Table 8.1. A breakdown of these data indicates that as the school district increases in size, more reliance for interviewing candidates is placed upon group judgment. As the school system decreases in size, the responsibility is generally carried out by the superintendent of schools. But as the discussion develops, the point will be made that a systematic approach to personnel selection which wisely uses available methods of quantifying the results of appraisal, as well as nonnumerical techniques, will necessarily involve group participation in the selection process.

Despite the fact that group judgment, like most techniques designed to measure individual fitness for a given position, has certain limitations, its use in the selection process should be encouraged. It has the advantage of revealing strengths and weaknesses of a candidate which may not be discovered when the appraisal is made by a single person. One of the weaknesses of the group estimate is that it may provide such differences of opinion that the chief executive, who is responsible ultimately for the selection of personnel, has difficulty in making a decision. This can be minimized, however, if the data-gathering process is comprehensive enough to provide the administrator with data designed to assist him in forming balanced judgments.

What Should Be Appraised?

The list of qualities and traits alleged to be essential to success in teaching is a long one. Despite numerous inquiries into the problem, including investigations of why teachers fail, pupil opinion, expert opinion, studies of good and poor teachers, and correlation studies of factors relating to teacher success, there is no final proof as to what individual factors actually determine success in teaching.

Since professional effectiveness depends upon a combination of behavioral characteristics, some of which are considered to be of more significance than others, many schools systems are inclined to develop a comprehensive appraisal program to secure as much meaningful information as possible about the characteristics of each applicant. The data are considered as means by which the selection team can better understand the total dimensions of each applicant, and through which judgments can be made as to whether the individual is likely to succeed in the position for which he is under consideration.

The characteristics about which data are gathered for each candidate generally include: mental ability, physical characteristics, professional qualifications, personal attributes, cultural background, and social adjustment. Some of the foregoing factors can be measured more precisely than others. Some administrators place more emphasis upon certain characteristics than they do upon others.[1] Figure 14, has been included to illustrate an appraisal form based on the foregoing categories. In addition, suggestions are included under each category to illustrate identification of the procedures or techniques to be used by the selection team in securing data relating to each factor to be appraised. No significance should be attached to the order in which the characteristics are listed, and it should not be assumed that the descriptions of each are intended to be definitive.

Figure 14 reflects a systematic approach to appraisal in that it: (1) establishes a uniform basis for appraising all candidates; (2) identifies the factors which administration deems essential; (3) links the appraisal instruments and procedures to the factors to be appraised; (4) furnishes a record of the judgments of the appraiser; (5) facilitates comparisons when group estimates are used.

The factors to be included in the appraisal of school personnel is an administrative decision of extreme importance. Consequently, the major aspects to be appraised are treated briefly in the succeeding paragraphs in order to indicate more fully the nature of each factor to be appraised, as well as the related instruments of evaluation which may be employed.

Despite the fact that valid and reliable instruments are not available to measure with infallible accuracy some of the items listed in Figure 14, school officials should not refrain from efforts to gather and to evaluate information on these characteristics. It is a fact of administrative life that some decisions must be made on a subjective basis. In the last analysis, selection must go on with the best available instruments and techniques, despite their acknowledged shortcomings. As uncertain as one may be of the data which some instruments of evaluation yield, their use is infinitely more preferable than that of selection on the basis of favoritism, church or political affiliation, or pressures from individuals or community power structures.

[1] For an extensive study of teacher behavior and its components, patterns, variations, and relationships see David G. Ryans, *Characteristics of Teachers* (Washington: American Council on Education, 1960). See also Robert B. Howsam, *Who's a Good Teacher? Problems and Progress in Teacher Evaluation* (Burlingame, Calif.: California Teachers Association, 1960), and American Association of School Administrators, *et. al.*, *Who's a Good Teacher?* (Washington: National Education Association, 1961).

Instructions for Appraising Candidate

This report is to be used in appraising candidates for teaching positions in Northwood School District. Characteristics to be appraised are located on the left side of the sheet; spaces for recording appraisal of each characteristic on the right. Suggested sources of data are listed under each characteristic. Rate the candidate A, B, C, D, or E on each of the categories listed below and on the reverse side of the sheet. At the bottom of the reverse side of this sheet make any comments which you believe will help in appraising the candidate's qualifications for the position under consideration. Appraisals should not be made until specifications for the position have been carefully analyzed. (See Figure 10 for illustration of position guide.)

Policy Governing Selection

It is to the interest of the Board of Education to attract, retain, and develop superior personnel for all teaching positions. Priority in selection should be accorded to candidates who, in the judgment of appraisers, possess those qualities conducive to successful teaching careers, and who represent good "survival risks."

MENTAL ABILITY

Does the candidate possess above-average intelligence? *Rating*
Does he demonstrate superior ability in oral and written expression? To what extent is he able to conceptualize his classroom role? His role in the school organization? In the profession?

Secure results of intelligence tests. Review college transcript. Conduct interview in depth to assess this characteristic. Check for record of outstanding achievements, honors, and experiences which give indication of mental alertness and judgment.

PHYSICAL CHARACTERISTICS

Is the individual's state of health conducive to effective *Rating*
service? Does he possess physical defects which restrict his ability to perform effectively? Does he have the physical energy and vitality which the position demands? Communicable diseases?

Secure results of medical examination required by district before employment. Analyze medical history of applicant. Secure judgments from several sources, including former employers.

A—Superior; B—Above average; C—Average; D—Below average; E—Inferior

196

FIGURE 14 *(Cont.)*.

PROFESSIONAL QUALIFICATIONS

To what extent does the candidate understand the pur- *Rating*
poses, programs, methods, and materials of instruction? To
what extent is the candidate career-minded? Does the
candidate have the potential to succeed as a classroom
teacher? Knowledge of subject? General cultural background?
Appraise this composite by referring to scores on National Teacher Examination, college transcript, observations of teaching ability, interviews,
recommendations from teacher education institutions, rating scales.

PERSONAL ATTRIBUTES

Does the candidate give indications of being responsible, *Rating*
understanding, poised, enthusiastic about teaching, ener-
getic, eager to improve his competencies, open-minded?
Arrive at tentative estimate on basis of interview. Check
recommendation blanks for information relating to personal characteristics. Secure judgments of other persons. Rating scales, paper-and-
pencil tests, and personality inventories may be employed.

EMOTIONAL ADJUSTMENT

Does the candidate adjust well to irritations, frustrations, *Rating*
criticism, confusion, difficult personal and professional
problems? Does he exhibit a reasonable degree of self-con-
trol, poise, tolerance?
If previously employed, check with employers; if inexperienced, check with teacher education institutions. Have several persons
conduct interview. Rating scales and personality inventories optional.

SOCIAL ADJUSTMENT

Is the candidate able to get along reasonably well with *Rating*
others? Can he cooperate with colleagues in solution of
professional problems? Is he secure in the presence of
colleagues?
Examine recommendations. Secure judgments of several persons. Interview candidate. Rating scales and other personality assessment techniques optional.

NAME OF APPLICANT   Age   Experience

Date   Composite Rating

Summary Statement: To what extent does the candidate possess the
qualifications for the position under consideration? List reasons for predicting success or failure. Would you advise employment?

Physical Characteristics

Optimum physical and mental health for school personnel are requisite employment characteristics about which there can be no argument. Professional personnel are expected to perform constantly at a high level of physical and mental efficiency, and every effort should be made to appraise the actual and potential physical condition of each applicant. Experience indicates that chronic illness on the part of staff members is conducive to waste and inefficiency. If staff illness and disability exist to any extent the educational program may suffer. In addition to interferences which develop in the educational program through physical incapacities of staff members, additional expenditures are called for when leaves of absence for extended illness and retirement due to disability occur. The argument here is not against normal illnesses; it is that efforts should be made to eliminate candidates for employment who are actually or potentially physically unfit to perform efficiently.

What should the school district do about appraising physical fitness? The minimum control should be a thorough physical examination by a qualified physician. A desirable program would include: (1) a thorough physical examination by an examining physician employed by the school district; (2) a neural examination by designated medical personnel; (3) physical standards specified by the school district; (4) medical forms which reflect the relation of the physical characteristics of the applicant to the physical standards established, and which will make for greater uniformity in the standards adhered to by medical examiners; (5) detailed instructions to medical examiners, indicating the purposes and the nature of the examination specified by the school district.

It is patent that physical health cannot be appraised any more accurately by observation than can intelligence. The expense of a program such as the one described is negligible when viewed in terms of its value to the school district.

Intelligence

The nature of the activities in which professional school personnel engage are such that one could hardly argue for putting a ceiling on intelligence for employment purposes. Yet, as Lieberman points out:

Although a high degree of intelligence would seem to be an obvious requirement for teachers if education is to be regarded as a profession, it is by no means universally regarded as such by educators. On the contrary, much educational literature, especially the literature expressly devoted to recruiting high school or college students to teaching, actually encourages young women and men to enter teaching by advancing the claim that only average or slightly above average intelligence is required for successful teaching.[2]

Admittedly, many teachers have been employed in recent years with little regard for a given level of intelligence. The fact that this is the case does not make the practice acceptable. What the intellectual level of a teacher should be depends upon how one views the teaching function. If it is assumed to be largely custodial in nature, then the intellectual demands need not be rigorous. If, on the other hand, the teaching function is viewed as embracing considerable creativity, imagination, planning, and academic sophistication, or as requiring excellence in those characteristics described in Figure 14, then it must be assumed that the intellectual qualities for school personnel must be of high order.

The most common procedure in appraising the intelligence of the applicant is to use I.Q. scores. These are generally available at the graduating institution, or can be derived through the application of standard intelligence tests.

Professional Qualifications

The problem of appraising the professional qualifications of a candidate, such as teaching skill, methods of instruction, and understanding of the teaching-learning process, important as they are, raises a number of practical considerations, such as: (1) the expense involved in observing teachers who reside in another district or state; (2) the time involved on the part of the applicant or the appraiser if extensive travel is required; (3) the difficulties in arranging to observe a candidate who is currently employed in another district; and (4)

[2] Myron Lieberman, *Education as a Profession* (Englewood Cliffs, N. J.: Prentice-Hall, Inc., 1956), p. 232.

arranging for the selection team to observe the applicant in an actual classroom setting.

Some districts use the National Teacher Examinations as one of the devices by which to determine the professional qualifications of the candidate. The results of examinations such as the foregoing, together with an analysis of the candidate's transcript, are practices often used in lieu of, or together with, classroom observation to arrive at an estimate of the candidate's professional qualifications. To a limited extent, judgments of other persons, as expressed in letters of recommendation, may have to be relied upon to secure information to supplement that derived from sources mentioned above. What the person or persons responsible for appraisal must keep in mind is the relationship of the candidate's qualifications to the specifications of the position under consideration. If this matter is emphasized, appraisal of professional qualifications will tend to become purpose-centered.

Academic and Cultural Background

Characteristics of a competent teacher certainly include a thorough knowledge of that phase of the curriculum for which she will be responsible. In addition, the teacher should possess a broad cultural background to supplement the technical skills and knowledge which the position requires. The Educational Policies Commission emphasizes this need in stating the principles which should govern the selection and education of teachers.

Every teacher should comprehend the purposes of public education in a democratic society and the contribution he makes through his teaching to the achievement of these purposes.

Every teacher should have both a liberal education and a knowledge in depth of the field in which he teaches. Specialization is essential, but alone is not enough. In the school of today the competent teacher must recognize and teach the relationships of his field to the whole of education and the whole of life.

Every teacher has the obligation to keep abreast of knowledge in his field and of developments in teaching materials and techniques which will help improve his performance.

Because of the prime importance of citizenship education in a democracy, every teacher should be well prepared to assume his own obligations as a citizen and should understand how the school may serve as an agency for developing civic responsibility.

Every teacher should have sympathetic understanding of boys and girls and should be familiar with scientific knowledge regarding child development and the psychology of learning.

Every teacher should understand the nature and purposes of guidance and should have had experience in individual and group guidance as a part of his training.

Teacher education should include supervised experience in dealing with actual classroom problems.[3]

Assessment of the academic and cultural background of the applicant requires several kinds of evaluations. The transcript of the college record is a starting point, for it will indicate something about the breadth and depth of academic preparation, the professional and nonprofessional course patterns, and general scope of cultural interests. Some of the larger city school districts specify certain types of preparation for newly appointed teachers, depending on the grade level of the assignment. These include a specific number of semester hours of credit in designated professional education courses, and in the major subject to be taught.

The general cultural examination, of which there is a variety, represents another form of evaluation which may be used to secure some indication of the relative cultural achievement of the candidate. The interview, too, may yield certain insights in this connection, provided it is carefully directed toward evaluating pertinent aspects of academic and cultural background, and provided the interviewer is skillful enough to elicit the type of information desired.

Personal-Social Adjustment

Nearly everyone would agree that personal, social, and emotional adequacy is equally as important as professional adequacy, and should be so regarded in the selection of school personnel. There are many kinds of techniques which are employed to secure data regarding personal-social adjustment, such as those reported by Wrightstone,[4] in-

[3] National Education Association, Educational Policies Commission, *The Contemporary Challenge to American Education* (Washington: The Association, 1958), pp. 14-15.

[4] J. Wayne Wrightstone, Joseph Justman, and Irving Robbins, *Evaluation in Modern Education* (New York: American Book Company, 1956), pp. 340-341.

cluding self-descriptive inventories or personal reports, rating scales of personal and social conduct, observational and anecdotal records, free association and projective methods, autobiographies, sociometric techniques, and situational tests.

Despite the variety of instruments of evaluation which have been introduced to study personal-social adjustment, appraisal of these characteristics is not an easy matter. Considerable training and skill are needed in applying these techniques, and in interpreting the results which they yield. For a majority of school districts, a comprehensive survey of the personal-social adjustment of each candidate creates practical problems which are difficult to surmount. The time required to make a careful appraisal, as well as the specialized personnel necessary to undertake this phase of appraisal, serve to illustrate the point. Despite these and other obstacles which enter into the appraisal of personal-social adjustment, there is reason to believe that such analyses are of considerable value to the appraiser.

Unfortunate as it is that the devices for measuring personal-social adjustment are, to a large extent, subjective, the importance of selecting employees who are adequate in this respect cannot be overlooked. The limitation of subjective evaluation, handicap that it is in appraising personnel, should not deter appraisal efforts. The positive effects of appraisal of this characteristic, even by subjective means, tend to outweigh the negative. This is to say that conscientious inquiry into this aspect of behavior will provide some insights which are helpful in making judgments. They should not be postponed because of the subjectivity of approach.

Administrative Considerations

The foregoing discussion has summarized pertinent characteristics which should be appraised in the process of screening applicants for positions in the school system. It should be apparent that considerable planning is necessary to design and to implement the appraisal program which is to serve as the basis for selecting school personnel. Quite obviously the leadership of the superintendent will influence the kind of program which is developed. Among the possible decisions with which he may be confronted are these:

1. What kinds of data are needed to appraise the competencies of candidates?

2. What characteristics should be selected for emphasis?

3. What types of instruments or techniques must be employed in appraising candidates?

4. What specialized personnel are needed to apply the appraisal techniques and to interpret the results? Are such personnel available within the system?

5. Does the school system have sufficient personnel to undertake the recommended appraisal program?

6. To what extent is clerical assistance needed?

7. What materials, tests, or other evaluating devices are needed?

8. How can the appraisal process be systematized, clarified, and routinized?

9. What are the budgetary implications of the appraisal program?

10. What forms are needed to conduct a well-organized and conscientious approach to staff selection, such as application blanks, inquiry blanks, appraisal records, interview blanks, etc.?

11. To what extent should consultant services be employed in planning the appraisal program?

12. How should personnel be organized to initiate and to maintain the program?

The purpose of the above list is to denote some of the problems which arise in the process of selecting school personnel. It would seem to be clear from the summary of the several characteristics presented earlier that the process is too extensive and too complicated to expect the superintendent of schools to be capable of appraising each behavioral trait. While it is agreed that the ultimate decision on the selection of a candidate is the province of the superintendent, it is fallacious to assume that appraisal of candidates, with all of the intangibles it involves, can be a one-man operation.

Analyzing the Results of Appraisal

Before data can be utilized by persons charged with the responsibility for selection of school personnel, the data must be processed or refined in order to make the analyses more meaningful.

Certain of the factors discussed previously can be quantified more readily than others. Raw scores from tests may be transformed into percentile ratings or standard scores. Some kinds of data permit the use of rating scales or rankings. Graphic profiles are also used to por-

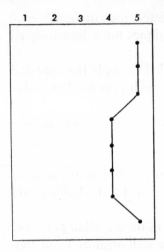

FIGURE 15   Illustration of qualification
profile used in selecting school personnel.

tray the results of evaluation, such as the qualification profile illustrated in Figure 15, which makes use of the outline of behavioral
characteristics referred to throughout this chapter.

While it is not the intent of this discussion to suggest specific
procedures for analyzing results, it should be emphasized that, whenever possible, information should be expressed in quantitative terms.
Where descriptive data cannot be quantified readily, judgments of
responsible persons or a consensus will have to be relied upon. The
point that leadership for systematizing the techniques and procedures
for analyzing test results lies with the superintendent of schools is
worth repeating.

While no one would claim that predictive devices for selecting
school personnel have been developed to the point where they are
infallible, it is surprising how much a carefully conceived and systematized procedure for selecting personnel will help to minimize the
problems involved in the selection process. By way of summary, it can
be stated that a definite administrative procedure for selecting school
personnel is a requisite for a well-managed school system. The minimum essentials of this procedure will include specifications defining:
(1) appraisal responsibilities; (2) types of information to be compiled; (3) techniques employed to compile the information; (4)
sources of information from which to compile data; (5) criteria to
govern appraisals; (6) procedures for summarizing results; and (7)
principles governing selection or rejection of applicant.

Little consideration has been given thus far to the selection of appraisers. The burden of selecting suitable persons for employment rests with the appraiser, and his competency in this matter is a factor of utmost importance. The personnel selected by the superintendent to assist him in the selection process should be those who possess the kind of balanced judgment which is basic to the selection process. To set up an elaborate selection procedure administered by incompetent appraisers is to vitiate the entire operation.

Eligibility List

Although the definition of an eligibility list probably varies somewhat among school districts, it is generally taken to mean that those persons responsible for selecting school personnel have designated as suitable for employment applicants who have met established qualifications and position specifications. The following description is illustrative:

The names of candidates who obtain a final composite score of seventy or better are listed in rank order, subject to approval of physical fitness, and this becomes the eligibility list which is sent to the Board of Superintendents for adoption.

The superintendent of schools, on the basis of the applicant's place on the eligibility list, recommends to the Board of Public Education the assignment of an applicant to a teaching position. . . . The Board takes formal action to effectuate the recommendation.[5]

Final selection of personnel should adhere to the merit principle which holds that vacancies should be filled by those candidates who best meet the established qualifications. Departure from this concept sooner or later invites abuses which lead to a staff of inferior quality. One of this century's greatest problems in the struggle for good government has been the development and control of sound personnel selection procedures. The advance from the spoils system to the modern career service concept has not been easy. Experience indicates that unless selection from the eligibility list is carefully controlled so that the merit principle operates, the integrity of the entire program is threatened.

[5] School District of Philadelphia, Pennsylvania, *Qualifications and Examination Procedures for Obtaining a Teaching Position in the Public Schools of the City of Philadelphia* (Philadelphia: The Board of Education, 1957), pp. 5–6.

Certification Audit

Before personnel nominations are made to the board of education, it is customary to require evidence from each candidate that he has satisfied certification requirements. This stage of the selection process would appear to be an appropriate time for the school system to make certain that certification requirements have been satisfied, in view of the fact that teaching personnel are frequently elected to positions only to discover at a later date that they cannot meet certification requirements. Moreover, there are legal ramifications to the matter, as Edwards points out:

> . . . a contract made by a teacher who does not possess the certificate required by law is void and not subject to ratification. If the law requires that a teacher hold a certificate at the date of making the contract, or at the time of beginning teaching, failure to have the certificate at the time required is fatal to the contract, and a subsequent procurement of the certificate will not validate the contract [6]

Nomination and Appointment

As noted earlier, ability to sustain the integrity of the personnel program depends upon a number of conditions, one of which is the separation of policy development and execution. In the personnel selection process, the chief executive should have the exclusive responsibility for making all recommendations for appointment to positions or jobs in the school district. The board of education, on the other hand, is responsible for approving employment recommendations.

Notification of Appointment

One of the very real difficulties in a selection process is that posed by the time factor. Many competent candidates are lost to competing systems because of the time lag between the initial interview and official election by the board of education. While every effort should be made to keep to a minimum the amount of time involved in se-

[6] Newton Edwards, *The Courts and the Public Schools*, rev. ed. (Chicago: University of Chicago Press, 1955), p. 444.

lecting a candidate, it is especially important that there is no delay in notifying candidates of official appointment.

Contracts

A contract is an agreement between two or more people to do or not to do certain things. A teaching contract is an agreement between the board of education and the teacher which specifies the nature of the personal services which the board intends to purchase in exchange for a specific sum of money.

Operationally, the contractual relationship between school personnel and boards of education varies considerably in both form and content. While local boards of education are permitted by law to contract for professional services, it is a legal requirement in about one-third of the states, the form being a standard contract prescribed by the state. In the majority of states, state education agencies have prepared contract forms for use by local boards of education.

Some idea of the nature, incidence, and trend of written contracts of teachers surveyed by the National Education Association is given in Table 8.2.

Table 8.2
Use of Written Contracts for Teachers

Practice	1950–51		1955–56	
	Number	%	Number	%
Which teachers sign contracts for their services?				
No teachers sign contracts	114	7	87	4
All teachers sign every year	909	56	1,187	61
All teachers sign on first employment only	336	21	247	13
Probationary teachers only	171	11	153	8
Probationary teachers and teachers when first placed on tenure	66	4	252	13
All teachers sign at every salary change	Not reported		18	1
When teachers are first placed on tenure only	9	1	3	*

* Less than one-half of 1 per cent.
Source: National Education Association, Research Division, *Teacher Personnel Practices, Urban School Districts, 1955–56*, Special Memo (Washington: The Association, 1956), p. 13; *Teacher Personnel Practices, 1950–51: Appointment and Termination of Service* (Washington: The Association, 1952), p. 21.

Term of Employment

One of the most important features of a teaching contract is the term of employment. Analysis of Table 8.3 is helpful in understanding general practices which are used by boards of education in specifying the term of employment. As a rule, the term of employment for a beginning teacher is a single year. As the data in Table 8.3 indicate, some school districts elect all teachers annually, regardless of the length of service. Underlying this practice is the idea that the board of education is under no obligation to renew a contract for the ensuing year, nor to state the reasons for nonrenewal. In effect, the teacher is not dismissed; he is simply not reemployed.

Table 8.3

Term of Employment for Teachers

Practice	Number of Districts	%
What is the prevailing practice with respect to the term of employment for teachers?		
Tenure or protective continuing contract	1,296	66
Spring-notification type continuing contract	419	21
Annual election	245	12
Periodic election other than annual	13	1

Source: National Education Association, Research Division, *Teacher Personnel Practices, Urban School Districts, 1955–56*, Special Memo (Washington: The Association, 1956), p. 13.

Two types of continuing contracts are identified in Table 8.3. In both cases the agreements remain in effect for an indefinite period. In the spring-notification type contract, however, the teacher must be notified on or before a given date if he is not to be employed in the ensuing year. This type of contract has little to recommend it, for a teacher's employment may be terminated at the end of the year, without cause, upon proper notification. An interesting feature of this type of contract is that the board of education must initiate action to dismiss the teacher; it cannot simply fail to elect, as in the case of the annual contract.

The protective continuing contract, which Table 8.3 indicates is in effect in the majority of school systems included in the sample, provides for permanent tenure of a teacher after a probationary period of a given number of years (usually three). A teacher may be dismissed during any year of the probationary period without showing cause. Employment of a teacher after the probationary period is tantamount to permanent tenure, although there are specific conditions under which a teacher may be dismissed who has acquired permanent tenure, such as incompetency or immorality.

The trend in protective continuing contracts from 1931 to 1956 is reassuring. In 1931, only 28 per cent of the cities had protective continuing contracts; in 1955–56 this figure stood at 66 per cent.

Contractual arrangements between the board of education and school personnel, as noted earlier, depends upon statutory requirements. When contracts are not prescribed by law, but are mandated by board regulations, they should conform at least to the following specifications:

A written agreement as opposed to an oral one
Specific designation of the parties to the contract
Statement of the legal capacity of the parties represented
Provision for signatures by the authorized agents of the board of education and by the teacher
Clear stipulation of salary to be paid
Designation of date of contract, duration, and the date when service is to begin
Definition of assignment [7]

In concluding this section, it may be well to recall the relationship of contracts for school personnel to the total selection process. The contract is another of the devices which is of very great value, not only in furthering the career service concept, but also in controlling the quality of personnel who enter the school systems and the teaching profession. It is a control to be used in preventive selection, so to speak, which is to withhold permanent tenure from probationary teachers who have proven to be unsatisfactory. This procedure is emphasized because it would appear to be infinitely more effective and realistic than the difficult process of dismissing unsatisfactory teachers who have gained tenure.

[7] Willard S. Elsbree and E. Edmund Reutter, Jr., *Staff Personnel in the Public Schools* (Englewood Cliffs, N.J.: Prentice-Hall, Inc., 1954), pp. 421–422.

Selection of Administrative Personnel

Importance of Careful Selection

The question of how to select capable administrators is an old one. Quite rightly, discussions of it usually involve consideration of the personal characteristics essential to administrative success, sources of administrative talent, and selection techniques.

The importance of selecting highly qualified administrators is generally recognized in public education, as it is in most every kind of organization. The case for improving the quality of school administrators is not difficult to establish. This we know:

1. The administrative problems in public education are becoming increasingly complex.

2. The knowledge needed in school administration has increased considerably over the years.

3. School systems are becoming extensive and expensive operations.

4. The responsibilities of school administrators are increasing.

5. The number and variety of administrative positions are increasing.

6. Administrative positions in education require extensive and intensive professional training.

7. Greater demands are being made for wider and more effective use in school administration of lay groups and professional staff members in the solution of school problems. This approach to administration, which requires a thorough understanding of group processes and democratic procedures, obviously calls for a different kind of leadership than one which adheres strictly to the line-staff concept.

8. The success of the educational enterprise has become increasingly dependent on the judgment of administrative personnel.

9. Social change will continue to create persistent problems which will require skillful administrative planning for their solution.

10. Increasingly, the administrator must spend his time with people rather than with things.

With so much riding on successful administrative performance, the cardinal importance of selecting suitable administrators is clear.

Basic Considerations

The selection process for administrative personnel has certain elements which are common to any personnel selection process. These include: (1) formulation of a program for selecting administrative personnel which is closely meshed with the total program for personnel development; (2) formulation of board policy governing objectives, responsibility for selection, and the compensation structure for administrative personnel; (3) description of administrative positions and their organizational relationships; and (4) definition of selection procedures, including the kinds of data needed for selection decisions.

Regardless of what plan is developed to select school administrators, it is well known that there are no quick and easy solutions to the problem of selecting the right personnel for administrative positions. Research in administrative selection has contributed useful suggestions, but few definitive answers. Until the research is more conclusive, much of the selection process will have to be tempered with experience gained from experiment and observation.

While the number of administrative positions in any school system is small in relation to the total number of professional and noninstructional personnel, the task is admittedly complex and time-consuming. But a mistake in selection can be so costly and destructive that no system can be satisfied with less than a diligent and painstaking effort to secure suitable administrative personnel.

Policy Decisions

It is generally recognized that public schools in the United States suffer from administrative deprivation. In some school systems there is but one professional administrator—the superintendent of schools. The attendance units in these systems will have no principals, only "head teachers." It is only in recent years that attention has been given to improving the adequacy of school administrative staffs. Four questions may help boards of education to reach some practical working decision on policies for selecting administrative personnel:

1. How many administrators are needed to staff our schools adequately?

2. What qualifications should members of the administrative staff possess?

3. What standards shall be established for selection purposes?

4. What arrangements shall be made for compensating administrative personnel?

Of course, answers to these questions will be influenced by many factors, such as tradition, economic conditions, the board's concept of administration, school size, and the attitude and understanding of the chief executive regarding the administrative process.

Certification of Administrators

A majority of the states have established controls governing the certification of school administrators. Table 8.4 contains the number and per cent of states issuing types of administrative certificates during the period 1900 to 1957. Analysis of these data indicates an increase in the number of states which control the certification of administrators, as well as an increase in the number of positions for which administrative certificates are provided.

Table 8.4

Number and Per Cent of States Issuing Types of Administrative Certificates, 1900–57 *

Type of Certificate	Prior to 1900 No.	%	1910 No.	%	1920 No.	%	1930 No.	%	1940 No.	%	1950 No.	%	1957 No.	%
Supt.	1	2	8	15	10	20	11	22	29	60	29	60	34	74
H.S. Prin.	0	0	6	12	10	20	14	29	21	43	19	39	35	76
Elem. S. Prin.	0	0	5	10	7	14	16	33	20	41	18	37	36	78
Gen. Adm.									7	14	8	15	11	24
Gen. Prin.									10	20	11	22	8	17
Supervisor									6	12	7	14	24	52

Source: Robert B. Howsam and Edgar L. Morphet, "Certification of Educational Administrators," Preprinted from *The Journal of Teacher Education* IX, No. 1 (March, 1958) and No. 2 (June, 1958), p. 38.
* Each state equals approximately 2 per cent.

The trend indicated in Table 8.4 toward strengthening certification requirements for administrators is encouraging. But there is an inference to be drawn from these data which is related to the selection of administrative personnel. There is wide variation among the administrative certification requirements. Further, in a few states the requirements are not as rigorous as they might be. It would be unwise, then, for any school system to depend solely on certification requirements as the selection criterion. In some states, for example, there are ten or more licensed administrators for every existing administrative position. Certification requirements are helpful in the selection process, but every system should consider them as minimal, and should establish standards which are high enough to secure administrators who have the necessary qualifications and competencies needed for the administrative positions under consideration. Howsam and Morphet, in their study of certification of educaitonal administrators recommend:

Local school districts are encouraged to seek personnel on the basis of job descriptions and required competencies. Anyone who is employed is required to hold the state certificate as a minimum. Local school districts are encouraged to establish higher standards and especially to select and place personnel on the basis of evidence indicating that they have the competencies needed for the positions involved. Each local school district develops a description of the position and competencies needed for work in the district and selects persons in terms of (a) possession of a certificate as required by law, (b) evidence of special preparation in the form of diplomas from accredited institutions, (c) such appropriate oral and written examinations as are considered desirable, (d) meaningful recommendations, and (e) personal interviews. Responsibility for determining whether the candidate has the qualifications needed for a position is thus placed on and held by the local district. However, the special problems encountered as a result of existing small districts are recognized, and provisions are made for assuring that they will have competent assistance when needed.[8]

Selection Procedures

Long-term Approach

Selection of school personnel, it has been said in this chapter, should be based upon policies and procedures which are the outgrowth of advance planning to meet the recurring problem of developing and

[8] Robert B. Howsam and Edgar L. Morphet, "Certification of Educational Administrators," Preprinted from *The Journal of Teacher Education IX*, No. 1 (March, 1958), and No. 2 (June, 1958), p. 8.

maintaining an effective school staff. This point of view embraces the following propositions:

1. That one of the major functions of school administration is the fashioning of a comprehensive program of personnel development.

2. That the selection of administrative personnel is a long-range consideration, which is initiated with the recruitment of teachers, at which time selection is based not only on the individual's qualifications for the position under consideration, but also on his suitability for future advancement.

3. That the personnel program should be designed to make possible effective development and utilization of personnel.

The intent of the foregoing discussion is to emphasize the necessity for long-range administrative planning for administrative personnel. All too frequently an administrative vacancy occurs in a school system, and, because of the absence of systematic planning, the choice of a successor may be the result of pressures for a "favorite son," political manipulation, lack of time to locate a suitable replacement, and so on. In effect, selection is made in default of planning.

One of the recurring problems in selecting members for the administrative staff is whether to choose from personnel within or from outside the system. Another question of importance, especially as it concerns the principalship, relates to the experience requirements to be established. Should selection of administrative personnel be restricted to those with administrative experience? If not, what selection techniques should be employed to predict administrative behavior in advance of performance?

Position Guides and Specifications

One of the techniques which has proved useful in selecting persons for administrative positions, and one which will help in arriving at solutions to questions such as the foregoing, is the position guide, commonly known as job description. As was pointed out in Chapter Five, position guides identify the basic and subsidiary functions of the position, the duties and responsibilities, as well as the relationship of the position to other positions in the school organization. As such, it forms the basis for preparing position specifications, so that those responsible for selection will have a clear understanding of the position and the competencies needed by the person who will fill it.

In effect, position guides and specifications will better enable those who are responsible for selection to assess the qualifications of candidates.

In those school systems establishing position specifications, certain specific requirements relating to preparation and experience are standard procedure. These may include an administrative certificate issued by the state, evidence of completion of graduate courses in administration and supervision, previous administrative or supervisory experience, and superior or successful teaching experience.

Talent Bank of Administrative Personnel

Underlying the personnel selection process, which must be considered as a means to developing an educated citizenry for our times, is the assumption that it should be designed to improve the quality of the school staff. With specific reference to the selection process as it pertains to administrative personnel, it is further assumed that:

1. The board of education, in consultation with the chief executive, will formulate specific guide lines for the selection of personnel.

2. That the chief executive will have authority over the selection of subordinates.

3. That the selection process will be formalized.

4. That procedures for recruitment, selection, and development will be predetermined for each administrative position.

These, and other points yet to be made, form a broad outline within which the selection process takes place. As mentioned earlier, the point of beginning in the selection of administrative personnel is at the time of recruitment, when efforts are made to select individuals who have the potential capacity to advance in the administrative echelon. This approach engenders an administrative talent bank from which the system can draw replacements for administrative vacancies as they occur.

The talent bank plan for developing administrative talent presupposes that considerable attention will be focused on it by the chief executive. Implementation of the plan will include such activities as:

1. Forecasting future administrative personnel needs.

2. Development and maintenance of an administrative personnel inventory, which would catalogue the administrative potential within the system.

3. Compilation of a record of pertinent information for each person included in the personnel inventory. The basic information would be provided by the individual, and relate to previous background, experiences, and accomplishments. To this would be added data from appraisal devices which school officials choose to employ in the selection process, such as results from tests, questionnaires, meaningful recommendations, interviews, and appraisal reports by staff members.

4. Provision for developmental opportunities within the school system which furnish one basis for predicting future administrative performance.

5. Provision for continuance of graduate education along lines which will be beneficial to both the individual and to the school system.

6. Periodic review of the personnel inventory to determine the progress of each individual under consideration as it pertains to his state of readiness to occupy an administrative post.

The foregoing plan, if pursued as a matter of policy, would mean that promotion to administrative positions generally would be from within the system. Whether this can or should be school policy cannot be answered here, for it depends upon a number of considerations. The talent inventory idea, however, does not necessarily exclude the selection of administrative personnel from outside the system, especially if persons within the system are not capable of meeting the position specifications.

Predicting Administrative Effectiveness

How to define and to predict administrative effectiveness are two interrelated problems which have long engaged the attention of students of school administration. While an inventory of administrative positions, including duties and responsibilities peculiar to each, is basic to the selection program, the characteristics needed by the individual to perform effectively in the position is of paramount importance. Those who are charged with the selection of school administrators must consider what mental, physical, personality, and character attributes are needed, and in what degree, to perform successfully in the position.

Many approaches have been used to predict administrative effectiveness, including the use of standardized tests, on-the-job observation, studies of traits of successful administrators, and measures of past administrative success.

While studies of desirable traits needed for success in school administration have been useful, it is generally conceded that mere possession of certain traits, such as intelligence and articulation, does not guarantee administrative competency. It is the effective use of these traits in administrative situations which is of primary importance. Similarly, it has become increasingly apparent that mastery of abstract knowledge of the field of school administration will not, in itself, make a competent administrator.[9]

The use of tests to select school administrators has not proved to be completely satisfactory. For example, Nunnery's study of standardized psychological tests in the selection of school administrators concludes that there is no single instrument which can serve as a best predictor. The results of projects aimed at determining the predictive value of selected standardized tests were reported to be inconclusive and somewhat conflicting.[10]

With the increase in the number and variety of positions in school administrative structures, it is becoming increasingly evident that different kinds of administrative competencies are essential to the effective functioning of the organization. The skills, knowledges, and abilities essential to the superintendency are not necessarily identical with those required by the principal, the business manager, or the director of instruction.

Briner's study of the qualities superintendents look for in selecting subordinate administrators revealed that the appraisals were based upon information grouped according to the following characteristics:

Physical and Character Image: Age, sex, race, appearance, mannerisms, sense of humor, family and social group relationships, personal interests, and a variety of values.

Levels of Professional and Personal Potential: Quality of oral and written expression, conceptualization of the purpose and need for public

---

[9] For an extended discussion of the competencies required in school administration, see Roald F. Campbell, John E. Corbally, Jr., and John A. Ramseyer, *Introduction to Educational Administration* (Boston: Allyn and Bacon, Inc., 1958), Chapter 10.

[10] Michael Y. Nunnery, "How Useful Are Standardized Psychological Tests in the Selection of School Administrators?" *Educational Administration and Supervision*, 45 (November, 1959), pp. 349–356.

education, educational and social philosophy, academic training, personality, cooperation with others, and use of rational techniques in observing and interpreting an educational problem.

Levels of Demonstrated Professional and Non-Professional Competence: Performance of administrative and teaching functions, use of special educational and non-educational knowledge, oral and written recommendations, and professional contributions.[11]

Lipham's study, which hypothesized that effective school principals would tend to rank higher than ineffective principals on certain measurable personality variables (activity drive, achievement drive, mobility drive, social ability, feelings of security, and emotional control) provides useful implications for selecting administrators. While the results indicated no significant differences between effectives and ineffectives concerning a number of characteristics such as age, intelligence, sex, years of graduate study, years of classroom teaching experience, and years of experience as a principal, the personal construct of the effective school principal was found to be different from that of the ineffective principal.[12]

While it is apparent that research has not provided definitive answers for the selection of school administrators, many of the findings are worthy of consideration. It is clear that the selection process can be improved if continuous attention is devoted to the systematic development of selection criteria, especially in defining the administrative behavior which is desired for each of the several administrative posts. Moreover, greater recognition needs to be given to the concept that the effective functioning of an organization depends more upon the development of an administrative team than upon the employment of individual administrators. The selection process should be designed to match not only the man and the job, but to locate the individual whose abilities will complement those of existing administrative staff members.

[11] Conrad Briner, "The Superintendent and the Selection of Subordinate Administrators," *Administrator's Notebook*, VIII, No. 6 (February, 1960), University of Chicago: Midwest Administration Center, 1960.

[12] James M. Lipham, "Personal Variables of Effective Administrators," *Administrator's Notebook*, IX (September, 1960), University of Chicago: Midwest Administration Center, 1960. See also: Ralph B. Kimbrough, "The Behavioral Characteristics of Effective Educational Administrators," *Educational Administration and Supervision*, 45 (November, 1959), pp. 337–348.

Selection of Noninstructional Personnel

In a broad sense, the principles and procedures advocated in this chapter for the selection of professional personnel are applicable in the selection of noninstructional personnel. There are reasons, however, for believing that we do not now have in general operation the kind of selection programs for noninstructional personnel that we ought to have. These reasons include the following:

1. Refusal of many boards of education to delegate to the chief executive responsibility for selection of noninstructional personnel.

2. Political control of the selection process.

3. Undervaluation of the role of the noninstructional employee.

4. Failure to accept the principle that the productivity of good workers is far greater than that of inferior workers.

5. The high turnover rate among noninstructional personnel.

6. The absence of formal systems of employee recruitment and selection in most school systems.

7. The disposition of school officials to underestimate the range of productivity among employees.

8. The widespread practice of employing mediocre rather than superior talent to fill noninstructional positions.

9. The general absence of classification plans of any kind for noninstructional personnel.

10. Failure to utilize fully available knowledge in the selection process.

11. The quantitative inadequacy of administrative staffs in many school systems which often leads to a lack of attention to noninstructional personnel.

Special Problems in Selecting Noninstructional Personnel

The range in types of noninstructional personnel is extensive. It varies from the unskilled laborer to the professional, who are employed to render service in such widely varying activities as maintenance, operation, transportation, food, health, safety, attendance, business, clerical, and law. The heterogeneity of these employees is in itself a factor which makes the establishment of a systematic plan for personnel selection a virtual necessity.

The size of a school system is also a factor which must be taken into consideration in predicating selection processes for noninstructional personnel. In the very small school system the chief executive, often because of the quantitative inadequacy of the administrative staff, generally performs all personnel functions directly, including recruitment, selection, development, and advice to the board on matters pertaining to personnel policy. The selection devices which he employs often depends upon the special competencies he may possess or develop in this area, or the assistance he may secure from personnel specialists.

The small number of candidates for a particular vacancy in a small school system also poses selection problems. Development of a comprehensive selection process, including the use of a variety of selection techniques, would not appear to be feasible in very small school systems for obvious reasons. Some of these difficulties can be overcome by the development of a part-time personnel officer, and by the employment of consultant service for assistance on special aspects of the selection process. In some school systems where the establishment of a formal selection process is not feasible, noninstructional personnel are employed on a trial basis, and their suitability for the job tested under actual conditions. This method has certain limitations, but the probationary plan may be more effective than exclusive reliance on the judgment of the employing officer.

Elements of the Selection Plan

The quality of noninstructional personnel employed in the school system can be improved, provided certain essential elements are given a place of primacy in the selection phase of the personnel function.

1. Careful consideration is given to the task of matching the *man* and the *job*. This means that each job is analyzed (job description) in terms of its duties and responsibilities. The job description furnishes the basis for defining (job specification) in detail the nature and scope of the job, and a description of the type of person required to perform it effectively. The job specification generally includes the minimum qualifications for employment.

2. Characteristics of the *man* required to perform the job are described as carefully as possible. Such characteristics as experience,

physical requirements, mental ability, age, education, and personality are defined in relation to the job to be filled.

3. Devices to be used to identify the extent to which the applicant possesses the characteristics needed to perform the job are predetermined. It is worth repeating that the devices used will vary from system to system. Use of the interview, recommendations, and application blanks is standard operating procedure for most school systems. The use of tests, in an attempt to supplement subjective judgment with more objective information, is increasing.

4. A system of job classification is established on the basis of job descriptions and specifications. The classification system may be used as the basis for the compensation structure for noninstructional personnel.

5. The administration, including the board of education, the chief executive, and the administrative staff, should not only understand the relationship between the selection function and staff quality, but they should plan continuously to make the selection program more effective. This will require sufficient professional personnel specifically prepared to perform the duties and responsibilities of selection. It will require the development of a systematic plan for selecting personnel. It will also necessitate continuous study of both the job classification plan and selection devices so that bases of selection will become progressively better.

The critical role of the selection process in the total personnel program is such that it demands the constant attention of administrative officials if it is to function effectively from one year to the next. If the selection process is to become increasingly effective, there must be continuous efforts to improve its validity. The ultimate test of the selection process is the quality of the performance of personnel employed. Continuous improvement of the selection program involves efforts to make the standard selective devices more effective. The point has not yet been reached, for example, where the application blank, the interview, and the reference are completely satisfactory. In addition to the improvements which can and are being made in these devices, new instruments of evaluation are being developed to aid those responsible for selection to do a more effective job of predicting performance. In fine, the selection program and the results achieved by it should be placed under constant and careful scrutiny to the end that the school system will be able to secure and retain the noninstructional personnel it ought to have.

Suggested Reading

Chamberlain, Leo M., and Leslie W. Kindred, *The Teacher and School Organization*, 3rd ed. (Englewood Cliffs, N.J.: Prentice-Hall, Inc., 1958).

Eastmond, Jefferson, *The Teacher and School Administration* (Boston: Houghton Mifflin Co., 1959).

Edwards, Newton, *The Courts and the Public Schools* (Chicago: University of Chicago Press, 1955).

Elsbree, Willard S., and E. Edmund Reutter, Jr., *Staff Personnel in the Public Schools* (Englewood Cliffs, N.J.: Prentice-Hall, Inc., 1954).

Finchum, R. N., *Administering the Custodial Program* (Washington: U. S. Government Printing Office, 1961), Chapter III.

The International City Managers Association, *Municipal Personnel Administration*, 6th ed. (Chicago: The Association, 1960).

Lieberman, Myron, *Education as a Profession* (Englewood Cliffs, N.J.: Prentice-Hall, Inc., 1956).

National Education Association, Educational Policies Commission, *The Contemporary Challenge to American Education* (Washington: The Association, 1958).

Nigro, Felix A., *Public Personnel Administration* (New York: Henry Holt & Co., Inc., 1959).

Ryans, David G., *Characteristics of Teachers* (Washington: American Council on Education, 1960).

Stone, C. Harold, and William E. Kendall, *Effective Personnel Selection Procedures* (Englewood Cliffs, N.J.: Prentice-Hall, Inc., 1956).

Yoder, Dale, *Personnel Management and Industrial Relations*, 4th ed. (Englewood Cliffs, N.J.: Prentice-Hall, Inc., 1956).

Induction of Personnel

CHAPTER NINE

Induction may be defined as a systematic organization effort to minimize problems confronting new personnel so that they can contribute maximally to the work of the school while realizing personal and professional satisfaction. A school system can recruit and select personnel, but until these individuals become fully cognizant of the work to be performed, as well as the environment in which it is to be performed, they cannot be expected to contribute maximally to the goals of the enterprise. Administrative attention to induction problems is a relatively recent undertaking, and its importance is becoming increasingly appreciated by all organizations of whatever purpose.

Development of an effective induction program is one way that organization can contribute to personnel security and satisfaction. Perhaps at no time in his period of service does the newly appointed staff member need more consideration, more guidance, and more understanding than he does between the day of his appointment and the day when he becomes a self-motivated, self-directed, fully effective member of the organization.

223

Every school administrator needs to realize that one of the emotional needs of every individual is a structure in which he can find a reasonable degree of security and satisfaction. The beginning school employee is no exception. He is apprehensive of many things—the community, his co-workers, his ability to succeed, his being accepted both socially and professionally. He is generally unaware of "the way we do things here." He is probably uninformed about school objectives, specific duties and responsibilities, school and community traditions and taboos, and personal and professional standards to which he is expected to adhere. These and other problems experienced by new school personnel are important enough to warrant administrative efforts which will result in planned programs of assistance for the individuals under consideration.

It is clear that the number of first-year teachers who leave the profession is higher than it ought to be, and that the loss is higher than the profession can long sustain, especially in a period when competition for professional personnel is becoming increasingly marked.

To say that school systems have not been concerned, or are not now concerned with problems of the inductee would be a gross misstatement. Many excellent programs are in operation. Yet, it is probably fair to say that, for many school systems, the approaches to induction problems have been of the curbstone variety rather than those which have been developed through systematic planning. It is to the matter of induction planning that the considerations following in this chapter will be directed. These include discussion of the range of induction problems, as well as the aims, elements, procedures, and responsibilities involved in a comprehensive induction program.

The terms *induction* and *orientation,* often used synonomously in the literature dealing with personnel administration, mean the process by which newly appointed personnel are assisted in making the necessary position and related adjustments. The process is conceived as beginning in the recruitment stage and ending when the inductee has made the necessary personal, professional, and social adaptations which enable him to function fully and effectively as a member of the school staff. It involves more than plans for making new personnel feel at ease in a new environment. The induction process, in its broadest sense, is an extension of the recruitment and selection programs, in which administrative efforts are designed to match the man and the position, to enable the man to achieve position satisfaction, and to utilize fully the satisfactions and the competencies of the man in attaining the goals of the educational program. Thus, the concept of induction discussed in this chapter is closely meshed with the chapters on recruitment and selection of personnel, and completes the series of three chapters in Part III dealing with satisfaction of personnel need.

Induction Problems

The increasing interest in induction problems of public school personnel is reflected in the number of recent investigations which have been undertaken, especially during the decade of the fifties. During this period several reports have pointed to faulty induction programs in the public schools, including those by the National Education Association, Eastmond, Wallace, Lane, Wey, and Fischer.[1] While these reports vary somewhat both as to purposes and as to conclusions, there is general agreement that the induction programs of school systems, on the whole, are far from satisfactory. Problems experienced by personnel newly appointed to school positions, as revealed by the foregoing investigations, may be listed summarily as follows:

1. Problems in becoming acquainted with and making adjustments in the *community*.

2. Problems involved in understanding the *school system*, its aims, policies, programs, procedures, controls, resources, organizational relationships.

3. Problems in becoming acquainted with the *position*, including courses of study, pupil personnel, and parents.

4. Problems in making acquaintances with other *school personnel*.

5. Problems of a *personal* nature, such as locating suitable living accommodations, health, and transportation facilities.

[1] (a) National Education Association, Research Division, "First-Year Teachers in 1954–55," *Research Bulletin*, XXIV, No. 1 (February, 1956), pp. 34–36; (b) Jefferson N. Eastmond, *The Teacher and School Administration* (Boston: Houghton Mifflin Co., 1959), p. 18; (c) Morris Wallace, "Problems Experienced by 136 New Teachers During Their Induction into Service," *North Central Association Quarterly*, 25 (January, 1951), p. 292; (d) Willard R. Lane, *The Induction of Beginning Teachers in Wisconsin Public Schools* (Madison: University of Wisconsin Doctoral Thesis, 1951); (e) Herbert W. Wey, "Difficulties of Beginning Teachers," *The School Review*, XIX, No. 1 (January, 1951), pp. 32–37; (f) Eugene Fischer, *A National Survey of the Beginning Teacher* (DeKalb: Northern Illinois State Teachers College, 1954).

Many of the difficulties of first-year teachers, such as those mentioned in the sources above, have been attributed to deficient programs of induction.

Community

It is an article of faith among educators that the community is an important conditioner of educational quality. Mort and Vincent have observed:

> The school is one of the cultural fruits of the community. What it is—good, bad, or indifferent—is in no small measure caused by certain characteristics of the community in which it happens to be. Beginning about 1935 a series of studies have investigated the various characteristics of communities and how they influence the school. The results of these studies can all be generalized in the following statement: More than any one influence, the community is responsible for the quality of education to be found in its schools. Despite three and a half centuries of writing by the educational philosophers, despite the changes that have occurred in Western civilization—and, especially in America, despite the efforts which have been made to rethink educational objectives in recent times, despite constitutional provisions which make education a state function—despite all these, certain factors of the local community soil in which the school grows have more to do with the quality of that school than any other influence.[2]

It should be noted also that the education of the school administrator involves a thorough understanding of school-community relationships. It is an interesting paradox, however, that studies of teacher induction point out consistently that the means employed to inform prospective or newly appointed teachers about the community, or to help them to make adjustments in the community, generally were less than satisfactory. As a matter of fact, the incidence of difficulties experienced by teachers in securing information about the community, and in making adjustments to the community, is serious enough to reinforce the contention that much more can and should be done administratively to assist inductees in becoming fully acquainted with the community structure and characteristics. If the relationship of the community to the school is as strategic as it is purported to be, then

[2] Paul R. Mort and William S. Vincent, *Introduction to American Education* (New York: McGraw-Hill Book Co., 1954), pp. 108–109.

it would appear that administration should help the school staff, especially newly appointed members, in understanding the community and its effect upon the school.

The inductee needs a variety of specific kinds of information, not only for making adjustments in the community, but for helping him to fulfill his role as an educator. Such items as community geography, economy, housing, government, religious agencies, educational resources, provisions for dealing with crime, public safety, health conditions and resources, opportunities for recreation, provisions for child care and family welfare, racial minorities and the foreign-born, and agencies for community planning and coordination are illustrative of the informational needs of the beginning teacher.

Taking the long view, the school has an important responsibility in raising the level of public understanding of education. The school also shares in the responsibility for community improvement. What the school staff contributes to these ends depends to a large extent upon staff understanding of the community. The induction program, it would seem, provides administration with favorable opportunities for helping the newcomer to become adjusted in the community, and for acquainting him with its problems and potential.

Position

Indications are that newly appointed personnel experience certain problems in understanding assignments, such as gaining a clear and workable understanding of the school's philosophy and objectives, understanding and using special school services, and learning to evaluate pupil achievement. It need not be argued that the position which the new employee is to assume is a most paramount consideration, the nature and function of which he should clearly understand. Several studies have indicated that newly appointed personnel need more help than they are getting in order to understand clearly the specific duties and responsibilities of the position. As Eye and Lane point out:

Of all the information which teachers want when they are applying for a new position, the most important is that concerned with the specific duties involved in the teaching assignment. In most cases, however, when a teacher receives information about the prospective position from a placement bureau, the notice states that it is "teaching English," or "teaching mathematics." If the teacher is fortunate in his interview, he may learn about some of the extra-class duties connected with the position. After reporting for duty, he may find that the originally stated commitments of the employing official constitutes only a small part of the duties that he is expected to perform. A more unfortunate situation is one in which the teacher has been told or led to understand that he is assigned to none of the classes for which he thought he was under contract to teach.[3]

The value of job and position descriptions in personnel administration has been emphasized repeatedly throughout this text. Every local school system could improve the manner in which the induction function is performed if it established systematic procedures for analyzing and describing the positions to be filled. If the positions are described in terms of duties and responsibilities to be performed, the recruitment, selection, and induction programs can be carried out much more effectively. These descriptions have a variety of uses, including:

1. Provision of facts describing the position to the candidate and to placement bureaus.

2. Provision of information to those responsible for the selection of personnel, so that the task of matching candidates and positions can be performed more effectively.

3. Establishment of a compensation plan for noninstructional personnel on the basis of job classification.

4. Minimization of the adjustment problems of newly appointed personnel.

Preparation of position descriptions should not only prevent applicants from accepting positions without adequate knowledge of inherent duties and responsibilities, but it should improve the performance of the total personnel function. The trend in school enrollments and developments in the reorganization of school administrative units means increases in staff size. This, in turn, demands improved personnel procedures designed to secure and retain competent personnel.

School System

Every organization faces the problem of informing its members of purposes, policies, and procedures. This task is even more incum-

---

[3] Glen G. Eye and Willard R. Lane, *The New Teacher Comes to School* (New York: Harper & Brothers, 1956), pp. 107–108.

bent upon the school than upon most other organizations, since staff members are involved in certain kinds of administrative activities. Enlightened participation by the staff member in carrying on the work of the school requires a clear understanding of the way in which the school operates, its controls, organizational relationships, lines of authority, and the myriad means through which the educational program functions.

Other School Personnel

Since the work of the school is carried on by and through people, the matter of human relationships becomes especially important to the beginning employee. Getting acquainted with other colleagues in the school system often poses difficulties for the new teacher. The initiative for making official contacts rests with school officials, who employ faculty meetings, social gatherings, professional association meetings, and other procedures to acquaint the new teacher with his colleagues. Data reported by Elliott in Table 9.1 illustrate the relative value of orientation procedures as judged by school personnel.

Personnel Adjustment

The personal problems which the individual experiences upon entering a new position and which are outside the realm of the actual school assignment merit attention at this point. These are the problems of every newcomer—locating suitable living accommodations, arranging transportation, finding banking facilities, and numerous details which must be attended to in the process of adjusting to the new environment. The ease with which the individual is able to cope with these problems is of concern to the administration. It is of concern because complete adjustment to the new assignment is not likely to be effected until anxieties involved in getting established are relieved.

It would be completely unrealistic to believe that school administration can help the individual to solve all of the many problems which he will encounter in the process of being inducted into the school system. Many problems must be resolved by the individual. But the school can help by a planned program of induction to minimize the kinds of difficulties which newly appointed personnel are

Table 9.1

Orientation Procedures Having Value as Reported by Superintendents, Principals, and Teachers

Orientation Procedure	Per cent of group indicating the procedure has value			
	Supt.	Prin.	Tchr.	Mean
1. Availability of pupil records to all new teachers	96	95	92	93
2. Faculty meeting at beginning of year to discuss over-all program	100	98	90	92
3. Individual conferences with principal	96	98	86	89
4. Assignment in major field of preparation only	100	88	85	87
5. Information in regard to teaching assignment for new teachers before school starts	93	90	84	86
6. Assistance in understanding the keeping of records	100	88	81	84
7. Assistance in understanding the school's method of evaluating pupil progress	92	90	82	84
8. Handbooks explaining the school policies	85	88	82	83
9. Principal's daily office hours for teacher consultation	80	90	81	83
10. Giving of information about community problems	88	85	79	81
11. Letters during the summer preceding the opening of school	100	83	77	80
12. Aid for new teachers in understanding the services rendered by the school	96	83	78	80
13. School socials for getting acquainted	96	83	78	80
14. Frequent departmental discussions	84	88	77	79
15. Group conferences with new teachers before opening of school	96	76	74	77

Table reads: 96 per cent of the superintendents, 95 per cent of the principals, and 92 per cent of the teachers say that this procedure has value for the new teacher. Of the total group 93 per cent say that this procedure has value for the new teacher.

Source: Bessie Marie Elliott, A Study Concerning the Orientation of New Teachers in the Metropolitan Area of St. Louis (St. Louis: Washington University Doctoral Dissertation, 1954), p. 71.

likely to encounter. This program, which will be discussed in the text following, is necessary not only to assure effective personnel performance, but to aid in the emotional adjustment with which every new employee is confronted. It is also necessary to provide assistance to enable the individual to become increasingly secure in his environment, and increasingly independent of administrative counsel and direction. A major goal of the program is individual self-direction.

Role of the Administrator

In assessing the administrator's role in the induction program, it will be helpful to refer to the description of the administrative process in Chapter Two. This process, it was noted, consists of the following components: (1) planning, (2) allocating, (3) influencing, (4) coordinating, and (5) appraising. These elements of administrative responsibility are useful in identifying the administrator's role in preparing plans for inducting newly appointed personnel. More specifically, he is responsible for conceptualizing the total induction process, for seeing that objectives of the induction program are established, for appraising existing induction plans, and for developing the induction program. To be clear on this matter, decisions relative to the induction process are not made personally and arbitrarily by the chief administrator. They are organizational decisions based upon board of education policy. Objectives of program, for example, stem from broad policies governing the total personnel function. In brief, responsibility of the administrator in planning to induct newly appointed personnel is not necessarily different from his responsibility for the educational program. With assistance from all operating levels, he will fix objectives, decide the kind of program which should be put into effect for achieving induction goals, assign staff responsibilities for specific program activities, coordinate staff efforts in various phases of the induction process, and appraise the effects of the program in terms of purpose.

Induction Goals for Administrative Action

It is hardly necessary to advocate or to argue here for establishment of objectives for the induction program. The great need is to convince boards of education and administrators of the efficiency of meaningful objectives. In developing goals, it must be realized that the more unified and concrete the objectives are, the more feasible will be the task of developing the total program. Induction goals commonly mentioned, and which may serve as useful guides to administrative planners are listed below:

1. The induction program should enable every newly appointed staff member to be fully informed about the community, duties and responsibilities of the position, nature of the school system, and the individual attendance unit to which the inductee will be assigned. This is tantamount to saying that one of the chief activities of the program will be that of furnishing newly appointed personnel with pertinent information to facilitate adjustment.

2. An important goal of the induction program is to make the new appointee feel, as soon as possible, that he is an integral part of the organization and the community which the school serves.

3. The ultimate aim of the induction program is to improve the quality of instruction. The induction program should provide for a continuation of efforts to determine the extent to which the man and the position are compatible, and, to determine whether the school system should accept the individual as a permanent member of the school staff.

4. An important part of the induction program is that of providing technical assistance to the newly appointed personnel. Whether it be assistance in understanding goals, or in developing attitudes and skills, the program should be designed to eliminate the possibility of teacher failure or maladjustment because he lacks assistance in his work.

5. The induction program should utilize total resources of the school, both human and material, in helping the inductee to reach a satisfying level of performance.

6. Position satisfaction and the increasing ability of new personnel to be self-directing are legitimate and practical ends of the induction program. To the extent that it is possible through administrative means, the conditions of employment should be conducive to position satisfaction and to increasing the ability of the inductee to perform at a level of efficiency which lessens the need for supervision.

In sum, the induction period, which begins during recruitment and ends when the inductee becomes a permanent member of the school staff, offers numerous opportunities for the school system to further its aims through improvement of the school staff. The next section deals with the content of induction programs.

Features of the Induction Program

An induction program is a plan for achieving induction objectives through a cycle of activities which are continuously in operation in the school system. A discussion of the features of a good induction program assumes a conviction on the part of the board of education and the school staff that a program is essential to staff development. It also assumes that the induction program is conceived to be a continuous planning responsibility. To be effective the program must be viewed as an administrative responsibility which requires a systematic approach similar to that employed in developing the school budget or the educational program.

Planning

The school system which is determined to develop a systematic program for newly appointed personnel rather than to assume a laissez-faire attitude and to let nature take its course will develop specific plans. These will include decisions as to the kinds of activities to be included in the program, definition of responsibilities for various activities, time sequence of the program, and procedures to be employed in appraising its effectiveness. Figure 16 illustrates a suggested organization for the induction of new teachers. Analysis of Figure 16 will point up some of the problems and decisions involved in program development.

Scope

The scope of the induction program will be determined by a number of factors, including past experience in personnel replacements, anticipated future need for new personnel, nature of the community, and size of the school staff. Induction problems will vary from one school system to another and the type of program developed for a given system will be the result of balanced judgment arrived at by giving due consideration to factors such as those referred to above.

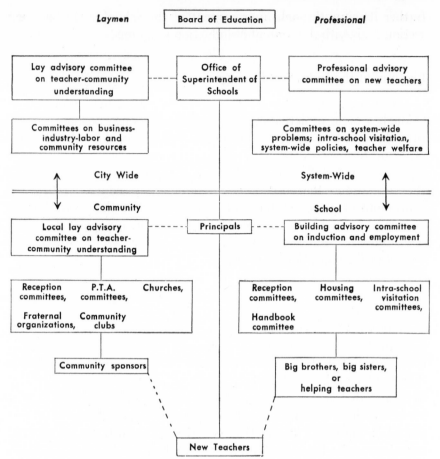

FIGURE 16 Suggested Organization for Induction of New Teachers. Glen G. Eye and Willard R. Lane, *The New Teacher Comes to School* (New York: Harper and Brothers, 1956), p. 353.

Timing of Program Activities

As noted earlier, the induction program properly begins during recruitment, and generally terminates upon completion of the probationary period. During this time span different types of induction activities will need to be undertaken to serve certain specific purposes. While these activities will be taken up in a later section, it should be noted here that the induction program will generally cover the following time span: (1) preappointment period, (2) interim period, and (3) probationary period. In order to achieve the purposes of induction, activities in the induction program will vary during each of the time sequences listed above.

Involvement

By way of illustration, it should be noted that a variety of persons and agencies are involved in the induction organization suggested in Figure 16. These include lay, professional, and building advisory committees, board of education, superintendent of schools, and various community organizations. Whatever the nature of the organization developed to implement the induction program, the relationships, duties, and responsibilities of people involved should be clearly defined.

Activities

Analysis of the goals of induction makes it apparent that a successful induction program will include activities which will enable the new appointee to: understand clearly the duties and responsibilities of the assignment; become acquainted with the community, the school system, and the school staff; develop the level of professional competence which the school system anticipates; make personal, social, and position adjustments; and deal more effectively with conditions conducive to security and satisfaction. A discussion of these activities is included in the text following.

Induction Procedures Preceding Appointment

A good induction program begins before the initial contact between the school and the applicant. It begins whenever a vacancy occurs. In announcing intention to fill the position which is vacant, the school system will have prepared a description of the position to:

1. Give direction to those responsible for recruitment and selection.

2. Make clear to the applicant the qualifications, duties, and responsibilities of the position.

3. Enable placement agencies to locate candidates who can meet the position requirements.

The school system interested in developing a good induction program should recognize that the first step involves clarification of the requirements of the position under consideration. When applicants are given false impressions of the position, the likelihood is that neither the interests of the school nor those of the applicant are served. In addition to position descriptions, it is the practice of some school systems to provide applicants with brochures describing characteristics of the community and of the school system.

The Interview

The initial interview between the school representative and the applicant provides an opportunity to furnish the latter with a variety of information which he is likely to need in making a decision to accept or reject the position.

A number of advantages flow from holding the interview in the school system. It provides the candidate with an opportunity to meet with administrative officials and school personnel, and to visit the community. If this procedure is followed, and efforts are made to furnish pertinent information needed by the applicant, a major step will have been taken to satisfy one of the goals of the induction program—that of providing the applicant with full and complete information about the position.

Induction Procedures Following Appointment

The realities of formal appointment to a position in the school system pose problems to the appointee which are different from those confronting him prior to appointment. These problems are of a nature that they can be solved most effectively with planned assistance from the school system.

Before Reporting

Certain preliminary steps can be taken by the administrator and his staff to minimize difficulties generally encountered by the appointee upon entering a new position. These include:

1. Letters of welcome from the board of education, the superintendent of schools, and the local teachers association.

2. Assignment of an experienced teacher to serve as a sponsor to the new teacher.

3. Preparation of a bulletin for teacher sponsors explaining aims of the induction program and responsibilities of sponsors.

4. Preliminary conference between sponsors and principal.

5. Conference between principal and the new appointee to discuss the latter's teaching load. The principal avoids the tendency to assign to the new teacher a heavy teaching load, behavior problems, exceptionally large classes, and other unusual assignments which make it difficult for the beginner to achieve a measure of success in the first year. The practice of making assignments, whenever possible, on the basis of teacher preference and of reducing the load of the inexperienced teacher during the first year is commendable.

6. Copies of the school handbook distributed to newly appointed personnel.

7. Inventory of living accommodations is prepared to assist newcomers in finding suitable quarters.

Activities described above highlight the importance of phasing the induction program. It is sound planning to begin the induction process prior to the time the individual assumes his responsibilities. Elimination of some of the problems of newly appointed personnel before the school term begins, such as those relating to living accommodations, assignment, and certain informational requirements, makes possible an earlier realization of their full service potential.

Before School Begins

There are numerous induction activities to be planned for new personnel for the period immediately preceding the opening of school. Among those widely used are the following:

1. *Preopening Conferences*

The preopening conference technique, which may assume a variety of forms, is universally employed in school systems. It provides opportunities to acquaint new personnel with members of the school staff and with plans and procedures which have been effected to operate the educational program. Some conferences involve the entire school staff; others are restricted to the building staff; some may be designed specifically for new personnel.

2. *Orientation to the New Position*

One of the major aims of the induction program is to help the appointee adjust readily to the new position. The building principal is generally responsible for this phase of the induction program. This involves planning sessions with the building staff to interpret plans for the coming year, acquainting new teachers with the building and site, explaining the inventory of teaching resources in the building and system, explaining plans developed for use of special facilities, such as the library and multipurpose rooms, interpreting curriculum guides and courses of study, identifying services which the principal will render to teachers, and outlining general school policies, procedures, and office routines.

3. *Orientation to the Community*

Since the work of the school and of the individual teacher is inevitably related to the life of the community, and since school personnel are in fact members of the community by virtue of their function, an investment of administrative time and effort in assuring the new teacher's acceptance into the life of the community would seem essential. Group conferences with parents of children assigned to the new teacher, receptions by the board of education, and other social activities, whether planned by the school or by community agencies, are useful means for helping the new teacher to make a satisfactory transition in the new environment.

Although the induction techniques listed above could be extended, the heterogeneity of school districts and the wide range of induction problems with which they are confronted rule out from this discussion a prescribed program to be followed. Each district should plan those induction techniques and activities best calculated to attain the goals of the program.

The Probationary Period

Responsibility for new personnel does not terminate with the opening of school. The dimensions of the induction concept range from recruitment to permanent tenure. Recruitment can improve the quality of the applicants. Selection attempts to improve the compatability of the man and the position. But until the appointee has had an opportunity to demonstrate his ability under actual conditions, and the school organization has had an opportunity to appraise the suitability of the appointee for the position, the appointment cannot be considered final. It is for this reason that the probationary period is becoming increasingly a matter of public school policy.

It is a fact that no inductee comes to the position completely trained and equipped for his new duties and responsibilities. It is also a fact that the best selection process is fallible. Administration cannot ignore its responsibility for planning and administering a follow-up program to place new personnel in assignments which will make maximum use of their abilities and will provide opportunities for personal satisfaction and professional growth.

The investment of time, money, and effort in recruiting, selecting, and inducting new personnel is considerable. The loss which the school district suffers is also considerable when the probationer's service is terminated. Since the school system is also on trial during the probationary period, a positive program of administrative services should be established to reduce the incidence of failure.

Administrative Provisions

What are the administrative responsibilities during the probationary period? The answer is that administration employs every means available, within the limits of manpower and financial resources, which will help inductees in the proper performance of their work. More specifically, this involves:

1. *Special Assistance*

An affirmative approach to the problems of the inductee assumes that although professional development is an individual process, this development can be helped when assistance is made available. This assistance may take a variety of forms. Practices commonly employed include planned consultation with supervisory officials, visits with master teachers, provision of special consultants in the individual school or on a system-wide basis, summer workshops, special library facilities, seminars for new appointees, and making available helping teachers or other forms of supervisory assistance.

2. *Appraisal*

Appraisal of the appointee's work during the probationary period is essential from the standpoint of the school and of the individual. The school is interested in knowing, for example, whether the initial placement has proved satisfactory, i.e., are the man and the position compatible? It is also interested in knowing whether his work is satisfactory, the extent and kinds of assistance needed, and what the school can do in providing assistance. It is interested ultimately in determining whether the individual should be granted permanent tenure. The individual, on the other hand, should know about his successes and shortcomings, which may proceed through a discussion of completed rating blanks or informal consultation.

3. *Adjustment*

Some of the induction activities undertaken prior to the opening of school may be extended during the probationary period to assure adjustment of the individual to the community, to his colleagues, and to his total living and working environment. Teachers who are anxious to work with church, social, and civic groups should be given encouragement and assistance in this direction. In brief, administrative efforts should be continued during the probationary period to enable the individual to become a fully adjusted, effective staff member.

The success of the school is dependent largely upon continuous development and maintenance of a competent staff. The carefully planned induction program can make a significant contribution to this end. The suggestion offered here, then, is that school administration should devise induction patterns and procedures by which newly appointed personnel can demonstrate their full potential for becoming permanent staff members. The investment in time, money, and effort is necessary not only to prevent the incompetent from gaining tenure, but to direct the growth and development of those individuals who have satisfied the administration that their retention will strengthen the school staff.

Legal Aspects of Probation

The probationary periods under state and local tenure periods are summarized in Table 9.2. Analysis of these data indicates that tenure

Table 9.2

Probationary Periods Under State and Local Tenure Provisions

State	Duration of probationary period
1	2
Alabama	3 years
Arizona	3 years
California	2 years: optional in districts with 60,000 ADA; 3 years: other districts
Colorado	3 years
Connecticut	3–6 months; Bridgeport; 3 years; Hartford, New Britain, New Haven, Stanford, Waterbury; 4 years: rest of state
Delaware	3 years
District of Columbia	2 years
Florida	3 years: state, Duval, Hillsborough, Orange, and Volusia counties
Georgia	3 years: De Kalb, Fulton, and Richmond counties
Illinois	2 years: outside Chicago; 3 years: Chicago
Indiana	5 years
Iowa	None
Kansas	3 years: Kansas City and Wichita
Kentucky	4 years [a]
Louisiana	3 years
Maryland	None: Baltimore; 2 years: outside Baltimore
Michigan	2 years
Minnesota	None: outside first-class districts; 3 years: Duluth, Minneapolis, St. Paul
Missouri	3 years: St. Louis
Montana	3 years
Nebraska	3 years: Lincoln and Omaha
New Jersey	3 years [b]
New Mexico	3 years
New York	1–3 years: outside rural districts; 5 years: rural districts
Ohio	3 years [c]
Oregon	3 years: Eugene, Portland, Salem, Klamath County, and Klamath Falls
Pennsylvania	2 years
Rhode Island	3 years
Tennessee	3 years
Washington	None
Wisconsin	3 years [d]

Source: National Education Association, Research Division, *The Teacher and the Law*, Research Monograph 1959–M3 (Washington: The Association, 1959), p. 34.

[a] Two years or less after having had tenure in another district.

[b] Unless a shorter time is fixed by the board.

[c] Three years out of the last 5, or 2 years following tenure in another district. Provisions differ for districts with fewer than 500 pupils.

[d] Two years in Milwaukee after having had tenure in another district.

laws generally require three years of probation. Four tenure laws make no provision for a probationary period. The data also indicate that probationary provisions vary considerably among the states, ranging from several months to five years. The probationary period also varies among districts within certain states. Further, some tenure laws permit the district to shorten the legal probationary period. Other tenure provisions permit extension of the probationary period under certain circumstances.

Suggested Reading

American Association of School Administrators, *Staff Relations in School Administration* (Washington: The Association, 1955).

Eastmond, Jefferson N., *The Teacher and School Administration* (Boston: Houghton Mifflin Co., 1959).

Elliott, Bessie Marie, A *Study Concerning the Orientation of New Teachers in the Metropolitan Area of St. Louis* (St. Louis: Washington University Doctoral Dissertation, 1954).

Eye, Glen G., and Willard R. Lane, *The New Teacher Comes to School* (New York: Harper & Brothers, 1956).

Heffernan, Helen, "Induction of New Teachers," *California Journal of Elementary Education*, XXVI, No. 1 (August, 1957), pp. 54–64.

Yeager, William A., *Administration and the Teacher* (New York: Harper & Brothers, 1954).

Maintaining

and Improving

Personnel Service

Development of Personnel

CHAPTER TEN

As noted earlier, this book is organized around three major areas of personnel administration. These are: determination of need, satisfaction of need, and maintaining and improving service. This chapter and the three which follow comprise Part IV. The central idea underlying Part IV is simply that personnel administration is a continuous function, one which must be carried on day in and day out, year in and year out, if the local school system expects to maintain an effective educational program. More specifically, personnel administration does not cease to function when vacancies for the ensuing year have been filled. It must concern itself with persistent problems of staff development, with appraising personnel, and with their general welfare, including health, tenure, leaves of absence, substitute service, associations, grievances, academic freedom, and retirement. Development of an administrative perspective for dealing with problems connected with the foregoing matters is emphasized throughout Part IV.

245

Dimension and Scope of Personnel Development

Definition

As considered here, development refers to provisions made by school administration to improve the performance of school personnel from initial employment to retirement. Several aspects of this definition will require further explanation in order to lend more meaning to the discussion which follows. While it is recognized that personnel can and should contribute to improving their effectiveness without administrative direction, attention in the text following will be focused upon those activities specifically planned and administered by school officials to promote the continuous improvement of personnel.

Another aspect of the definition is that development includes all school personnel—professional and noninstructional. While emphasis on the improvement of the professional staff is quite proper, the basis of the treatment which follows is total staff development.

A third aspect of the definition is that the personnel development program is aimed at three kinds of improvement: pupil achievement, instruction, and the educational program. This is to say that staff development is a means to an end, the end being improvement of the quality of pupil learning experiences. The process of facilitating the growth of personnel is necessarily related to improvement of pupil growth, and to improvement of the total educational program of which all personnel are a part.

Need for Personnel Development

The need for in-service education [1] or development has been recognized throughout the history of American education. How to correct deficiencies of the poorly trained teacher, to help the inexperienced, to keep staff members abreast of educational and social developments, and to stimulate professional growth have been perennial problems in public school administration. Numerous inventions have emerged over the years in response to the demand for staff improvement, including the reading circle, teachers' institutes, extension courses, summer schools, workshops, correspondence study, and

[1] The terms in-service education and personnel development are used interchangeably throughout this chapter.

conventions. The quest for more effective in-service education continues today, perhaps at a greater pace and in diverse directions, to provide opportunities for personnel to become and to remain professionally competent.

The concept of in-service education as a means of facilitating personnel development has never been seriously challenged. It is generally accepted, for example, that school personnel do not enter the profession as highly competent practitioners. There are differences in the extent and nature of their preservice education. Some teachers are graduates of a five-year program; others do not possess a bachelor's degree. There are differences, too, in the quality of preservice programs, which is to say that there is often little relationship between the preservice program and the actual demands of the teaching position. Thus, unevenness of teacher preparation as well as general immaturity of beginning teachers are factors which help to create the need for programs of personnel development.

Social and educational change are closely related. Expansion of knowledge in the twentieth century is so rapid, and the rate of obsolescence so swift that much of the knowledge acquired by personnel during the preservice period may be quickly outmoded. New understandings in chemistry, physics, and mathematics, for example, pose problems of educational change for the classroom teacher, as well as for the total educational program. Advances in the psychology of learning, in teaching methods, and in providing for individual differences are further examples of the need for continuous professional growth on the part of staff members in order to provide the quality of educational experiences appropriate for our times.

The current teacher shortage, critical as it is, threatens to compound the personnel problem. Many school districts have found it necessary to employ both inexperienced and unqualified teachers. The need for development programs for personnel in this category is apparent if they are to become reasonably effective in their work. While it would seem to be poor economy to spend public funds for development programs for the unqualified, instead of making the salary schedule competitive enough to attract superior personnel, some administrators are confronted with this dilemma.

The development program also helps to provide continuity in administrative leadership. The school system will exist for more years than those who serve it. The program should make possible improvement of administrators in their current assignments; it should also make available capable leadership for recurring administrative vacancies.

The development program is closely related to institutional change. The educational program, for example, is in constant need of revision to meet educational problems created by social change. In other sections of this chapter it will be noted that a carefully planned program, emphasizing continuing professional growth through cooperative staff action on the total school program, is one of the most important means for effecting school improvement.

Policies for In-Service Development of Personnel

Circumstances point to increased acceptance of in-service development of school personnel as an important and appropriate function of school administration. Prospects for further advances in the concept of staff development, and in provisions for its implementation are favorable. This trend may be attributed in part to:

1. Widespread interest in the improvement of school personnel.

2. Benefits which have been derived from development programs in education, industry, government, and the military.

3. Realization that many curriculum-instructional problems can be solved through in-service programs emphasizing cooperative staff action.

4. Demand for securing increased returns from funds expended for school personnel.

5. Unsatisfactory conditions which develop in the classroom and in the educational program when the stimulus to professional improvement is lacking.

6. The fact that pupil growth can be facilitated and enriched by teacher growth.

7. The emerging concept that school administration has an obligation to provide opportunities and assistance to the person committed to a career of service in education to enable him to derive personal and professional satisfaction from his endeavors.

Purposes of In-Service Education

Policies, programs, and appraisal of in-service education are governed by purposes. These are generally considered to be: (1) improvement of total staff competency, (2) improvement of the educational program, and (3) improvement of the competency of the individual staff member.

While the above purposes are concerned with professional personnel, there is no doubt that they can be applied equally well to noninstructional personnel. It is necessary to recognize also that the broader intent of these specific aims is to improve the quality of education at every level of the school system.

Questions of Policy

The variety of activities, personnel, and agencies which characterize a comprehensive in-service program is illustrated in Table 10.1.

Table 10.1

Elements of a Program of In-Service Education

Personnel	Activities	Agencies
School Board	School Board Institutes, Conferences (State, Local, County, Regional) Reading Material, Short Courses, Visitation, Surveys	Local School System
		Universities
		Colleges
Professional Teachers, Principals, Superintendents, Supervisors, Division and Service Department Heads	Conferences, Workshops, Special Assistance for New Teachers, Curriculum Committees, Surveys, Staff Meetings, Cooperative Study of Special Problems Involving Staff and Consultants, Graduate Work, Demonstrations, Exchange Visits, Individualized Activities, Research Projects, Extension Courses, Intervisitation.	State Education Agency
		Professional Organizations
		Community Agencies
		Intermediate Units
		School Study Councils
		Libraries
		Regional Accrediting Associations
Noninstructional Clerical, Operational, Maintenance, Service	Workshop, Institutes, Short Courses, Conferences, Lectures, Demonstrations, Reading Materials, On-the-job Instruction	Advisory Groups

One of the fallacies in the thinking of many board members and administrators about in-service programs is that they can be developed without systematic attention to policies which should govern their operation. The in-service program requires many policy decisions in order that its operation be planned and directed systematically. Since the development of personnel is as essential an administrative function as the provision of funds and facilities, or the maintaining of interrelationships with the community, its effectiveness is equally dependent upon systematc planning.

Formulation and adoption of an in-service program involves several issues or problems upon which policy decisions are required. Among the more important of these are:

1. To what extent should the local school system engage in in-service development of personnel?

2. For whom shall the program be designed?

3. How shall responsibility be allocated for initiating, directing, and appraising the program?

4. What policies are needed to ensure time, staff, facilities, and resources to stimulate and strengthen the program?

5. What studies need to be undertaken to develop the program?

6. What kinds of activities shall be included in the program?

7. What steps should be taken to guarantee that in-service needs will be provided through the budgetary process?

8. What steps should be taken to ensure program balance?

9. What provisions shall be made for continuous review of the program?

The foregoing problems point up the need for certain policy decisions by the board of education to enable the chief executive and his staff to plan and to implement the in-service program. The discussion which follows will examine the implications of these policies.

Authorization

It must be conceded that many school systems do not have genuine policies which deal broadly, constructively, and intelligently with problems of in-service education. This is due in part to the narrow concept of economy which all too frequently dominates policy makers. Many board members are not opposed in principle to a comprehensive program of personnel development; they are opposed to paying for it. Others do not comprehend the consequences of failure to establish an in-service program which will develop and maintain the kind of staff which is necessary to achieve the aims of the enterprise. These and other conditions pose a challenge to the school administrative group to convince the community, through its elected representatives, that a broadly conceived program of in-service development is essential to the growth and development of pupils; that the expenditures will produce educational returns; that failure to deal with the problem realistically leads to undesirable consequences in the form of a static school program and a staff whose competencies are never fully developed nor utilized to serve the interests of the school.

If the board of education is to fulfill its responsibility to the community to attract and to develop a competent school staff, it must commit itself in this direction. It must, in effect, make a declaration of intentions as to what it wants to happen as regards the development of personnel, what it is willing to support financially. It goes without saying that these intentions or convictions are most effective, emphatic, and capable of being implemented when crystallized in the form of written policy. Policies in writing provide the administrator and his staff with the authorization needed to plan the in-service program. They chart the direction in which the policy makers wish the administration to proceed. It is true that policy is not a panacea. While it does not produce plans and programs automatically, it creates the understructure for problem solving.

Absence of stated policy sometimes means that the chief executive can make his own policy without board interference or control. If it happens that the policy is whimsical, inconsistent, or overemphatic on a particular aspect of development, negative results can be expected. In the final analysis, personnel learn to perform their responsibilities in one way rather than another. The contention here is that staff development can be more purposeful, more meaningful, and more effective if it is determined and directed by policy.

Program Scope

The scope of the program of in-service education is directly related to objectives of the educational enterprise. A primary function of the administrator is to recruit, select, induct, and develop personnel to carry out the aims of the school. Policy should make it possible to provide whatever in-service activities are necessary to carry out this function.

The extent to which a local school district should go in formulating the in-service program is a matter of board policy. This policy will depend upon certain conditions, such as extent of in-service needs, financial ability, and the attitudes of school officials. These are known to vary from one administrative unit to another.

Policy must indicate for whom the program is to be designed. Will it be for teachers only? Or should it include administrators,

Table 10.2

Number and Per Cent of Districts Reporting Various Practices with Respect to Financing In-Service Training Activities

Kinds of Activities	FINANCED BY DISTRICT						Total Districts Using Activities
	Wholly No.	%	Partly No.	%	Not at all No.	%	
Conferences	152	46.8	46	14.1	127	39.1	325
Consultant Services	148	48.7	56	18.4	100	32.9	304
Correspondence Courses	2	3.4	1	1.7	56	94.9	59
Demonstration Teaching	98	63.6	6	3.9	50	32.5	154
Exchange Teaching	22	46.8	3	6.4	22	46.8	47
Exhibits	109	50.5	20	9.3	87	40.2	216
Experimentation	108	66.7	17	10.5	37	22.8	162
Extension or Evening Courses	6	3.5	10	5.7	158	90.8	174
Faculty Meetings	150	44.9	6	1.8	178	58.3	334
Intervisitations	146	64.9	10	4.4	69	30.7	225
Institutes	114	46.9	45	18.5	84	34.5	243
Lectures	65	52.4	25	20.2	34	27.4	124
Teacher Study Groups	104	46.8	29	13.1	89	40.1	222
Workshops	151	49.4	50	16.3	105	34.3	306
Preparation and Evaluation of Instructional Materials	123	52.1	19	8.1	94	39.8	236
Teacher Orientation Program	172	63.5	12	4.4	87	32.1	271
Radio or TV Programs	14	35.0	4	10.0	22	55.0	40
Courses Conducted by District	40	63.5	7	11.1	16	25.4	63
Other	6	66.7	1	11.1	2	22.2	9

Source: California Teachers Association, Research Bulletin 120, *District In-Service Training Programs—A Survey of Policies and Practices* (San Francisco: The Association, 1959), p. 12.

noninstructional personnel, and board members? Quite obviously, scope is an important ingredient of policy, for program planning and financing are inextricably related to it.

A clear understanding of the implications of program scope may be gained by reference to Table 10.2. These data, which illustrate in-service activities and attendant fiscal policies in selected California school districts, indicate the nature of the decisions which need to be made not only about the activities which comprise the program, but also about the extent to which each of the activities will be supported by public funds.

Responsibility

No policy statement relating to the in-service program would be complete without reference to the matter of responsibility. It is gen-

Table 10.3

Number and Per Cent of Districts Reporting Certain Individuals and Groups as Responsible for Administration of In-Service Training Program

Person or Group	General Direction of the Program		Determination of the Staff		Determination of the Scope and Content		Determination of Time Scheduling		Original Initiation of Program	
	No.	%	No.	%	No.	%	No.	%	No.	%
Superintendent	209	54.5	201	52.5	160	41.8	177	46.2	200	52.2
Associate Superintendent	7	1.8	6	1.6	8	2.1	4	1.0	10	2.6
Assistant Superintendent	79	20.6	74	19.3	67	17.5	61	15.9	47	12.3
Deputy Superintendent	7	1.8	7	1.8	6	1.6	4	1.0	3	0.8
Other Central Office Staff	65	17.0	63	16.4	81	21.1	69	18.0	38	9.9
Teacher Administrative Committee	52	13.6	61	15.9	142	37.1	104	27.1	52	13.6
Teacher Association	16	4.2	16	4.2	30	7.8	20	5.2	11	2.9
County Office	92	24.0	97	25.3	88	23.0	75	19.6	80	20.9
Principal	27	7.0	29	7.6	40	10.4	30	7.8	15	3.9
Other	17	4.4	25	6.5	31	8.1	30	7.8	13	3.4
No Response	16	4.2	36	9.4	32	8.4	34	8.9	55	14.4

Table 10.3 (continued)

Number and Per Cent of Districts Reporting Certain Individuals and Groups as Responsible for Administration of In-Service Training Program

Person or Group	RESPONSIBILITY									
	Selection or Formulation of Specific Activities		Evaluation of the Program		Determination of Requirements for Participation (when not purely voluntary)		Determination of Eligibility for Participation		Selection of Participants (where enrollment is invitational)	
	No.	%	No.	%	No.	%	No.	%	No.	%
Superintendent	138	36.0	164	42.8	211	55.1	162	42.3	120	31.3
Associate Superintendent	6	1.6	6	1.6	5	1.3	3	0.8	4	1.0
Assistant Superintendent	57	14.9	62	16.2	59	15.4	53	13.8	52	13.6
Deputy Superintendent	4	1.0	5	1.3	1	0.3	4	1.0	4	1.0
Other Central Office Staff	86	22.4	83	21.7	46	12.0	59	15.4	69	18.0
Teacher Administrative Committee	156	40.7	157	41.0	44	11.5	65	17.0	79	20.6
Teacher Association	20	5.2	35	9.1	6	1.6	8	2.1	11	2.9
County Office	83	21.7	85	22.2	22	5.7	33	8.6	46	12.0
Principal	35	9.1	32	8.4	35	9.1	31	8.1	28	7.3
Other	28	7.3	30	7.8	18	4.7	22	5.7	25	6.5
No Response	43	11.2	48	12.5	85	22.2	94	24.5	109	28.4

Source: California Teachers Association, Research Bulletin 120, *District In-Service Training Programs—A Survey of Policies and Practices* (San Francisco: The Association, 1959), p. 14.

erally accepted that responsibility for in-service development of personnel belongs to the superintendent of schools. Not only should this point be clarified by policy, but the general nature of his responsibility and that of other administrative officials involved in the program should be clearly identified. The general outline of in-service responsibilities of the chief executive include: (1) determining development needs; (2) encouraging staff participation in in-service programs; (3) establishing programs to meet immediate and long-range needs; (4) providing time, resources, and facilities to implement the program; (5) evaluating results of existing programs; (6) planning for the continuous improvement of the school staff; and (7) delegation of responsibilities to staff members involved in the administration of the program.

Responsibility for the in-service development of school personnel is a continuing obligation of the chief executive. He and his staff have the duty of translating policy to specific aims, programs, and practices, assigning its execution to staff members, and appraising outcomes. In sum, the chief executive must have unsplintered authority to make certain that the school system will be staffed today and tomorrow with personnel who will contribute maximally to the purposes of the enterprise. The contribution of the board of education to this end is the establishment of policy which gives full-scale backing to the chief executive to create imaginative approaches to the problems of in-service education. This is a prerequisite for staff improvement.

Results of a study of the responsibility for administration of in-service programs in selected California school districts appear in Table 10.3. They reveal variations in administrative practices, as well as the substantial role of the superintendent of schools in initiating, directing, and appraising in-service programs.

Background Studies

Formulation of policy to guide thinking and action about the program of in-service education necessarily involves collection and refinement of certain kinds of information. What are the immediate needs for in-service education? The long-term needs? What kinds of programs will be needed? What personnel will be involved? Will additional staff members be needed to maintain the in-service program? What are the short- and long-run financial obligations of the proposed programs? What priorities need to be established? Is it financially feasible to maintain both a competitive compensation structure and a good program of in-service development? Answers to these and related questions are prerequisite to the major and minor decisions needed to establish a course of action.

The assumption that decisions should be based on pertinent data leads logically to the idea that board policy should authorize a series of studies designed to provide a clear understanding of the various alternatives to accomplish the program objectives, as well as to indicate the advantages and limitations of each possible course of action. The economy of such systematic planning is readily apparent. A variety of short-run decisions with little or no relation to purpose or to long-run considerations is extremely uneconomical. Policies and programs for in-service development, just as for capital improvement or guidance programs, require intensive study and careful planning.

Programs

There is an intrinsic relationship between programs and policy. The chief executive, in recommending a program of in-service education to the board of education for adoption, must consider various forms and methods of staff improvement for attaining purpose. As illustrated in Table 10.4, devices now employed in the in-service program are increasing in variety and scope. The program recommended to the board by the chief executive, with the enlisted judgment of the school staff, involves selection of the most appropriate of in-service approaches from the many which now exist and which are constantly emerging. Typical of problems involved in deciding means and procedures are the following: To what extent should consultant service be used? To what extent should individualized activities, such as professional reading, extension, and summer courses be encouraged and supported? Should the school system participate in regional school board institutes? What kind of curriculum materials center is needed? Procedural considerations such as the foregoing are closely related to policy, since decisions made concerning them usually involve expenditure of public funds, determine the nature and scope of the improvement activities in which school personnel will engage, and affect the quality of the educational program. The point is that effectiveness of the personnel improvement program will depend in part upon the appropriateness of procedures employed. As will be noted in the section of this chapter devoted to programing of in-service education, planning of basic and derivative improvement programs will require more time, more imagination, and more skill on the part of administrators. The quiet revolution which is taking place in the theory and practice of staffing schools places increased emphasis upon experimentation and research in order to adapt in-service programs to changing conditions.

Table 10.4
What Administrators Do to Improve Instruction

1. Encourage teachers to use a variety of instructional techniques.
2. Involve the staff in formulating an in-service training program.
3. Utilize demonstration teaching to acquaint teachers with various teaching methods (respondents mentioned the following methods: lecture, recitation, laboratory, seminar, and project).
4. Use faculty meetings to discuss ways in which instruction might be improved.
5. Use democratic leadership methods while conducting instructional meetings (respondents stressed the avoidance of administrative domination of the meetings).
6. Conduct research projects in different subject areas and grade levels in an effort to improve instruction.
7. Devise an intra- and inter-visitation program for administrators and teachers.
8. Secure resource personnel to assist in workshops and other instructional meetings.
9. Acquire and administer standardized tests to indicate strong and weak instructional areas and individual differences.
10. Evaluate and follow up instructional workshops, conferences, and demonstration.
11. Encourage the grouping of students to provide for individual differences.
12. Obtain new equipment to make instruction in specific subject areas more meaningful.
13. Organize orientation programs to assist new teachers.
14. Suggest special instructional projects, such as science fairs, student banking programs, field trips, and job experience programs that will make subjects more lifelike and meaningful.
15. Prepare handbooks, guides, and worksheets to assist teachers in improving instruction.
16. Suggest to teachers various methods of dealing with classroom disciplinary problems (respondents mentioned the use of student courts, self-discipline, suspension, etc.).
17. Use tact in offering constructive criticism to teachers.
18. Demonstrate to teachers the effective use of audiovisual equipment.
19. Explain new instructional procedures to parents (respondents stated that this would gain parental support for the instructional program and, therefore, strengthen it).
20. Provide released time for teachers to attend instructional meetings (respondents mentioned the use of substitute teachers, holidays, etc.).
21. Provide more time for classroom instruction by relieving teachers of menial tasks (respondents suggested that menial tasks could be handled by student assistants, full-time administrative secretaries, etc.).
22. Use community facilities and resources.
23. Employ the assistance of the staff in the selection of audiovisual and other instructional equipment.
24. Allot sufficient time for observing and supervising instruction.
25. Arrange extension classes for the professional improvement of the staff.
26. Conduct follow-up studies involving graduates of the institution.
27. Discuss homework assignments with teachers.
28. Encourage the reading of professional articles and books to improve instructional techniques.
29. Encourage the use of lesson plans to improve the instructional program.
30. Follow up classroom visits with teacher conferences.
31. Lengthen class periods to improve instruction (respondents suggested 60-minute periods for secondary classes—30 minutes for recitation and 30 minutes for supervised study).
32. Pay staff members' expenses for attending professional conventions.
33. Prepare and issue agenda prior to instructional meetings.
34. Prepare devices for the evaluation of instructional aids.

Source: William T. Bush, "What Administrators Do to Improve Instruction," *Phi Delta Kappan*, XLI, No. 2 (November, 1959), p. 64.

Programs for In-Service Development of Personnel

A program, as the term is used herein, is a plan of what is to be done. It is a comprehensive plan to achieve specific objectives, based upon policy decisions which chart the broad course of administrative action. It involves determination of how the in-service program is to be carried out, selection of activities, time span, personnel involved, how the money will be spent, physical facilities required, appraisal procedures, and organization for putting the program into effect.

Program Premises

The image of an in-service program for a local school district is difficult to characterize because of the great diversity of conditions which affect formulation of the program, as well as the emerging nature of the concept of in-service development. The discussion which follows does not attempt to be prescriptive; rather, the intent is to outline features of a comprehensive program, and to offer a few guiding ideas for its implementation.

1. *Chief responsibility of school administration for the in-service program is to create both climate and opportunities for self-improvement.* Administration does not develop people; people develop themselves. Administration can do much to facilitate self-development, but the key to personal improvement is internal rather than external.

2. *Proper emphasis of the in-service program is fundamental rather than remedial.* The local school system cannot be expected to assume responsibility for a program geared to filling gaps created by inferior preservice programs. Closer working relationships between local school systems and teacher education institutions are necessary to reach a satisfactory solution to this problem. The local school system has a primary obligation to clarify the kinds of competencies needed by the personnel it employs through position analysis. Teacher education institutions, on the other hand, should strive to make preservice programs more effective. A major portion of the in-service program could then be focused upon solution of curriculum-instructional problems.

3. *Programs of in-service education in schools have as their primary purpose improvement of both the quality of the educational*

program and the competency of the total staff. Continuous growth of school personnel is important, and opportunities to meet this need should be included in the design of the in-service program. But there are other kinds of growth which in-service education seeks. Growth in ability to work as a member of a group, in social skills, and in ability to shoulder professional responsibilities are examples of outcomes as necessary as academic proficiency. One of the advantages of gearing in-service education to the study of curriculum-instructional problems is the opportunities provided for individual and staff growth, as well as for betterment of the educational program.

4. *Supervision, in-service education, and curriculum development are intrinsically related.* The symbolic figure on which our extensive educative effort is centered is the educated man. It represents the purpose for which the school system organizes contributing instrumentalities—manpower, materials, methods, and money. It is also the *raison d'etre* for in-service education, supervision, and curriculum development—three major functions in the program for the improvement of instruction. Spears, in commenting on the integrity of these three administrative approaches to instructional improvement, notes that:

> The in-service program cannot be separated either in spirit or function from curriculum planning and supervision, the three representing overlapping features of the program for instructional improvement.
>
> It is fair enough to conclude that the in-service training program blankets in the other two, curriculum planning and supervision; it represents the entire organized effort of a school system to assure teachers' growth on the job. For its activity, its things to do, it draws especially upon the improvement of the instructional program—curriculum planning. Since much of the time of supervisors is directed toward this same goal, the in-service movement has likewise commandeered the effort of supervision.
>
> It is impossible to conceive an in-service program existing in a school system without curriculum study as its common carrier. Deprived of curriculum improvement in the classrooms of the participating teachers, inschool growth would become an individual matter, and the effort would be diffused into a miscellany of disconnected activities that are followed by teachers as individuals. The in-service idea secures its quality in the organization of teacher effort toward a common goal.[2]

[2] Harold Spears, *Curriculum Planning Through In-Service Programs* (Englewood Cliffs, N.J.: Prentice-Hall, Inc., 1957), pp. 43–44, 315.

The close relationship among the three functions under consideration requires particular attention by the administrative staff to make certain that all organized improvement efforts are unified and coordinated for the purpose of making the teaching-learning process more effective. When any of the functions becomes an appendage of the other, the total program for the improvement of instruction tends to become inoperative.

5. *Relationships and functions of personnel responsible for coordinating and implementing the in-service program are clearly defined.* One of the most difficult problems in implementing an in-service program is the matter of staff organization. As a matter of organizational principle, the in-service program should not be divorced from the system-wide program for the improvement of instruction. Stated another way, the in-service program should be conducted within the regular administrative framework established for coordinating and implementing the over-all instructional program. Figure 17 illustrates the administrative plan in operation in the Wilmington, Delaware, Public Schools for developing the in-service education program.

Acceptance of the foregoing premise, however, does not relieve the administration of the necessity for clarifying the nature of the program to be undertaken, who is to be responsible for initiating, implementing, and appraising the various activities which comprise the program, what the relationships are to be among the personnel to whom responsibilities have been delegated.

Experience suggests that the foregoing problems are not solved easily. In-service organizational patterns are exceedingly diverse, due in part to the varying nature of school administrative units. The in-service organization for schools responsible to the intermediate administrative unit, for example, generally differs from that of large city school systems.

From the premise that in-service education can best be promoted through improvement of the educational program, the broad outlines of the in-service organization can be deduced. Certain curriculum-instructional problems will need to be attacked on a system-wide basis, others at the individual building level. In some cases the system-wide program forms the basis for many in-service activities at the building level.

FIGURE 17 Responsibility, function, and duties of the committee on professional growth, Wilmington, Delaware, Public Schools.

COMMITTEE ON
PROFESSIONAL GROWTH
Chairman: Superintendent
Secretary: Director of Personnel

MEMBERSHIP:
Ex officio
Director of Elementary Education
Directory of Secondary Education
Director of Vocational Education
Director of Child Development
and Guidance

Elected for one year
2 from supervisors' group
1 each from food service, maintenance, clerical and department chairman groups
3 principals: 1 elementary, 1 senior high, 1 junior high
1 classroom teacher from each building or group under one principal

Executive Committee
All members ex officio
4 elected from membership for one year

Reorganization scheduled for October of each year

RESPONSIBILITY:
The Committee on Professional Growth is directly responsible to the Superintendent and reports only to him.

FUNCTION:
The development of a program of in-service training designed to increase the professional competency of the staff.

DUTIES:
1 Survey the professional activities in operation in the schools in order to discover the needs and interests of all personnel.
2 Plan and administer a program of inservice training which will meet the needs and interests of all personnel in individual schools, on a city-wide basis or for the individual teacher.
3 Recommend the program to be approved and the budget appropriation necessary to finance it.
4 Provide the stimulation necessary for the exchange of ideas and for the development of new projects whose activities will supplement and challenge the thinking of all groups.
5 Cooperate with the director of personnel in the approval of the inservice training program directly related to salary increments.

Source: Wilmington Public Schools, *Administrative Organization and Functions* (Wilmington, Delaware: Board of Education, 1961), p. 30.

Results of a study of organizational patterns for in-service education programs in selected Texas schools are reported in Table 10.5. These data indicate that the most common type of organization for in-service programs for the schools under consideration is the subject area. Most of the suggested organizational patterns were used by a majority of the school systems.

Table 10.5

Organizational Patterns for In-Service Education Programs

Type of Organizational Pattern	Number of School Systems
System-wide	44
Building faculty	40
Subject area	56
Special interest group	37
Grade level	44
Child study	11

Source: The West Texas School Study Council, *A Look at Curriculum Practices and Trends in Public Schools* (Lubbock: The Council, 1959), p. 60.

Whatever the nature of the in-service program decided upon, and whatever types of organizational patterns are employed to implement the program, attention should be given by school administration to allocation of responsibilities among central office and building unit personnel. The contribution of the organization to the success of the in-service program will be more effective, and administration of it considerably simplified if the interrelationships of the superintendent, assistant superintendent for instruction, supervisors, coordinators, directors, principals, department heads, consultants, and committees are clarified.

Programs for Classroom Personnel

Whether major responsibility for initiating and maintaining the in-service program is allocated to central office personnel, the building unit, a teacher-administrative committee, or an intermediate administrative unit, a major task is to determine the kinds of in-service education problems which are most significant. While it is true that no school system has ever had a shortage of problems, the success of the program depends upon identification of those problems which have significance for the personnel involved in their solution. Clues to in-service problems come from a number of sources, such as appraisals of the staff and of the educational programs, interviews, complaints, reports of accrediting associations, opinion polls, and suggestions from the teaching staff.

In-Service Activities

Activities which comprise the in-service program for classroom teachers are numerous and varied. They are aimed at improvement of both the educational program and the general ability of each staff member to function effectively in his current position assignment. They involve individual and cooperative effort. They are directed toward helping teachers solve persistent problems such as are illustrated below:

1. To develop skill in individualizing classroom instruction.

2. To acquire a mastery of the subject matter for which the teacher is responsible.

3. To understand and acquire skill in using modern classroom techniques.

4. To acquire ability in the use and interpretation of devices for appraising pupil growth.

5. To provide instructional leadership and to maintain control of the classroom.

6. To develop an understanding of the function of education in a society, its relations to the social, economic, and governmental structures.

7. To recognize weaknesses in the educational program and to participate with other staff members in studying means for effecting improvements.

8. To work with other teachers to provide continuity in learning experiences of children and youth.

9. To help the school system to develop meaningful educational objectives.

10. To participate in the solution of problems which are of common concern to staff personnel.

Avenues for encouraging growth in these areas may take the form of workshops, group conferences, teachers' meetings, visitation, exchange teaching, intervisitation, professional writing, graduate work, participation in the evaluation of a school program, preparation of a course of study, participation in experimental programs, and in system-wide planning for improving the educational program. These and other approaches have been effective in the conduct of in-service programs. When backed by leadership and resources, there is reason to believe that in-service programs are a school system's best insurance against professional inactivity and deterioration.

Motivation of Teachers

One of the most difficult administrative aspects of the in-service program is to secure maximum staff participation. As the conviction of the worth of in-service education has increased, there has been a tendency on the part of administrators to extend the opportunities for professional growth and to devise various arrangements for wider staff involvement. The financial incentive, a proven stimulus to action, has been used frequently to promote participation in professional activities. Among the plans for relating financial and personal incentives to in-service participation are the following:

1. Relating in-service requirements to the salary schedule. Many such plans require evidence of professional improvement as a basis for eligibility to further salary increments. Equivalent credit for specified types of in-service activities is sometimes granted in lieu of college credits.

2. Teachers are paid a stipend for writing courses of study.

3. Tuition for graduate work is paid from public funds.

4. Expenses for attending workshops, conferences, and similar professional meetings are paid by the local school system.

5. Remuneration for attendance at local or regional in-service activities.

6. District increases annual salary by one-tenth every three years for participation in specified activities.

7. Promotion to administrative or supervisory positions based upon outstanding contribution to in-service program.

8. According tenure to probationary teachers who have participated successfully in the in-service program.

Money is indeed important for motivational purposes, but it is no substitute for administrative leadership. The design of the in-service program, for example, has a considerable effect on its ability to provide experiences which are conducive to staff improvement. There is general agreement that programs are most likely to be effective when:

1. Teachers participate in the planning process.
2. Problems are of significance to those who participate.
3. Released time is provided.
4. Resources are available, including consultants, facilities, and funds.
5. The budgetary process is fully utilized to project the immediate and long-term program needs.
6. Experimentation and invention are encouraged.
7. Individual, building, and system activities are related in such a way as to promote both professional growth and improvement of the educational program.
8. Administrative provisions for professional growth are extensive.
9. The climate for improvement is positive.

Variation among local school systems precludes the idea that what constitutes a suitable program of in-service education is at all places and at all times the same. The kind of plan which will be most effective in a given school system depends upon continuous planning, experimentation, and refinement of procedures based upon appraisal of results achieved. This approach will minimize uncritical imitation, a tendency which emphasizes the fashionable rather than the applicable.

Programs for Administrators

In-Service Education of Administrators Essential

The array of crucial problems confronting modern public education such as mounting enrollments, shortages of competent personnel, increasing competition for the tax dollar, the impact of accelerated social change upon the educational program, resistance to social integration, and the demands of special interest groups calls for a high order of leadership in school administration. Whether the administrator be a superintendent, principal, or staff member related to either office, the scope of his functions is wide and demanding in personal, professional, and leadership qualities. As in the case of the classroom teacher, the preservice program cannot possibly provide all of the experience necessary to effective on-the-job performance. Further, the changing demands of school administration makes necessary the continuing professional growth of administrators during their total period of service.

The Board and Administrative Development

It can be stated without reservation that no effective program of in-service development for administrators is possible without the understanding, cooperation, and support of school boards and citizens. They must understand, first and foremost, that there is a close relationship between professional improvement and improvement of educational opportunities within the local school system. An equally important understanding is that in-service programs require financial support. Professional leave policies, travel, participation in cooperative studies of administrative problems, and other program activities mean public expenditures and board sanction. A third awareness needed by boards and citizens is that policies are necessary to encourage the continuous professional development of its chief executive and administrative staff. The point of this statement is that without some sort of enabling rules, administration is hardly in a position to develop a thoroughgoing program. Clarification of the program can best be achieved through a sound budgetary process, where the responsibility for developing plans is lodged with the superintendent and his administrative staff. Board and citizen appraisal of plans, as expressed in the budget, leading to formal budget approval, would, in effect, establish policy and give direction to the program.

Practices and Resources

An illustration of practices and resources for the continued professional development of school administrators is shown in Figure 18. One of the important observations which can be gained from analysis of Figure 18 is that the most productive type of in-service program is one which involves the active participation of a variety of interrelated agencies and institutions, such as professional schools and associations, state education agencies, administrators, and local school systems. The cooperative activities of these groups provide avenues not only for the solution of educational problems, but for

RESOURCES

PRACTICES	Professional School	Professional Association	State Education Department	School Boards Association	Local School District	Individuals	Other
RESEARCH	do	finance	do and finance	finance	finance and use	do	foundations
WORKSHOPS	do	encourage	consultation	encourage and finance	do and finance	participate	
CLINICS	do	encourage and finance	consultation	encourage and finance	finance and participate	use	
SCHOOL STUDY COUNCILS	services and consultation	encourage	consultation	encourage and finance	finance and participate	participate	
COURSES	do	encourage	encourage	encourage	finance	do	
CONSULTATION	do	do	do	encourage	finance	use	
PROFESSIONAL LEAVE POLICY	encourage	encourage	encourage and finance	encourage	finance	use	
TRAVEL	encourage	encourage	encourage	encourage	encourage and finance	do	Fulbright, foundations, etc.
PERSONNEL PRACTICES	consultation	consultation	consultation	encourage	develop	participate	best practices in business and industry

FIGURE 18 Practices and resources for continued development of administrators.

From the Cooperative Development of Public School Adminsitration in New York State, *Toward the Improved Preparation of Administrators in the Public Schools*, Resource Manual 2 (Albany: State Education Department, 1954), p. 25.

the growth and development of school administrators as well. The suggestions contained in Figure 18, it should be noted, augment the traditional developmental activities which are generally individualized, such as reading, writing educational articles or books, and serving as an instructor in college courses.

It is worth noting that efforts to provide opportunities for the improvement of school administrators are widespread and radiate in many directions. Professional associations, universities, state departments, intermediate units, and school study councils are continuously, but separately, attempting to better the quality of school administrators. These efforts are often uncoordinated, resulting in neglect of administrators in certain areas of a state, or in failure to provide a single, comprehensive program to meet varying developmental needs. Further exploration of means for coordinating the total efforts of all agencies and institutions interested in the in-service education of administrators should lead to identification and clarification of functions which each group can best accomplish.

One of the major concerns of the local school system lies in the development of a realistic in-service program for principals and supervisory personnel, since they constitute a majority of the administrative staff. Criticisms of existing in-service programs for principals and supervisors point generally to the lack of well-planned programs and to the absence of realism in program activities. Urging principals to garner additional college credits, to attend conventions, and to write articles for professional journals does not add up to a challenging in-service program. A strong defense can be made for an in-service program which is developed locally, which clearly identifies problems of vital concern to principals, which is supported by funds to secure appropriate consultant services, and which constantly employs a variety of techniques to further the professional growth and development of the participants.[3]

Programs for Noninstructional Personnel

Personnel development is an essential function of school administration. Until recent years, however, this task has been narrowly

---

[3] For a detailed discussion of in-service programs for school principals see: Kenneth E. McIntyre, *Selection and On-the-Job Training of School Principals* (Austin: University of Texas, 1960), Chapter IV.

conceived. In-service education programs, for example, have been focused almost exclusively on professional personnel, despite the fact that every school system employs noninstructional personnel, depends upon them for the performance of business and clerical services, operation and maintenance of the school plant, preparation of food, and transportation of children to and from school. In the catalogue of arguments advanced in support of training programs for noninstructional personnel, the following are worthy of emphasis:

1. Training of noninstructional personnel is inevitable in every school system, whether by formal or informal means, by plan or by chance, and whether effective or ineffective. The newcomer must learn what to do and how to do it. The experienced employee must learn to do better the work for which he is responsible. Training which is essential can be improved if it is conceived as a part of overall personnel policy.

2. Training makes the difference between operating efficiency and inefficiency.

3. Noninstructional personnel contribute to realization of the educational program.

4. Machines, tools, and building equipment operated by noninstructional personnel are becoming increasingly numerous and complex, and require more extensive training.

5. Personnel incompetency is a violation of the principle that full value should be received for each tax dollar expended. Money wasted on incompetent personnel reduces the funds available for the support of the educational program.

Planning Decisions

Since effectiveness of noninstructional personnel contributes to realization of the educational program, the design, development, and maintenance of plans for improving the competency of these employees become an important facet of the personnel function.

Through application of principles developed in this and other chapters for the continuing improvement of personnel, there is reason to believe that the services under consideration can be measurably improved. Among the major problems involved in developing a training program for noninstructional personnel are the following:

1. What are the general and specific objectives of the program?
2. What personnel shall participate?
3. What kinds of training are needed?
4. How are the training needs to be identified?
5. Who shall train?
6. What methods of instruction shall be used?
7. What shall be the content of the training program?
8. What shall be the length of the training program?
9. When shall the training be given?
10. What are the program budgetary requirements?
11. What shall be the organization for administering the program?
12. What administrative policies are necessary to initiate and to maintain the program?
13. What arrangements shall be made for appraising the program?

Since many of these problems have been analyzed in detail in other texts, the brief review provided below is designed to illustrate the relationship between policy decisions and the program for improvement of noninstructional personnel.

Essential to the improvement program under consideration is the necessity for its being recognized and supported as a matter of board personnel policy. Unless and until noninstructional employees are considered as members of the school personnel team, and this consideration is recognized through clearly established policy, a thoroughgoing training program is inconceivable.

Organization

Organization for the training program of noninstructional personnel raises familiar questions of allocation of responsibility and authority. The central administrative staff, as always, is responsible for initiating, planning, coordinating, and appraising the training program. But the central staff will not conduct all the training; much of it will be delegated to subordinate supervisors, such as the assistant superintendent in charge of facilities, or clerical, cafeteria, and transportation supervisors. The central office can assist in the over-all training programs. This includes helping administrators in charge of noninstructional personnel to: (1) appraise training needs; (2) become acquainted with on-the-job training techniques, such as conducting conferences, workshops, and demonstrations; (3) develop plans to enable noninstructional personnel to become increasingly aware of job requirements and the anticipated levels of performance effectiveness; (4) engage in continuous study of methods and procedures for simplifying noninstructional tasks; (5) find time, funds, facilities, and personnel to implement the training program; (6) appraise the effectiveness of the training program and revise it periodically in light of the findings derived from continuous study.

Ultimate responsibility for the training program must rest with the chief executive, though many duties are delegated to subordinates. He is, in effect, chief instructional agent for the total improvement program.

Types of Training Programs

Types of training programs referred to below are those for which the board of education assumes responsibility. These may be categorized as either preservice or in-service. The former type is generally provided for prospective employees prior to employment; the latter may be provided after employment but prior to a specific assignment, after assignment, or both. The kinds of programs developed depend in part upon the number of employees, types of training requirements, and availability of resources for conducting the program. Larger school systems generally find it advantageous to conduct their own training programs, especially when the services of local staff members can be utilized, and can be augmented by training personnel from agencies in nearby urban centers. Small schools, on the other hand, often depend upon such agencies as the intermediate unit, school study councils, or cooperative arrangements with other districts to provide training programs.

Resources

There are various agencies whose services can be utilized in the conduct of the training program. These include colleges and universities, state and federal agencies, national professional organizations, and commercial organizations. Decisions governing the training resources to be used from within and outside of the school system require analyses of training needs and priorities. This will facilitate the process of deciding how resources of the foregoing agencies can be utilized effectively and appropriately in the training program.

Methods

As the list in Table 10.6 makes clear, the variety of training methods which may be employed both on-and-off the job is extensive. The key problem is to select those specific techniques which are most appropriate for the training needs which have been established by a thoroughgoing training survey.

Table 10.6

**Types of Training Methods Employed in Programs for
Noninstructional Personnel**

Type	Example
Demonstrations:	Use of power equipment for cleaning floors, mowing lawns, and snow removal
Short Courses:	Care and cleaning of buildings, operation of vehicles
Inspection:	Operation of a central warehouse or cafeteria
Courses:	Use of business machines for school accounting
Seminars:	The conduct of workshops and conferences
Lectures:	Orienting new personnel to job assignments
Laboratory:	Techniques of mass feeding; testing school supplies
Instruction:	Supervised instruction for those new to an assignment, including rotation of assignments
Conferences:	Safety education for bus drivers
College Courses:	To enable supervisory personnel to meet changing certification requirements

The foregoing illustrations, which are largely group-centered, are not indicative of the entire range of training possibilities. Individual instruction, both on-and-off the job, including extension and correspondence courses, reading, and apprenticeship plans are additional avenues for extending the scope of the program.

Not a great deal of evidence can be derived from existing research to indicate the comparative effectiveness of the various types of training methods. Training results depend upon many factors, especially the quality of planning devoted to the training program, the caliber of the trainees, and the competency of personnel in charge of the operation.

The substance of what has been said and implied in the foregoing paragraphs adds up to something like this: satisfactory service to implement the educational program depends upon improvement of noninstructional personnel, as well as the people by whom they are directly supervised. It depends also upon a systematic training program for all noninstructional personnel, which utilizes a variety of available resources and methods, is given full-scale backing by board of educational policies, is placed under unit control with the chief executive responsible for administering the program, and is organized in such fashion that administrative and supervisory relationships are clearly understood.

Programs for Board Members

Public education in the fifty states, as indicated in Table 10.7, is an extensive operation involving basic administrative units ranging from one-teacher rural schools to large metropolitan systems, serving

Table 10.7

Highlights of the Public School Enterprise, 1959–60 and 1960–61

Elements	*1959–60*	*1960–61*
Basic administrative units	40,148	37,153
Board members in basic units	175,630	166,820
Superintendents in basic units	13,440	13,392
Pupil enrollment	36,037,937	37,244,284
Instructional staff	1,464,930	1,526,079
Total receipts (billions)	16.5	17.6
Total expenditures (billions)	15.2	16.4

Source: National Education Association, Research Division, Research Report 1960–R15, *Estimates of School Statistics, 1960–61* (Washington: The Association, 1960), p. 5.

more than 37 million pupils. Policy determination and general supervision over local district operations rests with local boards of education, made up of appointed or elected lay persons.

Effective performance of board of education functions means that persons who serve in this capacity must understand, among other things, the role of the school in American society, as well as the role of the local board of education as a lay planning and appraising body. The shifting composition of school board membership is such that few members are prepared initially, or remain in office long enough to be able to cope with the many problems with which they are continuously confronted. Yet, for all the criticism which has been leveled at boards of education, it is generally recognized as a sound device for carrying out the local education function. It is also acknowledged that if boards of education, which are continuing bodies, are to operate at maximum efficiency, measures are needed which will increase both their understanding of school problems and their effectiveness as decision makers.

Problem Areas

Of the many problems which arise in connection with school board membership, the following appear to be continuously perplexing:

1. How to acquaint new board members with their duties and responsibilities.

2. How to develop harmony and team spirit within a board.

3. How to help board members to understand the difference between the legislative and executive functions.

4. How to get board members to develop and adhere to written policies.

5. How to help boards learn what good schools are and what they can do.

6. How to provide board members with useful information about their schools.

7. How to acquaint board members with the finance, program, plant, and personnel functions.

8. How to help boards interpret the role and needs of the school to the community.

9. How to help board members take an interest in the improvement of education at the local, state, and national level.

10. How to develop effective board-superintendent relations.

11. How boards work with lay advisory committees.

The points listed above are not new. They represent the kinds of troublesome problems which confront most boards and board members, and which, if they are to be minimized, require positive action.

Improving the Effectiveness of Board Members

It is well to recognize that problems of boards and board membership are recurring. The changing composition of these bodies, as well as the omnipresent issues in public education, calls for planned and directed experiences which will be helpful in the development of responsible leadership.

Problems involved in helping board members to perform their functions effectively are difficult. Participation in improvement activities is not only voluntary but limited because of the inability of many members to devote substantial amounts of time to this purpose. Studies [4] of this problem indicate there is a great wealth of ideas for the practical and effective development of school board members, but the number of school systems utilizing these ideas is limited. Space permits only a brief summary here of some of the practices used by boards to learn about good schools. These are listed in Table 10.8. The wide variety of practices and procedures available is such

Table 10.8

Practices for Improving the Effectiveness of Boards of Education

Board members participate in the activities of national and state school board associations.

Board members are furnished a variety of pertinent reading material, including books, pamphlets, journals, and research studies.

The professional library of the local school system contains materials sufficient to meet the informational needs of board members.

Board members engage in interschool visitation.

State education agencies provide opportunities for board members to learn more about their functions and how they can be performed more effectively.

Universities cooperate with local school districts in providing a variety of experiences designed to improve the ability of board members to deal with educational problems.

Provisions are made for board members to participate in clinics, workshops, and institutes.

Board members are provided with descriptions of outstanding educational practices.

The board of education engages consultants to assist it in the solution of specific educational problems.

Provisions are made to acquaint new members with the purposes, practices, problems, and potentialities of public schools.

Boards continually study ways of establishing and maintaining effective policies.

[4] See Daniel R. Davies and Ellwood Prestwood, *Practical School Board Procedures* (New York: Chartwell House, Inc., 1951).

that any school system can provide a development program if it wishes to do so. With so much riding on the decisions made by boards of education, efforts to prepare them better for the task appear to be eminently worthwhile.

Suggested Reading

American Council on Education, *College and University Business Administration*, Vol., 2 (Washington: The Council, 1955), p. 88.

Committee on Employee Training in the Public Service, *Employee Training in the Public Service* (Chicago: Civil Service Assembly, 1941), pp. 67–68.

Davies, Daniel R., and Ellwood L. Prestwood, *Practical School Board Procedures* (New York: Chartwell House, Inc., 1951).

Douglas, Harl R., *Modern Administration of Secondary Schools* (Boston: Ginn & Co., 1954), p. 109.

Hunt, Herold C., and Paul R. Pierce, *The Practice of School Administration* (Boston: Houghton Mifflin Co., 1958), p. 319.

The International City Managers' Association, *Municipal Personnel Administration*, 6th ed. (Chicago: The Association, 1960).

Koontz, Harold, and Cyril O'Donnell, *Principles of Management* (New York: McGraw-Hill Book Co., 1955), pp. 435–436.

McIntyre, Kenneth E., *Selection and On-the-Job Training of School Principals* (Austin: University of Texas Press, 1960).

Moore, Harold E., and Newell B. Walters, *Personnel Administration in Education* (New York: Harper & Brothers, 1955).

National Society for the Study of Education, Part I, Fifty-Sixth Yearbook, *In-Service Education for Teachers, Supervisors, and Administrators* (Chicago: University of Chicago Press, 1957).

Spears, Harold, *Curriculum Planning Through In-Service Programs* (Englewood Cliffs, N.J.: Prentice-Hall, Inc., 1957).

Tuttle, Edward M., *School Board Leadership in America* (Danville, Ill.: The Interstate Printers and Publishers, 1958).

The University of the State of New York, *Operation and Maintenance*, School Business Management Handbook No. 7 (Albany: The State Education Department, 1955).

Wiles, Kimball, *Supervision for Better Schools*, 2nd ed. (Englewood Cliffs, N.J.: Prentice-Hall, Inc., 1955).

Yeager, William A., *Administration of the Noninstructional Personnel and Services* (New York: Harper & Brothers, 1959).

Appraisal of Personnel

CHAPTER ELEVEN

The discussion which follows identifies and analyzes the nature and function of appraisal as it applies to personnel administration. The chapter is divided into two problem areas: (1) appraisal of the general personnel function, and (2) appraisal of personnel performance. The former approach is macroscopic in that it views appraisal of the personnel function at large; the latter miscroscopic in the sense that attention is focused on an important and complex appraisal problem—personnel performance.

Meaning of Appraisal

"Appraisal" is one of those terms which is both fashionable and controversial. In the lexicon of the classroom teacher it often becomes synonymous with "merit rating." As such, the concept has acquired negative implications. Mere mention of the word is suggestive of a device to determine the financial worth of the employees' service to the school district. This state of affairs has tended to obscure the broader meaning of appraisal and its function in school administration.

A Major Function of the Administrative Process

Appraisal,[1] as the term is used herein, refers to one of the major functions of the administrative process. In the cyclic activity of the administrative process plans are developed and put into operation. Appraisal is concerned with the effects of the plans and procedures in relation to attainment of organizational purpose.

Each component of the educational operation—plans, programs, personnel, plant, funds—is a means for attainment of purpose. Each has a purpose subsidiary to, but essential in, realization of the general aim of the school system. Hence, each component of the administrative process should be appraised continually in terms of (1) its operational effectiveness, and (2) its contribution to the larger aims of the enterprise. The school plant, for example, is appraised to determine its suitability to house the educational program, its capabilities for future use, its present utility and economy of operation, as well as its ability to contribute to educational results desired. The recruitment program is judged in terms of its success in attracting qualified and competent personnel. Thus viewed, appraisal is an omnipresent function of school administration, an aspect of the administrative process which seeks to keep means and ends in balance. It is concerned with the extent to which and how well organizational purposes are achieved, as well as the effect of each operational activity upon the general aims of the school. It is a useful step in developing a framework for analyzing problems of and planning solutions for both individual and total operations.

Why the Personnel Function Should Be Appraised

Appraisal attempts to determine effects of plans, policies, procedures, and programs in terms of organizational purpose. Since attainment of aims depends so heavily upon human effort, judgments of this effort and the conditions related to it are inevitable.

Knowledge of effects of personnel effort, and of action taken to maintain and to improve it, is useful not only to the board and to the administration, but to the personnel who are making the effort and to the community which must make decisions concerning the scope and support of school operations.

[1] Appraisal and evaluation are used interchangeably throughout the text

Appraisal helps the board and administration to determine, for example, whether the personnel recruitment program is attracting competencies needed to staff the school program, whether the selection process is conducive to staff quality, and whether the program of in-service education is helping to improve both personnel and program.

Certainly the community and school personnel have an interest in appraisal. Contraction or expansion of the educational program is, in the final analysis, a financial decision which rests with the citizenry. Support which administration requests for its program ought to be based upon defensible needs, needs which are determined by careful appraisal. No one knows better than the modern school administrator that people do appraise their schools, quite often voluntarily. A positive appraisal program which is utilized to inform the community of the status and needs of the school system is an inherent administrative necessity, as well as an effective means for neutralizing rumors and unfounded criticisms.

Appraisal of the individual school employee is vital to improvement of his performance. It is inevitable if his strengths and weaknesses are to be identified, and if he is to be given constructive counsel as to steps to be taken to improve his performance.

Whether appraisal in a school system goes on consciously or unconsciously, formally or informally, methodically or unsystematically, it does go on, day by day. It will go on better, however, if the significance of appraisal is recognized, if accepted as a necessary function of the administrative process, and if particular attention is paid to problems created by its use.

What Areas of the Personnel Function Should Be Appraised?

Essential Questions

The personnel function in a school system is primarily concerned with (1) attracting, developing, retaining, and motivating personnel needed to attain the aims of the enterprise, and (2) creating the conditions and climate conducive to these ends. In order to determine how well the personnel function is carried out in a given school system, a number of factors need to be analyzed. Among essential questions to be dealt with are the following:

1. To what extent does the personnel program contribute to improvement of instruction?

2. Are the personnel goals of the school system designed to achieve its larger purposes?

3. Is the school system attracting personnel needed to staff the school system?

4. Are the quantity and quality of personnel satisfactory?

5. Is the compensation structure planned to attract and retain qualified personnel?

6. Is the recruitment program effective?

7. How well does the selection process function?

8. Does the personnel program provide extensive and appropriate opportunities for individual and staff growth?

9. Does the supervisory program enable personnel to do their best work?

10. Are the provisions for working conditions, benefits, security, opportunity, individual growth, and personal recognition satisfactory?

The answer to each will help to shed light upon the nature of the personnel program, call attention to variation in practice and theory, and provide information to serve as a basis for future planning. It will aid in judging how well the total personnel function is being conducted, and to what extent it contributes to organization purpose. As such, it may be looked upon as the galvanism of change, since it provides the means for analyzing existing personnel provisions in relation to a conceptual framework—a body of principles to guide the formulation, implementation, maintenance, and adjustment of personnel policies.

Who Appraises the Personnel Program?

Organizational Responsibility

If there is validity to the contention that performance of professional personnel is the prime determinant of the quality of American education, it would seem to follow that the school personnel program is everybody's business. The board of education, its executive officer and staff, organizational personnel, and the community at large have a responsibility for appraising personnel provisions and their effects upon the educational program. Moehlman has exemplified this concept in Figure 19. If this illustration is extended in terms of the agents, activities, and means, the concept of total organizational re-

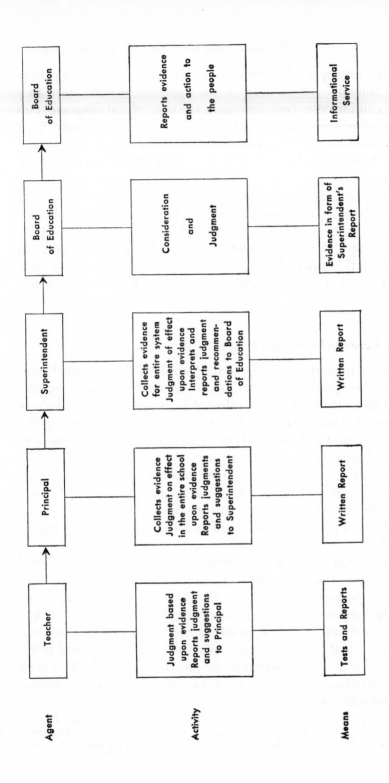

FIGURE 19 Appraising the Results of an Activity

Source: Arthur B. Moehlman, *School Administration*, 2nd ed. (Boston: Houghton Mifflin Co., 1957), p. 260.

sponsibility for appraisal becomes apparent. Noninstructional personnel, for example, are included in the appraisal process, since they must be considered as contributors to the educational program. This same line of reasoning holds for the citizens of the community, for it is they who ultimately have considerable influence upon the amount of funds to be spent for education in relation to the total needs of government.

In addition to appraisal agents within the school organization, the role of external agents should be noted. These include outside consultants, accrediting agencies, the state education agency, and citizen advisory groups. How these resources can be organized and employed effectively in the appraisal process presents major administrative problems, a discussion of which will be found in a later section of this chapter.

How the Personnel Function Is Appraised

It can be understood readily that appraisal of the personnel function, like the appraisal of other administrative functions, may take a variety of forms. It may be conducted by personnel from within or outside of the school system, or by a combination of both, such as the school staff and a citizens' advisory group. It may be continuous or periodic, planned or in response to pressures, system-wide or building level, focused on a single problem or the entire range of personnel considerations. It may involve few or many persons. It may be used to determine the status of personnel provisions, to assess the operational effects of policies, or to identify ways by which changes can be effected.[2]

The appraisal process is continuous, cyclical. It is initiated when a plan is put into operation, such as an in-service program, to achieve a particular purpose. Effects of the plan are analyzed, interpreted, recorded, and appraised. Effectiveness of the plan is judged in terms of outcomes achieved, i.e., pupil growth, staff growth, program improvement. The extent to which present plans deviate from desired objectives is reviewed, and reasons for the differences studied. The cycle begins again when the action needed is decided upon, and the revised plan is put into operation.

[2] Guidelines for conducting the appraisal of a school or a school system are discussed in Edgar L. Morphet, R. L. Johns, and Theodore L. Reller, *Educational Administration: Concepts, Practices, and Issues* (Englewood Cliffs, N. J.: Prentice-Hall, Inc., 1959), Chapter 23.

The process of appraising the personnel function can be maintained effectively when:

1. There are broad policy decisions making provisions for, and encouraging, the improvement of the personnel function.

2. All aspects of the personnel function are subject to continuous appraisal.

3. There is continuous planning by the administration.

4. There is emphasis upon objectifying the appraisal processes through research and experimentation.

5. The total staff is involved in the appraisal process.

There is every reason to believe that the idea of a planned appraisal program will continue to gain adherents in school administration. The core of the program will be the local school staff, which makes use of specialized appraisal agents and agencies for the continuous study of the personnel function.

Using the Results of Appraisal

Appraisal generally reveals problems requiring organization action. The compensation structure may be faulty, staffing loads out of balance, and personnel turnover well beyond expectations. The administrative task, then, becomes one of developing new plans, putting them into effect, and reappraising the results. Certainly this is not as easy as it sounds. It is one thing to say that the salary structure is obsolescent, but quite another thing to bring about a revision which is acceptable to both school personnel and the taxpayers. In view of the fact that organizational change involves cooperation of school personnel and approval by the board and community, it would seem that two major uses should be made of the results of appraisal. The first would be interpretative—to inform school personnel, board members, and citizens of the results of appraisal, and of their educational implications. A second use would be improvement planning. An essential instrument for planning is the school budget. While it must be recognized that budgeting is not all there is to improvement planning, the budget is where virtually all planning is resolved. It is the major process by which needs revealed by appraisal are generally compiled, reviewed, defended, approved, eliminated, or reduced. The budget may also be looked upon as a device for protecting the gains made in the personnel program as the planning and appraising activities are continually carried on for its betterment.

Perhaps one of the most valuable assets of the budget is the conflict which it inevitably produces between the desirable and the possible. No device is more serviceable than the budget for advancing preferred personnel policies, and for using the results of appraisal to indicate the extent to which there are deviations between practice and acceptable standards. The wise administrator uses the budget to stress ideals; he uses the results of appraisal to indicate how practice deviates from the ideal, as well as to chart the course of action which needs to be followed to achieve the objectives which the organization has for its personnel. The board of education, on the other hand, assesses what is possible, then establishes personnel needs on a priority basis. This calls for appraisal of those personnel needs which are most appropriate to the attainment of purpose—a process which produces greater understanding of the goals, programs, procedures, and the action needed for their improvement. It is an effective method of making circumstances conform to plans.

Appraisal of Individual Performance

In the course of administering the affairs of a school system, judgments of organizational personnel are inevitable. While there are many reasons for appraising individual performance, a compelling one is to improve the effectiveness of each staff member so that he contributes maximally to the attainment of purpose.

Appraisal of organization personnel properly begins during the recruitment and selection processes, when qualifications of the individual are judged in relation to district employment requirements. It continues throughout the entire service period for reasons such as the following:

1. Determine whether the individual should be retained in the organization on a permanent basis.

2. Ascertain the potential of the individual to perform various kinds of tasks.

3. Place the individual in the organization where he can render maximum service to the school system.

4. Improve performance.

5. Uncover abilities.

6. Transfer, promote, or dismiss personnel.

7. Provide a guide for salary advancement.

8. Point up in-service education needs.

9. Test the validity of the recruitment and selection processes.

Few are they who question the need for appraisal of individual performance. The real problem is to develop and improve valid appraisal procedures. A second problem is to create greater understanding of the limitations of appraisal devices so that the results derived from them will not be misused.

Complexity of Personnel Appraisal

Appraisal of personnel effectiveness poses numerous and nettlesome problems. While it is generally agreed that the most dependable approach to appraising teacher effectiveness is to appraise the results or products of teaching, i.e., the growth of the learner, this ideal is hard to come by. The results of teaching, for example, are not always immediately apparent. In addition, problems involved in determining what pupil changes should be measured, how they can be measured, and whether changes are due primarily to the effectiveness of the teacher or to other environmental influences are such that this approach has not yet reached the stage that it can be applied satisfactorily.[3]

A second, though indirect method of appraising personnel effectiveness involves evaluation of those attributes of teacher behavior which are deemed to be effective in producing desirable changes in pupils. This may involve appraisal of either teacher behavior in the actual process of instruction, or rating of teacher attributes considered to be important in effective instruction. The problems involved in determining what aspects of teaching to appraise and what means shall be used for appraising them are illustrated in the lists contained in Table 11.1. These inherent difficulties, coupled with criticism of and resistance to personnel appraisal, make it one of the most formidable problems facing administrators.

While it must be recognized that existing means for appraising personnel effectiveness are imperfect, this fact is of little comfort to the administrator who faces the hard realities of making judgments about organization personnel in matters concerning promotion,

[3] For a detailed discussion of the problems involved in appraising teacher characteristics, see David G. Ryans, *Characteristics of Teachers* (Washington: American Council on Education, 1960).

transfer, dismissal, or salary advancement. This is a way of saying that the difficulties in appraisal must be faced, and continued efforts made to objectify the entire appraisal process. The alternative is to rely upon general impressions, uncontrolled and unsystematic judgments, which have been responsible in part for the opposition which commonly attends institutional appraisal of its personnel.

Table 11.1

Appraisal of Classroom Activities to Determine Teacher Competence

Classroom Activity	Examples of Appraisal Techniques
Provisions for individual differences	Observation, check lists, rating scales
Encourage critical thinking	Test results
Organization of instruction	Review of plans, observation, interview
Quality of assignments	Check list, rating scale
Appraisal of pupil growth	Records, reports, test results
Use of instructional aids	Ratings, observation
Application of principles of learning	Check list, observation
Stimulation of pupil interest	Written reports, interview, observation
Breadth of instructional techniques	Check lists
Instructional planning	Analysis of plans, observation
Relationship of instruction to objectives	Analysis of plans, observation, tests
Classroom management	Rating scales
Developing pupil work habits	Observation, reports

Personnel Appraisal Techniques

Various techniques are employed to appraise the professional performance of school personnel. These include:

- Teacher self-evaluation
- Ratings of teachers by pupils
- Ratings of teachers by school administrators
- Evaluation by supervisors
- Evaluation of teachers by colleagues
- Evaluation of teachers by special committees
- Evaluation of teachers by outside professional experts
- Evaluation of teachers by lay citizens
- Evaluation of teachers on the basis of concrete evidence of the character of instruction

- Evaluation of teachers on the basis of cumulative personnel record information
- Teacher evaluation based on pupil changes
- Evaluation of teachers on the basis of nonstructured written responses
- Evaluation of teachers by means of questionnaires and examinations [4]

Analysis of the foregoing techniques for appraising effectiveness of professional personnel indicates that most are designed to appraise teacher behavior or concomitants considered to be related to instructional effectiveness. Each method, of course, has proponents and opponents. Each has alleged advantages and disadvantages.

Regardless of the plan used to appraise the performance of either professional or noninstructional personnel, the ultimate aim is to improve the service rendered by the individual to the school district. All of the activities in the appraisal process, whether they relate to development of personnel performance standards, to procedures used to measure teacher effectiveness, to collecting and recording information concerning performance, to counseling and guidance efforts, should be designed to foster personnel improvement. The appraisal process which fails to do this falls short of achieving its primary purpose.

A well-organized school system will establish an appraisal process which utilizes numerous techniques for appraising personnel performance. Evidence gathered by appraisers will be recorded in a cumulative record system which provides the basis for judgments of personnel performance. It will include appropriate anecdotal data, records of the results of appraisal, and any other type of data which is likely to be useful to the administration in its efforts to improve the service rendered by school personnel.

Administrative Application of Personnel Appraisal

The continuous movement of personnel into, within, and out of an organization poses difficult administrative problems. Within any

[4] Jefferson N. Eastmond, *The Teacher and School Administration* (Boston: Houghton Mifflin Co., 1959), pp. 402–407. See also Robert B. Howsam, *Who's A Good Teacher? Problems and Progress in Teacher Evaluation* (Burlingame, Calif.: California Teachers Association, 1960).

given year it is likely that new personnel will be employed, others will be transferred, dismissed, promoted, or advanced in salary. The movement of persons within the organization often involves changes in status, which is inevitably accompanied by changes in the feelings, attitudes, and modes of behavior of persons thus affected. Administration of change in personnel status within the organization presents problems in human relations, which, if not dealt with effectively, tend to reduce total organizational efficiency.

While it is hardly within the capabilities of the best and wisest administration to operate a school system in which personnel problems of the sort referred to above do not arise, it is demonstrably possible to minimize these problems through continuous planning and appraisal.

Experience of various kinds of organizations indicates that the core function in personnel administration is to place each individual in a position which is compatible with his interests and abilities. The appraisal process is closely linked to this core function in a variety of ways. It is related to the selection of personnel. It is necessary in determining how effectively the man performs in the assigned position. It is also the means by which evidence is gathered upon which to base decisions concerning the transfer, reassignment, dismissal, promotion, and improvement of personnel. Unfortunately, there is no neat system to recommend for dealing successfully with these problems. But there are certain principles which have been developed empirically and which have been utilized successfully by administrators in dealing with personnel problems. It is to a consideration of some of the major problems growing out of the continuous mobility of personnel within the organization, as well as to certain principles which should be operative in effecting appropriate solutions, that the remainder of this chapter is devoted.

Transfer of Personnel

The term transfer, as used herein, refers to the movement of personnel from one position, office, department, or school to another. The movement is generally horizontal, and may or may not involve increased responsibilities or compensation. Transfer should not be confused with reassignment, which means a change in assignment within the same office, department, division, or school. In general, transfers are initiated either by the administrative staff or by organization personnel. They apply to both professional and noninstructional employees.

Transfer of school personnel is an important aspect of school administration, one which deserves more attention from a policy standpoint than it is usually accorded in most school systems. Some understanding of the extent of the transfer problem can be gained from the outline contained in Table 11.2.

Table 11.2
Types of Personnel Transfer Problems

Transfers Initiated by the Administration Due to	*Transfers Initiated by Personnel Due to*
1. Enrollment increases or decreases	1. Desire to work in a new school
2. Changes in the organization of instruction	2. Personal friction
3. Unsatisfactory service	3. Physical reasons
4. Technological advances in maintenance and operation affecting work load of noninstructional personnel	4. "Blind alley" jobs
5. Deterioration in personal relationships	5. Monotony and stagnation
6. Planned experience for future administrative service	6. Desire to work in schools which are not racially mixed, which are not in low-income areas, and which are not obsolescent
7. Efforts to identify future administrative talent	7. Desire for advancement in status or compensation
8. Necessity of maintaining a well-balanced faculty in every school	8. Desire to work nearer home
9. Unsuitability of employee to position	

Analysis of the data in Table 11.2 makes it evident that every school system should give attention to establishment of personnel transfer policies and procedures. Central to this consideration is the welfare of school children. A plan which places senior members of the faculty in the "favored" schools and the inexperienced teachers in the "difficult" schools does not meet this criterion.

While it is not the purpose of this discussion to prescribe what type of transfer plan should be established in a given district, there are certain important decisions which need to be made in developing a course of action. These include:

1. When will transfers be made? It is advisable to establish a mini-

mum amount of experience personnel are required to render in a general assignment before a transfer can be effected. The underlying reasons for this control are to enable the administration to appraise the performance of the individual, to determine the suitability of the original placement, and to avoid interruptions in the instructional program.

2. What are the circumstances or conditions for which transfer requests will be considered? It is quite obvious that the conditions under which transfers will be granted should be clearly defined. The plan should set forth circumstances under which the administration may initiate the transfer, as well as conditions under which it will grant transfers requested by personnel. It is important that these conditions are publicized in the employee handbook or through other media so that misunderstandings concerning the transfer plan are minimized. It should be clearly understood by personnel that they have no inherent right to a given position, and that the welfare of the school has a priority over the welfare of personnel.

3. What limits should be established as to the number of personnel who may be transferred? Some school districts limit the number of transfers which may take place during a school year. This control is designed to maintain staff stability, especially in "undesirable" schools.

4. What procedures should be followed in processing transfer requests? In establishing the transfer plan, attention needs to be given to development of a uniform application for requesting transfer, administrative routing of the request, supporting information accompanying the request, persons charged with acting upon the request, and notification of the individual of the decision reached by the administration.

5. What administrative cooperation is necessary in effecting transfers? The administrator who receives an employee who has been transferred because of unsatisfactory service is usually skeptical. Transfers of this nature require extensive counseling and guidance, as well as cooperation from the receiving administrator in helping the individual to make a satisfactory adjustment to the new position. It is a matter of record that individuals perform satisfactorily in one situation and not in another. Unless there is broad understanding among administrators of aims of the transfer plan, its chances for success are not very good.

Transfers should be encouraged whenever they are in the interest of the individual and the school system. The transfer is a valuable administrative device for improving staff development and flexibility. It should be construed as a means of putting into practice the concept that administration has a continuous responsibility for matching men and jobs.

Continuous appraisal of transfer policies and procedures should make it possible to improve the operation. It should help administration secure information on the scope of the transfer problem, on the effect of transfers, on improvement of service, and on those aspects of the transfer plan which are effective as well as ineffective. Fundamental to the success of the transfer plan is continuous appraisal of personnel performance, for the information which it yields is essential in making judgments and decisions about transfer problems.

Promotion of Personnel

Promotion is generally taken to mean an advance in status or position. Frequently it implies a change in duties, responsibility, and compensation. It belongs to the cluster of administrative problems relating to movement of personnel into and out of the organization —recruitment, selection, placement, transfer, and separation. It is unnecessary to stress the point that the promotion problem is a significant aspect of personnel administration. The school system is dependent upon availability of qualified replacements at all administrative levels. Opportunity for promotion is related to recruitment and retention of personnel. It is also necessary so as to maximize desires and interests of personnel from a status standpoint.

The effect of promotion practices upon personnel morale should be mentioned. Negative effects of promotions made solely on the basis of loyalty, friendship, consistent agreement with administrative viewpoints, showmanship, and favoritism are generally recognized. It is due in part to the harmful effects which these and other promotion practices have had upon all types of organizations that increasing attention is being devoted to improvement of promotion policies.

The problem of developing policy on promotion is extremely delicate. Many school administrators contend that for the typical system:

1. Administrative deprivation is such that the opportunity for promotion is extremely limited.

2. Competition for administrative positions, with the higher compensation incentive, has resulted in a loss of many excellent classroom teachers.

3. In-service development of classroom teachers is centered upon preparation for administrative positions rather than upon improvement of teaching performance and/or the educational program.

4. Extensive encouragement of classroom personnel to prepare for administrative positions has a detrimental effect upon the maintenance of a potent teaching staff.

In light of these conditions, they argue, administration should not exalt the relatively few promotional opportunities, but should concern itself more with improving conditions of work and compensation to retain able personnel in the classroom. In support of this argument the proponents note that the number of certified administrators is far in excess of available administrative positions. While it is true that the supply of administrators generally exceeds demand, this does not rule out the need for establishment of a systematic promotion plan in the local school district. Unless there is a planned program to produce leaders, the chances are good that they will not be secured by "doing what comes naturally." The promotion problem, if left to chance, will probably lead to practices not conducive to maintenance of staff morale.

Advancement of personnel from within the system as opposed to selection from the outside is another problem to be considered in developing promotion policy. The argument generally advanced for promotion from within is that it is essential to establishment of a career service. Without such a policy, it is claimed, it is difficult to attract or to retain promising personnel. Unless there is assured opportunity for promotion, the competent person looks to other systems or to other areas of service where his talents will be recognized and for which there will be greater financial rewards.

The danger that some see in the promotion-from-within concept is inbreeding and stagnation, as well as denial of freedom of choice to the administrator. Unavailability of properly qualified candidates within the system to meet the specifications of a vacancy illustrates this point.

A guiding principle in developing policy would seem to be that of encouraging promotion from within, unless there is reason to believe that vacancies can best be filled through competition from the outside. If proper steps are taken to attract, retain, and develop a staff of high quality, there is every reason to believe that promotion from within can meet most of the needs for higher administrative positions. It is possible through a carefully planned development program for administration to identify administrative capabilities within the system, to provide opportunities in which such capabilities can be assessed, and to establish a talent bank from which to fill vacancies as they occur. Such a program would tend to minimize the "inside or outside" issue, since it would create a long-range plan for providing administrative personnel as needed.

A third problem involved in developing a system for promoting personnel is the basis upon which candidates are selected for promotion. This is, in effect, a problem of appraisal for which there is no perfect solution. Attempts to objectify the promotion process have led to the use of competitive examinations, rating devices, seniority plans, and planned experiences, such as job rotation, internships, or assistantships. While these efforts have helped to improve opportunities for promotion, and have fostered the principle of merit promotion, there is no single method which is completely dependable. A combination of several or all of these methods, including application of position guides, generally secures results more satisfactory than those derived from the use of any single criterion.

While it would be difficult to discuss in this chapter all of the ramifications of developing a sound system of promotion, it is practicable to suggest a number of guidelines. These may be listed as follows:

1. Clearly defined policy statements should be developed by the board of education, indicating its intent with respect to promotion of all organizational personnel. Procedures for implementing policy should be clear and unequivocal on these points: how vacancies in higher positions are to be filled, the extent to which opportunities are available for promotion from within the organization, the means by which promotable persons are to be identified, the bases upon which promotion is to be decided, the conditions under which selection for higher positions will be made from outside the organization, the extent to which administration will assist personnel in preparation for higher positions, whether or not opportunity for promotion is

system-wide, and the personnel responsible for carrying out the promotion policy.

2. In its broadest sense, promotion should be viewed as the culmination of a series of related developmental activities, beginning with the recruitment of personnel, the aim of which is to attract those individuals who appear to possess potential for future advancement. Placement, supervision, in-service development, and transfer activities are so integrated that the decision to promote will be based on a long-term appraisal and developmental process aimed at minimizing unsatisfactory appointments resulting from hasty action.

3. Promotion is based upon a planned program of appraisal designed to assess the individual's past and current performance, as well as his capacity for growth and development in assignments contemplated by the administration. A combination of appraisal devices is desirable to enable appraisers to make judgments of qualifications of the individual in relation to position specifications.

4. In order to minimize prejudice and injustice, the appraisal of promotable persons should involved judgments of more than one administrator.

Dismissal of Personnel

Dismissal of personnel in any organization is seldom easy or pleasant. Generally it is undertaken with reluctance. It is a matter of deep concern to every school system, one which deserves particular attention because it represents the loss of a considerable investment of time, money, and effort, and often creates unfavorable attitudes toward the school system on the part of persons directly or indirectly involved. On the other hand, elimination of incompetent personnel from the school system is an imperative administrative responsibility, one which must be exercised in behalf of the welfare of the organization.

Legal aspects of dismissal add to complexities of the problem. Statutory provisions, contracts, civil service regulations, and collective bargaining agreements are designed to protect personnel from losing their jobs unfairly. The conditions under which dismissal may be effected are generally prescribed to the point where the basis of any such action on the part of the school district must be defensible and supported by appropriate evidence.

The concern of any organization should not be to discover less painful methods for dismissal of personnel. Its primary aim should be to minimize the necessity for such action. It is inevitable that dismissal problems will arise in any organized endeavor, despite careful efforts to recruit, select, place, orient, supervise, and develop personnel suited to the service for which they are employed. But there are certain kinds of administrative action which can be taken from a preventive standpoint. The initial selection of personnel is a point of beginning. It is the better part of wisdom to attempt to discover incompetents before they enter the system, or before they are granted tenure, than it is to dismiss permanent members of the staff. Many personnel problems develop and fail of solution because they are ignored, or because administration fails to establish machinery to deal with them realistically. The school that has developed a thoroughgoing appraisal program to assess capabilities of personnel for permanent service in the system has taken a major step in prevention of personnel problems that lead to dismissal.

Two kinds of appraisal activities appear to be necessary in dealing with the matter under consideration. The first involves continuous appraisal to discover strengths and weaknesses in individual performance. Appropriate counseling and guidance services should be available to enable personnel to recognize and to take the necessary steps to overcome any shortcomings which may exist.

Continuous appraisal of individual performance is also necessary to accumulate a solid array of evidence of unsatisfactory performance which, if necessary, can withstand the rigors of judicial review in the event that dismissal is warranted.

A second type of appraisal relates to examination of reasons for the dismissal of personnel. Who is dismissed? What are the reasons for dismissal? Was dismissal necessary because of administrative inaction during the period of service? Does the dismissal reflect administrative errors? The point to be made is that a certain amount of self-examination by administration is necessary to correct any conditions induced by shortcomings in the administrative process.

A clear-cut statement of policies and procedures governing dismissal of personnel is needed in every school system. This should enable staff members to know what is expected of them, that dismissal cases will be treated fairly, that the facts will be carefully considered, and that dismissal proceedings are not initiated until informal corrective efforts have failed to secure the level of service which is expected.

Appraisal and Salary Advancement

It has been stated earlier in this chapter that appraisal of personnel performance is a necessary administrative function, the main purpose of which is improvement of service. Broadly conceived, this function involves certain major tasks, such as elimination of incompetents, appropriate placement of personnel, identification of strengths and weaknesses in performance, and provision of services and opportunities for encouraging staff self-improvement. Consequently, appraisal of personnel performance must be considered as an essential administrative function, whether or not the organization decides to link teacher competence to salary provisions.

The advantages and disadvantages of merit salary schedules have been so thoroughly analyzed during the better part of the past three decades that it appears superfluous to repeat them here.[5] The real difficulty in relating teacher competence to salary provisions is one of appraisal, a central problem out of which others evolve, including such questions as what shall be appraised, who appraises, what means shall be used to appraise, and how appraisals are translated into monetary rewards.

Those who advocate relating quality of service to compensation do so largely on the grounds that personnel differ in the quality of service which they render, that these differences must be recognized financially in order to attract and to retain professionally effective personnel. The argument has force, and appears to persist despite opposition which is historical in character.

That professional performance as a factor in teachers salaries will neither be universally accepted nor rejected appears to be a reasonable assumption. It is to be anticipated that experimentation in relating compensation to performance will continue. The continuing controversy over "merit rating" points to the need for increasing research

[5] For comprehensive treatments of this problem see New England School Development Council, *Teacher Competence and Its Relation to Salary* (Cambridge: The Council, 1956); Jefferson N. Eastmond, *The Teacher and School Organization* (Boston: Houghton Mifflin Co., 1959); and Charles S. Benson, *The Economics of Public Education* (Boston: Houghton Mifflin Co., 1961).

and experimentation to test, to refine, and to improve procedures which have been developed. A summary of the major points in the literature regarding the use of merit recognition in the personnel compensation structure would include the following:

1. Advance planning for merit salary programing is a primary consideration. This includes definition of what is to be evaluated, how it is to be evaluated, and how the evaluations are to be translated into financial rewards.

2. Appraisal of individual performance should be conceived as a comprehensive, long-term undertaking. A single rating for salary purposes is contrary to sound concepts of appraisal.[6]

3. The compensation structure should be competitive in design to attract and to retain competent personnel without application of merit provisions. Recognition of professional performance should be in addition to a competitive salary schedule and should not constitute a threat to the existing financial status of personnel.

4. Clarification of major and subsidiary goals will help to resolve the difficulties encountered in appraising performance.

5. A program for recognizing performance should be the product of staff planning. Attempts to impose plans externally developed have been generally unsuccessful. Those who are directly affected by the plan should participate in its planning and operation.

6. The professional as well as the classroom role of the teacher should be considered in making decisions as to what aspects of performance should be appraised.

7. A system of checks and balances should be built into the merit plan so that major decisions are not the responsibility of a single individual.

8. The unusual amount of staff time required to administer a merit program is such that additional personnel will probably be needed. Lack of personnel to administer the program and to refine the instruments of appraisal are serious deterrents to the success of a merit plan.

9. The broad purpose underlying merit is the improvement of service. Teacher-evaluator conferences should become an essential phase of the appraisal process so that improvement of personnel can be furthered.

[6] This point is developed extensively in New England School Development Council, *op. cit.*, pp. 91–102.

10. Potentialities of personnel self-evaluation should be recognized in the over-all appraisal plan.

As the general level of salaries for school personnel increases, greater demand for improvement of professional performance should be anticipated. Personnel within the local school system, working cooperatively, must assume the major role in formulating appraisal plans and procedures for the improvement of teaching and learning. The nature of the appraisal problem demands continuous and extensive experimentation, involving a wide variety of appraisal techniques. If there are significant advantages to be attained by linking salaries and performance, such as improved teaching, attraction and retention of personnel, increased public support, and greater desire for professional improvement, the possibilities seem too attractive to reject categorically.

Personnel Records and Appraisal

A formidable administrative asset in the appraisal process is a systematic means for gathering, interpreting, and utilizing personnel data which has probative value, and which may be employed in developing an appraisal history for each member of the organization. Such a system would include forms, reports, and records. A *form* may be defined as a standardized method of recording data; *reports* utilize forms to communicate information; *records* are the accumulation and organization of information which is regarded as of more than temporary significance. Records and reports, according to Yoder, are distinguishable but related. Reports are made to create a record. They may be conserved as records. Records sometimes become parts of a report, and reports may be built up from records.[7]

While there are many reasons for maintenance of personnel records, including legal requirements, the unreliability and inefficiency of individual memory, the wide demand for personnel information, and the necessity for transmitting such information to a variety of persons and agencies, the central purpose of appraisal records should be the improvement of service.

In the text following, which is suggestive rather than exhaustive, two kinds of personnel information are considered as starting points

[7] Dale Yoder, *Personnel Principles and Policies,* 2nd ed. (Englewood Cliffs, N.J.: Prentice-Hall, Inc., 1959), p. 566.

in establishing or reorganizing record systems. The first category includes personnel records which should be centrally available. These include:

1. *Personal:* Date and place of birth, race, church affiliation, marital status, special interests, community and general cultural activities, travel, health, emotional and social adjustment.

2. *Academic:* These data relate to formal schooling, including dates and types of institutions attended, diplomas and degrees granted, courses taken, academic standing, activity participation, honors achieved, special awards, and outstanding achievements.

3. *Professional:* (a) Experience within the district; when employed, duties assigned, annual salary record, building or system-wide responsibilities in addition to regular assignment; (b) professional experience outside of the district; where employed, when employed, duties assigned, annual salary record, nonteaching assignments.

4. *Certification:* Complete record of all certificates granted, including types, date, issuing authority, and current validity.

5. *Nonteaching Occupational Experience:* Complete record of all occupational experience other than teaching, including military service.

The second group of records would bring together in one place the appraisal history of each member of the school organization. This would be, in effect, a central or master record file of past and current data relating to the judgments, opinions, and observations of the actual and potential performance of personnel in the organization. There are numerous sources from which the appraisal record can be developed. These include, for example:

1. Appraisals made during the recruitment stage, including judgments of recruiting officials, statements from persons in charge of undergraduate training programs, and letters of recommendation and their validation.

2. Appraisals made during the selection process, including the results of tests, physical examinations, and interviews.

3. Appraisals of past experience, such as those provided by administrative officers in school systems where the individual has been previously employed.

4. Appraisals provided by principals and supervisors, which are ordinarily required as a part of the routine evaluation of all personnel.

5. Records of professional activities of staff members, such as in-

service activities, publications, contributions to the improvement of the educational program, and graduate work pursued.

6. Ratings for salary purposes.

7. Records of commendations and awards.

8. Records of performance in various positions held in system.

In short, the appraisal record should include information which would be of value in helping administration to improve the performance of each staff member. On the basis of the record system outlined above, each administrator is in a better position to discharge his appraisal responsibility to the children, the staff member, the board of education, and the community.

Criteria which can be applied in appraising the personnel record system include the following:

1. Is the personnel record system capable of yielding readily those items of information essential to the performance of the personnel function? There are numerous occasions when personnel data are needed for planning and appraisal purposes. Cost of a proposed salary schedule, sources of position applications, cost of leaves of absence, annual need for substitute service, personnel eligible for retirement, expenditures for collateral benefits, reasons for resignations, transfers, and dismissals are illustrations of administrative considerations which involve collection, refinement, and interpretation of personnel data. It goes without saying that many personnel problems are ignored or go unrecognized because the personnel record system has not been organized or manned to provide pertinent data.

2. How readily can current, accurate, complete data be secured from the personnel record system? The ability of any organization to collect, store, and retrieve data has increased considerably with the introduction of automatic data-processing equipment. The day must be anticipated when dependence on electromechanical devices for much of school record keeping and analysis will be standard procedure. Careful planning will make possible a wide variety of useful personnel data from the district's master record system. While the processing of records by mechanical means has the advantage of routinizing the record-keeping operation and reducing the time needed to secure essential information, it also makes available more time and more pertinent, accurate, current data for planning and appraising the entire personnel function.

3. To what extent are the records protected against loss by fire,

theft, and examination by unauthorized personnel? Certain arrangements are necessary to protect documents and records from theft, possible loss, and misuse by unauthorized persons. Administrative controls should be established to direct the preparation, use, duplication, storage, and issuance of records.

4. Is the record system reviewed periodically to determine items which can be eliminated from or added to current files? Changing conditions make necessary constant surveillance of records so that time, effort, and space is not devoted to amassing irrelevant information.

5. Does the school district have a comprehensive plan governing the preparation and use of personnel reports? What personnel data are needed, when and by whom they are prepared, and the purposes they are intended to serve are all matters of procedure which should be given consideration in planning personnel records so that the right information is available at the right time.

It may be suggested, finally, that personnel records, when properly designed, can also serve as the basis for detecting flaws in personnel policy. Record analysis should make possible a measure of the quality of personnel recruited, recruitment sources, and placement, transfer, and dismissal problems. This is to say that the record system facilitates appraisal of the total personnel function, its strengths as well as areas where corrective measures are needed.

Suggested Reading

Eastmond, Jefferson N., *The Teacher and School Administration* (Boston: Houghton Mifflin Co., 1959).

Morphet, Edgar L., R. L. Johns, and Theodore L. Reller, *Educational Administration: Concepts, Practices, and Issues* (Englewood Cliffs, N.J.: Prentice-Hall, Inc., 1959).

National Industrial Conference Board, *Forms and Records in Personnel Administration*, Studies in Personnel Policy, No. 175 (New York: The Board, 1960).

Nigro, Felix A., *Public Personnel Administration* (New York: Henry Holt & Co., Inc., 1959).

Stahl, O. Glenn, *Public Personnel Administration*, 4th ed. (New York: Harper & Brothers, 1956).

Walters, J. E., *Basic Administration: The Process of Planning, Organizing, Managing, Appraising, and Controlling* (Ames, Iowa: Littlefield, Adams and Co., 1959).

Wasserman, Paul, *Measurement and Evaluation of Organizational Performance: An Annotated Bibliography* (Ithaca, N.Y.: Graduate School of Business and Public Administration, Cornell University, 1959).

Whitehill, Arthur M., *Personnel Relations* (New York: McGraw-Hill Book Co., 1955).

Wiles, Kimball, *Supervision for Better Schools*, 2nd ed. (Englewood Cliffs, N.J.: Prentice-Hall, Inc., 1955).

Yeager, William A., *Administration and the Teacher* (New York: Harper & Brothers, 1954).

General Welfare of Personnel:

BASIC PROVISIONS

CHAPTER TWELVE

This chapter is based upon the assumption that all organizations of whatever purpose face a common problem of promoting the welfare of its members. If we begin by examining the meaning of the word "welfare" it will help to clarify the intent of the discussion which follows. The dictionary defines the term welfare as work done among employees to improve conditions of labor and morale, often called *personnel work.* The question may well arise at this point as to whether the total personnel function could be properly considered as a systematic approach to the improvement of the conditions of employment. While it can be argued that there is more to personnel administration than improving conditions of employment, there is no doubt that welfare problems in any organization require considerable administrative emphasis.

Welfare provisions to be treated herein—leaves of absence, substitute service, health, grievances, academic freedom, associations, tenure, and retirement—are crucial, since they affect organizational stability and, perhaps indirectly, its capability to achieve purpose.

303

For the most part, welfare provisions pertain to the security of the individual during and after his term of service in the organization. The majority of states have enacted legislation governing some of the matters under consideration. Statutory compliance, however, is not a substitute for problem solving. Within the legal framework there is considerable leeway for creative approaches to the improvement of welfare provisions in local school systems.

Leaves of Absence

A leave may be defined as absence from employment, by permission, with or without compensation, for a stated period of time, without severing the employment relationship. Regardless of the size of the school district, leave policies and procedures are essential, as may be seen from the variety of leave requests listed in Table 12.1. Increasingly, school systems of all sizes are initiating or improving provisions governing leaves of absence.

Table 12.1

Illustration of Types of Leaves of Absence

Personal illness	Maternity leave
Family and personal bereavement	Marriage
Exchange teaching	Brief or extended leaves of absence for
Religious holidays	professional reasons, such as research
Travel or study	or serving professional organizations
Attending educational conferences, meetings, or conventions, or to receive degrees	Opportunity leaves
	Jury and witness duty
	Civic leaves
Sabbatical	
Military leave	
Temporary active military duty	

Although a leave of absence plan serves many purposes, it should be conceived as an investment in the improvement of instruction. In safeguarding the physical and mental health of the school staff, in maintaining employment security, and in fostering professional growth and morale, the leave plan is not considered to be an end in itself, a collateral benefit, nor a generous gesture of the board of education. The investment is made on the assumption that it will ultimately produce conditions of employment conducive to the improvement of instruction.

Characteristics of Leave Plans

It is customary, and frequently mandatory for school systems to establish provisions governing the absence of personnel due to illness and other reasons.

Illness leave plans can be classified as either (1) limited, or (2) unlimited. The limited type plan, frequently established by statute, generally contains provisions governing:

1. The number of days allowed each year for sick leave.
2. The cumulation of leave days from year to year, including the total days which can be accumulated.
3. The number of days for which sick leave is granted with full or part salary.
4. Verification of the illness.
5. Adoption of board regulations extending the period of leave with pay in excess of statutory provisions.
6. Nonapplication of sick leave provisions in the event absence is due to injury incurred while personnel are engaged in remunerative work unrelated to school duties.

According to the data contained in Table 12.2, some states determine the amount of sick leave on the basis of length of service, some specify how many days of sick leave are mandatory at full pay, while others leave this matter to the discretion of the local board.

The unlimited sick leave plan, which as yet has been adopted in only a small number of school districts, places no limit upon the number of days personnel may be absent due to illness. This type of leave may provide for full or part pay, or a combination of both. In the latter case, full pay is granted for a limited number of days, after which time part pay is granted without time limitation.

Leaves of absence for purposes *other than illness* are less often prescribed by statute or included in local board leave policies. These include leaves for (1) professional development, (2) professional service, (3) civic duties, and (4) personal matters. Death in the immediate family, professional study, exchange teaching, maternity, and attendance at educational meetings account for a majority of leaves granted in the nonillness category.

Table 12.2
State Sick Leave Provisions

State	Mandatory at full pay	State board authorized to regulate sick leave	Local districts authorized to exceed mandatory number of days at full pay	Part pay provided at end of full-pay period	Amount of unused full-pay leave which may be accumulated
	1	2	3	4	5	6
Alabama	Amount at discretion of local board				20 days
Alaska	10 days				30 days
Arizona					50 days
California	10 days		X	At discretion of local board [a]	Indefinitely
Connecticut	10 days				At least 60 days
Delaware	10 days				120 days
District of Columbia	10 days		X		Temporary teachers, 20 days; probationary and permanent teachers, 75 days [b]
Florida	6 days				72 days in the twelfth year
Georgia	1–¼ days for each completed school month				Not cumulative
Hawaii	10 days			20 days mandatory	30 days
Idaho	5 days				20 days
Illinois	10 days			5 days mandatory	30 days
Indiana	7 days				60 days
Iowa	5 days				35 days

State				
Louisiana		10 days		
Maine		Amount at discretion of local board		25 days
Maryland	X	10 days	At discretion of local board	Law silent
Mississippi		Amount at discretion of local board		
Nevada		Amount at discretion of local board [a]		At discretion of local board
New Jersey	X	10 days	At discretion of local board	Indefinitely
New York		Amount at discretion of local board		
North Carolina		Up to maximum of 5 days		
Ohio		5 days		Law silent
Oklahoma		Amount at discretion of local board		
Oregon	X	10 days		Law silent
Pennsylvania	X	10 days		30 days
Tennessee		1 day for each month taught		36 days
Vermont		10 days		20 days within same school district
West Virginia		Maximum, 5 days, at discretion of local board		20 days, provided the board has established a sick-leave fund
Wisconsin	X	5 days [e]		At least 30 days

[a] For more than five months, pay is at the discretion of the local board, subject to rules and regulation of the state board.

[b] Up to 25 days leave may be granted for service before July 1, 1949, but the total shall not exceed 75 days.

[c] Increasing 1 day for each year of consecutive employment to 9.

[d] Up to a maximum of 10 days in 1 school year, 20 days for 2 school years, or 30 days for 3 school years.

[e] State aid shall not be paid any district except first-class districts for any year in which teachers' contracts do not so provide.

Source: National Education Association, Research Division, *The Teacher and the Law*, School Law Series Research Monograph 1959 M–3 (Washington: The Association, 1959), p. 64.

State Sick Leave Provisions

A digest of state sick leave provisions is contained in Table 12.2. Analysis of these data indicates that most states having sick leave mandates specify a minimum leave period and permit accumulation of unused full-pay leave. Several states authorize local districts to exceed the mandatory number of days at full pay.

Guidelines for Administering the Leave Program

A comprehensive leave program, which increasingly appears to be an organizational necessity, calls for resolution of many and varied issues, including:

1. What are the reasons for which leaves of absence should be granted?

2. What should be the limit on the number of teachers on non-illness leave at one time?

3. What eligibility requirements should be established for each leave category?

4. What conditions shall attach to each type of leave, type of application required, salary on return to service, service required after return from leave, notice required, priority factors, report on use of leave, assignment upon return to service, termination of leave, and notice of intention to return to service?

5. How can abuse of absence privileges be minimized?

6. What arrangements are necessary for safeguarding the education of pupils?

7. What priorities should the leave program be given in the budget?

8. How can the school staff help to plan the leave program cooperatively?

While it is unnecessary to prescribe here what the leave program for any school system should be, there are certain principles generally accepted as being related to its operation. As suggested throughout this text, written policies formally adopted by the board of education give an administrative plan meaning and direction. The leave program is no exception, as can be judged from the illustration in Table 12.3, which outlines the leave policies and procedures in effect in the Chicago public schools.

Analysis of a school district's experience with the operation of a leave plan over a period of years is a useful starting point. One of the purposes would be to determine possible leave eventualities which may arise, frequency of occurrence, budgetary demands of the leave program, privileges which are subject to abuse, and suitability of existing administrative controls.

A study of leave practices in California school districts suggests certain criteria which should be employed in implementing or evaluating leave policies. These include:

1. The improved quality of instruction should be the primary purpose in granting leaves.

2. Planning of policies should involve the cooperative effort of all persons concerned.

3. Policies must support the legal provisions of the state, and should be free from conflict with these provisions.

4. Policy statements should allow leeway for the exercise of administrative judgment in individual cases not covered specifically by the majority of circumstances.

5. The various types of absence leaves should be treated separately.

6. Adequate financing should be considered in terms of the needs of teachers and the ability of the district to support them.

7. Policies should include proper protection for the taxpayer, but should be constructed primarily for the protection of the majority of honest teachers.

8. The education of pupils must be protected through an adequate plan for providing qualified substitutes for teachers who are absent on leave.

9. Adequate plans and records should be worked out to provide for the efficient administration of adopted policies.

10. Policies must include provisions for keeping personnel informed of current practices and recent changes.

11. Provisions should be made for periodic review and revision of policies.[1]

Continuous reexamination of leave policies may well include consideration of their relationship to the extension of research and study of problems which have both immediate and long-range implications

[1] Noel MacHenry Shutt, *Leave of Absence Policies for Certificated Personnel in California School Districts* (Los Angeles: University of Southern California, Doctoral Dissertation, 1959), pp. 30–31.

Table 12.3

Leaves of Absence: An Illustration of Policy Application

Kinds of Leave	Application	Eligibility	Conditions of Leave	Termination of Leave	Compensation
Personal Illness	Form T-Per. 109 (Application for Illness Leave of Absence) is filled out and signed by teacher and principal after a continuous absence exceeding ten consecutive days. If possible, application should be made prior to tenth day. Leave includes first ten days of absence.	Regularly appointed teacher	Leave may not exceed five months in any school year nor be in excess of five months in any two consecutive years and the teacher's position is held open. If extension is granted, even though absence is not consecutive, teacher's position is declared vacant.	The teacher notifies principal by two o'clock on the second school day prior to date of return to duty.	Salary is allowed in accordance with sick pay rule.
Extension of Leave for Personal Illness	Prior to termination of leave for Personal Illness request for extension is made on form T-Per. 109 (Application for Illness Leave of Absence) and forwarded to Bureau of Teacher Personnel.	Regularly appointed teacher	Extensions are granted for an additional period not to exceed fifteen school months. If extension is granted teacher's position is declared vacant.	Teacher notifies Bureau of Teacher Personnel at least ten school days before expiration or prior to termination of leave. Bureau of Teacher Personnel authorizes the	None.

	Application / Notice	Eligibility	Conditions	Notification of Return	Salary
	A doctor's certificate or other proof of continuous serious illness is presented with the application.		N. B. When leave has been granted for a period of two full years no further leave for illness is allowed until after the expiration of two full years from the date of return.	teacher to make an appointment for a health examination by Board of Education health examiner.	Salary is allowed in accordance with sick pay rule.
Illness in Family	Form T-Per. 109 (Application for Illness Leave of Absence) is filled out and signed by teacher and principal.	Regularly appointed teacher	Leave may not exceed five school months within two consecutive years. Leave is granted because of serious illness of a member of immediate family, i.e., one who resides with the teacher.	Teacher notifies principal by two o'clock on the second school day prior to date of return to duty.	Salary is allowed in accordance with sick pay rule.
Death in Family	Notice is given to principal on date of death.	Regularly appointed teacher	Period of absence may not exceed five days from date of death to date of the burial, both dates inclusive, plus the necessary time for return to Chicago when funeral is held out of the city.	Teacher notifies principal by two o'clock on the school day prior to the date of return to duty.	Salary is allowed in accordance with sick pay rule.

Table 12.3 (*cont.*)

Kinds of Leave	Application	Eligibility	Conditions of Leave	Termination of Leave	Compensation
Religious Holidays.	Written notice is given to the principal two school days in advance of non-attendance.	Regularly appointed teacher	Absence may not exceed three days in any one school year. Leave is granted only when the religious denomination has officially set aside the day as a religious holiday on which members may not engage in gainful employment.	Date of return is determined when leave is granted.	Leave is granted with pay less the amount payable for substitute service.
Travel or Study.	Teacher applies by letter to Bureau of Teacher Personnel.	Three years of continuous satisfactory active service as a regularly appointed teacher	Four major courses must be completed within one year, or the teacher must engage in travel of such a nature as will improve his efficiency.	Upon return teacher presents to Bureau of Teacher Personnel credentials from an accredited institution of learning showing courses completed, or an itinerary of travel.	None.
Attending Educational Conferences,	Teacher presents written application on Form T-Per. 100 to principal	Regularly appointed teacher	Degree is being conferred on teacher.	Upon return teacher presents brief written report to the Department	Leave is granted with pay

Meetings or Conventions or to Receive Degrees.	three weeks in advance of expected date of leave.		Meeting or convention is educationally advantageous to work of school.	of Personnel.
Sabbatical	Form T-Per. 47 (Application for Sabbatical Leave of Absence) is filled out, signed and presented to Bureau of Teacher Personnel at least two school months previous to effective date of leave. N. B. Deadline date announced in bulletin of General Superintendent of Schools each semester.	Six years or more of continuous satisfactory service as a regularly appointed teacher.	Leave is granted for a definite period not less than five school months nor more than ten school months. Leave starts the beginning of a semester and terminates at end of a semester. Study: Completion of four major resident courses during a leave of ten school months in an accredited institution of learning. Travel: Continuous bona fide travel designed to improve the service of the teacher to the school system.	The following verifications are presented to the Bureau of Teacher Personnel before return to duty. Study: An official transcript of credits bearing the seal of the university and the signature of the registrar. Travel: A verified report indicating places visited, dates, length of stay, and in case of foreign travel, a passport.	Salary is allowed less amount payable for substitute service, less any amount earned in the Sabbatical Leave activity if such compensation has been approved in advance. When amount earned is greater than his regular salary less substitute's pay the teacher receives no pay from the Board of Education.

Source: Abridged from *Handbook of Policies and Procedures* (Chicago: Chicago Public Schools, 1961), pp. 34-35.

for the improvement of the educational program. Most school districts have nettlesome problems which cannot be attacked, simply because of a lack of manpower and because available personnel do not have the time to concentrate for an extended period of time on problem solving. Liberalizing sabbatical provisions which would make possible release of personnel on full salary to engage in research and study on problems of concern to the school system is a matter which should come high on the list of policy priorities.

Recommendations of the Advisory Committee on Compensation for the professional staff in Scarsdale, New York, embodies the foregoing concept. The committee advocated a system of school improvement fellowships designed to free teachers from regular duties so that they can have time and money to carry out projects of importance to the schools. The fellowships, as viewed by the committee, (1) may involve absence from regular duties for an extended period of time, and (2) may require salary payments for nonteaching duties. Possibilities include:

1. Full expenses (travel and tuition) and partial salary to make possible a summer devoted to appropriate university work.
2. Relief from classroom duties with full pay for a period of three months to work on curriculum development in Scarsdale.
3. Five months leave-of-absence at full pay to pursue a textbook writing project.
4. A year's leave-of-absence with travel expenses and enough salary to prevent loss of income for a teacher who takes a position in a foreign school.[2]

Substitute Service

An important adjunct to the leave-of-absence program is a plan for providing suitable substitute service. It goes without saying that unless there are qualified replacements for personnel who are absent, the leave plan is incomplete and indefensible. The incongruity of a liberal leave-of-absence plan which results in periodic low-level instruction is not likely to engender public confidence and support. While the reasons often given for the generally inferior quality of substitute service are numerous and varied, they are not completely convincing.

[2] Union Free School District No. 1, Scarsdale, New York, *Report of Advisory Committee on Compensation for Professional Staff to the Board of Education* (Scarsdale, New York: Board of Education, 1961), p. 2.

It is generally agreed that substitute service in many school systems can be improved through deliberate and continuous planning.

Persistent Problems

Inability to recruit sufficient and qualified replacements accounts for many of the problems attending substitute service. This is especially true in school districts not located near population concentrations. For a substantial proportion of small school districts, some of the suggestions which follow will be largely academic, because of the unavailability of personnel who can be induced on short notice to travel the distances involved and to work for the day-to-day rates which districts offer. The substitute service problem in the small school district, like many other problems inherent to it, appears destined to lie unresolved, as it has for years, until such administrative units are reorganized.

It is argued by some administrators that the day-to-day substitute plan has not, and in all likelihood will not, produce satisfactory results. Supporters of this view advance the following limitations:

1. Most qualified teachers who would ordinarily be available for substitute service have been employed on a regular basis because of the personnel shortage.

2. The substitute teacher list generally includes a substantial proportion of incompetents.

3. Personnel absence can no longer be looked upon as an unusual occurrence, since an increasing number of teachers are inclined to take full advantage of the number of allowable days granted under leave or disability plans.

4. The cost differential between permanent and day-to-day substitute service is not great enough to continue the generally inferior service which results from the latter plan.

5. The difficulty of predicting need.

6. The inordinate amount of administrative effort required to recruit, select, and supervise the day-to-day substitute.

7. The difficulty of involving temporary personnel in the regular school program.

8. The increase in disciplinary cases which attend the use of substitute teachers.

One of the difficulties which confronts the administrator in analyzing these arguments is the lack of evidence dealing specifically with the substitute service problem. Does this paucity of information result from an assumption that the day-to-day substitute plan is the most satisfactory approach conceivable? Or does it mean the continued neglect of an old problem ever new?

Arguments favoring abolition of traditional substitute teacher plans have force, and are especially applicable in school districts where replacements are needed continuously. It is quite reasonable to assume that most administrators would favor an arrangement whereby permanent personnel would be employed instead of substitute teachers. The cost factor, however, has been a major deterrent. But the level of instruction which could be maintained through a permanent corps of reserve teachers would appear to offset the many disadvantages of the part-time substitute system. It can be argued that the permanent corps would produce greater educational returns for the increased investment, whereas the part-time approach involves substantial expenditure of public funds without appreciable returns.

What Schools Can Do to Maintain Instructional Standards during Absence of Regular Personnel

Replacements for absent teachers is a problem which no longer can be treated as an administrative or budgetary happenstance. It must be viewed as an important task essential to the maintenance of a satisfactory level of instruction. Like any other recurrent need, it requires development of a course of action, reenforced by board policies and budgetary provisions. The solution lies in a balanced, multilateral approach, including:

1. Formulation of a specific plan to be followed in the administration of personnel replacements. (See Table 12.4.)

2. Specifications for personnel replacements.

3. A permanent, specialized corps of replacements to meet minimum district needs, to be composed of highly competent personnel, deliberately selected and trained to deal with the special problems of substitution. A salary advantage is suggested because of the exacting nature of the assignment.

4. A second group of temporary teachers to be employed seasonally when the replacements cannot be filled by the permanent corps suggested above. This group to be recruited and selected on the basis of criteria designed to employ personnel able to perform in this capacity.

5. Responsibilities for carrying out the details of the replacement plan are clearly defined. This includes administrative responsibility for development, assignment, and full utilization of the permanent corps of replacements, as well as recruitment, selection, orientation, supervision, and appraisal of temporary personnel.

6. Preparation of a handbook for temporary employees which will routinize procedures to be followed and which will help to clarify and to minimize the problems usually encountered.

7. Advance planning in each building unit by the principal and regular staff regarding the preparation of plan books to be followed in the event of absence. This matter is important, since the continuity of education by replacement depends upon clear instructions.

8. Continuous appraisal of the replacement plan. Records of the daily, monthly, and yearly absence rates are necessary to enable administration to determine, for example, the feasibility and cost of employing permanent replacements. Many other aspects of the plan must be appraised, such as the reasons for absence, the predictable need for temporary personnel, and the effects of whatever plan is employed upon the quality of instruction.

Should the present trend in the reduction of administrative units throughout the nation continue, remaining units will be larger, and increases in staff size and personnel absence problems must be anticipated. Unless more effective solutions are devised, administrative difficulties and instructional losses usually associated with teacher absence can be expected.

Health of School Personnel

Few are they who would contend that the physical and mental status of school personnel is unimportant. The conviction that physical and mental efficiency of the school staff affects the quality of personnel performance is widespread. But the fact remains that in many school districts the well-being of the school staff is considered to be a personal rather than an administrative responsibility.[3] Whether or

[3] An NEA Research Division report indicates that of 1973 school districts reporting. 52 per cent had no specified provisions for a thorough health examination for teachers, 49 per cent of 902 districts reporting required teachers to pay for the expense of the health examination, 24 per cent of 1973 districts reporting had no specified provision for chest x-ray. National Education Association, Research Division, *Teacher Personnel Practices, Urban School Districts, 1955–56.* Special Memo (Washington: The Association, 1956), p. 32.

Table 12.4

Illustration of Substitute Service Procedure

SUBSTITUTE TEACHERS

A. *Securing a Temporary Certificate*

Procedure for securing position of substitute teacher in the Chicago Public Schools:

1. The applicant must secure a temporary certificate issued by the Board of Examiners, who require credentials certifying:

    (1) For elementary school: A Bachelor's Degree including fifteen semester hours in education

    (2) For high school: A Bachelor's Degree including 18 semester hours in education and 18 to 24 hours in the field for which application is made

2. The applicant must pass a health examination and present satisfactory evidence of freedom from tuberculosis

3. The applicant must present a loyalty affidavit as required by law

B. *Application for Position*

When the temporary certificate has been granted, the applicant obtains a payroll number and attendance blanks from the Division of Teacher Payroll. These are signed by the principal for every day a teacher works, and it is the teacher's responsibility to forward these to the Division of Teacher Payroll every two weeks.

The applicant then registers in the Office of the Division of Substitute Teacher Assignment. He obtains a school directory and a copy of the rules and regulations for substitutes. Temporary certificates expire June 30 of the cur-

C. *Requirements for Employment in the TET Group*

The Chicago Board of Education has authorized the employment of elementary teachers who meet the requirements for temporary certificates as full-time temporary teachers at the first year of the appropriate lane of the salary schedule. By the end of a year of employment as a full-time temporary teacher, the teacher is expected to meet full requirements for and take the examination for a regular certificate in either the Kindergarten-Primary grades or the Intermediate-Upper grades.

When a teacher employed under this temporary plan secures a regular certificate to teach and is regularly appointed, his salary will be adjusted so as to give full credit for his accumulated teaching service during the period of temporary employment up to the maximum provided for in the rules. The teacher should consult the Circular of Information issued periodically by the Board of Examiners regarding the general requirements for admission to the examinations and should secure an announcement from the Board of Examiners to determine when the examinations are scheduled.

D. *Requests for Substitute Teachers*

Calls for substitute work are processed only through the office of the Division of Substitute Teacher Assignment. A record of the time a request for a substitute teacher is received and the time the substitute teacher accepts the assignment is kept in the office of this division.

Table 12.4 (cont.)

rent year. Applications for temporary certificates for the following school year may be made any time during and after the spring vacation. Processing of applications requires time and they should be submitted early to assure processing before the opening of schools in September. A new payroll number is issued between the close of the school year in June and the opening of the new school year in September; this new payroll number must be obtained before the substitute teacher is allowed to work in September.

E. *Efficiency Rating*

Principals must submit efficiency marks, once a month, for all substitutes serving three or more consecutive days. The efficiency mark is based on quality of work, appearance, cooperation, punctuality, and remaining in one assigned position until released by the Division of Substitute Teacher Assignment. It is permissible to issue marks for less than three days. An unsatisfactory rating should be accompanied by an explanatory letter.

Source: Chicago Public Schools, *Handbook of Policies and Procedures* (Chicago: Chicago Public Schools, 1961, pp. 32–33).

not this indifference stems from a broader economic postulate which holds that public expenditures should be limited to "basic needs," and which reflects a widely held opinion that the attitude of government for the welfare of people should be one of "laissez faire," is difficult to discern.

Provisions for the Health of Personnel

A desirable feature of school personnel policies is a plan for encouraging and assisting all school employees to keep mentally and physically fit. This is an obligation which every district owes to the children and staff personnel for whom it is responsible. The intent of the plan would be to reduce personnel absence, to secure maximum personnel performance, and to carry out the general objectives of the school health program. There are at least four areas around which provisions should be developed to promote the well-being of school personnel. These include (1) preemployment health standards; (2) periodic examinations during employment; (3) provision of advisory medical service and emergency treatment; and (4) formulation of sound personnel policies conducive to job satisfaction. Details of the foregoing provisions are treated briefly in the text following.

Preemployment Health Standards

A principle of considerable repute in school administration is that selection of personnel should be based upon standards indispensable to satisfactory performance. One such standard which should be applied to all candidates for employment in the public schools is sound health, including mental, physical, and emotional vigor. At the base of any plan for maintaining a healthy staff is the preemployment health examination, which is aimed at eliminating applicants mentally and physically incapable of meeting health standards established by the district.

Statutory provisions in certain states provide a basis for the health examination. According to Table 12.5, there is considerable variation among the states in health examination requirements. Some states have no requirements; in others, a health examination is prerequisite to employment. Periodic health examinations during employment are required in some states; in others, the matter rests with the local board.

Preemployment health standards of local districts should go beyond minimum state requirements. A commendable arrangment is the cooperative development of personnel health standards by school and medical authorities. This approach will enable the school district to establish uniform specifications for the examination of applicants for positions in the school system. Expenses incidental to the administration of the preemployment examinations should be planned for in the annual budget. This expenditure can in no sense be considered a charity, since it is a control measure exercised for the protection of children.

Periodic Examinations

It is apparent that the preemployment examination is but one phase of a program to promote the physical, mental, and emotional fitness of school personnel. In order to maintain personnel health standards, a systematic procedure should be developed which would (1) make provisions for periodic medical examinations and chest x-rays; (2) prescribe administrative action to be taken in the event that a report indicates that an individual needs medical attention, or is a source of contagion; and (3) indicate the procedure to be followed upon the return of an employee after a leave of absence due to illness.

Among the purposes to be served by periodic health examinations are the prevention potential, detection of physical, mental, and emotional disorders of a serious nature, placement of individuals, especially those approaching retirement or those suffering from physical incapacities, in positions which are compatible with personnel physical capacity. The bus driver whose vision may be impaired or the maintenance worker who is a potential risk on a ladder-climbing or window-cleaning assignment illustrate the point.

Advisory Medical Services

A comprehensive plan for promoting the health of the school staff, which takes into consideration both the welfare of children and that of the individual employee, should include advisory medical service. There are special occasions, for example, when the physical, mental, or emotional fitness of an employee to perform his duties is subject to question. Some school boards, under its regulations, reserve the right to require any school employee to submit to a special examination.

Table 12.5

State Provisions for Health Examinations

State 1	General medical examination 2	Examination for tuberculosis and other communicable diseases 3	Examination for tuberculosis only 4
Alabama			Before employment and triannually thereafter by laboratory tests and X rays.
Alaska	Required annually.		
Arizona			Before employment and therafter may be required as often as twice a year; tests not specified.
Arkansas		Before employment.	Before employment only; X ray and laboratory tests if deemed necessary.
California	As required by local board.		Required every two years; X ray or intradermal tuberculin test may be used.
Connecticut	As deemed necessary.		As necessary; tests not specified.
Delaware			Periodical X rays.
District of Columbia	Before employment.		Required annually by X ray.
Hawaii			As necessary; laboratory tests if deemed necessary.
Idaho			Required annually by X ray.
Illinois	As deemed necessary; as required by local board.	Required annually.	
Indiana			Before employment and triannually thereafter by laboratory tests and X rays.
Kansas	As required by local board.		
Kentucky	As required by local board.		

State		
Maine	Required annually.	Required annually by tests prescribed by state school and state health officers.
Maryland	Required annually.	Required annually; law silent as to test.
Massachusetts		As necessary; by intradermal tuberculin test.
Minnesota		As necessary; tests not specified.
Missouri	Before employment.	
New Hampshire	Before employment and thereafter as deemed necessary.	As necessary; tests not specified.
New Jersey		As necessary; tests not specified.
New Mexico		Required annually; law silent as to tests.
New York	As required by local board.	
North Carolina	Required annually.	Required annually by tests prescribed by state school and state health officers; may include X ray.
Ohio		As necessary; tests not specified.
Oregon	Before employment.	Before employment only; tests not specified.
Pennsylvania		As necessary; by X ray.
South Carolina		As necessary; by tests prescribed by state board of health.
South Dakota		Required annually by tests prescribed by state school and state health officers.
Tennessee	Before employment and thereafter as deemed necessary.	As necessary; tests not specified.
Utah	Before employment.	
Virginia		As necessary; tests not specified.
Washington	As required by local board.	As necessary; tests not specified.
West Virginia	As required by local board.	As necessary; tests not specified.
Wisconsin		Periodical X rays in districts of less than 500,000 population.

Source: National Education, Research Division, *The Teacher and the Law*, School Law Series Research Monograph 1959-M3 (Washington: The Association, 1959), p. 19.

There are also examples of personnel malingering at public expense, and, when suspected, are required by regulations to submit to special examinations.

The over-all point of this discussion is that certain administrative machinery is necessary to make advisory medical service available to the board of education, and under special circumstances, to school personnel. In the latter instance, there is no suggestion that extensive medical services should be provided to personnel at public expense. Rather, it points to the availability of a medical referral service which can be utilized by administration when special personnel problems arise and which require bilateral medical advice and information.

Conditions of Work and Personnel Health

Broadly conceived, the total personnel function is concerned with the health and general welfare of the school employee. Administrative practices which can exert a favorable influence on the health of school personnel include security in employment, fair compensation, leaves of absence, health and accident insurance, workmen's compensation, retirement plans, credit unions, equitable assignments, clerical assistance, decent housing, suitable instructional space and materials, academic freedom, and effective leadership. Taking the long view, the factors in the total personnel program relevant to the health of school personnel are numerous; each needs to be appraised periodically to determine its effect in enhancing the conservation of staff health.

Grievances

The dictionary defines a grievance as a just or supposed ground of complaint. Every school system probably has its share of each category. Whether a grievance is real or imagined, automatic means for the redress of human dissatisfactions are not yet available. Unless there is an established procedure for recognizing and initiating action to deal with grievances, which are inevitable in organized human effort, consequences generally come to the surface in the form of poor morale and ineffective performance.

The causes of grievances are legion, ranging from misunderstandings to administrative neglect of human relations. The pattern of grievances in public schools deviates considerably from that existing in business and industry. On the whole, public school personnel generally have greater job security than nonpublic employees. The nature of employment is different, as is the compensation structure, the job classification problem, the objectives of the enterprise, and the employer-employee relationship. Hence, the grievance problems are different, but they do exist. Procedures for handling grievances in the public schools also vary markedly from that of private enterprise. Until recent years, very few school systems had established formal grievance machinery of any kind for the examination and solution of personnel complaints. Most difficulties were handled by an "open-door policy" of the chief administrator. Commendable as this practice may be it will not suffice as a comprehensive plan for coping with staff discontent. There is need for a more systematic, constructive approach which aims primarily at minimizing the number of grievances which arise. This entails a willingness on the part of administration to encourage organization personnel to indicate sources of dissatisfaction and to enlist their judgment in remedying unsatisfactory conditions. Staff involvement in development of appropriate policies and procedures would appear to be a cornerstone in any plan to deal positively with grievances.

The anatomy of most grievance machinery is fairly simple, consisting of a prescribed series of steps, or line of appeal, beginning with presentation of the problem to the immediate superior. If the employee finds no redress at one level, it is possible for him to take the case to higher officials in order of authority, such as principal-superintendent-board of education–state education agency. A general feature of the process is a committee which acts in an advisory capacity as well as a liaison body between the aggrieved and the administration.

Several authorities insist that the psychological effect resulting from mere availability of grievance machinery to organization personnel is far more important than the manner in which it is utilized. When sincere administrative efforts are made to deal with personnel problems, the number of cases which run the full line of appeal are likely to be minimal.

The number of grievance cases will be fewer when administrators at the operating level closest to the employee are able to identify the seeds of discontent. Sensing an incipient problem, dealing with it promptly, tactfully, and informally often forestalls the need for complicated grievance procedures.

The foregoing comments can be summarized by saying that foremost among the conditions necessary for dealing with staff disagreements, complaints, misunderstandings, or dissatisfactions are the following:

1. A policy declaration by the board of education which clearly indicates its intent toward the expression and consideration of grievances.

2. Administrative procedures for implementing grievance policy. This includes preparation of a personnel guide or handbook which indicates: (a) what constitutes a grievance; (b) how the grievance is presented; (c) to whom it is presented initially; (d) steps in the line of appeal, and the routine to be followed in each step; (e) the time limits within which each phase of the grievance process should be completed.

3. Constant assessment of conditions of employment to locate and deal with problems which generate situations conducive to personnel dissatisfaction.[4]

Professional Organizations

Relationship of Organizations to Personnel Welfare

Closely akin to improvement of the general welfare of school personnel are various education associations and organizations which have been established to help solve some of the general professional problems standing in the way of the advancement of education, such as promoting professional standards, improving the quality of service rendered, furthering the social and economic status of the membership, and enhancing the cause of education.

The foremost fact about the professional organization is that it is essential not only to the cause of public education, but to the welfare of each and every member of the profession. The individual teacher cannot, through his efforts alone, bring about conditions and controls necessary to the development and maintenance of a strong teaching profession. Singly, he is unable to mobilize, finance, and direct the collective effort needed to improve salaries, tenure and leave of absence provisions, and retirement benefits. His own efforts

[4] Grievance machinery for public school systems is discussed in National Commission for the Defense of Democracy Through Education, *Taking the Grief out of Grievances in Public School Systems* (Washington: National Education Association, 1958).

are never powerful enough to focus attention and to secure action on the challenging educational issues with which the nation and the world are confronted.

The nature of American society and the influence which organized groups exert upon it leave little room for argument about the necessity for professional associations in the field of education. The rapid development of organized labor in the twentieth century, the gains which have been achieved for its membership, and the power of its influence in national affairs attests to the importance of collective action. The concept of group organization is part of the fabric of the American scene. It is reasonable to assume, furthermore, that it will continue to be a salient feature of every major occupational endeavor.

Variety of Educational Associations

The number and variety of educational organizations in the United States is so extensive that a separate publication would be necessary to catalogue and to describe in detail their purposes, membership, activities, and organizational patterns.[5] They now exist at national,[6] regional, state, and local levels.

That there is a proliferation of educational organizations, that their memberships have increased substantially in the twentieth century, and that they have provided useful services to teachers—these facts by themselves have not made such groups immune from criticism. On the contrary. The shaft of opinion is frequently directed at the ineffectiveness of educational organizations to an extent that they have become a subject of controversy within and outside of the profession.

Criticism

Only in recent years has the role of educational organizations come under serious examination.[7] This is reflected in the paucity of litera-

[5] *The Education Directory,* published annually by the United States Office of Education, identifies more than 500 national and regional education associations.

[6] Organizations which are national and international in scope include: National Education Association, American Federation of Teachers, World Confederation of Organizations of the Teaching Profession, Institute of International Education, Phi Delta Kappa, Delta Kappa Gamma, American Council on Education, Association for Childhood Education International, National Congress of Parents and Teachers, National School Boards Association, and National Citizens Commission for the Public Schools.

[7] For an evaluaton of the National Education Association, see *Progressive Education.* Vol. 34, No. 4 (July, 1957), Entire issue.

ture dealing with the appraisal of these groups. Since the influence of educational organizations is potentially a powerful one in advancing the cause of education in a free society, it would appear that one of the greatest services the profession of education can render to itself is a reexamination of the role which this institution is to serve in the future. Included in such an analysis would be consideration of the criticisms which have been directed frequently at educational organizations, such as:

1. Educational organizations are increasingly taking on the characteristics of labor unions.

2. Educational organizations fail in a most important function—self-criticism.

3. Some state associations have not given enough support to strengthen state departments of education on the grounds it would threaten organization status.

4. Educational organizations devote an excessive concern to teacher welfare.

5. Educational organizations neglect philosophical issues.

6. Lack of organizational unification in education reduces its tremendous potential.

7. The objectives of educational organizations are too limited.

8. Educational organizations are dominated by administrative personnel.

9. Organizations are weak where they should be strong—at the local level.

10. Organizations fail to deal internally with highly controversial issues, such as civil rights.

11. Voluntary membership weakens the influence of educational organizations.

12. Educational organizations do not take effective action to implement the professional standards which they espouse.

13. Efforts of organizations, especially at the state level, are not directed primarily at improving the quality of personnel performance.

14. Organizations protect the incompetent.

15. Approaches used by some associations in dealing with local administrators and local boards of education are not conducive to the improvement of school-community relations.

The foregoing statements are not intended as a blanket indictment of education associations. They do not represent the findings of exhaustive research. They are opinions, published and unpublished, which point up some of the important problems and issues confronting agencies which are important adjuncts of the profession. The discussion which follows focuses further attention upon several of the more important issues relating to education associations and the implications for improving their effectiveness.

Issues and Problems of Educational Organizations

Unification

The question of whether an educator should join the N.E.A. or the A.F.T. is one which has received considerable attention in educational literature. While strengths and weaknesses of each organization are frequent topics of conversation, the divisive and debilitating effects of more than one organization representing the nation's educators has not been given the benefit of the careful scrutiny which it deserves. Exhortations on the salutary effect of organizational competition are not difficult to come by. But surely there is some dissipation of effort in dual representation; certainly there is some loss in organizational strength; certainly there are conflicting positions on larger educational issues which lead to public and professional confusion. While it is not to be anticipated that the unification of organizational effort can be resolved readily, the potential of organizational solidarity cannot be overlooked, for it could mean the largest professionally organized group in the nation. Lieberman, in arguing for a more decisive role for organizational leadership, suggests:

A teachers' organization which is not affiliated with labor, which is free both from administrator domination and also from an unimaginative and unproductive hostility toward administrators, which aggressively advocates teacher control over entry to the teaching profession as well as collective bargaining, which is ready to take a new look at such shibboleths as local control of education, which is adamant on such matters of principle as the elimination of racial segregation from public education, which takes the lead instead of dragging its heels in the introduction of such things as educational television or a new personnel structure in education—such an organization might well replace the N.E.A. as the predominant teachers' organization in the United States. In any case, the development of a teachers' organization along the lines suggested is one of the most important educational needs of this generation.[8]

[8] Myron Lieberman, *The Future of Public Education* (Chicago: University of Chicago Press, 1960), p. 198.

The unconventional approach suggested by Lieberman to revamp the conceptual basis of the professional organization in education will invite criticism, to be sure, for it is one of the few drastic proposals which have been offered to challenge the effectiveness of existing organizational endeavors. Few will question the need for certain reforms in professional organizations for educators. The functions which they should perform and the methods adopted to implement these functions appear to be significant issues which need to be joined.

Method of Operation

The struggle by educators to secure a just share of the nation's economic productivity, to establish working conditions conducive to job satisfaction, and to advance the cause of education generally has taken a variety of forms, including organized as well as unorganized means. The tendency to seek representation to advance the welfare of educators appears to be on the increase.[9] This leads to a consideration of the necessity for collective bargaining by professional organizations in negotiating solutions to personnel problems in public education. Proponents of the idea claim that the present framework for dealing with welfare issues is wholly ineffective and needs to be replaced by a plan which gives organizations the legal right to negotiate with boards through collective bargaining. The opponents, which include both educators and lay people, are inclined to reject any approach which embraces "labor tactics." The issue, restated in a different way, reduces itself to these questions: Should public employees adopt policies similar to those used in business and industry to achieve professional status? If not, what can be done to improve the effectiveness of the present structure so that the aims may be achieved without resort to methods used by labor and industry? The issue involves a choice of values, and is not one which can be settled completely by educators. The consequences of inaction on the part of educational organiza-

[9] Two recent court actions are of interest in this connection. The supreme court of Michigan held that teachers were "public employees" within the meaning of a statute that created a labor mediation board and clothed it with authority to mediate grievances "of a group of public employees" when petitioned so to do. (See Lee O. Garber, "Labor Board Can 'Mediate' Teacher Salaries," *The Nation's Schools*, 65, No. 4 (April, 1960), pp. 98–100. Another case centered around the legality of a Montana School District to enter into a "Masters Agreement" with the Teachers' Union. (*Benson et al. v. School District No. 1 of Silver Bow County et al.* [Mont. Sup. Ct., No. 9908, June 29, 1959]).

tions, however, may well lead to some form of group representation for educators which is independent of the profession. It is a challenge of serious proportions to all educators, then, to devote particular attention to the image which they would have the professional organization become, to the functions they would have it perform, and to the methods which they would have it employ operationally.

Related Issues

The problems and issues involved in educational organizations are so complex that they will not be treated extensively here.[10] It is necessary to point out, however, that high among the major issues in need of extended consideration are the following:

1. Should membership in a major professional organization be compulsory?

2. Should it be made a condition of employment?

3. Should the dues structure of the professional organizations be radically altered to secure revenues which are needed to deal more effectively with professional problems?

4. How can the leadership of associations at all levels be improved?

5. What should be the relationship among national, state, and local associations?

6. Should administrative personnel be excluded from organizations which are generally structured for teachers?

7. Should membership in associations be differentiated according to professional training?

8. What should be the relationship of the local association to the local school administration?

These problems and issues, like so many others in education, will require extensive analysis and understanding before satisfactory solutions are attained. It is part of the responsibility of peronnel administration to provide opportunities for staff members to examine the courses of action which need to be taken to solve some of the pressing problems of educational associations, for the welfare of any single teacher cannot be completely provided for without benefit of group action.

[10] Two scholarly and provocative documents by Lieberman, which include extended treatments of educational organizations are recommended: Myron Lieberman, *Education as a Profession* (Englewood Cliffs, N.J.: Prentice-Hall, Inc., 1956), and *The Future of Public Education* (Chicago: University of Chicago Press, 1960).

Academic and Personal Freedom

Free minds for free men is a concept which is both inspirational and historical in character. It is a matter of considerable import in personnel administration, the ultimate concern of which is to facilitate the teaching-learning process. If children and youth are to be free to learn, the teacher must be free to teach. The relationship is an intimate one which personnel administration seeks to guarantee.

Much has been written lately about academic freedom. The decade covering 1950–1960, referred to as the "difficult years" in the matter of academic freedom, has been witness to various and subtle attempts to restrain freedom of expression in educational institutions. Counterattempts to prevent such restrictions have been equally vigorous.[11] The 1958 Lazarsfeld report on academic behavior and inquiry, involving 2451 social scientists in 165 participating colleges and universities, reveals numerous incidents involving academic freedom.[12] While similar data are not available to indicate the extent of problems relating to academic freedom in the public schools, it appears to be a reasonable assumption that threats to the intellectual, political, and personal freedom of the teaching community do exist.

A Working Definition

The concept of academic freedom means different things to different people. To some it means an absence of restraint on scholarship; to others it means the right to present conflicting and unpopular points of view in the classroom. Some would place certain limitations upon academic freedom; others would not. Some maintain that academic freedom is a matter which concerns only university faculties; others hold that it refers to the liberty to inquire, to discuss, and to interpret any aspect of culture at all levels of instruction. Some believe it refers solely to teacher freedom. Increasingly, it is argued that student freedom is equally involved.

In the discussion which follows the term academic freedom refers

[11] An indication of the concern about academic freedom is shown in the following number of entries under this category in the *Education Index*: 1950–53 (145); 1953–55 (124); 1955–57 (85); 1957–59 (25); 1959–60 (12).

[12] Paul F. Lazarsfeld and Wagner Thielens, Jr., *The Academic Mind—Social Scientists in a Time of Crisis* (Glencoe, Ill.: The Free Press, 1958).

to the extent to which professional personnel are able to exercise intellectual independence and to encourage it in the classroom. As such, it is not to be considered a special kind of privilege for the educator, but a condition essential to free inquiry for the student and the teacher. It is basic to freedom of learning.

Forms of Restraint

Examination of the restraints which have been imposed upon students and teachers provides a wide range of illustrations. These include:

1. Elimination of certain textbooks from the classroom which are unacceptable to a particular segment of society.

2. Restrictions on the teaching of alleged controversial issues, such as socialized medicine, communism, socialism, fascism, the right of organized labor to bargain collectively, sex education, building a new social order, and so on.

3. Restriction of teachers from participating in political activities.

4. Requirement of all educators in institutions receiving state aid to take a special loyalty oath.

5. Restrictions on the purchase of teaching materials which are conspicuously controversial.

6. Restraints on educators from holding public office.

7. Dismissal of fifth-amendment teachers.

8. Legislation forbidding a certain subject to be taught.

9. Denial of student organizations permission to invite guest speakers who are "controversial."

10. Denial of teachers the right to join education associations or unions.

11. Elimination of experimental curriculums, methods, or textbook series on the grounds that they are "progressive."

12. Restriction of teachers from expressing political, economic, or religious views.

The point of concern in these and other forms of restraint upon the academic and personal freedom of public school personnel is that safeguards are needed in local school systems to ensure conditions conducive to the teaching-learning process. The difficulties in achieving these safeguards, however, are formidable. There are boards of education who see no point in establishing policies on academic and personal freedom. Some have come to believe certain restraints in these areas are not only desirable, but outright necessities. An equally significant consideration is that threats to the personal and academic freedom of personnel cannot be minimized unless protective measures are established by the board of education. The following paragraphs are devoted to an examination of this problem, especially the kinds of constructive action which can be taken by boards of education, administrators, communities, and teachers which will contribute to the preservation of the freedoms under consideration.

Responsibilities of the Board

To an appreciable extent, the academic and personal freedom of school personnel depends upon what the board of education wants or permits. This is so because of what might be referred to as the doctrine of organizational accountability, or the responsibility of authorities in an organization for the actions of personnel under its direction. If conditions are to prevail which make possible the development and maintenance of intellectual independence in the local school system, the board of education must take certain steps to see that these conditions are established.

What are the positive steps which can be taken by the board of education to encourage and to protect the freedom essential to growth of the democratic ideal? Although the board can do many things, its first obligation is to understand clearly the purposes of education in a democratic society, for the events which take place in a classroom—the discussions, the methods and materials employed—must be appraised in terms of purpose.

Another step which the board can take is to make clear the kind of conduct which it expects the staff to maintain within and outside of the academic scene. Some of the more important aspects of this conduct may be suggested by the following questions: How does the board expect the staff to deal with controversial issues? Does the board, for example, see the need for emphasizing the basic moral and intellectual commitments inherent in a democracy? To what extent is the board committed to the principle that the development of the curriculum is a professional task? If the board is clearly committed to this principle, does it resist pressures to eliminate certain textbooks? Does it resist attempts to make changes in the curriculum which are not approved by the professional staff? Does the board support the principle that a teacher outside the classroom has no less freedom than any other citizen? Does it support his freedom to express his convictions on political, economic, and religious subjects? These questions, and countless others, call for policies by the board of education which will safeguard personnel in their responsibilities as teachers and as citizens.

In brief, the board and the community have an important responsibility for establishing the climate within which academic freedom can flourish. While a precise formula for doing this has not yet been written, much can be accomplished if the board is alert to its responsibilities in the area under consideration. This includes a willingness to examine all criticisms of the school and its staff objectively, to avoid hasty action to satisfy pressure groups, to establish machinery for dealing with charges or attacks against school personnel, and to develop policies designed to provide personnel with the security necessary to the maintenance of the ideals of public education.

Responsibility of the Administrator

The responsibility of the administrator for maintaining academic and personal freedoms of the school staff is both difficult and delicate. His task is to give support, meaning, and direction to the principles of academic and personal freedom. This means, among other things:

1. That he must be a student of our civilization, its cultural heritage, values, and ideals. Without these understandings, his ability to provide leadership in the areas under discussion is limited.

2. That he must exercise selectivity in the employment of personnel, for the beliefs and attitudes of the teaching staff determine the extent to which free exercise of the intellect obtains in the classroom.

3. That he exercise the authority delegated to him as educational leader of the school system to establish educational objectives, curriculums, and methods which encourage the development of intellectual independence.

4. That he makes every effort to resist attempts to limit or to destroy intellectual freedom.

5. That because of his unique position in the educational hierarchy, he is obligated to interpret fully and clearly to the board, the

community, and the school staff the broader implications of the professional's need for intellectual freedom.

It is because of the long tradition that the teacher should be a nonpolitical, no-issue citizen, that his task should be confined to an understanding and maintenance of the status quo, that the role of the administrator is both difficult and challenging in seeking solutions to the problems under discussion. But the great social changes which have occurred in America and in the world place upon him a major share of the responsibility for encouraging the development of free minds, for creating an intellectual climate conducive to this end, and for protecting the schools against restraints and attacks on the freedom of teaching and learning.

Responsibilities of the Teacher

Two kinds of responsibility should be stressed in connection with the teacher and academic freedom. One pertains to the teacher's obligation to conduct the teaching-learning process in keeping with the principles upon which academic freedom rests. There is little point to the establishment of elaborate academic safeguards if the spirit of inquiry is not encouraged by the school staff. If controversial issues are ignored, if varying points of view are not tolerated, if the right to dissent is forbidden, if the teacher is careful not to bring up controversial topics, if he evades an opinion solicited by students, where does this leave us? In certain respects it leaves us with students who have little understanding of the scientific method, or with citizens who are unable to make intelligent decisions because their education was conducted in an atmosphere where the spirit of free inquiry was not encouraged.

There is, however, the difficult question of the levels at which such educational experiences are appropriate. As Fuchs points out:

Until the learner has reached some stage of responsibile maturity, not only must conduct be restrained to a larger extent than later, but the learning process must be affirmatively conditioned to secure the transmission to the newcomer of the prevailing cultural heritage. It is a delicate matter, as every parent and professional educator knows, to transmit the wisdom of the past and of the present consistently with freedom for the learner and with the attitude of devotion to basic beliefs, accompanied by tentativeness of view, that, in our culture, must somehow be communicated. Yet, clearly, at an early age in the learner's course, the more certain knowledge and the relatively prevalent attitudes must be conveyed. Gradually criticism and questioning, accompanied by methods of evaluation and of arriving at independent conclusions, can be developed until the stage of complete freedom, testing all knowledge and all values without destroying them, is reached.[13]

Thus, determination of the manner in which, the degree to which, and the time at which intellectual independence is encouraged become some of the staff's most challenging professional responsibilities and opportunities.

Finally, there is another kind of teacher responsibility related to academic freedom. This is the self discipline inextricably related to freedom. It is the obligation to maintain those standards of personal and professional integrity which are in keeping with the noble purpose the teacher serves. The standards of teaching, learning, and scholarship to which he adheres must be conducive to the attainment of the aims of the educational system. This is, in reality, academic freedom's justification.

Suggested Reading

American Association of School Administrators, *Administering a Sick-Leave Program for School Personnel* (Washington: The Association, 1954).

American Association of School Administrators, *Health in Schools*, rev. ed. (Washington: The Association, 1951).

American Association of University Professors, "Academic Freedom and Tenure and Academic Retirement: Statements of Principles," *American Association of University Professors Bulletin*, 43, No. 1 (Spring, 1957) pp. 112–120.

American Civil Liberties Union, "Academic Freedom Academic Responsibility: Their Meaning to Students, Teachers, Administrators and the Community," *American Association of University Professors Bulletin*, Vol. 42, No. 3 (Autumn, 1956), pp. 517–529.

Corey, Arthur F., "Professional Organizations and You," *N.E.A. Journal*, 46, No. 7 (October, 1957), pp. 453–454.

[13] Ralph F. Fuchs, "Intellectual Freedom and the Educational Process," *American Association of University Professors Bulletin*, 42, No. 3 (Autumn, 1956), pp. 471–472.

Haag, Jessie Helen, *School Health Program* (New York: Henry Holt and Co., Inc., 1958).

Harris, Chester W., ed. *Encyclopedia of Educational Research*, 3rd ed. (New York: The Macmillan Co., 1960), pp. 1362–1363.

Kirk, Russell, *Academic Freedom—An Essay in Definition* (Chicago: Henry Regnery Co., 1955).

Lieberman, Myron, "The Influence of Teachers' Organizations upon American Education," in *Social Forces Influencing American Education*, Sixtieth Yearbook of the National Society for the Study of Education (Chicago: The University of Chicago Press, 1961), Chapter VIII.

Lyfford, Joseph P., "Social Science Teachers and the Difficult Years," *American Association of University Professors Bulletin*, 43, No. 4 (December, 1957), pp. 636–645.

Mark, Max, "The Meanings of Academic Freedom," *American Association of University Professors Bulletin*, 43, No. 3 (September, 1957), pp. 498–506.

National Education Association, Department of Classroom Teachers, *Conditions of Work for Quality Teaching* (Washington: The Association, 1959).

National Education Association, Educational Policies Commission, *Professional Organizations in American Education* (Washington: The Association, 1957).

National Education Association, Research Division, *The Teacher and the Law*, School Law Series Research Monograph 1959-M3 (Washington: The Association, 1959).

Pfiffner, John M., *The Supervision of Personnel* (Englewood Cliffs, N.J.: Prentice-Hall, Inc., 1958).

General Welfare:

TENURE AND RETIREMENT

CHAPTER THIRTEEN

Two of the most constructive concepts for improving both the effectiveness of the school system and the general welfare of public school personnel are those relating to tenure and retirement. Both may be thought of as security measures which society establishes in behalf of personnel entrusted with the education of its children. In its finest intent, tenure is a necessary safeguard to provide continuity of employment for the competent, to prevent unjustified dismissals, and to maintain staff stability and academic security in the interests of carrying out the proper function of the school system. Retirement, on the other hand, is viewed as an arrangement between the district and organization personnel which provides a financial safeguard after withdrawal from duty because of age or disability.

As the following discussion intends to make clear, tenure and retirement practices affecting public school personnel are shaped by statutory provisions and court decisions. Within the legal framework, however, a heavy responsibility rests with local school officials for realizing the intent of tenure and retirement arrangements. Much of the emphasis in the text which follows is aimed at developing an

339

understanding of the constructive utilization of tenure and retirement provisions in personnel administration for the general welfare of school personnel.

Characteristics of Tenure

Tenure, in the broadest sense, embodies a system designed to provide educators with continuing employment during efficient service, and which establishes an orderly procedure to be followed before their services are terminated. Salient features of the tenure system include:

1. Completion of a specified probationary period, the duration of which is generally three years. The probationary period is construed to mean a temporary appointment, during which time the individual is carefully supervised and appraised in terms of the extent of his ability to render efficient service to the school organization.

2. Automatic tenure status at the end of the probationary period to personnel who meet established requirements.

3. An orderly procedure for the dismissal of personnel. This includes provision for notifying the individual that his services are unsatisfactory, as well as a reasonable opportunity to show improvement before notification of intent to dismiss is given.

4. Notice of the intent to terminate the services of the individual in the event that the desired improvement in service has not been attained. Written notice of the intent to dismiss details the specific reasons for the action which is contemplated.

5. A hearing before local school authorities which provides an opportunity for the accused to defend himself against the charges.

6. The right to appeal an adverse decision to higher educational authorities, and to the courts.

The meaning and operation of tenure laws are not always understood by some persons within the professional ranks, nor by many lay citizens as well. Perhaps this lack of understanding has given rise to the relatively high incidence of tenure litigation, as well as to the refusal of a few legislatures to support any kind of tenure legislation.[1]

Let us consider, first, the legal nature of tenure. In general, tenure is construed to be a privilege granted by the state rather than an obligation which the state owes to the educator. The latter has no inherent right to permanent employment merely because he has com-

[1] States without tenure laws in 1960 are listed in Table 13.1.

plied with state certification requirements, or because he has served a probationary period during which he rendered service which was satisfactory in the eyes of his employer. It is generally held by the courts that a tenure statute is not in the nature of a contract between the state and the teachers affected by it; that an act of the legislature is only an expression of current legislative policy; that the acts of one legislature do not necessarily bind future legislatures unless the intent to do so is clear.[2]

The phrase "permanent employment" is frequently the cause of many misinterpretations of tenure legislation. Customary practice is to grant permanent tenure after an individual has served a probationary period. Permanent tenure, however, does not necessarily mean that the local board of education has no authority to effect changes affecting persons who have gained tenure status. It does not mean, for example, that the board, so long as its actions are not arbitrary and capricious, cannot transfer a teacher from one school to another. Tenure of employment and tenure of assignment are not necessarily synonymous. Nor does it mean that tenure teachers cannot be reassigned to different positions. If the board decides to reduce the size of the staff because of declining enrollments, mere existence of tenure legislation does not prevent the board from taking such action. In brief, it is generally not the intent of tenure laws to prevent boards of education from making necessary changes which involve tenure personnel. Permanent employment does not mean the absolute absence of change in the conditions of employment. If this were so, administrators would be powerless to cope with the day-to-day personnel problems with which they are confronted.[3]

Tenure Objectives

Among the objectives most frequently cited for establishing tenure for professional educators, the following are representative:

1. To guarantee professional personnel security of employment during satisfactory service.

[2] Newton Edwards, *The Courts and the Public Schools*, rev. ed. (Chicago: University of Chicago Press, 1955), p. 467.
[3] For a more detailed treatment of the nature of tenure and tenure status see Lee O. Garber, "Making Teacher Tenure Laws Work," *The Nation's Schools*, 58, No. 5 (November, 1956), pp. 63–64. Also Newton Edwards, *The Courts and The Public Schools*, rev. ed. (Chicago:' University of Chicago Press, 1955), Chapter XVII.

2. To protect personnel against unwarranted dismissal of any kind.

3. To encourage academic freedom in the classroom.

4. To prevent the incompetent from gaining permanent employment in the profession.

5. To maintain staff stability and to promote job satisfaction.

6. To ensure school personnel no less personal freedom outside of the classroom than any other citizen.

7. To assure the community that its schools will be staffed with personnel who are at liberty to encourage student freedom of inquiry and expression.

State activity in tenure legislation is generally defended on the basis of social benefit. The state seeks to improve the school system through the tenure instrumentality, which is designed in part to protect the people and their children from incompetent teaching. The state's purpose in protecting the teacher against arbitrary acts which are inspired by political, personal, or capricious reasons is to enable him to exercise his civil rights and to render effective professional service. The point of emphasis here is that tenure legislation is not a unilateral action by the state to establish an occupational haven for the incompetent. Tenure is designed to serve not only the interests of professional personnel, but the state, the people and their children, and the local school system. There are few matters in personnel administration more in need of solution than that of making tenure laws serve the social interest mentioned above. Every school system which has the authority to grant tenure can contribute in part to the solution of the problem by injecting far more consideration into tenure decisions than that which is usually accorded this important personnel function.

Tenure Practice

An outline of the nature and extent of tenure practice in the several states is contained in Table 13.1. Examination of these and related data reveals:

1. There is a lack of uniformity in existing contract and tenure provisions for public school personnel.

2. The range in tenure practice is considerable, varying from no tenure provisions whatsoever in a few states to state-wide coverage of all teachers in other states.

3. In some states tenure provisions are not identical for all school districts.

4. Tenure generally does not include all professional personnel. Whether superintendents are covered by the tenure provisions in some states is a moot question.

5. Some laws apply to one city or county only.

6. In some states the laws are not equally applicable to all teachers.

7. A substantial portion of public school personnel is not accorded essential tenure provisions.

8. Legal arrangements governing the duration of employment in the several states vary from the annual contract, which affords the least protection, to the tenure law which gives assurance of continuing employment after completion of the probationary period, and which provides an orderly procedure for dismissal.

Conditions Governing Duration of Employment

Table 13.1 categorizes major types of employment contracts in operation in the several states for public school personnel. Although the language contained in tenure provisions varies considerably from one state to another, and makes for difficulty in providing clear-cut descriptions of the different kinds of contractual arrangements, outstanding features of the contracts listed in Table 13.1 are summarized below.

Permanent Tenure. This generally means a statutory guarantee, which may have either partial or state-wide application, of continuing employment after successful completion of a probationary period, and which entitles the teacher to a notice of intent to dismiss, statement of charges, a fair hearing, and the right to appeal.[4]

Continuing Contracts. States providing continuing contracts are noted in Table 13.1. One type, referred to as the spring-notification contract, provides that a teacher's contract will be automatically renewed for the ensuing school year unless notice of nonrenewal is given by a specified date. Under this type of contract, no reasons for

[4] The National Education Association defines a tenure law as "one which (a) provides for continuing employment of teachers who, under its terms, have acquired permanent tenure, or continuing contract status; and (b) requires boards to comply with prescribed procedural provisions of notice, statement of charges, and right to a hearing before a tenure teacher can be dismissed, or before nonrenewal of the teacher's contract of employment can be effective." National Education Association, Research Division, "Teacher Tenure Laws," *Research Bulletin,* 38, No. 3 (October, 1960), p. 81.

dismissal are necessary, since the teacher is not dismissed; he is simply not reemployed.

Another kind of continuing contract, not specifically referred to in Table 13.1, provides that a statement of the reasons for dismissal accompany notice of nonrenewal of the contract, and that the teacher may request a hearing. For the most part, continuing contract arrange-

Table 13.1

Type of State Tenure or Contract Provisions in Effect, 1960

1. STATES WITH TENURE LAWS

State-wide without exception

Alabama	Iowa	New Hampshire
Alaska	Kentucky	New Jersey
Arizona	Louisiana	New Mexico
Connecticut *a*	Maine	Pennsylvania
Delaware	Maryland	Rhode Island
District of Columbia	Massachusetts	Tennessee
Florida *b*	Minnesota	Washington
Hawaii	Montana	West Virginia
Idaho		

Less than state-wide—exceptions as noted

California: Optional in districts with average daily attendance under 850 pupils
Colorado: Subject to local adoption in small districts
Illinois: Excludes districts under a board of directors
Indiana: Excepts township schools
Michigan: Two different laws have been enacted, both subject to local adoption
New York: Certain rural districts not covered
Ohio: Optional in districts of under 800 pupils

In certain places only

Georgia: DeKalb, Fulton, and Richmond Counties
Kansas: Kansas City and Wichita
Missouri: St. Louis
Nebraska: Lincoln and Omaha
Oregon: Districts with average daily attendance of more than 4500, and districts where tenure was in effect prior to September 1, 1958
Wisconsin: County and city of Milwaukee

Table 13.1 cont.

2. STATES WITHOUT TENURE LAWS

State-wide continuing contract of spring-notification type	*Annual or long-term contracts*
Arkansas	Mississippi
Nevada	North Carolina
North Dakota	South Carolina *d*
Oklahoma	Texas
South Dakota	Utah
Virginia *c*	Vermont *d*
	Wyoming *d*

---

a Special local tenure laws govern certain cities.
b Special local tenure laws govern certain counties.
c Subject to local adoption.
d Statutes silent on permissible length of contract term.
Source: National Education Association, Research Division, School Law Summaries, *Tenure and Contracts* (Washington: The Association, 1960), p. 3.

ments, such as those described above, cannot be considered as genuine tenure provisions.

There are variations of continuing contracts, however, which are considered to provide to the teacher what is tantamount to permanent tenure since they fulfill the major criteria of genuine tenure laws.

Annual and Long-term Contracts. A term contract provides for employment for a specific period of time. The duration of employment under a term contract is usually one year, although it should be noted in Table 13.1 that some states authorize long-term contracts. Whether the contract is on an annual basis or longer, the teacher whose contract has not been renewed has no right to notice or hearing unless these provisions are so stipulated in the contract. It goes without saying that term contracts do not embody the tenure concept.

Improvement in Tenure for Public School Personnel

Despite the fact that tenure coverage for public school personnel has not yet attained a level which is regarded to be satisfactory, the one clear point which should be recognized is that considerable progress has been made in this direction in a relatively short period of time. In 1930, for example, the majority of the states had no tenure laws for teachers. As indicated in Table 13.1 the situation in 1960 is quite different. Only a few states have yet to enact some form of tenure legislation.

It is universally recognized that while progress made in tenure legislation is encouraging, laws of most states can and should be materially improved. In some instances, for example, the law provides only token protection.

While it is easy enough to bring into bold relief the present shortcomings of tenure legislation, it is fairly certain that solution to many tenure problems does not reside completely in strengthening tenure statutes, essential as such action generally is deemed. Opportunities at the local level to improve tenure by other than legislative means are considerable, and to this the efforts of personnel administration can be properly directed. Selective elimination of probationary personnel, clarification of policies on transfer, reassignment and promotion, definition of seniority rank in the event of staff reduction, development of procedures to cope with problems relative to reduction in status or compensation, means by which probationary teachers are dismissed, definite board policies on tenure which are in keeping with or exceed state tenure laws—these and other measures will help to provide desired staff competency and security which is requisite to effective performance.

The Tenure Process

The treatment in the foregoing sections of the broad subject of tenure legislation is, by intent, brief and selective. Its object is to show the interrelationship between tenure problems and personnel administration. In this section an effort will be made to view the tenure process in perspective, and to illustrate contributions which personnel administration can make to staff improvement and welfare in various facets of the total tenure process. In the final analysis, it is clearly against the interests of the public, the children and youth, and the local school system to allow incompetents to gain continuing employment status. But it is also clearly in the interests of society to prevent the loss or dismissal of competent personnel. The tenure process must be considered as one means by which both ends can be served.

Each of the phases of the process, including the probationary period, the tenure privilege, termination of service, and the right of appeal, will be discussed. The suggestions offered are intended to be illustrative rather than prescriptive.

The Probationary Period

Permanent appointments to the school staff, reference to which has been made at various points throughout this text, represent long-term commitments in administrative judgment, public trust, and school revenues. As such, tenure decisions take on added significance and cannot be treated casually or in an offhand manner. Perhaps this is why the probationary period is considered to be a matter of strategic importance in tenure considerations.

There are at least four purposes which personnel administration can attain during the probationary period. The first has to do with an assessment of the individual—his present competency and future potential, his compatability as a member of the working team, and his ability to serve the future staff needs of the organization. Another purpose is the contribution which the organization can make to the development of the individual through careful supervision and appraisal. A third purpose is to validate the original selection and placement. The probationary period provides an opportunity over an extended period of time to determine whether the original choice and placement were, in effect, faulty. Finally, and most important, the probationary period provides an opportunity for selective elimination which will permit the organization to employ on a permanent basis only those who meet the terms of excellence required for such appointments.

Several major questions relating to the probationary period should be considered for procedural reasons by local boards of education. These include the following:

1. Are experienced teachers new to the district required to serve a probationary period? If so, what should be the length of the probationary period?

2. Should notice of unsatisfactory work be given during the probationary period? If so, how frequently?

3. Should professional growth requirements be established for probationary teachers? If so, what should be the nature and scope of the requirements?

4. Should teachers be allowed to serve more than one probationary period?

5. Should substitute service count toward fulfillment of the probationary period?

6. What procedures should be followed when dismissal of probationary teachers is contemplated?

Answers to these and other questions pertaining to teachers serving a probationary period are sometimes set forth in the laws of certain states. In others, the laws are completely silent. Regardless of presence or absence of specific legislation, many problems can be avoided if the local board of education takes positive steps to clarify the operational aspects of the probationary period. When policies and procedures governing probationary personnel are reduced to written form to provide greated understanding by those affected, the likelihood is that this approach will be conducive to solutions to the problems under consideration.

Measures which should be taken by the organization during the probationary period to assure a capable and stable teaching corps include:

1. Consistent attention of the administration to the orientation and in-service development of the probationer.

2. Provision of funds for an extensive in-service program.

3. Consistent appraisal of, and counseling with, temporary personnel by the administrative head of each attendance unit, aided by the supervisor, department head, and key teachers assigned to this role.

4. Continuity in the selection process, including early dismissal of those who are decidedly inferior or barely acceptable. Those in the latter category present some of the most difficult administrative decisions relating to tenure.

It is recognized by educators that the factors which interfere with and frequently prevent development and maintenance of a capable staff are numerous and vexing. For example, teacher shortages and lack of funds for recruiting and retaining personnel of high caliber often tempt some administrators to ignore the qualitative aspects of staffing, one consequence of which is that the incompetent are permitted to gain tenure status. It is also apparent that as the proportion of ineffective staff members increases, the ability of the district to recruit and to retain superior personnel tends to decrease. The sheer waste of time, money, administrative effort, and educational opportunities incurred through the admission of unsatisfactory personnel to the profession is so staggering that it must be avoided. No better opportunity exists to minimize errors of judgment in these matters than in the recruitment, selection, and probationary processes.

The Tenure Privilege

Acceptable practice in implementing the tenure principle calls for: (1) assurance of continuing employment after successful fulfillment of the probationary period; (2) termination of employment only for defensible cause; and (3) limitations on the dismissal procedure. In return for the tenure privilege there are certain obligations which all tenure personnel are expected to assume. Without going into detail, this involves, for one thing, adherence to the code of ethics for the teaching profession.[5] The bilateral character of tenure assumes that the local board of education will protect the employment security of personnel during efficient service. It assumes also that personnel will fulfill obligations attending the service for which they are employed.

Some of the tenure problems which frequently create difficulty are those which do not involve dismissal proceedings, such as transfer and reassignment, reduction in salary, demotion, and the abolition of positions due to enrollment, curriculum, or financial exigencies. While the right of administrators to transfer and to reassign personnel is recognized generally by the courts, demotions under some tenure laws invoke the tenure process. It can be argued forcefully that administration has the obligation to accord all personnel who are to be demoted in status or salary the right to be notified, a written statement of reasons for the action, and a fair hearing. The principle of seniority should be adhered to in the event that reduction in teaching positions is necessary.

Termination of Service

On the basis of past experience or statistical probabilities, it is a certainty that school districts from time to time must dismiss tenure personnel. In many cases this is not so much a reflection on the individual as it is on the recruitment, selection, placement, and appraisal

[5] See *NEA Handbook, 1960–61* (Washington: National Education Association, 1960).

processes in operation. As most everyone knows, there are personnel whose immoral, intemperate, or insubordinate behavior leaves the administration no choice but dismissal, and that there are legal channels for accomplishing this purpose. But the individual whose regressive inefficiency becomes the cause for dismissal proceedings is another problem, especially if the incidence of such cases is excessive. While reasons why competent persons gradually become incompetent have not been clearly isolated, there are grounds for assuming that some of the responsibility can be laid on the institutional doorstep. Some staff members stagnate because of lack of opportunity; others become inefficient because of excessive teaching loads; some fail because of lack of proper supervision; others do not succeed in spite of their willingness to succeed. The point of concern here is that the organization does not fail in its effort to provide optimum climate and conditions of employment conducive to success. Until the organization does its utmost to match the man and the job, and to create the many conditions which attend job satisfaction and success, dismissal is hardly the conscionable, though it may be the only remaining approach.

In general, the causes and procedures for dismissing a tenure teacher are set forth in the statutes, although there is considerable variation in the statutory language and in the interpretations possible under the different tenure laws.

Notice of the decision to separate a tenure teacher from the school system should, of course, follow legal procedure, and, in addition, provide ample time for the teacher affected to search for another position. In most tenure laws, notice of the intent to dismiss must be given within a specified time limit prior to the dismissal. It is worth noting at this point that should the teacher propose to withdraw from service, he should give school authorities notice in ample time to secure a replacement. Typical requirements in the state laws range from 30 to 60 days' notice.

A fair hearing, preceded by written notice of intent to dismiss, including a statement of the charges against the accused are among the essentials of an acceptable tenure law. Those in charge of the hearing should: (1) provide opportunity for the accused teacher to be heard in his own defense; (2) permit the accused to have counsel and to present witnesses; (3) have a stenographic record of the hearing prepared in case of appeal.

In the event that the results of the hearing are not in favor of the accused, and the dismissal action stands, the statutes generally provide opportunity for administrative (state superintendent, state board of education) as well as ultimate appeal to the courts.

Suggestions for Minimizing Tenure Litigation

Although resort to the courts by teachers for legal redress from dismissal actions which are capricious, illegal, and arbitrary is sometimes necessary, it is generally agreed that involvement of school officials and personnel in legal controversy can be minimized. Garber, in reviewing the causes and procedures for dismissing a tenure teacher, offers the following suggestions to board members for decreasing litigation.

1. In dealing with its personnel, a school board should always act in good faith. Any attempt to evade the operation of the law is debatable on the ground of ethics. Nevertheless, whenever a school board is convinced of the fact that the continued employment of a particular tenure teacher is not in the best interest of the boys and girls, for any reason, not only is it justified in attempting to dismiss that teacher but its duty is to do so.
2. When dismissal is required by the circumstances, it should be achieved in the legal manner.
3. A tenure law does not give a teacher a vested right to continued employment.
4. A school board may dismiss a teacher on tenure status for reasons of economy or when his services are no longer required because of curricular or program changes.
5. A school board may transfer a tenure teacher from one position to another in the same system, as long as the position to which he is transferred is not of lower grade or rank, and as long as it does not decrease his salary.
6. Where the statute specifically enumerates the causes for dismissing a permanent teacher, courts generally hold that the enumeration is exhaustive and a board may not dismiss a teacher for any cause not mentioned in the statute.
7. Where the statute permits the board to dismiss a teacher for "good and just cause," the board has wide latitude, but it may not act arbitrarily and capriciously.
8. Where the statute sets up specific procedures for notifying a teacher

of charges and for granting him a hearing, the board, if its action is to be legal, must follow the statute, as the mode is the measure of the power.

9. While the courts will not, necessarily, void a board's action if it departs slightly from the statutory procedure, a board, in order to be on the safe side, should be satisfied with nothing less than a rigid compliance with the statutes.

10. Before taking any action toward the dismissal of a teacher, a school board should familiarize itself with the law as found in the statutes and in court decisions. Even this is not sufficient. It should employ counsel to guide it in each step it takes. Tenure laws are complex. A board that decides to operate without an attorney is destined to encounter numerous difficulties.[6]

Tenure for Administrators

There is something of a tradition in American education that the principles of tenure should apply to teachers but not to administrators. Justification of this practice has been an issue of long standing. The arguments, both pro and con, are not greatly dissimilar from those relating to the need for, or the undesirability of, tenure for teachers.

From the standpoint of the actual tenure coverage for administrators in the several states, superintendents are seldom mentioned in the tenure laws, the result of which has been that tenure coverage of administrative positions is often left to judicial interpretation.[7]

Since very little is known about the relationship of the length of service of an administrator and the quality of the school system which he administers, it is likely that the issue of administrative tenure will continue. The fact that the term of office of the superintendent of schools is not generally fixed by law has probably given impetus to the assumption that this position affords, at best, tenuous employment. Examination of the available data regarding this problem, however, seems to indicate that there is much more stability in the superintendency than had been traditionally assumed. A 1960 report of a study conducted by the American Association of School Administrators concludes that superintendents are less mobile than is commonly

[6] Lee O. Garber, "Causes and Procedures for Dismissing a Tenure Teacher," *The Nation's Schools*, 58, No. 2 (December, 1956), pp. 73–74.

[7] Chester W. Harris, ed., *Encyclopedia of Educational Research*, 3rd ed. (New York: The Macmillan Co., 1960), pp. 1382–1384.

thought. The mean time in the present position for the administrators included in the sample was nine years.[8] A report by Spalding and Hummel on the tenure of the superintendents in cities above 200,000 population indicates similar findings. This report also notes that during the past 25 years, 17 out of 109 terminations in the cities under consideration were due to dismissal, which, according to the authors, is a rebuff to the assumption that the majority of superintendents are forced to resign because of the whims of the school board. Period data reported by Spalding and Hummel on the average annual turnover of superintendents of schools in cities above 200,000 in population are shown in Table 13.2.

Table 13.2

Average Annual Turnover of Superintendents of Schools in Cities above 200,000

Period	Total Positions Filled	Per cent of Average Annual Turnover
1933–1937	20	10
1938–1942	18	9
1943–1947	29	14.5
1948–1952	17	5
1953–1957	26	9.3

Note: (Years 1933–47, 40 cities; 1948–57, 56 cities).
Average Annual Turnover of Superintendents
Tenure?" *American School Board Journal*, 137 (September, 1958), pp. 37–38.

The logic of the argument against tenure for superintendents, which the present discussion supports, is straightforward. It acknowledges the difficulties inherent in the superintendency, its responsibility for supporting unpopular views on occasion, and the requirement for constantly dealing with issues and difficult decisions. It recognizes the pressures and problems which are constant threats to the security of the position. But it contends that this is in the nature of the leadership role in any organization, a condition which no amount of tenure by law can mitigate.

The view of the no-tenure advocates that the chief administrator

[8] American Association of School Administrators, *Professional Administrators for American Schools*, Thirty-eighth Yearbook (Washington: The Association, 1960), p. 24.

is expendable—that the hold on his position should be the least secure of any in the organization—is posited on the principle that the entire system and the attainment of its mission is closely related to his effectiveness. If he is ineffective an impasse develops, and the system falls short of attaining its intended purpose. This principle also holds that there is a difference in tenure considerations for the chief administrator and the teacher. The latter is accorded the privilege of tenure so that he may seek and speak the truth. The administrator's function is a much more encompassing one. He must link purposes, programs, personnel, plant, and principles into a coordinated effort so that the system may go forward. When he fails in this effort, the principle holds that his dismissal is warranted. It may be argued that tenure may be of some value as a guarantee of security. But a position of such strategic importance can become untenable despite any protection which tenure may provide.

The demands of the superintendency in modern America are such that the chief administrator cannot meet the full obligations of the office without entailing risk. Leadership in any organization is a risk venture, an exposed position which can best be secured by capable performance. The right to leadership must be continuously earned. It cannot be guaranteed by law.

An arrangement which appears to be more satisfactory than permanent tenure for the superintendent is a statutory term of office or a contract of sufficient duration which will provide ample opportunity to demonstrate his ability. Salaries which are high enough to attract and to compensate administrators for the prevailing risks and the absence of tenure will help. An administrative staff which is numerically and qualitatively above average may contribute to his effectiveness. But in the final analysis, no way has yet been found to guarantee security in the superintendency, and at the same time, to eliminate the risk element.

Retirement

Provision for the health and welfare of persons who withdraw from service because of age, years of service, or disability appears to be one of the values to which our society is committed. The twentieth century has been witness to a series of commendable developments aimed at making life more satisfying and secure for the aged and infirm. For the nation as a whole these include enactment by Congress of the original Social Security Act of 1935, and subsequent amendments; [9] passage of workmen's compensation laws, development of life insurance plans by private companies, and general emergence of pension and retirement systems in business, industry, and government.

During the twentieth century and more especially in the 1950–1960 decade, efforts to provide improved benefits for educators have been vigorous, the consequence of which has been emergence of a variety of plans covering retirement, life insurance, and medical expense protection. All states now have retirement systems (either state or local) for public school teachers; [10] some or all teachers are covered by social security in thirty-eight states; [11] seventy-six per cent of the four-year institutions of higher education, it is estimated, have retirement plans.[12]

The necessity for providing retirement and related benefits, then, is no longer at issue. The emerging pattern of the federal, state, and local units of government uniting with the educator to establish suitable benefits is a heartening one, despite existence of unsatisfactory features in some of the retirement systems. The major task ahead in benefit planning for educators appears to be maintenance and improvement of existing systems to the point where they become effective contributors to the objectives of education.

Objectives of Retirement Systems

Before beginning an analysis of retirement systems, it may be useful to examine some of the major reasons for their existence and perpetuation. Strangely enough, the problems involved in retirement planning have not aroused the interest of the profession to the extent that a majority of its members have been actively engaged in seeking more satisfactory solutions. Adjustments in retirement systems are

[9] 1939, 1946, 1950, 1952, 1954, 1956, 1957, 1958, 1960, 1961.

[10] National Education Association, Research Division, School Law Series Research Monograph 1959-M3, *The Teacher and the Law* (Washington: The Association, 1959), p. 80.

[11] National Council on Teacher Retirement, Retirement Income Series, Number 17, Revised, *Social Security Coverage of Public School Teachers* (Washington: NEA Research Division, 1961), p. 3.

[12] William C. Greenough and Francis P. King, *Retirement and Insurance Plans in American Colleges* (New York: Columbia University Press, 1959), p. 4.

inevitable. Inflation continues to diminish the value of retirement allowances. Moreover, the prospect of an extension of the benefits of the Social Security Act and their application to existing retirement systems call for increased understanding and wise decisions by school personnel. If the reasons underlying retirement systems are better understood, it is likely that staff members will participate actively in establishing arrangements which are conducive to these ends. The discussion which follows treats the major objectives of retirement planning.

What Should a Retirement System Accomplish for Its Members?

One of the fundamental contributions of a retirement system is to enable individual staff members to live in dignity, in satisfaction, and in security throughout the retirement period. In one sense, retirement planning seeks to alter the time-honored relationship between old age and economic destitution. It also seeks to alter the relationship between old age and dependence by systematic economic planning. Few are they who relish the thought of depending upon friends, relatives, and institutions for their very existence after gainful employment has been terminated. In short, the retirement system should help its members to realize, during the period of retirement, protection against economic and physical hazards, as well as a measure of independence which permits fulfillment of a wide variety of pursuits and ambitions. The system should do for the individual what he generally cannot or will not do for himself—to set aside a portion of his income during his productive years which is returned to him in the form of deferred salary and benefits when his period of service has ended.

The sense of security which the retirement system provides for the individual during his active years is also a matter which should be given added emphasis. When the individual understands that the retirement system provides certain benefits to him in the event of disability, or to his survivors in the event of his death, some of the anxiety and uncertainty about the future course of events for himself and his family will be eased.

Accordingly, the retirement plan should help to release more of the creative energy and efforts of school personnel to make possible a more effective daily and long-term performance in the service for which they are employed. In fine, the retirement system should contribute to improvement of the quality of education. This, it would seem, is its primary mission.

What Should a Retirement System Accomplish for the Institution?

A retirement system yields certain important benefits to the institution which should be recognized. First, there is general acceptance of the idea that benefits provided by the retirement system are conducive to more effective personnel performance as well as to greater loyalty to the profession. While there is no incontrovertible proof to support this assumption, it serves as an important supporting hypothesis in retirement planning. The fact that the compensation structure in public education is generally regarded as less than satisfactory makes the retirement system an important contributing device for securing satisfactory service.

Second, is the fact that public education is in keen competition with business, industry, government, and various other employers for trained manpower. If education expects to recruit and to retain its share of the limited supply of qualified personnel, it must be prepared to offer retirement and related benefits which are as attractive as those in other occupations. A sound retirement system often offsets some of the attractiveness of positions which are long on salaries, short on retirement benefits. In deciding upon a career, college men and women of today are prone to give extensive consideration to retirement benefits which are available in the several occupational fields. As improvements in the retirement systems for educators are effected, the possibilities for recruiting more able persons for careers of service in education will be enhanced.

A third advantage of a retirement system to the institution is that it provides an orderly means by which the services of staff members may be terminated when they are no longer capable of rendering effective service. Without a retirement system, institutions are compelled, for humane reasons, to retain personnel even though they have outlived their periods of usefulness. Thus the ability of the administration to effect an orderly retirement of personnel enables it to attract competent recruits and to make promotions more feasible. The broad intent of the retirement system, then, is aimed at increasing staff competency, stability, morale, and human satisfaction.

Retirement Systems: A General Description

The purpose of this section is to set forth prominent features of retirement systems to enable the beginning administrator to gain an understanding of their operation, problems, and potential for increasing staff effectiveness. The discussion is not designed to be definitive, for variations in retirement plans of the several states and the application of social security to these plans are so extensive as to make a comprehensive treatment herein neither feasible nor desirable. Questions relating to the nature of an individual system can best be answered through the administrative organization created for this purpose or through the services of state and local professional associations.

Administration

Retirement systems for educators are administered characteristically by an official governmental body, commonly known as the state retirement board. While there is considerable variation among the states in the constituency of board membership, many typically consist of both ex-officio and elected officers. Board members usually serve without compensation, but are reimbursed for expenses. Some states subsidize administrative costs entirely. In others, they are shared equally by the state and system members. In a few states, administrative costs are borne exclusively by the retirement fund. Other state legal provisions relating to the administration of the retirement system include employment of an executive secretary, actuarial service, and establishment of a medical board for dealing with applications for disability retirement.

A business enterprise so extensive as a state retirement system, involving management of millions of dollars, as well as the welfare of thousands of school personnel, is no ordinary administrative undertaking. It is generally accepted that most state retirement systems have not attained the level of administrative effectiveness of which they are capable. A public retirement system, haphazardly run, can be no more successful in its operations than a poorly managed private business. Certain details of retirement administrative machinery have been frequently identified as faulty. These include:

1. Lack of balanced representation on retirement boards in some states. It is generally agreed that the interests of both the public and system members should be represented on the governing board. No such ideal is possible in those states where appointments are purely political in character, or in those where members are denied representation. A board whose membership consists of both state officials and those elected by the system at large should provide the balance essential to the development of policies for maintaining a sound retirement system.

2. Poor relations between administration and system members. A marked absence of good relations exists in some states between retirement boards and their clients. Inability of participants to secure prompt, accurate information about system operation or about the periodic status of member accounts has been a general source of dissatisfaction. Integration of social security with retirement systems has, in some instances, created considerable confusion and misunderstanding, as well as the need for extensive administrative efforts to inform members about the operational aspects of such plans. It should be possible for members to secure readily answers to any and all questions pertaining to the operation of the retirement system. Moreover, it is a cardinal responsibility of the governing body to take such steps as are necessary to keep system members constantly informed of the provisions, operations, and problems of the retirement plan.

3. Lack of system adaptability. It has become increasingly evident that retirement systems need to be responsive to social change. A state with retirement provisions which are outmoded—which do not provide reasonable financial security for the participants, which make for inequity in cost distributions, which ignore the problem of reciprocity —will have serious difficulties in attracting and retaining qualified personnel to staff its schools.[13]

Membership

There are differing membership bases among the several state retirement plans for public school personnel. In some states, membership includes all public school employees, professional as well as noninstructional. In others, participation is limited to faculty members.

[13] For details of retirement systems see National Education Association, Research Division, *Abstracts of State Retirement Systems* (Washington: The Association, issued periodically).

A few states define membership to mean faculty members, administrative officers, and clerical workers.

Some states establish a waiting period as an eligibility requirement. Participation is generally compulsory for all regularly employed personnel, but there are exceptions in some states for special classes of employees.

If it is assumed that one of the aims of personnel administration is to promote the general welfare of school personnel, considerable thought and care must be devoted to development of a plan which will operate continuously from recruitment through the retirement period to inform staff members about the benefits and obligations of retirement membership, including contributions, options, and procedural requirements. This calls for a comprehensive system of personnel records, publication of retirement information, and individual counseling through which information on most retirement problems can be furnished readily.

Contributions

It is possible to finance retirement plans by at least three different methods: (1) the contributory plan, in which members pay all costs; (2) the noncontributory plan, in which a unit of government, such as the state or municipality pays the entire cost, and (3) the joint contributory plan, in which costs of the plan are shared by the members and governmental units, such as the state and/or school district. Retirement systems for school personnel are preponderantly of the joint contributory type, since this is the only equitable approach to the operation of a sound retirement system.

Contributions to the retirement system under a joint contributory plan are actuarially determined to produce an annuity in accordance with the benefits established in the plan. The rate of contribution is based upon the age and sex of the member at the time of entry. Members contribute a percentage of the current salary, which is supplemented by public funds to meet the costs of the plan. Because of the differences in the several retirement systems, the percentage contributions are not uniform.[14]

[14] The Wyoming retirement system is supported by contributions of members equal to 2 per cent of the first $4,800 of salary, which is matched by public funds. In California, individual contributions range from 7.46 per cent at age 20 to 12.72 per cent at age 59 or over.

Public contributions to the joint contributory system are made by means of pay-as-you-go or reserve plans. Under the pay-as-you-go plan the governmental unit appropriates annually its share of whatever benefits are due those who have retired. This is also known as the cash disbursement plan, and is seriously deficient on several counts. Since future costs are not actuarially determined, and since there is no provision for a reserve fund to earn interest to pay part of the cost of the benefit, unpredicted liabilities must be met by increasing contributions or decreasing benefits.

Experience has shown that a sound joint contributory plan requires an actuarial reserve system. This involves: (1) determining future benefit costs on an actuarial basis; (2) requiring public and individual contributions to be paid concurrently; and (3) holding total contributions in trust until benefits are paid. The salient advantage of a reserve plan is that the public contribution is made during the individual's years of active service. Both public and individual contributions are then combined to form a reserve, which, when invested, accumulates interest to pay for part of the benefit costs.

Benefit Formulas

One of the significant elements in a retirement plan is the benefit formula, which stipulates the basis upon which the allowance of the retirant is determined. The major types of benefit formulas may be classified as (1) money purchase, (2) fixed benefit, and (3) a combination of (1) and (2).

The fixed benefit plan provides retirement benefits in a fixed amount or at a fixed percentage—such as 1/70 of the average annual salary during the highest five years' compensation for each year of service; or 1.5 per cent of the average salary of the highest five consecutive years for each year of service.

The money purchase plan provides for computation of the retirement allowance in two portions: an annuity, the value of which is determined actuarially on the basis of employee contributions, and a pension, the value of which is determined actuarially on the basis of employer contributions.

A variation of the foregoing plan provides for an annuity on an actuarial basis and a pension at fixed rate.

Each of the foregoing plans has strengths as well as limitations.

The fixed benefit plan is easy to interpret, but frequently criticized on the grounds that benefits based upon unpredictable future salary levels virtually excludes the possibility of sound reserve financing. Adverse economic conditions could conceivably affect benefits under any type of plan. If state revenues are insufficient to pay the obligations which fall due, if interest earnings on investments decline, if costs continue to exceed revenues, objectives of any formula will be difficult to realize.

Retirement Age

Provisions governing age of retirement are standard features of state plans. While provisions are by no means uniform, they often cover the following circumstances:

1. Age at which retirement is voluntary.
2. Age at which retirement is compulsory.
3. Period of service required for disability retirement.
4. Period of service required as a condition for voluntary or compulsory retirement.
5. Provisions for extension of service when the normal retirement age has been attained.
6. Authority responsible for granting service extensions.
7. Effect of early retirement on benefit allowances.
8. Conditions by which full allowances may be received under voluntary retirement.
9. Retirement prior to eligibility for social security benefits.

Flexibility is one of the hallmarks of a sound retirement system, and there are evidences to indicate that increasingly plans for teachers are developing this characteristic. Every system should make it possible for members to retire early if they so desire, or if physical or mental conditions make it necessary. Indeed, the system should anticipate various human exigencies, and attempt to make progressive adjustments in the structure for coping with them. Right or wrong, a compulsory retirement age is a firmly established practice in many state systems, as well as in many types of business and industrial organizations. Within recent years, however, sentiment has been increasing to modify the compulsory age limit provision in state retirement systems. Many contend that the decision as to whether or not an individual should retire when he reaches the normal retirement age is one which properly belongs to local school officials and not to the state retirement board.

More than one superintendent of schools, on the other hand, has argued that involuntary retirement is an administrative necessity, despite the reasonable defense which can be mustered in opposition to the practice. They contend that the difficulties involved in extending the period of service beyond the normal retirement period for some teachers and not for others are numerous and delicate. Such extensions, they say, usually create more administrative problems than they solve.

In the immediate years ahead the assault on involuntary retirement will continue, based on arguments that life expectancy is increasing, that older teachers are more healthy and vigorous than ever, and that they are needed to fill the gap caused by shortages in trained manpower. Furthermore, it is not difficult to envision the day when older teachers will want to extend the normal period of service simply because the retirement benefits which they receive may well be insufficient to maintain a decent standard of living.

The age at which an individual retires is usually dealt with administratively by one of the following methods:

1. No compulsory age limit. Each member makes his own decision as to retirement, regardless of his ability to serve.

2. Gradual retirement, sometimes with decreasing load coupled with a reduction in salary.

3. Compulsory retirement, without exception, at a specified age.

4. Extension of normal retirement age, continuance of employment being at the discretion of the local board of education.

5. Voluntary retirement earlier than the normal retirement age.

From many standpoints, compulsory retirement has advantages superior to other plans, one of which is to enable the institution to plan intelligently with the individual for his retirement and replacement. But the circumstances are so varied from one school to another in regard to this problem that there is no defensible reason for suggesting exclusive adherence to a single approach.[15]

---

[15] Arguments in behalf of and suggestions for administering "selective retirement" are contained in B. J. Chandler and Paul V. Petty, *Personnel Management in School Administration* (Yonkers-on-Hudson, New York: World Book Company, 1955), pp. 373-378.

Vesting

If a teacher dies while in service, or withdraws before fulfilling age or service requirements, is she or her survivors entitled to full ownership of all benefits which have accumulated through her and her employer's contributions? Retirement vesting provisions vary considerably among the several systems, as the following outline of practices indicates:

1. Only the employee contributions, with interest, are returned.
2. Only the employee contributions, without interest, are returned.
3. Total contributions are returned. Provisions vary with respect to return of interest.
4. Employees who have served a specified number of years may leave contributions on deposit and receive deferred annuity beginning at a specified age.

The foregoing statements, which are intended to indicate in a general way the range in vesting practices in retirement plans for school personnel, point up an issue which is becoming increasingly prominent in retirement legislative considerations.

As efforts are made to adjust retirement plans to new and changing conditions, modification of outmoded vesting provisions is an urgent necessity. Quite aside from the principle of fairness and justice to the individual is the need for vesting provisions which will enable educators to move to positions which are in keeping with their interests without forfeiture of a portion of accrued benefits which the total contributions to their accounts have earned. In other words, system members should be entitled to full ownership of the benefits which are created for them by the total contributions. Students of retirement plans recommend that withdrawal of the equity should be in the form of an annuity rather than a cash settlement.[16]

Creditable Service

Most retirement systems have established policies regarding the extent to which credit is granted for service outside the state or for service in the state prior to enactment of the retirement plan. As examples, no out-of-state service is creditable in Alabama. Prior service

[16] See William C. Greenough and Francis P. King, *Retirement and Insurance Plans in American Colleges* (New York: Columbia University Press, 1959), p. 75.

creditable includes all state service prior to 1941 if the member was in service on the date the system was established. In Pennsylvania, a member may purchase credit for out-of-state service not exceeding ten years. The total number of years purchased cannot exceed the number of credited Pennsylvania service or ten years. In Ohio, there is no limit on purchased service credit as a teacher or any other type of public employment. Included in the definition of outside service in some states are full-time and continuous substitute teaching service, Fulbright scholarship or exchange teaching, out-of-state public school administrative service, military service, federal civilian service, and service in any state institution.

Reciprocity

Statutory and administrative provisions in retirement laws are such that it is very difficult for a teacher to transfer from one state to another, or in some cases to another position in the same state without forfeiting certain retirement benefits. Some progress has been made in this direction in the decade of the fifties. A number of intrastate reciprocity agreements have been effected. This refers to agreements between or among retirement systems within a state, such as the State of Missouri and the Teachers of Kansas City.

Increasingly, arrangements are also being made for granting deferred annuities, and for credit for prior outside service, all of which contribute to easing the problem of personnel mobility.[17]

Formidable as the task may be, an optimum solution to reciprocal retirement service can be arrived at only through greater interstate cooperation. One of the strengths of the federal social security system is the unconditional right of members to change positions, regardless of location, without forfeiting benefits.

Retirement Allowances and Benefits

Most plans make it possible for a member to have his retirement allowance paid to him by one of several different methods, such as:

1. A single life annuity whereby the retirant receives the benefits guaranteed in the formula throughout his life. Monthly allowances under this plan are larger than those of the other options. Under this

---

[17] See National Council on Teacher Retirement, Retirement Income Series No. 8, "Reciprocity Progress," (Washington: NEA Research Division, 1959, mimeographed).

option, however, no protection is provided for a beneficiary or an estate.

2. A reduced annuity whereby a lesser allowance is paid to the member throughout his life and then to his survivor throughout his (her) life.

3. A reduced annuity whereby a lesser allowance is paid to the member throughout his life, and then the balance of the accumulated allowance is paid to the beneficiary.

The foregoing options refer to allowances members receive *after they retire* as well as income arrangements for beneficiaries. A related consideration centers around provisions made for survivors of members who die *before they retire*.

According to a National Education Association study:

1. It is customary for retirement systems to refund accumulated contributions of a deceased member to his estate or a named beneficiary.

2. A few systems also pay an additional lump-sum benefit. At least 16 teacher retirement systems pay monthly survivors' benefits. With one exception these monthly benefits are in lieu of the refund of the accumulated contributions of the member. In only four of these systems are teachers covered by social security. (Survivors benefits under social security are in addition to those provided by the retirement system.)

3. In nine systems survivors' benefits are payable immediately upon the death of the member and are not contingent upon the age of the widow.

Depending upon the system, and upon designated circumstances, benefits are available to widows, children, and dependent parents.[18]

Practically all state retirement systems provide a disability benefit, but there are differences in the service requirements for eligibility and in the range of benefits payable. A 1959 National Education Association study of the disability benefits in 55 retirement systems for teachers reported that 10 systems required 15 years of service as a prerequisite; 45 systems reported benefits payable for disability after 10 years of service. Monthly disability benefits payable under a given set of conditions ranged from $15 to $232.50.[19]

[18] National Council on Teacher Retirement, Retirement Income Series Number 11, *One Criterion for Evaluating Retirement Benefits for Teachers* (Washington: National Education Association, 1959), pp. 83–85.

[19] *Ibid.*, p. 65.

Disability benefits for teachers under workmen's compensation laws should also be included in the benefit structure. The majority of states provide state-wide compulsory coverage for teachers under workmen's compensation laws, but to be eligible, disability must be incurred in line of duty. This is not the case in state retirement systems.[20]

Variation in Retirement Allowances

One of the few studies to evaluate retirement allowances provided for teachers by state and local systems indicates wide variations in the return per teacher contribution. Using the monthly return per $100

Table 13.3

Retirement Income and Return per $100 of Contributions,
at Age 65 with 25 Years of Service, Ending June 30, 1958
Representative Retirement Systems

Monthly Allowance Men	Return per $100 Contributed by Teacher	Monthly Allowance Women	Return per $100 Contributed by Teacher
$ 60.91	$2.47	$ 52.04	$2.11
92.29	4.36	139.72	4.04
141.97*	8.45	140.73*	8.37
146.33	5.37	152.92*	5.92
148.50*	7.50	163.27*	8.62
234.37*	6.45	231.08*	6.97
244.51*	4.64	240.42*	4.39
248.07	6.66	248.07*	6.66
272.42	4.74	270.49	4.38
292.00	7.10	292.00	7.10

* Includes social security benefits.
Source: National Education Association, Research Division, "How to Evaluate Retirement Allowances," *NEA Research Bulletin*, 38, No. 2 (May, 1960), pp. 62–63.

of contributions as the appraisal criterion, the National Education Association study revealed that a high monthly retirement allowance does not always mean a high return on the amount contributed. This fact is illustrated in Table 13.3. According to these data, two women

[20] For a detailed discussion of workmen's compensation coverage of teachers, see National Education Association, Research Division, School Law Series, Research Monograph 1959-M3, *The Teacher and the Law* (Washington: The Association, 1959), pp. 68–73.

in different systems, entitled to monthly allowances of $140 are getting disproportionate returns on contributions per $100—one getting $4.04, the other $8.37. Two men in different systems receive monthly allowances of $272.42 and $141.97; one getting a return of $8.45 per $100 of contributions, the other only $4.74. The systems paying the largest dollar amount do not necessarily yield the largest return in terms of teacher contributions.

It cannot be construed from the foregoing data that the systems paying the highest return on contributions are superior in every respect to other systems. The broad implication is that more systems frequently need to assess the relationship between contributions and returns, as well as the reasons for unusual variations which may exist in these factors.

Retirement and Social Security

Background

On August 14, 1935, President Franklin D. Roosevelt signed into law a significant piece of social legislation known as the Social Security Act. Congress has since passed various amendments to the act, notably in 1939, 1950, 1954, 1956, 1958, 1960, and 1961.

The Social Security Act consists of nine distinct programs, the general aims of which are to keep individuals and families from destitution, to keep families together, and to give children the opportunity of growing up in health and security. The nine programs may be classified as follows:

Social Insurance	*Public Assistance to the needy*	*Children's Services*
(a) Unemployment insurance	(a) Old-age assistance	(a) Maternal and child health services
(b) Old-age, survivors, and disability insurance	(b) Aid to the needy blind	(b) Services for crippled children
	(c) Aid to dependent children	(c) Child welfare services
	(d) Aid to the permanently and totally disabled	

It should be mentioned that while the Social Security Act is a federal law, the only program which the federal government operates is the OASDI (old-age, survivors, and disability insurance). The other eight programs are operated by the states, with federal cooperation.

The Social Security Administration, in cooperation with the U.S. Treasury, administers OASDI.[21]

Social Security and Public School Personnel

The evolving nature of the Social Security Act makes it apparent that it is destined to play an increasingly significant role in the general welfare of public school personnel. The brief résumé of the OASDI provisions, listed in Table 13.4, indicates the retirement income, disability insurance, and survivors benefits available under the system.

Examination of the provisions contained in Table 13.4 makes it clear that OASDI cannot, by any stretch of the imagination, be considered a substitute for a sound retirement system, for this has never been its intent. But OASDI has certain advantages, especially the survivor benefits which, as indicated earlier, are not generally available in existing retirement systems. The 1960 amendments which provide disability insurance at any age, is also a feature which is not characteristic of the typical state retirement system for teachers.

The fact that personnel may move from one state to another without forfeiting any rights or benefits to which they are entitled adds to the system's value as an instrument for enhancing general welfare.

The chief dissatisfaction with OASDI, from the teachers' standpoint, is that the benefits are not proportionately related to the individual's salary nor to his contributions. Because the system is heavily weighted in favor of low-income groups the yield on dollars invested in social security is lower than the yield from dollars invested in the retirement system. The very real danger in social security, however, is its tendency to provide increasingly for the individual's welfare, the costs of which ultimately may be too great for educators to shoulder along with those of a sound retirement system.

The benefits illustrated in Table 13.4 are based upon equal contribution rates (3⅛ per cent in 1962) for both employer and employee on the latter's average monthly earnings. This rate is scheduled to increase until in and after 1968 it will be 4⅝ per cent.

As an example, an employee who earns $4800 a year (the maxi-

[21] U.S. Department of Health, Education, and Welfare, *A Brief Explanation of the Social Security Act* (Washington: U.S. Government Printing Office, 1959), pp. 3–6.

Table 13.4

Examples of Monthly Income Benefits Available Under Social Security

Average yearly earnings after 1950	$800 or less	$1200	$1800	$2400	$3000	$3600	$4200	$4800
Retirement at 65 / Disability benefits	$40.00	59.00	73.00	84.00	95.00	105.00	116.00	127.00
Retirement at 64	37.40	55.10	68.20	78.40	88.70	98.00	108.30	118.60
Retirement at 63	34.70	51.20	63.30	72.80	82.40	91.00	100.60	110.10
Retirement at 62	32.00	47.20	58.40	67.20	76.00	84.00	92.80	101.60
Wife's benefit at 65 or with child in her care	20.00	29.50	36.50	42.00	47.50	52.50	58.00	63.50
Wife's benefit at 64	18.40	27.10	33.50	38.50	43.60	48.20	53.20	58.30
Wife's Benefit at 63	16.70	24.60	30.50	35.00	39.60	43.80	48.40	53.00
Wife's benefit at 62	15.00	22.20	27.40	31.50	35.70	39.40	43.50	47.70
Widow 62 or over	40.00	48.70	60.30	69.30	78.40	86.70	95.70	104.80
Widow under 62 and 1 child	60.00	88.50	109.60	126.00	142.60	157.60	174.00	190.60
Widow under 62 and 2 children	60.00	88.50	120.00	161.60	202.40	236.40	254.00	254.00
One surviving child	40.00	44.30	54.80	63.00	71.30	78.80	87.00	95.30
Two surviving children	60.00	88.50	109.60	126.00	142.60	157.60	174.00	190.60
Maximum Family Benefit	60.00	88.50	120.00	161.60	202.40	240.00	254.00	254.00
Lump Sum Death Payment	120.00	177.00	219.00	252.00	255.00	255.00	255.00	255.00

Source: U.S. Department of Health, Education, and Welfare, *Your Social Security*, Revised to Include Changes Effective August, 1961 (Washington: U.S. Government Printing Office, 1961), p. 9.

mum salary taxable), contributes $150 per year for OASDI benefits. The employer also contributes $150 per year for this employee. The total contributions of $300, then, provides a monthly retirement income at age 65 of $127. Under the 1960 amendments, benefits can be paid to disabled workers at any age.[22] As indicated in Table 13.4, reduced benefits are payable starting at age 62. In addition to the lump sum death payments ranging from $120 to $255, survivor benefits under designated circumstances are payable, depending upon average monthly earnings of the deceased employee.[23]

Social Security Coverage for Teachers

For reasons which are historical in character, the extent of social security coverage for teachers differs among the states. Although Congress passed the original Social Security Act in 1935, it was not until 1950 that coverage of federal old-age and survivors insurance was extended to public employees who were not members of a local or state retirement system. Since virtually all teachers were covered by a state or local retirement system, abandonment of a retirement system was the only means by which teachers could become eligible for social security. Several states pursued this course of action.[24]

A 1954 amendment to the Social Security Act made it possible for public employees who were members of a retirement system to be included in the program by means of a referendum. In 1956, the Act was further amended so that in certain named states, retirement systems for public employees could be divided into two parts for referendum purposes—those who desired to be covered by social security and those who did not. Congress has since extended the list of states wherein divisional coverage is authorized. This procedure was necessary in some states because constitutional provisions prohibit

[22] U.S. Department of Health, Education, and Welfare, Social Security Administration, *Changes in Old-Age, Survivors, and Disability Insurance Under the Social Security Amendments of 1960* (Washington: U.S. Government Printing Office, 1960), p. 2.

[23] The foregoing discussion has presented in outline form only the salient features of OASDI. Questions pertaining to individual benefits should be discussed with the local office of the Social Security Administration.

[24] Delaware, Iowa, Mississippi, Oregon, South Dakota, Utah, Virginia, and Wyoming. These states have since adopted new retirement systems. See National Council on Teacher Retirement, Retirement Income Series Number 17 revised, *Social Security Coverage of Public School Teachers* (January, 1961), (Washington: NEA Research Division, 1959), pp. 2 ff.

impairment of existing retirement contractual obligations between public employees and their employers.

Data contained in Tables 13.5 and 13.6 indicate the arrangements which states have made to utilize social security benefits for retirement purposes. Examination of these data indicates that by 1961, some or all teachers in 38 states were covered by social security, but through several different approaches, such as:

1. Supplementing existing retirement systems with social security benefits. No change in existing retirement formula.

2. Coordinating retirement systems with social security. Retirement system modified to adjust to OASDI.

3. Integrating retirement systems with social security by an offset method which reduces the retirement allowance by the benefit (or a percentage thereof) due from social security.

Table 13.5

Retirement and Social Security Coverage for Elementary and Secondary Public School Instructional Staff State-Wide Application

Full supplementation: No modification of existing retirement system	*Co-ordination:* Existing retirement system modified to adjust to OASDI	*Integration:* Offset method used to adjust to OASDI
1	2	3
Alabama, 1955	Indiana, 1955	Delaware, 1953
Arizona, 1953	Michigan, 1955	New Jersey, 1955
Idaho, 1957	Mississippi, 1952	Utah, 1953
Iowa, 1953	New Hampshire, 1957	
Kansas, 1955	North Carolina, 1955	
Maryland, 1956	Oregon, 1953	
Nebraska, 1959	South Carolina, 1955	
South Dakota, 1951 [a]	Virginia, 1952	
Washington, 1955		
Wyoming, 1953		
West Virginia, 1956 [b]		

[a] South Dakota repealed its retirement law at the time social security was adopted. A new retirement law was enacted in 1959.
[b] By county referendums; all counties now covered.
Source: National Council on Teacher Retirement, Retirement Income Series Number 17, Revised, *Social Security Coverage of Public-School Teachers* (Washington: N.E.A. Research Division, 1961), p. 3.

Table 13.6

**Retirement and Social Security Coverage for Elementary
and Secondary Public School Instructional Staff
Limited Application** [a]

Full supplementation: Adoption in some districts or counties; no modification of existing retirement system	Divisional basis [b]		
	Full supplementation or co-ordination [c]	*Co-ordination*	*Offset*
1	2	3	4
Georgia, 1956 [d]	New York, 1957	Hawaii, 1957	Pennsylvania, 1957
Montana, 1955	Wisconsin, 1957	Minnesota, 1959	
North Dakota, 1956		Tennessee, 1957	
Oklahoma, 1955–56			
Texas, 1956 [d]			

[a] Some school employees in Arkansas, California, Maine, Missouri, Vermont, and the Virgin Islands are covered.

[b] California, Connecticut, Florida, Massachusetts, Rhode Island, and Vermont are authorized by amendments to Social Security Act to adopt OASDI on the divisional basis, but have not done so.

[c] New York and Wisconsin retirement system members may elect on an individual basis to be covered on full supplementation or co-ordination basis.

[d] Authorized to adopt OASDI on divisional basis by amendments to Social Security Act (Georgia, 1956; Texas, 1960), but adopted by local counties or districts.

Source: *Loc. cit.*

4. Permitting some districts or counties to adopt social security without modifying the state retirement system.

5. Supplementing state retirement systems by coordinating or integrating with social security on a divisional basis.

The foregoing arrangements have made it possible for more than half of the public school teachers, as well as thousands of noninstructional personnel, to be covered by social security. There is a high degree of certainty that in the years ahead OASDI will be universally utilized in improving and extending retirement plans for public school personnel.

Issues and Problems in Retirement Planning

Many teachers retiring today at age 65 are the recipients of retirement benefits which have been secured by a struggle which has been going on for the greater part of their lives. State or local retirement plans have been established for virtually all teachers, as well as for thousands of other school personnel. More than half of all professional personnel are members of the social security system. Considerable improvement has been effected in the actuarial bases of retirement plans, retirement and disability benefits strengthened, and many features of retirement plans liberalized to accommodate the various needs of members of retirement systems. Taking the long view of developments in retirement plans for educators, the gains achieved have been sizable.

Impressive as this list is, it is hardly safe to conclude that the profession is not confronted with major problems in this area. It is a matter of fact that there is a lag between desirable standards for retirement plans and actual practice. Every retirement system is currently confronted with both immediate and emerging problems which must be squarely faced and answered by educational associations, individual members of retirement systems, and legislative bodies. Some of the more significant issues are discussed briefly in the following pages.

Compulsory Retirement

One of the persistent issues in retirement plans is the age at which an individual should retire from active service. The lengthening span of life, the short supply of professionally qualified personnel, and the inadequacy of many retirement allowances are among the factors which heighten the demand for extending the retirement age limit. Among the questions which need to be given consideration in this regard are the following: Should a compulsory age limit for retirement be set by the retirement board? If not, what should be the nature of authority granted to local administrative units for dealing with the retirement age problem? If the local board has the authority to establish policies governing the age of retirement, should retirement be left to the discretion of the board or to the individual? What are the advantages and limitations of gradual retirement?

Retirement Allowances

Experience has indicated that retirement allowances have not been sufficient for most retirants to maintain a reasonable standard of living.

One of the critical problems confronting retirement systems is that of increasing retirement allowances without making the cost to members inordinately expensive. The movement to liberalize retirement benefits by adopting survivor benefits, increasing disability benefits, and raising the basic allowances have generally resulted in increased contributions by employer and employee. There is every reason to believe that retirement allowances will increase generally, the cost of which will increase accordingly. What must be recognized as a matter of plain fact is that the benefits of any retirement plan depend upon the amount of contributions. If greater benefits are desired, some of the burden for achieving this end must be shared by system members. Furthermore, it should be clear that no retirement or social security system will provide for all of the retirement needs of the individual. No retirement plan is designed to provide for the needs of its members beyond certain minimum essentials. To the individual rather than the system belongs a full measure of responsibility for planning security measures beyond those guaranteed by the retirement plan.

Several efforts have been made in recent years to deal with the problem of the decreasing purchasing power of retirement allowances. In some cases, bonuses or cost-of-living allowances have been granted to retirants as a means of supplementing low retirement income. Tax deductions for retired persons and the use of a variable annuity are other means which have been employed to cope with this problem. The variable annuity plan permits members to invest part of their and their employer's contributions in common stocks which provide an annuity income. The annuity increases as stock prices and dividends increase, and decreases when they decline. This approach, now in operation since 1952 in college retirement planning, deserves serious consideration by teacher retirement systems as one means of offsetting the decreasing purchasing power of retirement allowances.[25]

Social Security

The dilemma presented by the social security program in relation to teacher retirement plans is that its ultimate direction cannot be safely predicted. With each new session of Congress there are various

[25] A detailed explanation of the variable annuity is contained in William C. Greenough and Francis P. King, *Retirement and Insurance Plans in American Colleges* (New York: Columbia University Press, 1959), Chapter III.

attempts to amend the provisions of OASDI. Medical care for the aged, for example, is a continuing issue, and its ultimate resolution will undoubtedly affect future policy decisions on this matter by state retirement systems.

There is also the possibility that the social security program will become more social and less individual, meaning that it is quite within the realm of the possible for social security to become so extensive and expensive that the need for both a retirement system and a social security program will be debatable. The compelling problem at the moment is for retirement systems to develop plans which can make effective use of both systems so that the objectives of both can be realized. The day is already at hand when some teachers are contributing almost 10 per cent of their salaries for retirement and social security benefits, and boards of education are suddenly appreciating the reasons for the dramatic upsurge in expenditures for fixed charges in the annual budget. If the point is reached when social security and/or retirement absorbs a disproportionate share of the teacher's income, there will be little opportunity for her to make investments to produce income beyond that due her from either or both of the foregoing sources. The question of whether we need the social security system is no longer at issue. We need it, but we also need more foresight, more coordination, and more planning to combine all welfare plans into a genuine security structure.

Insurance

Plans for life insurance, hospital-surgical-medical insurance, and major medical expense insurance are fast becoming standard features of the occupational structure. Before too many years have passed, it can be assumed that such provisions will be made a part of the general welfare pattern for all public school personnel. Whether this should be accomplished by federal, state, or local plans, however, is a matter which deserves continuing study.

Much could be accomplished if it were possible to effect intelligent coordination of retirement and insurance planning among the various governmental agencies. Social security planning is largely independent of that engaged in by public school retirement systems, the result of which is an unnecessary duplication of various kinds of welfare provisions.

Enough has been said to illustrate the fact that retirement and insurance planning has not reached the point where all plans are completely satisfactory. But in spite of many unsolved problems, much has been achieved in providing for the welfare of public school personnel.

Suggested Reading

Burns, Eveline, M., *Social Security and Public Policy* (New York: McGraw-Hill Book Co., 1956).

Department of Health, Education, and Welfare, *Social Security Handbook on Old-Age, Survivors, and Disability Insurance* (Washington: U.S. Government Printing Office, 1960).

Department of Health, Education, and Welfare, *Social Security in the United States* (Washington: U.S. Government Printing Office, 1959).

Municipal Finance Officers Association of the United States and Canada, *Retirement Plans for Public Employees* (Chicago: The Association, 1958).

National Education Association, Committee on Tenure and Academic Freedom, *Trends in Teacher Tenure thru Legislation and Court Decision* (Washington: The Association, 1957).

Turnbull, John G., Arthur C. Williams, Jr., and Earl F. Cheit, *Economic and Social Security: Public and Private Measures against Economic Insecurity* (New York: The Ronald Press Co., 1957).

Selected Bibliography

1 School Personnel: An Overview

Bredemier, Harry C., and Jackson Toby, *Social Problems in America: Costs and Casualties in an Acquisitive Society* (New York: John Wiley & Sons, Inc., 1960).

De Young, Chris A., and D. Richard Wynn, *Introduction to American Public Education*, 4th ed. (New York: McGraw-Hill Book Co., 1960).

Morse, A. D., *Schools of Tomorrow-Today* (New York: Doubleday & Co., Inc., 1960).

National Society for the Study of Education, *Social Forces Influencing American Education*, Sixtieth Yearbook, Part II (Chicago: University of Chicago Press, 1961).

Pounds, Ralph L., and James R. Bryner, *The School in American Society* (New York: The Macmillan Co., 1959).

Thayer, V. T., *The Role of the School in American Society* (New York: Dodd, Mead & Co., 1960).

Thelen, H. A., *Education and the Human Quest* (New York: Harper & Brothers, 1960).

379

2 The Personnel Function in School Administration

American Association of School Administrators, *Staff Relations in School Administration* (Washington: The Association, 1955).

American Management Association, Personnel Division, *Personnel Function: A Progress Report* (New York: The Association, 1958).

Flippo, E. B., *Principles of Personnel Management* (New York: McGraw-Hill Book Co., 1961).

International City Managers' Association, *Municipal Personnel Administration*, 6th ed. (Chicago: The Association, 1960).

Jucius, Michael J., *Personnel Management*, 4th ed. (Homewood, Illinois: Richard D. Irwin, Inc., 1959).

National Industrial Conference Board, *Statements of Personnel Policy*, Studies in Personnel Policy, No. 169 (New York: The Board, 1959).

Northcott, C. H., *Personnel Management*, 4th ed. (New York: Pitman Publishing Corp., 1960).

Pigors, Paul, *Personnel Administration*, 4th ed. (New York: McGraw-Hill Book Co., 1961).

Scott, Walter D., Robert C. Clothier, and William R. Spriegel, *Personnel Management*, 6th ed. (New York: McGraw-Hill Book Co., 1961).

Stahl, O. Glenn, *Public Personnel Administration*, 4th ed. (Harper & Brothers, 1956).

Strauss, George, and Leonard R. Sayles, *Personnel: The Human Problems of Management* (Englewood Cliffs, N. J.: Prentice-Hall, Inc., 1960).

Yoder, Dale, *Personnel Management and Industrial Relations*, 4th ed. (Englewood Cliffs, N. J.: Prentice-Hall, Inc., 1956).

Yoder, Dale, *Personnel Principles and Policies*, 2nd ed. (Englewood Cliffs, N. J.: Prentice-Hall, Inc., 1959).

3 The Human Element in Personnel Administration

Argyris, Chris, *Personality and Organization* (New York: Harper & Brothers, 1957).

Barnard, Chester, *Functions of the Executive* (Cambridge: Harvard University Press, 1938).

Bendix, Reinhard, *Work and Authority in Industry* (New York: John Wiley & Sons, Inc., 1956).

Bidwell, Charles E., "Administration and Teacher Satisfaction," *Phi Delta Kappan*, 37 (April, 1956), pp. 285–288.

Boulding, Kenneth, *The Organizational Revolution* (New York: Harper & Brothers, 1953).

Culbertson, Jack A., Paul B. Jacobson, and Theodore L. Reller, *Adminis-trative Relationships: A Casebook* (Englewood Cliffs, N. J.: Pren-tice-Hall, Inc., 1960).

Dale, Ernest, and Lyndall F. Urwick, *Staff in Organization* (New York: McGraw-Hill Book Co., 1960).

Davies, Daniel, and Laurence Iannacone, "Ferment in the Study of Or-ganization," *Teachers College Record*, 60, No. 2 (November, 1958) pp. 61–78.

Davis, Keith, *Human Relations in Business* (New York: McGraw-Hill Book Co., 1957).

Dubin, Robert, *Human Relations in Administration* (Englewood Cliffs, N. J.: Prentice-Hall, Inc., 1956).

Griffith, Daniel, *Human Relations in School Administration* (New York: Appleton-Century-Crofts, Inc., 1956).

Gross, Neal, Ward Mason, and Alexander McEachern, *Explorations in Role Analysis* (New York: John Wiley & Sons, 1958).

Heckman, J. L., Jr., and S. G. Huneryager, *Human Relations in Manage-ment* (Cincinnati, Ohio: South-Western Publishing Co., 1960).

Homans, George C., *Social Behavior* (New York: Harcourt, Brace and World, Inc., 1961).

Merrihue, Willard V., *Managing by Communication* (New York: Mc-Graw-Hill Book Co., 1960).

National Industrial Conference Board, *Charting the Company Organiza-tion Structure*, Studies in Personnel Policy, No. 168 (New York: The Board, 1959).

National Industrial Conference Board, *Following Up Attitude Survey Findings*, Studies in Personnel Policy, No. 181 (New York: The Board, 1961).

National Industrial Conference Board, *Improving Staff and Line Rela-tionships*, Studies in Personnel Policy, No. 153 (New York: The Board, 1956).

National Industrial Conference Board, *Preparing the Company Organiza-tion Manual*, Studies in Personnel Policy, No. 157 (New York: The Board, 1957).

Newcomb, Robert, and Margaret Sammons, *Employee Communications in Action* (New York: Harper & Brothers, 1961).

Niles, Mary Cushing, *The Essence of Management* (New York: Harper & Brothers, 1958).

Roethlisberger, F. J., *Management and Morale* (Cambridge: Harvard Uni-versity Press, 1940).

Smith, Henry Clay, *Psychology of Industrial Behavior* (New York: Mc-Graw-Hill Book Co., 1955).

Smith, Henry Clay, *Personality Adjustment* (New York: McGraw-Hill Book Co., 1961).

Weber, Max, *From Max Weber: Essays in Sociology* (New York: Oxford University Press, 1946).

Whyte, William H., Jr., *The Organization Man* (New York: Simon and Schuster, Inc., 1956).

4 Staff Personnel: Quantity

Chruden, Herbert J., and Arthur W. Sherman, Jr., *Personnel Management* (Cincinnati, Ohio: South-Western Publishing Co., 1959).

Finchum, R. N., *Administering the Custodial Program* (Washington: U. S. Government Printing Office, 1961).

Finchum, R. N. *Organizing the Maintenance Program* (Washington: U. S. Government Printing Office, 1960).

Sargent, Cyril G., and Eugene Belisle, *Educational Administration: Cases and Concepts* (Boston: Houghton Mifflin Co., 1956).

5 Staff Personnel: Quality

American Association of School Administrators, *Professional Administrators for America's Schools* (Washington: The Association, 1960).

Byers, Kenneth M., Robert Mantilla, and Elmer V. Williams, *Elements of Position Classification in Local Government* (Chicago: Civil Service Assembly, 1955).

Central School Boards Committee for Educational Research, *Quality Control Guide* (New York: Teachers College, Columbia University, 1958).

Griffith, Daniel E., David L. Clark, D. Richard Wynn, and Laurence Iannaconne, *Organizing Schools for Effective Education* (Danville, Ill.: The Interstate, 1961).

Lieberman, Myron, *Education As a Profession* (Englewood Cliffs, N. J.: Prentice-Hall, Inc., 1956).

McKenna, Bernard H., "Patterns of Staff Deployment Related to School Quality," Institute of Administrative Research, Teachers College, Columbia University, *Research Bulletin* 1, No. 3 (April, 1961).

National Education Association, Educational Policies Commission, *An Essay on Quality in Public Education* (Washington: The Association, 1959).

Vincent, William S., "Quality Control: A Rationale for Analysis of a School System," Institute of Administrative Research, Teachers College, Columbia University, *Research Bulletin* 1, No. 2 (January, 1961).

6 The Compensation Structure

Benson, Charles S., *The Economics of Public Education* (Boston: Houghton Mifflin Co., 1961).

Burke, Arvid J., *Financing Public Schools in the United States*, rev. ed. (New York: Harper and Brothers, 1957).

Johns, R. L., and E. L. Morphet, *Financing the Public Schools* (Englewood Cliffs, N. J.: Prentice-Hall, Inc., 1960).

Mort, Paul R., W. C. Reusser, and J. W. Polley, *Public School Finance*, 3rd ed. (New York: McGraw-Hill Book Co., 1960).

National Education Association, *Materials on Salaries Available From the National Education Association*, ARL 61–1 (Washington: The Association, 1961).

National Education Association, Research Division, Research Memo 1961–62, *Index or Ratio Salary Schedules For Teachers* (Washington: The Association, 1961).

National Education Association, Research Division, *Review of Literature on Personnel Rating in Business and Industry*, Research Memo 1961–11 (Washington: The Association, 1961).

National Education Association, Salary Consultant Service, *The Use of Index Ratios to Determine Salary and Salary Schedules of Supervisory and Administrative Personnel* (Washington: National Education Association, Salary Consultant Service [undated]).

National Education Association, *Selected References on Merit Salary Schedules*, ARL 60–8 (Washington: The Association, 1960).

Ovsiew, Leon, and William B. Castetter, *Budgeting for Better Schools* (Englewood Cliffs, N. J.: Prentice-Hall, Inc., 1960).

Thomas, Lawrence G., *The Occupational Structure and Education* (Englewood Cliffs, N. J.: Prentice-Hall, Inc., 1956).

Tickton, Sidney G., *Teaching Salaries Then and Now—A Second Look* (New York: The Fund for the Advancement of Education, 1961).

7 Recruitment of Personnel

Elsbree, Willard S., and E. Edmund Reutter, Jr., *Staff Personnel in the Public Schools* (Englewood Cliffs, N. J.: Prentice-Hall, Inc., 1954).

Maloney, P. W., *Management's Talent Search: Recruiting Professional Personnel* (New York: American Management Association, 1961).

Stone, C. Harold, and William E. Kendall, *Effective Personnel Selection Procedures* (Englewood Cliffs, N. J.: Prentice-Hall, Inc., 1956).

Strauss, George, and Leonard R. Sayles, *Personnel: The Human Problems of Management* (Englewood Cliffs, N. J.: Prentice-Hall, Inc., 1960).

8 Selection of Personnel

Bellows, Roger M., and M. Frances Estep, *Employment Psychology: The Interview* (New York: Rinehart & Co., Inc., 1954).

Coladarci, Arthur, "Administrative Success Criteria," *Phi Delta Kappan*, 37 (April, 1956), pp. 283–285.

Cronbach, Lee J., and Goldine C. Gleser, *Psychological Tests and Personnel Decisions* (Urbana, Ill.: University of Illinois Press, 1957).

Katz, Robert L., "Skills of an Effective Administrator," *Harvard Business Review*, XXXIII (January–February, 1955), pp. 33–42.

Stone, C. Harold, and William E. Kendall, *Effective Personnel Selection Procedures* (Englewood Cliffs, N. J.: Prentice-Hall, Inc., 1956).

Tiffin, Joseph, and Ernest J. McCormick, *Industrial Psychology*, 4th ed. (Englewood Cliffs, N. J.: Prentice-Hall, Inc., 1958).

9 Induction of Personnel

American Association of School Administrators, *Teacher Orientation* (Washington: The Association, 1956).

Chamberlain, Leo M., and Leslie W. Kindred, *The Teacher and School Organization*, 3rd ed. (Englewood Cliffs, N. J.: Prentice-Hall, Inc., 1958).

Eastmond, Jefferson N., *The Teacher and School Administration* (Boston: Houghton Mifflin Co., 1959).

Strickland, Evert Clark, *A Survey and Appraisal of Orientation Programs for New Teachers in the Elementary and Secondary Public Schools of Ohio* (Columbus, Ohio: Ohio State University Doctoral Thesis, 1955).

Waite, William W., *Personnel Administration* (New York: The Ronald Press Co., 1952).

10 Development of Personnel

Douglass, Harl R., Rudyard K. Bent, and Charles W. Boardman, *Democratic Supervision in Secondary Schools*, 2nd ed. (Boston: Houghton Mifflin Co., 1961).

Hunt, Herold C., and Paul R. Pierce, *The Practice of School Administration* (Boston: Houghton Mifflin Co., 1958).

International City Managers' Association, *Municipal Personnel Administration*, 6th ed. (Chicago: The Association, 1960).

Miller, Delbert C., and William H. Form, *Industrial Sociology* (New York: Harper & Brothers, 1951).

National Society for the Study of Education, *In-Service Education for Teachers, Supervisors, and Administrators,* Fifty-Sixth Yearbook, Part I (Chicago: The University of Chicago Press, 1957).

Rabdert, Karl G., "A Philosophy of Personnel Development," *Business Horizons,* 3 (Winter, 1960), pp. 46–53.

Spears, Harold, *Curriculum Planning Through In-Service Programs* (Englewood Cliffs, N. J.: Prentice-Hall, Inc., 1957).

11 Appraisal of Personnel

Abrahamson, Stephen, and Richard Wolf, *A Study of Devices Used in Rating Teachers' Performance in Public Schools in Western New York* (Buffalo: School of Education, University of Buffalo, 1957).

Adams, Robert Winthrop, *The Complete Employee: Handbook for Personnel Appraisal* (Chicago: Public Administration Service, 1959).

Brown, Milon, *Effective Supervision* (New York: The Macmillan Co., 1956).

Hagman, Harlan, and Alfred Schwartz, *Administration in Profile for School Executives* (New York: Harper & Brothers, 1955).

Likert, Rensis, "Measuring Organizational Performance," *Harvard Business Review,* XXXVI, No. 7 (March–April, 1958), pp. 41–50.

Luck, Thomas J., *Personnel Audit and Appraisal* (New York: McGraw-Hill Book Co., 1955).

National Industrial Conference Board, *Forms and Records in Personnel Administration,* Studies in Personnel Policy, No. 175 (New York: The Board, 1960).

Walters, J. E., *Basic Administration: The Process of Planning, Organizing, Managing, Appraising, and Controlling* (Ames, Iowa: Littlefield, Adams and Co., 1959).

Wasserman, Paul, *Measurement and Evaluation of Organizational Performance:* An Annotated Bibliography (Ithaca, N. Y.: Graduate School of Business and Public Administration, Cornell University, 1959).

12 General Welfare of Personnel: Basic Provisions

Haag, Jessie Helen, *School Health Program* (New York: Henry Holt & Co., Inc., 1958).

National Education Association, Commission for the Defense of Democracy Through Education, *Taking the Grief Out of Grievances in Public School Systems* (Washington: The Association, 1958).

National Education Association, Department of Classroom Teachers, *Conditions of Work for Quality Teaching* (Washington: The Association, 1959).

National Education Association, Educational Policies Commission, *Professional Organizations in American Education* (Washington: The Association, 1957).

National Education Association, Research Division, *The Teacher's Day In Court: Review of 1960,* School Law Series Research Report 1961-R7 (Washington: The Association, 1961).

13   General Welfare of Personnel: Tenure and Retirement

Committee on Public Employee Retirement Administration, *Retirement Plans for Public Employees* (Chicago: Municipal Finance Officers Association, 1958).

Eastmond, Jefferson N., *The Teacher and School Administration* (Boston: Houghton Mifflin Co., 1959).

Edwards, Newton, *The Courts and the Public Schools,* rev. ed. (Chicago: University of Chicago Press, 1955).

Elsbree, Willard S., and Edmund R. Reutter, Jr., *Staff Personnel in the Public Schools* (Englewood Cliffs, N. J.: Prentice-Hall, Inc., 1954).

Fricke, Cedric V., *The Variable Annuity* (Ann Arbor, Michigan: Bureau of Business Research, School of Business Administration, University of Michigan, 1959).

Greenough, William C., and Francis P. King, *Retirement and Insurance Plans in American Colleges* (New York: Columbia University Press, 1959).

Harris, Chester W. (ed.), *Encyclopedia of Educational Research* (New York: The Macmillan Co., 1960).

National Education Association, Research Division, *Trends in Teacher Tenure Thru Legislation and Court Decision* (Washington: The Association, 1957).

National Education Association, Research Division, *The Teacher and the Law,* School Law Series Research Monograph 1959-M3 (Washington: The Association, 1959).

Index

387